W9-CGN-916

International Security and Democracy

Pitt Latin American Series

Billie R. DeWalt, *General Editor*
Reid Andrews, *Associate Editor*
Carmen Diana Deere, *Associate Editor*
Jorge I. Domínguez, *Associate Editor*

International Security and Democracy

*Latin America and the Caribbean
in the Post-Cold War Era*

Edited by Jorge I. Domínguez

University of Pittsburgh Press

Created under the auspices of the Inter-American Dialogue

Published by the University of Pittsburgh Press, Pittsburgh, Pa. 15261

Copyright © 1998, University of Pittsburgh Press

Manufactured in the United States of America

Printed on acid-free paper

10 9 8 7 6 5 4 3 2 1

LIBRARY OF CONGRESS CATALOGING–IN–PUBLICATION DATA

International security and democracy : Latin America and the
    Caribbean in the post–cold war era / edited by Jorge I.
    Domínguez.
        p.   cm. — (Pitt Latin American series)
      Includes bibliographical references and index.
        ISBN 0–8229–4054–x (acid-free paper). — ISBN 0–8229–5659–4
    (pbk. : acid-free paper)
      1. Latin America—Foreign relations—1980– 2. Caribbean
    Area—Foreign relations. 3. Security, International. 4. Civil
    supremacy over the military. I. Domínguez, Jorge I., 1945– .
    II. Series.
    F1414.2.I65 1998
    327.8—dc21   97–33897

A CIP catalog record for this book is available from the British Library.

❧ Contents

❀ Tables

🪬 Preface

Today there are few matters more crucial to the construction of democracy in the Americas than how governments deal with an array of new security challenges. The hemisphere has changed in important ways in the last several years. Until recently, and particularly since the Cuban Revolution of 1959, the U.S. government viewed political developments and conflicts in Latin America largely through a cold war lens.

Although such a lens has not entirely disappeared, the ending of the cold war has opened up opportunities to view the region's security concerns and challenges in a fresh light. To date, however, there has been no systematic effort to illuminate this transformed regional context and to explore its importance and implications for hemispheric cooperation and peace.

This volume is the culmination of such an effort. Under the intellectual guidance and direction of Jorge Domínguez, a professor at Harvard University and a member and associated fellow of the Inter-American Dialogue, the project analyzes the intersection between regional security issues and the democracy-building process in Latin America. Such a focus fits squarely with the Inter-American Dialogue's long-standing commitment to strengthening democratic practice and institutions in the hemisphere. As part of this general concern, for many years the dialogue has also highlighted the importance of subordinating the military to civilian control and authority.

Domínguez assembled fifteen of the hemisphere's leading analysts—many with extensive practical experience—to participate in this important effort. The chapters cover a wide range of topics—from strains on weak Caribbean states as a result of the illicit drug trade to the implications of Argentine participation in UN peacekeeping operations throughout the world. Though diverse in coverage and varied in approach, the chapters share a fundamental concern with how democratic governments in the hemisphere can more effectively deal with the often delicate and complex balance between international security challenges and domestic peace and stability.

This project has proceeded in various stages. A March 1995 workshop enabled the authors to establish a common and coherent intellectual framework and to sharpen their arguments and positions. The chapters also benefited considerably from a full-day conference in September 1995 that gave project participants a chance to engage in a productive exchange and discussion with the Washington policy community. The conference brought together an impressive range of participants, including representatives of the hemisphere's academic community, the military, government officials, and key policy analysts.

Many others also deserve credit for their role in this project. We are especially grateful to Javier Corrales and Robert Hemmer for their translations of several chapters, and to a number of Inter-American Dialogue staff members: Jenny Pilling, for her work in organizing the conference; Nicola Lowther, for supervising the resulting publication; Jane Marcus, for performing a variety of crucial tasks; and Abby Horn, for skillfully managing the project's final phase. We appreciate as well support provided by Jennifer Cordero and Danielle Jetton. Dialogue interns who contributed to this project include Julie Olker, John White, Alex Gross, and Sarah Connelly.

The Inter-American Dialogue's research and publications are designed to improve the quality of public debate and key issues in Western Hemispheric affairs. The Dialogue is both a forum for sustained exchange among leaders and an independent, nonpartisan center for policy analysis on U.S.–Latin American economic and political relations. The Dialogue's hundred members—from the United States, Canada, Latin America, and the Caribbean—include former presidents and prominent business, labor, academic, media, military, and religious leaders. At periodic plenary sessions, members analyze key hemispheric issues and formulate recommendations for policy and action. The Dialogue presents its findings in comprehensive reports circulated throughout the Americas. Its research agenda focuses on four broad themes—democratic governance, inter-American cooperation, economic integration, and social equity.

The Inter-American Dialogue wishes to express its gratitude to the U.S. Institute of Peace and the Swedish International Development Agency for their support for commissioning these essays, the March 1995 workshop, the September 1995 conference, and the publication of this volume. We are also pleased to acknowledge the broader support that the Dialogue has obtained from the Ford and A. W. Mellon Foundations and the Carnegie Corporation of New York. Finally, we are grateful to Harvard University's David Rockefeller Center of Latin American Studies, and to Harvard's Weatherhead Center for International Affairs, for providing Jorge Domínguez with research support for this project.

—Michael Shifter, *Program Director, Democratic Governance, Inter-American Dialogue*

—Peter Hakim, *President, Inter-American Dialogue*

◈ Acronyms

AOR	Areas of responsibility
APEC	Asia-Pacific Economic Council
BEA	Batallón del Ejército Argentino
BED	Special Brigade for Disarmament
CAA	Conference of American Armies
CANARGUS	Joint Canadian, U.S., and Argentine flying unit
CARI	Argentine Council on Foreign Relations
CARICOM	Caribbean Community and Common Market
CASC	Central American Security Commission
CBM	Confidence-building measure
CEDOH	Documentation Center in Honduras
CEPAL	Comisión Económica para América Latina (see ECLA)
CIAV	International Support and Verification Commission
CICAD	Inter-American Drug Abuse Control Commission
CIVS	International Verification and Follow-up Commission
CLADDE	Latin America Center for Defense and Disarmament
CLO	Central Liaison Office
COCOM	Coordinating Committee on Export Controls
COPAZ	The National Commission for the Consolidation of Peace
COPEI	Christian Democratic Party, Venezuela
CSBM	Confidence- and security-building measure
DEA	U.S. Drug Enforcement Administration
DFT	Deployment for training
DHL	U.S. courier service
ECLA	Economic Commission for Latin America (see CEPAL)
EPIC	El Paso Intelligence Center
EPS	Sandinista People's Army
FLACSO	Latin American Social Science Faculty
FMLN	Farabundo Martí National Liberation Front

FSLN	Sandinista Front for National Liberation
FTA	Argentine Task Force
FTB	Fast torpedo boat
GDP	Gross domestic product
HCA	Humanitarian and civic action
HONLEA	Heads of National Law Enforcement Agencies
IADB	Inter-American Defense Board
IAEA	International Atomic Energy Agency
IAPF	Inter-American Peace Force
IBERIA	Multinational navy exercise
IDA	Instituto de Desarollo Agrario
IISS	International Institute for Strategic Studies
IMARA	Argentine Navy Marine Infantry
IMET	U.S. international military education and training
JAG	Judge Advocate General
JCS	Joint Chiefs of Staff
MERCOSUR	Southern Cone Common Market
MID	Militarized Interstate Disputes
MINUGUA	United Nations Mission in Guatemala
MINURSO	United Nations Mission for the Referendum in Western Sahara
MIRBMs	Medium and Intermediate Range Ballistic Missiles
MNF	Multinational Force
MOD	Minister of Defense
MOU	Memorandum of Understanding
MRC	Military Regional Conflict
MTCR	Missile Technology Control Regime
NAFTA	North American Free Trade Agreement
NATO	North Atlantic Treaty Organization
NGO	Nongovernmental Organization
NORAD	North American Aerospace Defense
NPT	Non-Proliferation Treaty
NSD	National Security Doctrine
OAS	Organization of American States
ONUC	United Nations Mission in the Congo
ONUCA	United Nations Observer Mission in Central America
ONUMOZ	United Nations Observer Mission in Mozambique

ONUSAL	United Nations Observer Mission in El Salvador
ONUVEN	United Nations Observer Group for the Verification of Elections in Nicaragua
OPBAT	Operation Bahamas and the Turks and Caicos
OSD	Office of the U.S. Secretary of Defense
PAM	People's Action Movement
PICE	Argentina-Brazil Economic Cooperation and Integration Program
PKO	United Nations Peacekeeping Operation
RIAL	Latin American International Relations
RSC	Regional Security Coordinator
RSS	Regional Security System (Caribbean)
SAFTA	South American Free Trade Area
SAM	Surface-to-air missile
SELA	Sistema Económico Latinoamericano [Latin American Economic System]
SICOFAA	System of Cooperation of American Air Forces
SIPAN	Amazon Protection System
SIVAM	Amazonian Watch System
SSU	Special Service Unit
SWAT	Special Weapons and Tactics
TIAR	Inter-American Treaty for Reciprocal Assistance
UN	United Nations
UNAMIR	United Nations Assistance Mission for Rwanda
UNAVEW	United Nations Mission in Angola
UNCRO	United Nations Force in Croatia
UNDCP	United Nations International Drug Control Program
UNDOF	United Nations Disengagement Observer Force
UNDP	United Nations Development Program
UNEF	United Nations Emergency Force
UNFICYP	United Nations Force in Cyprus
UNIKOM	United Nations Iraq-Kuwait Observation Mission
UNIMIH	United Nations Mission in Haiti
UNIMOG	United Nations Group of Military Observation in Iran-Iraq
UNIPOM	United Nations India-Pakistan Observation Mission
UNITAS	Annual multinational naval exercise
UNMIBH	United Nations Force in Bosnia-Herzegovina
UNMOP	United Nations Force in Previaka, former Yugoslavia

UNPREDEP	United Nations Force in Macedonia
UNPROFOR	United Nations Protection Force
UNTAC	United Nations Transitional Authority in Cambodia
UNTAES	United Nations Force in Eastern Slavonia
UNTAG	United Nations Transition Assistance Group for Namibia
UNTSO	United Nations Truce Supervision Organization
UPS	United Postal Service
URNG	Guatemalan National Revolutionary Union
USACOM	U.S. Atlantic Command
USCENCOM	U.S. Central Command
USIA	U.S. Information Agency
USMC	U.S. Marine Corp
USSOCOM	U.S. Special Operations Command
USSOUTHCOM	U.S. Southern Command

International Security and Democracy

Chapter 1

Security, Peace, and Democracy in Latin America and the Caribbean

Challenges for the Post–Cold War Era

Jorge I. Domínguez

The prospects for peace and security in the Americas improved as the cold war ended in Europe.[1] Peace settlements were reached in the civil wars in Nicaragua (1989–90), El Salvador (1992), and Guatemala (1996). The Cuban government stopped providing military support to revolutionaries in El Salvador, Guatemala, and Chile. And Colombia's M-19 movement, El Salvador's Farabundo Martí National Liberation Front, and Guatemala's National Revolutionary Union transformed themselves from guerrilla organizations into political parties. Nonetheless, as David Mares's chapter in this book shows, Latin American countries have been involved in a militarized interstate dispute with a neighboring country on average nearly once a year for the past century.

The cold war had fogged the lenses needed to see Latin America's own security concerns.[2] The ending of the cold war in Europe[3] left other long-standing regional peace and security issues essentially unchanged—a point made vivid by the war between Ecuador and Peru in early 1995. The centrality of the cold war for international relations since 1945 nearly monopolized the attention of governments in the United States and Europe. As a result, only some of Latin America's security concerns have received sustained scholarly and policy attention from international observers. On the other hand, the centrality of military coups for political stability, and the concern over democracy, focused decision makers and Latin Americanist scholars on the domestic aspects of the role of the armed forces and on civil-military relations, diverting their attention from international security issues.

This study proceeds at two levels. First, there are the issues that affect the countries of Latin America and the Caribbean in their relations with each other. These include long-standing territorial disputes and subregional balances as well as new efforts to establish means for cooperation to foster peace and security; for some of the countries, there are also threats to their stability from nonstate and substate military forces. At another level, the concern over peace and security links the United States and the countries of Latin America and the Caribbean. Nonstate violence, for example, facilitates drug trafficking from Latin America and the Caribbean into the United States. Moreover, the United States participates in inter-American military institutions, such as the Inter-American Defense Board and the Inter-American Defense College, and takes the lead in the design and implementation of joint military maneuvers with various armed forces of the hemisphere. In addition, the United States, among others, is a formal guarantor of peace settlements between some Latin American countries (such as the "Rio Protocol" between Peru and Ecuador) and is sometimes perceived as an informal guarantor of settlements and balances in the region.

In this book, we focus our inquiry at the intersection of concerns between international security and democratization. We examine international peace and security issues in the hemisphere both to understand potential conflicts and also because international security issues, regimes, norms, rules, and procedures are among the factors that affect and shape civil-military relations and the consolidation of democracy.[4]

In this chapter, I argue that major transformations have occurred in the relations among countries of Central and South America that have for the most part improved the prospects of peace. The practice of cooperative security has spread throughout these regions and been consolidated in the Anglophone Caribbean. Nevertheless, an array of conventional and unconventional threats to security persists; some new threats stem from the unexpected consequences of otherwise worthwhile outcomes. Moreover, the development of cooperative security faces important obstacles in the hemisphere. One of these obstacles, regrettably, is the complex relationship between the prospects for improved interstate relations, on the one hand, and the consolidation of democratic constitutional government, on the other. At the same time, the persisting unreformed inter-American security institutions and procedures detract from the consolidation of constitutional government in Central and South America.

Four Security Dilemmas

1. Will my attempt to enhance my own international security so frighten my neighbor that we will both end up less secure at greater cost? The classic security dilemma that states face in an anarchic international system has also been a part, of course, of interstate relations in Latin America.[5] The government of country X seeks to improve its national security by acquiring new weapons, professionalizing its armed forces, or otherwise improving its military capabilities. The government of country Y becomes alarmed and responds in kind—all of which may leave X and Y both better armed and less secure while incurring greater costs. Arms races are one result of the response of states to this security dilemma.[6] In this book, the chapters focused on the southernmost countries of South America (the Southern Cone) illustrate the ways in which governments and scholars think about this enduring problem and try to find means to overcome it.

2. Will my attempt to consolidate the stability of my country's domestic democratic politics so frighten my neighbor that we will both end up less secure? This dilemma is much less self-evident, in part because there is now strong scholarly[7] and policy[8] agreement based on a statistical observation: stable democratic regimes do not make war against each other. Yet several of the chapters in this book explore whether there is a connection between attempts to consolidate democratic politics, on the one hand, and increased interstate tensions, on the other.

In the experience of Latin America and the Caribbean in the twentieth century, the principal threat to the stability of constitutional government has come from the armed forces. Revolutionary or guerrilla threats have been frequent and salient but rarely successful. In the midtwentieth century, the development of national security doctrines in nearly all Latin American states focused the professionalization of the armed forces on improving the capacity to respond to "domestic threats" to stability.[9] These threats stemmed allegedly from the prospects of violence from communists or others; in time, these threat perceptions induced the armed forces to seek to shape the structure and management of the economy and civil society. By the late 1970s, only a handful of Latin American countries (plus most of the Anglophone Caribbean) retained constitutional governments in which civilians elected in free and competitive elections held the key posts. In the name of order, the armed forces of Latin America contributed to havoc.

Despite the retreat of military rule throughout the region, the armed forces exist everywhere in South and Central America except for Costa Rica and Panama. Only in the island Caribbean have armed forces been abolished (or never been created) in several countries (see chapter 9, by Ivelaw Griffith). What, then, should be the mission of these armed forces? Given a history where a domestically focused military had been the principal threat to constitutional government, in the 1990s some civilian governments eschewed assigning internal missions to the armed forces if such could be avoided. The principal remaining option to safeguard domestic stability was to assign external missions to the armed forces: my neighbor may be my enemy. Thus the attempt to consolidate democratic politics in countries with residual but still important elements of domestic instability may enhance the likelihood of interstate conflict. Michael Desch's chapter calls attention to this theme; this theme echoes in the chapters dealing with the Southern Cone.

3. Will my attempt to reduce the likelihood of interstate conflict and consolidate the stability of my country's domestic democratic politics through military demobilization create a threat of domestic disorder? Or, what do you do with soldiers when they stop being soldiers? The swift demobilization of combatants in Central America in the absence of ready employment alternatives, as the chapters by Caesar Sereseres and Fernando Zeledón make evident, has contributed to the creation of armed gangs of former soldiers or former guerrillas who threaten the stability of various governments and contribute to a crime pandemic. The chapter by Carlos Escudé and Andrés Fontana also recalls military unhappiness with the downsizing of Argentina's armed forces and the persisting concern about the future activities of those who may yet be demobilized in the intelligence services.

4. Will my attempt to combat violent gangs and drug traffickers in my country threaten the stability of constitutional government? In some countries as different as Nicaragua and Colombia, the level of nonstate violence has remained very high. There is doubt that the police could cope effectively with this violent criminal activity. Consequently, it may be prudent to call the armed forces into combat against such nonstate forces.

Once this decision is made, the armed forces find themselves with an internal mission. This internal mission may improve relations with neighboring countries and with the United States because such violent nonstate forces might support drug traffickers while threatening a subregion and because this mission distracts armed forces away from conflicts with neighbors. Yet such an internal mission, in the 1990s as in the 1960s, might lead the military down the slippery slope toward politics. Even if military coups are avoided or, if attempted, fail, the armed forces may come to play a decisive role within a formally constitutional government. Certainly in many Latin American countries the armed forces have claimed very high prerogatives as well as the right to veto, and to participate in the making of, key national policies.[10]

These dilemmas cannot be ignored; nor can they be easily resolved. On the other hand, their impact should not be exaggerated. From the early 1980s to the early 1990s, South America's aggregate military expenditures relative to the region's gross domestic product held roughly steady at about 2 percent. Except in Brazil, Colombia, and Venezuela, the weight of military expenditures on the economy has been declining, most markedly so in Argentina. The number of soldiers in South America's armed forces has fallen from about 1.1 million in the early 1980s to below 900,000 in the early 1990s. (As Francisco Rojas's chapter makes evident, however, the spillover of the Peru-Ecuador war may exacerbate the problem: As Peru and Ecuador rearm in the wake of their 1995 war, Chile may believe that it must rearm to counter a strengthened Peruvian military establishment.)[11] In Nicaragua, El Salvador, Panama, and Haiti, both military expenditures and the size of the armed forces shrank considerably in the 1990s as a result of the end of civil wars in the first two countries and the change of political regime in the latter two cases. Guatemala's armed forces are being downsized as well, following the end of this country's civil war. Central America has undergone very substantial military demobilization since 1989. For Latin America as a whole (including Cuba), in the early 1990s military expenditures represented only about 1.5 percent of gross national product—the smallest proportion for any region of the world. The number of soldiers per thousand people fell from about 4.5 during the first half of the 1980s to about 3.5 in the early 1990s. Consequently, the impact of the classic security dilemma has certainly been constrained.[12]

Moreover, Argentina, Brazil, and Chile well exemplify dimensions of the classic security dilemma but their interstate relations perhaps have never been better, as we see below. The armed forces of Colombia have long been engaged in matters of domestic security but they have not overthrown a constitutional government since the 1950s. The armed forces of Peru have fought a brutal domestic war for fifteen years but that did not prevent them from fighting short wars against Ecuador as well in 1981 and in 1995 or from engaging in smaller-scale militarized interstate disputes at other times. A crime pandemic, regrettably, can be observed nearly everywhere in Latin America, whether there has been substantial military demobilization or not. In short, we should be appropriately concerned with the dilemmas sketched above but we ought also to explore the ways and the reasons why their effects can be constrained or overcome.

International Subregional Balances and Transformations

Since the 1880s, international subregional balances, that is, relatively stable distributions of military and other capabilities among key states, have helped to preserve the peace in South America. When balances are stable, a state is less likely to fear that the security-enhancing efforts of its neighbors will weaken its own security.[13]

There have been very few interstate wars in Latin America in the twentieth century, a period when, as Mares's chapter shows, only nine wars have had at least eight hundred battlefield deaths. On the other hand, militarized interstate disputes are not uncommon, occurring on average almost every year. Typically, force is actually used, not merely threatened, in these disputes.

From the 1960s to the 1980s, moreover, preparedness for war increased markedly in South and Central America. In those years, war broke out between El Salvador and Honduras, Peru and Ecuador, and Argentina and the United Kingdom. Argentina and Chile mobilized militarily against each other and came to the edge of war in 1978, as did Guatemala and the United Kingdom and Guatemala and Belize. Less severe but still serious disputes developed between Chile and Bolivia, Chile and Peru, Argentina and Brazil, Venezuela and Colombia, and Venezuela and Guyana. These interstate disputes were not "side-shows" put on by "out-of-control" military, nor did they occur only when authoritarian governments ruled. Instead, these issues represent the legacies of the histories of these states since their independence.

A Diplomatic Transformation in the Southern Cone

From the late 1970s to the early 1990s a diplomatic transformation in interstate relations occurred in the Southern Cone (see chapters by Escudé and Fontana, Mônica Hirst, and Rojas). Until 1979, relations between Argentina and Brazil were very tense. Military missions envisaged combat against each other. The two countries were engaged in the early stages of a nuclear arms race. In November 1979, the military dictatorships of Argentina, Brazil, and Paraguay signed the Itaipú-Corpus Treaty. At the simplest level, this agreement governed the distribution of waters in the Paraná River system to permit the construction of two large hydroelectric projects, one led by Brazil, the other by Argentina.

Yet this treaty engineered not just dams but peace. Additional agreements were reached between Argentina and Brazil that greatly reduced the probability of military confrontation, began a process to reduce the likelihood of a nuclear weapons race, and would lead in 1985 to important accords on economic integration. In 1990, Argentina, Brazil, Paraguay, and Uruguay signed the Treaty of Asunción, committing themselves to the establishment of a common market (MERCOSUR), which was effectively launched on January 1, 1995, and dramatically lowered trade barriers. Argentine-Brazilian trade boomed from the late 1980s into the 1990s. Also in the early 1990s, Argentina and Brazil signed a nuclear safeguards agreement to provide for transparency and mutual guarantees in their respective nuclear power industries.

In 1978 the military governments of Argentina and Chile mobilized for war against each other; Argentina's military government had refused to accept an international arbitration award concerning the lands and waters in the Beagle Channel, even though the Argentine government had been bound in advance to abide by the outcome. War was prevented thanks to the Pope's mediation. In 1984 Argentina (then under a democratic government) and Chile (still under military rule) signed the Treaty of Peace and Friendship whereby Argentina accepted the award of the disputed Beagle Channel islands to Chile. Argentine-Chilean relations continued to improve across the board. Trade and other economic relations intensified also during the first half of the 1990s. And as Escudé and Fontana, and Rojas, show, twenty-three of the remaining twenty-four unresolved boundary disputes were settled in the early 1990s thanks to a joint decision by democratically elected presidents Patricio Aylwin and Carlos Menem.

Though problems remain, the transformation of interstate relations among the three major Southern Cone countries is unprecedented in their international history. In each case, through acts of statesmanship the governments of the three countries chose to eschew military conflicts for the sake of the wider long-term prospects of collaboration. In each case, decision makers responded to their analysis of the balance of power, military capabilities, and the capacity of each country to sustain war. They stepped back from the brink. These factors, not the type of political regime, were the key to the change in course. Clearly authoritarian regimes were just as capable of making peace or coming to the edge of war. Clearly the mere fact of having a democratic political system did not automatically cause peace.

An "Intermestic" Transformation in Central America and the Caribbean

In Central America and the Caribbean there have been intertwined changes at both the international and domestic levels regarding security issues—hence the neologism *intermestic*.[14] The end of the cold war in Europe had a decisive impact on security issues in Central America and the Caribbean (in contrast to its negligible impact on security issues in South America).[15] The Soviet Union collapsed, and none of its successor states was capable of continuing support for the Cuban government or for guerrilla organizations in the Americas. Already in the late 1980s, a much weakened Soviet Union curtailed its assistance to Nicaragua. In the 1990s, Cuba posed no conventional military threat to its neighbors; it also got out of the business of supporting revolutions in other countries. In 1983, the United States and several Anglophone Caribbean countries overthrew the Marxist-Leninist government of Grenada, making it easier to establish relations of political cooperation among the conservative Anglophone Caribbean societies of which Anthony Maingot has written.[16]

Faced with Soviet decline and collapse, and with Cuban decline, the United States under President George Bush's administration changed its policies in Central America, facilitating thereby negotiated peace settlements in Nicaragua and El Salvador.[17] The Clinton administration, in turn, fostered the negotiated peace settlement in Guatemala. The changes at the international level were not the only reasons for these domestic settlements, of course, but they contributed to them powerfully.

As Sereseres and Zeledón demonstrate, however, new security issues arose within Central America.[18] The demobilization of the armed forces and of guerrilla forces left many former soldiers and former guerrillas fully armed. The much less capable states of the region—weakened by years of war and the economic depression of the 1980s—did not succeed in retrieving all the weapons in the hands of former combatants. These weapons contributed to an illegal arms traffic; the specialists in violence added to the region's crime woes. The need to reincorporate demobilized troops and insurgents into society and economy places great burdens on government budgets and absorbs a significant portion of international assistance. In Central America, Sereseres argues, there is a security vacuum in which nonstate forces may disrupt social, economic, and political processes. The weapons beyond the control of the state threaten public order in every way. Various associations and institutions seek to foster cooperation in this subregion, among them the Central American Parliament, the Central American Security Commission, the association of police chiefs, and various interstate economic institutions, but their capacity is well short of the task.

Historically, to be sure, organized international nonstate military forces had been the scourge of Central America and the Caribbean. They were born in the age of international pirates. Beginning in the late 1950s, ideology and politics motivated many nonstate forces; instances of these motivations have become rare. In the 1990s, most nonstate military forces are no longer communist rebels but mainly the instruments of criminal organizations seeking enrichment, in a way returning to the age of the pirates.

In the Anglophone Caribbean, since the late 1970s criminal elements have at some point severely threatened the security of Dominica and of St. Vincent and the Grenadines and, as Maingot points out, have seriously infiltrated various governments in this subregion. As Griffith and Maingot note, in the Caribbean (as well as in Central America) the growth of drug traffic poses substantial and varied security threats. Police and military forces as well as civilian government leaders can be corrupted. The use of force becomes routinized; levels of violence increase or remain high. Criminal organizations, Maingot reminds us, can purchase governments and intimidate critics, relying at times on assassination.

The Anglophone Caribbean's Regional Security System (RSS), Griffith tells us, has played a constructive role; there are other security-related organizations, several of which include the United States, Canada, and the United Kingdom. The Anglophone Caribbean, moreover, is thick with political and economic institutions. But, Barbados excepted, these organizations have been no match for the equally thick array of criminal forces described in Maingot's chapter.

Because at the very core of the intermestic transformation is the weakening of most of the states of Central America and the Caribbean—they lack the domestic or international resources to govern effectively—the prospects for within-region cooperation are problematic. All of the governments that belong to their subregion's multilateral institutions are strapped for funds. Only Guatemala retains a large military establishment, and in the eastern Caribbean only Barbados's forces combine sufficient capacity, professionalism, and integrity. Faced with international organized crime that is well armed and funded by drug trafficking, and faced as well as with substantial substate violence (most of it criminal and some of it in Central America from demobilized soldiers), none of these governments or multilateral institutions can cope with security threats unless they receive substantial international backing from the United States and other countries.

Still, at this moment of intertwined international and domestic crises, the U.S. government has greatly cut back its economic assistance to all of these countries. The Soviet Union's successor states have stopped it altogether. The United Kingdom and Canada have reduced their aid to the Anglophone Caribbean. Other (though not all) donor countries have also scaled back their commitments to these subregions. Peace is not at hand.

Toward Cooperative Security?

One consequence of the diplomatic transformation in the Southern Cone has been the effort to anchor the relations among the states in the region on bases other than the traditional balancing of power. To maintain the peace by means other than conventional balancing, states must cooperate over security.[19]

Cooperative security seeks to reduce the prospects and scope of international aggression through the preventive association of participating states to protect their joint security. Within geographic regions, cooperative security requires participating states to reconfigure their military establishments to reassure each other about their respective intentions. Governments reduce the likelihood of war or other severe conflicts in various ways. They foster transparency in the security policies of each country, thus reducing the probability of acting on rumor or false information. They strengthen international institutions to maintain the peace, resolve disputes, and promote collaboration to address joint problems, and they develop bilateral cooperation to address specific joint security concerns. Reciprocal confidence-building measures become an integral part of national strategies. As Paul Buchanan notes in his chapter, cooperative security strategies also reorient military missions toward external, multilateral peacekeeping and peacemaking missions. Participating states supply peacemaking and peacekeeping forces when called upon by international institutions.

In a conventional approach to security, deterrence is achieved by acquiring the means to repel an attack from beyond the nation's borders and to inflict great costs on the attacker's forces and perhaps also on the attacker's country. In a cooperative approach to security, deterrence is achieved through the transparency of military procedures and information and through confidence-building measures that engage the armed forces of any given set of countries. In each case, the armed forces play a key role in the defense of the homeland, but they do so in quite different ways.

Ultimately, the goal might be to create what Karl Deutsch and his associates called pluralistic security communities.[20] Within a certain territory, a security community is achieved once people attain a sense of community and of institutions and practices strong enough and widespread enough to assure, for a long time, dependable expectations of peaceful change among its populations. This sense of community requires a belief on the part of actors in a group that they have come to agreement on at least one key point: that common social problems must and can be resolved by processes of peaceful change, that is, by institutionalized procedures without resort to large-scale physical force. Within pluralistic security communities, separate governments retain their legal independence. The United States and Canada are part of a pluralistic security community, as are the members of the European Union.

Examples of Cooperative Security

Each of the major South American countries has pursued at least some aspects of cooperative security policies, but each has done so in distinctive
ways. Rojas's chapter illustrates Chile's specialization in strengthening international institutions. Its government hosted the meeting of the Organization
of American States (OAS) in 1991 that issued the Santiago Declaration, committing the member states to respond to interruptions of constitutional government anywhere in the Americas. Chile supports changes in the charter of
the Inter-American Defense Board in order to subordinate it to the OAS and
to enable the board to operate in the security field under civilian authority.
Chile participates actively in the world economy and has made its own economy open and transparent. It played a leading role as a founder of the World
Trade Organization (WTO), it participates actively in the Asia-Pacific Economic Council (APEC), it has applied to join the North American Free Trade
Area (NAFTA), and it has promoted and signed trade expansion treaties with
a great many countries.

Hirst's chapter illustrates Brazil's specialization in subregional affairs.
Brazil has greatly improved its relations with Argentina through the creation
of MERCOSUR (which also includes Uruguay and Paraguay), the signing of
the quadrapartite nuclear safeguards agreement with Argentina and the International Atomic Energy Agency (in force since March 1994), and bilateral
measures of cooperation in various fields including security. As both Hirst
and Escudé-Fontana indicate, the armed forces of Brazil and Argentina have
redeployed away from battle-readiness at their border and have frequent exchanges of military information and personnel to reassure each other. The
armed forces of Argentina and Brazil have at times assisted each other and
participated in one another's military exercises. And, for the first time ever, in
September 1996 the armies of Argentina and Brazil undertook a joint exercise (Operation Southern Cross) in the Argentine province of Corrientes focused on planning and implementing a peacekeeping mission under UN
auspices.

The chapter by Escudé and Fontana illustrates Argentina's own specialization in cooperative security: unilateral initiatives. Argentina unilaterally
scrapped the Cóndor 2 ballistic missile development project, submitted its
nuclear industry to full-scope safeguards under the International Atomic Energy Agency, and signed the Nuclear Non-Proliferation Treaty. (In coordination with Brazil and Chile, it also ratified the Treaty of Tlatelolco binding itself not to build nuclear weapons.) The Menem government also drastically
cut the military budget, abolished military conscription, and launched a pro-

gram to privatize or shut down industries that had been operated by the armed forces.

Key disputes have also been resolved between Argentina and Chile. This process began through papal mediation over the Beagle Channel confrontation and was continued through bilateral negotiations between the governments of Argentina and Chile to settle most though not yet all of their boundary disputes. (International institutions have played no significant role in dispute resolution in the Southern Cone, however.)

Another example of successful conflict resolution was the treaty signed between Venezuela and Trinidad-Tobago in April 1990 to settle their dispute over jurisdiction in the Gulf of Paria waters.

The Anglophone Caribbean governments cooperate extensively with each other on many matters through formal institutions and informal means; most of the smaller island countries lack armed forces. As Griffith indicates, in October 1982 five Eastern Caribbean countries (Antigua-Barbuda, Barbados, Dominica, St. Lucia, and St. Vincent and the Grenadines) established the previously mentioned Regional Security System (RSS). St. Kitts-Nevis joined it soon thereafter. Some RSS forces participated in the 1983 invasion of Grenada led by the United States. (Grenada joined the RSS in 1985.) In the summer of 1990, RSS forces were deployed to Trinidad to assist the constitutional government in overcoming a coup attempt; and in November 1994, RSS troops and police were deployed to St. Kitts-Nevis following a mass prison riot. Anglophone Caribbean forces also joined other peacekeepers in Haiti following the September 1994 intervention authorized by the United Nations and led by the United States.

The Anglophone Caribbean best exemplifies the principles of cooperative security: transparency, participation in joint endeavors, and an external orientation under multilateral auspices. The problem for these countries is the lack of resources to address the principal threat to their security, namely, violence from nonstate forces.

In Central America, the principal instrument associated with the concept of cooperative security was the transparency created by United Nations and OAS personnel who helped to enforce and supervise the peacemaking processes in Nicaragua and El Salvador; observers from these organizations will monitor the Guatemalan peace process and may well have the same effect. As the armed forces of Nicaragua and El Salvador downsized, the threat to interstate peace declined. International institutions helped not just to monitor settlements but also to resolve disputes. Zeledón shows that the International Court at The Hague in September 1992 issued a definitive settlement of the territorial dispute between El Salvador and Honduras that had led to the so-called Soccer War between them in 1969. The court's ruling dealt with both mainland boundary issues and maritime delimitation in the Gulf of Fonseca. Despite numerous practical difficulties, the two governments accepted the ruling and have been attempting to implement it.

In sum, Central and South America and the Caribbean illustrate various approaches to maintain and foster peace consistent with the principles of cooperative security. Yet these chapters show as well several obstacles to the consolidation of a cooperative security strategy.

The Obstacles to Cooperative Security

Many confidence-building measures were designed to reduce the level of tension and lower the likelihood of accidental conflict between adversaries. The broader concept of cooperative security, however, is designed to foster the conditions that would make war unthinkable between countries. Within a full framework of cooperative security practices, countries would not aim their armed forces at each other but only at wider threats in the international system, to be addressed by multilateral institutions. There are a number of obstacles to realizing this hope in Central and South America.

1. Is there an enemy and a risk of military conflict? Countries that consider each other potential enemies may make effective use of certain confidence-building measures but are not likely to create and participate in a dense network of cooperative security procedures.

Only President Menem's Argentina approximated a policy that nearly stated that the country had no enemies other than nonstate actors (e.g., terrorists). The principal exception remained Argentina's claim over the South Atlantic islands in dispute with the United Kingdom, though the Menem government was committed to proceeding by peaceful means to resolve this issue. Thus Argentina foresaw no likelihood of military conflict with its South American neighbors.

In contrast, Chile has continued to perceive several potential enemies. Bolivia continued to claim some territory from Chile to permit its direct access to the Pacific Ocean. Attempts to resolve this dispute remained unsuccessful. For example, in 1993 Bolivian Foreign Minister Ronald McLean resigned because President Jaime Paz Zamora disapproved of the foreign minister's efforts to settle this long-standing dispute with Chile.[21] Under Presidents Aylwin and Fujimori, Chile and Peru made substantial progress to address the legacies remaining from the territorial settlement and delimitation treaties of 1883 and 1929 but have yet to agree on important details mainly because of divided opinions in Peru. One by-product of the 1995 war between Ecuador and Peru was Peruvian rearmament (in 1996 Peru purchased at least fourteen MiG-29 combat aircraft from Belarus), which provided one additional stimulus to Chile to allocate several billion dollars to purchase advanced aircraft as well. One territorial issue remained unsettled between Argentina and Chile—the delimitation of the Southern Cone's glaciers. The Chilean armed forces have also been more disposed to think that the near-war event of 1978 between Argentina and Chile might recur.

In Central America, Sereseres and Zeledón note the practical difficulties to settling some long-standing territorial and boundary disputes—even to demarcate the Honduran-Salvadoran boundary on the ground according to the agreed-upon judgment of the International Court. In 1997, five years after the Court's decision, only 81 of 234 miles of the border had been properly demarcated. Thousands of Salvadoran peasants, threatened with the loss of their lands and a forcible change of citizenship, have resisted the court's judgment; their protests in September 1994 led to Salvadoran and Honduran military re-deployments toward the common border. There is also some potential for interstate hostility, mostly between Guatemala and Belize, but also between Honduras and Guatemala regarding the Montagua River and between Nicaragua and Colombia over the San Andrés archipelago. Moreover, in the Caribbean, a long-standing territorial dispute continues to simmer between Guyana and Venezuela, whereby the latter claims over half of Guyana's national territory.

2. Is there a shared strategic vision? Governments that agree on their assessment of the nature of the international system, the sources of threats, the goals that must be pursued, the tasks to be achieved, and the means to reach objectives are much more likely to cooperate in matters of security.

There is a difference between Argentine and Brazilian views about the international role of the United States. In a sharp break with historic Argentine policies, the Menem government chose to bandwagon with the United States on nearly every international issue. Until the election of Fernando Henrique Cardoso to the presidency of Brazil in late 1994, the Brazilian government, in contrast, had perceived possible dangers to its international standing from the role of the United States. U.S.-Brazilian relations improved considerably since Cardoso's inauguration, though these suspicious views about the U.S. role linger within the Brazilian armed forces.

Brazil seeks a permanent seat on the United Nations Security Council in part to balance the perceived inordinate weight of the United States. Brazil aspires to substantial technological independence and has resisted international constraints on the development of its nuclear power industry. As Hirst reminds us, Brazil has not signed the Nuclear Non-Proliferation Treaty and it continued to insist on its right to access to missile technology for peaceful purposes. Brazil has been reluctant to endow the OAS with a pro-democratic interventionist bias.[22] The Brazilian armed forces have been concerned that the international environmental movements, with the support of the U.S. government, may infringe on Brazilian sovereignty over much of the Amazon River basin.

Similarly, as Sereseres makes clear, in Central America perhaps only Guatemala's armed forces have a strategic vision and, consequently, do not share it with anyone else in the subregion. The Guatemalan armed forces think of themselves as triumphant in the war against an insurgency that lasted for several decades; they are also proud to have achieved their success with virtually no international assistance.[23]

3. What should be the role of formal procedures and institutions? Under cooperative security, governments must have similar or, at least, compatible policies toward international institutions in order to provide support, facilitate their operation, and lower the transaction costs of various activities.

In contrast to Argentine and Chilean emphasis on strengthening the role of various international institutions and formal procedures, the Brazilian government, as noted above, has been much more reluctant to follow this path. Specifically with regard to issues of bilateral cooperative security, Brazilian officers are prepared to practice transparency in bilateral relations with the Argentine armed forces but not to institutionalize such practices if they were to reduce their own margin of discretion. As a consequence, the institutionalization of confidence-building measures in the Southern Cone lags well behind the record between the former adversaries of the Warsaw Pact and the North Atlantic Treaty Organization (NATO).

In Central America and the Caribbean, various governments and military establishments have rather different perspectives on the role of international institutions. Lacking armies, Panama, Haiti, Costa Rica, and various island countries of the Anglophone Caribbean necessarily emphasize and rely on international institutions and other forms of cooperation to provide for their own security. Nicaragua, El Salvador, and Guatemala are at the other end of the spectrum: at critical junctures their governments had no choice but to accept the decisive role of some international institutions on their domestic affairs, though Guatemala's army remained most skeptical of the role of foreign entities in the country.

4. Nontraditional sources of insecurity, Griffith, Maingot, Sereseres, and Zeledón note, require other forms of action. Confidence-building measures and most of the schemes concerning cooperative security were designed for relations between states. The threat from drug traffic–related violence or from substate forces (guerrillas, criminal gangs) calls attention to relatively new and complex problems. With regard to these matters, confidence building and transparency between states may well be irrelevant. At issue is the ca-

pacity of these states, with the support of stronger countries from outside the region, to mobilize resources to overcome rather novel but powerful threats that already erode their sovereignty and break the peace.

Curiously, although many confidence-building measures were developed during the cold war in Europe to ameliorate tensions and manage disputes between the United States and the Soviet Union and their respective allies, remarkably little confidence building has been constructed to address the one remaining severe cold war interstate dispute in the Americas, namely, relations between the United States and Cuba.[24]

In sum, despite the widening practice of cooperative security, Central and South America do not yet have a cooperative security regime, that is, a set of agreed-upon norms, rules, and institutions to govern the security relations between them. They are still far from creating a pluralistic security community. Nonetheless, there are already partial security regimes. The creation of these nascent security regimes is a hopeful trend that deserves to be nurtured and supported.[25]

The "Local" Effects of United Nations Peacekeeping Missions

Antonio Palá's chapter describes the substantial Latin American participation in United Nations peacekeeping missions.[26] He shows that Argentina alone accounted for half of the total Latin American contribution to such missions in the early 1990s through 1995 (because of budget constraints, however, Argentina's contributions to UN missions was cut in half in 1996). Sereseres calls attention to an important distinction between different forms of participation in these missions: Most countries in Latin America only contribute a small number of individuals to United Nations missions; their participation is unlikely to have much impact on the home forces. Argentina and Uruguay, however, have participated through relatively large units that are already having a substantial effect on the home armed forces. By 1997, nearly ten thousand people, just from the Argentine army, had participated in such UN missions. And, in 1996, Brazil for the first time became the largest contributor of forces to UN missions.[27]

Ricardo Lagorio, Palá, and Escudé-Fontana all argue that Argentine participation in United Nations missions helps to secure international peace, contribute to stable civil-military relations in a democratic Argentina, and reduce the likelihood that the Argentine armed forces could threaten Argentina's neighbors, given that such large contingents are deployed in faraway lands. Participation in peacekeeping missions also provides experience for conflict resolution while it enables the Argentine armed forces to focus more on their professional capabilities for international missions than on potential threats from their neighbors. Their arguments are telling and persuasive.

Palá and Lagorio show that participation in UN missions improved the professional competence of the Argentine military, enhanced the interoperability of the Argentine armed forces with those of many NATO countries, and gave substantial combat (in the Gulf War, 1990–91) and semicombat (in Croatia in the early 1990s) experience to Argentine military personnel. Pala demonstrates that Argentine participation under United Nations auspices in several operations of particular interest to the United States (the Gulf War, the intervention in Haiti in 1994) helped to improve the nature and extent of military collaboration between the United States and Argentina and contributed to the upgrading and modernization of Argentina's armed forces. He also shows how the Argentine military budget, and the income received by Argentine military personnel, was bolstered by participation in these missions.

What is to prevent any country that improves its military capabilities to serve in United Nations missions from using these assets to gain advantage over its neighbors, however? Argentina's engagement in international military activities has featured two processes. One has been participation in UN collective security and peacekeeping activities. The combat and semicombat field experience Argentine forces gained under United Nations auspices in the Gulf War against Iraq (an example of collective security) and in Croatia (an example of peacekeeping) could, in principle, be applied closer to home. The second process has been the construction of a wartime military alliance with the United States in the Gulf War and in the blockade of Haiti in 1994. In 1997, the U.S. government announced its formal intention to designate Argentina as its extra-NATO ally, a distinction it will share just with Israel and Egypt. This can be a concern for the armed forces of Brazil and Chile, each of which has at times disagreed with preferred U.S. security policies in the Americas.

Argentina's praiseworthy response to the calls for peacekeeping participation far from home could indirectly and unintentionally heighten a neighboring country's insecurity, particularly Chile's. In this fashion, an unexpected consequence from Argentina's contribution to generate international public goods may be the recurrence of the classic "security dilemma" between Argentina and some of its neighbors. Brazil's increased participation in UN missions in the mid-1990s could pose similar concerns for its neighbors.

In its relations with the United Kingdom, Argentina has addressed this worry with creativity. It deployed substantial forces to the United Nations peacekeeping operation in Cyprus where Argentine personnel worked alongside British forces. Similarly, the Menem government worked effectively to develop a full panoply of confidence-building measures with its neighbors. Were these policies to continue, in the medium and long term they ought to overcome the residual fears that its neighbors may harbor from Argentine participation in overseas UN missions.

The decision to participate in cooperative security arrangements poses a second risk, which is exactly the opposite of the one just discussed. Many peacekeeping tasks are closer to policing than to truly military tasks. The more an armed force redesigns its mission, training, and equipment to respond to peacekeeping operations, the fewer resources it will have to maintain the more traditional aspects of military professionalism. Tension may develop within the armed forces or between them and civilian governments for these reasons.

At issue more generally is whether the armed forces of Latin American countries would be comfortable with defining their missions to resemble those of the armed forces of Canada. The Canadian armed forces participate in collective security and peacekeeping missions under NATO and UN auspices. The Canadian armed forces have substantial experience with confidence building and many cooperative security measures. They are among the most professional and competent armed forces in the world. But Canada is not threatened militarily by its powerful neighbor to the south, and the Canadian armed forces are not designed to deter an invasion by its neighbor. The armed forces of most Latin American countries are unwilling and unlikely to give up this last mission.

Internationalist peacekeeping service under United Nations auspices—a public good—may provoke tensions between the sending country's civilian government and its armed forces. This suggests a third risk of participation in such missions, as highlighted by Carlos Romero's chapter. Romero calls attention to the critical importance of securing the domestic bases of support for an activist foreign policy before as well as while engaging in such a policy. He demonstrates that Venezuela's international engagement lacked sufficient support within the country. The civilian government had paid insufficient attention to explaining its activist foreign policy to its own military and it had failed to equip its own armed forces for the tasks they would be asked to perform.

In 1989 and 1990, Romero shows, the Venezuelan armed forces deployed hundreds of military officers and troops to Honduras and Nicaragua as peacekeepers under United Nations forces to help monitor a cease-fire in the Nicaraguan civil war and, eventually, to help to disarm the Nicaraguan Resistance (the "Contras") in the aftermath of the Sandinista electoral defeat and the inauguration of President Violeta Chamorro. They were part of an important mission—the first time that a Military Observer Group operated in the Americas and the first time worldwide that such a group would be used to demobilize and disarm irregular forces. Nonetheless, the Venezuelan officers and soldiers lacked the equipment necessary to carry out their mission; they had to ask other countries for assistance.

As professional Venezuelan officers reflected on this experience, some wondered about the competence and even the legitimacy of a government of Venezuela, and its high military command, that would send the nation's military on a mission for which they were unprepared and which required "begging" from others to carry it out. These circumstances fed into the unhappiness of some Venezuelan military officers with the government of President Carlos Andrés Pérez and contributed to their participation in the two failed military coup attempts carried out in Venezuela in 1992. The destabilization of Venezuelan democracy was, therefore, in part the unintended consequence of having generated an international public good—service in Nicaragua under UN auspices.

The estrangement of the Venezuelan military from civilian authorities did not begin with Venezuela's deployment of hundreds of soldiers to secure the peace in Nicaragua, nor was the deployment in itself the decisive factor in launching the subsequent coup attempts, but the decision to deploy troops and the practical operational problems of the implementation of this deployment contributed to military estrangement.

The Venezuelan case is sobering. Cooperative security and UN peacekeeping missions begin at home. Civilian governments require the professional advice of their own armed forces to be able to serve overseas in any mission, and above all they must explain and seek to persuade the military that such engagement is in the nation's interest. Absent such crucial steps, participation in United Nations missions may undermine democratic political stability, as it nearly did in Venezuela.

Latin America's experience with substantial participation in United Nations peacekeeping missions is too recent and too limited to shed sufficient light on a key question: does such participation help to consolidate democratic institutions in the sending country? At present, the evidence is inconclusive. Such participation contributed to weakening constitutional government in Venezuela but seems to have helped to strengthen it in Argentina. The relationship between security, democracy, and peace, of course, goes beyond participation in UN missions; we turn now to examine it.

Democracy and Peace: A Bias for the Status Quo?

Rare as war typically is between countries governed by civilian constitutional governments, and rare as war has been in South America, Ecuador and

Peru fought each other for a week in 1981 and for several weeks in 1995 while they were both governed by constitutional presidents—civilians who won free and competitive elections. Short of war, severe militarized interstate disputes have also occurred between democratic regimes (Venezuela and Colombia over maritime demarcation in the late 1980s, for example). As David Mares puts it, countries in Latin America that we commonly define as democratic are unaffected in their decision to use force in their foreign policy by whether or not the country with which they have a dispute is democratic. In South America, republics do go to war against each other.

As the chapters by Mares and Desch make clear, therefore, the spread of democracy throughout Latin America may have an indeterminate relationship to the maintenance of the peace. The infrequency of war in this region cannot be explained in terms of long traditions of consolidated democratic polities; on the contrary, the reduction in the incidence of war was first achieved in the 1880s—prior to the extension of the suffrage and the generalized acceptance of the practice of free and competitive elections. Democracy alone does not guarantee the peace of the region; democratic and nondemocratic governments have engaged in practices that make war less likely, as noted, for example, in the discussion of South America's diplomatic transformation. Nor are democracies any less likely than nondemocracies to engage in militarized interstate disputes with each other.

There are additional indications that democratic procedures in Latin American and Caribbean countries may make it more difficult to settle longstanding territorial disputes. Consider the effects of certain procedures and institutions that are central to the notion of constitutional democracy: the role of Congress, parties, and elections. In the 1980s and 1990s, several attempts to settle territorial disputes failed in Congress because of the adversarial competitiveness of political parties.

Venezuela's democratic politics, for example, has made it much more difficult to resolve the boundary dispute with Colombia.[28] The Venezuelan Congress has helped to derail several attempts to negotiate and settle this dispute.[29]

In May 1993, Chile and Peru signed the Lima Convention to resolve all outstanding disputes related to their boundary. In Peru, the democratic opposition to President Fujimori seized on this agreement to weaken Fujimori's political standing during the early stages of his campaign for reelection. In 1994, Fujimori had to withdraw the treaty from parliamentary consideration to prevent its defeat.

In 1991, Presidents Aylwin and Menem agreed to settle the twenty-four outstanding boundary disputes between Chile and Argentina. Twenty-two were handled readily through executive action; the Laguna del Desierto dispute was submitted to binding international arbitration, won by Argentina in October 1995. The delimitation of the Southern Cone glaciers had to be submitted to Congress, however, because the treaties in force did not cover the subject. In the Argentine Congress, the Radical Party opposed ratification; it obtained enough support from Peronist members of Congress to prevent it. This dispute remains unsettled.

Similar problems concerning the relationship between democratic institutions and procedures, on the one hand, and the making of peace, on the other, are evident in Central America. Consider the example of relations between Belize and Guatemala.[30] After years of formal and informal negotiations, on August 15, 1991, Guatemala recognized Belize's independence, which had been declared nearly ten years earlier. In tacit exchange, Belize agreed to some changes in its maritime boundaries to satisfy Guatemalan desires for access to the Caribbean Sea. The changes would allow Guatemalan ships to use a navigation channel in the Gulf of Honduras that would otherwise have been exclusively Belizean. In May 1993, Guatemalan President Jorge Serrano, who had reached the settlement with Belize, was forced to resign from office after his attempt to stage a coup against the Congress, the courts, and the political parties failed. In the weeks that followed, the successor civilian government publicly considered revising the settlement with Belize, though the issue subsequently subsided. In the meantime, an election campaign was under way in Belize.

On June 30, 1993, the opposition United Democratic Party won the Belizean national elections and assumed office. As he had promised during the election campaign, the new prime minister, Manuel Esquivel, moved to suspend the Maritime Areas Act that had given Guatemala the previously negotiated unimpeded access to the Caribbean Sea. Alarmed, the U.S. and British governments pressured the Esquivel government not to cancel the act outright; the United Kingdom threatened to pull out of its defense agreement with Belize if Esquivel were to proceed. Esquivel backed off. He appointed a study group to look into the issue. This incident was contained thanks to the coercion of the U.S. and British governments. Nonetheless, the democratic electoral process destabilized the security relationship between Belize and Guatemala. And the problem remains unresolved: In August 1997, troops from Belize crossed into territory claimed by Guatemala, and peopled by Guatemalans, to destroy crops.[31]

Some democratic procedures have served to make and consolidate the peace. Consider the most dramatic example. The 1984 Argentine-Chilean Treaty concerning the Beagle Channel faced considerable opposition from the armed forces and from others in Argentina. President Raúl Alfonsín chose to submit the treaty to a national plebiscite. The overwhelming support for the treaty, registered in that plebiscite, was decisive; it enabled the Argentine government to accept its "loss" in the Beagle Channel for the sake of a far greater long-term gain in interstate security and the prospects of cooperation with Chile.

Paradoxically perhaps, the fact that the military governments in Argentina, Brazil, and Chile began the rapprochement with their neighbors augurs well for the prospects of the consolidation of peace. Democratically elected civilian presidents were able to continue and build on the decisions of the armed forces to shy away from war. In Argentina, the policy of improving relations with Brazil, begun by the military government, has been subsequently developed by governments of the two major parties, the Radicals and the Peronistas. In Brazil, the policy of improving relations with Argentina, also begun by the military government, has been developed thereafter by four civilian presidents who span a broad spectrum of political opinion. And in Chile, the rapprochement with Argentina, begun by the government of General Augusto Pinochet, was advanced further by the successive governments of the Concertación Democrática, a coalition constituted of parties of the Center and Center-Left. The process of democratization, and the results of electoral turnover, confirmed the policies begun by the military governments and converted what could have been narrowly based decisions of specific political leaders or parties into the policies of the respective states toward each other. Democratic procedures made interstate commitments to peace more credible.

These observations suggest the hypothesis that, with regard to interstate security issues in Latin America and the Caribbean, democracies exhibit a status quo bias: they find it difficult to alter the status quo. They find it difficult to make the peace (though as the Beagle dispute settlement illustrates, not impossible). They find it difficult to break the peace (though as the Ecuador-Peru conflicts of 1981 and 1995 show, not impossible either). The most successful pattern of peacemaking and peacekeeping since the 1970s, evident especially in the Southern Cone, has begun with a military government and been continued by a civilian government. For a secure peace, in still fragile democracies the armed forces must be included in the consensus agreeing to make and keep the peace; once this has occurred, constitutional governments sustain the peace. In this fashion, democracy has contributed in a more subtle way to the consolidation of peace and to reduce the likelihood that democratic governments would wage war against each other.

The examples of partially frustrated efforts to settle all outstanding territorial disputes between Chile and Peru, Argentina and Chile, and Guatemala and Belize, moreover, call attention to an additional factor that might make it more feasible for democracies to contribute to ensure the peace: the need for government and opposition parties to agree to the broad outlines of a settlement in advance of its formal submission to Congress. Such agreements have become fairly common with regard to economic policy decisions but have yet to become the norm with regard to interstate security. Interpartisan agreements "commit the future." In supporting the settlement, today's opposition effectively guarantees that the accord will endure even if the opposition were to win the next national elections.

In the Western Hemisphere, democracy alone does not make or keep the peace. Democratic contributions to the maintenance of peace require active political efforts to obtain the support of the armed forces and the civilian opposition in order to engage neighboring countries in a diplomatic process that may in due course secure the peace.

Inter-American Security Relations

Inter-American military institutions and procedures are legacies of international wars that have ended and of threats to domestic order whose significance has vanished or declined greatly.[32] Founded in January 1942 to contribute to the defense of the Americas during the Second World War, the Inter-American Defense Board precedes both the Inter-American Treaty for Reciprocal Assistance (the Rio Treaty) and the Organization of American States (OAS).[33] The board has had an ill-defined relationship to the OAS. The board's members are military officers on active duty. In 1962, the Inter-American Defense College was founded. Its curriculum focuses on the strategic social, economic, political, and military problems of the Americas. The students are colonels and lieutenant colonels (or equivalent ranks) from the board's member countries.[34] The service chiefs of the various countries also meet on a regular basis around a common theme. These fora include the Conference of American Armies, the Inter-American Naval Conference, and the System of Cooperation of American Air Forces. Another forum is the Joint U.S.-Mexican Defense Commission. In addition, there are regularly scheduled routine military exercises for the air forces and the navies; Operation UNITAS for the navies of the hemisphere has been a major, visible operation for many years. (See the discussion in Buchanan's chapter.)

In democracies, the armed forces should be subordinate to civilian authority, but none of the multilateral institutions and procedures mentioned above are formally subordinate to their proper civilian authority: The Inter-American Defense Board and College are not subordinate to the Organization of American States.[35] The OAS, alas, bore some responsibility for this failure; not until 1992 did the OAS establish a Special Committee on Hemispheric Security (its first president was Argentine Ambassador to the OAS

Hernán Patiño Meyer). Similarly, the army and air force chiefs from various countries meet, but not until July 1995 had the defense ministers ever met. Though the United States has civilian secretaries of the army and of the air force, they do not even attend the inter-American conferences of the respective military services they lead.

Earlier in this chapter, I note that the mechanisms for cooperating over security issues are still underinstitutionalized in the Southern Cone and underfunded in Central America and the Caribbean. The inter-American military organizations and procedures may be overinstitutionalized, however. They have successfully resisted efforts to change them even when the case for change is compelling.

The fate of these institutional and procedural legacies was off the formal agenda at the first-ever Defense Ministerial meeting held at Williamsburg, Virginia, in 1995. For example, U.S. Defense Secretary William Perry referred to the need to "support an expanded role for the Inter-American Defense College for the education of civilians in national security studies," but the six principles agreed to at Williamsburg did not address these issues.[36] The second Defense Ministerial, held at Bariloche, Argentina, in October 1996, once again touched on the role of the college in fostering defense studies, but the Bariloche declaration failed to grapple with a key question: how to properly subordinate this college to international civilian authority.[37]

Holding these Defense Ministerial meetings, nonetheless, has been important and useful. In many countries that have recently adopted the policy of appointing civilians as defense ministers, the meetings contributed to the legitimacy and standing of this new practice. In Brazil, which lacks a defense ministry, the meetings added to the urgency of considering the utility of effecting a change in the organization of the cabinet and in the government's relation to the armed forces. Everywhere, the meetings required the military services to cooperate to prepare for the event, and nearly everywhere as well the military services and the defense ministry had to cooperate with the foreign ministry.[38]

Thus even modest changes in procedures can generate important consequences. Further changes in inter-American institutions and procedures (subordinating the Inter-American Defense Board to the OAS, altering the curriculum of the Inter-American Defense College to empower civilians to govern, inserting civilian participation in other hemispheric meetings where security issues are discussed) may well have salutary effects for the consolidation of security and democracy.

Yet these institutions and procedures are unlikely to be reformed unless the U.S. government is prepared to commit substantial attention and effort to such changes. Desch's chapter argues forcefully and persuasively that U.S.

policy attention, interest, and commitment over security issues in Latin America are likely to decline substantially in the years ahead as a consequence of the end of the cold war in Europe.

In the short run, however, there has been considerable U.S. attention to security issues in the Americas. As the cold war was ending, in December 1989 the United States invaded Panama. In September 1994 the United States intervened in Haiti under authorization from the United Nations. U.S. and hemispheric concern over the timing and form of a political transition in Cuba has heightened. The United States continues its military presence in Honduras through Joint Task Force–Bravo, as Sereseres reminds us.[39] The U.S. government strongly supports Latin American participation in confidence-building measures and in United Nations peacekeeping operations. Defense Secretary Perry even committed the scarcest of all resources—his own time—to focus U.S. military attention on Latin America (he stepped down in January 1997 as the second Clinton administration began).

There remains, nevertheless, a mismatch between several U.S. objectives and the self-perceptions of most Latin American armed forces (except, perhaps, those of Argentina). Most of the armed forces of the region are not yet ready to sign on to the stated U.S. preference for cooperative security and participation in United Nations missions as the key defining features of the military establishments of Latin America and the Caribbean.[40] Indeed, some of the armed forces in Central and South America are not even fully committed to civilian supremacy over the military within the context of constitutional democracy. Which vision of the future will prevail remains uncertain, though much still depends on the willingness of the United States to make a sustained commitment to foster security and democracy in the Americas.

Conclusions

"The primary function of Latin American armed forces has always been the maintenance of internal order." This was the operative sentence of the December 1955 U.S. National Intelligence Estimate for Latin America, the first since the end of Harry Truman's presidency and the last before Fidel Castro's landing in eastern Cuba to begin an insurgency.[41] It was accurate in many ways, but it underestimated—as similar attitudes have always underestimated—the self-perception of the armed forces of Latin American countries that they play a fundamental role in the defense of the homeland. More importantly, these typical U.S. views have contributed over time to U.S. unpreparedness for events such as the Ecuador-Peru war in 1995.

The diplomatic transformation in the Southern Cone and the intermestic transformation in Central America and the Caribbean have closed as well as opened chapters of insecurity and violence in the history of these subregions. Especially in Central America and the Caribbean, international nonstate and domestic substate violence have risen dramatically to threaten international and internal stability, while some legacies of territorial and boundary disputes remain evident in these subregions and in South America.

Giant steps have been taken in Central and South America since the late 1970s to promote international security and consolidate the peace. These policies have occurred concurrently with the region's democratization but they preceded it; their enduring success is not guaranteed by the fact of democratization alone. The consolidation of the peace continues to require sustained political attention to build civic-military coalitions to support it.

In its early stages, however, the attempts to consolidate democracy may increase the risk of interstate conflict. As democratic governments seek to reduce the likelihood of military interference or coups, they urge their armed forces to look for missions beyond the country's boundaries. In so doing, they risk international conflicts even as they hope to reduce the risk of domestic conflict. In order to make the consolidation of democracy compatible with the consolidation of peace, the Americas require domestic and international leadership to resolve extant disputes and to secure the bases for civilian supremacy over the armed forces within countries and in the governance of inter-American security institutions.

Contrary to the U.S. National Intelligence Estimate just quoted, in order to secure democracy the U.S. government should recognize the continuing, perhaps rising importance of the external missions of Latin America's armed forces, to collaborate with them professionally, and to help focus them on a sustained basis on addressing cooperatively the joint problems of international security within and beyond the hemisphere. Only then will it be possible to break out of the security dilemmas that still face the region, and only then will security, peace, and democracy stand a good chance of success throughout the Americas.

Chapter 2

The Use of Force in Latin American Interstate Relations

David R. Mares and Steven A. Bernstein

In the 1980s interstate war threatened to break out in Latin America. The Argentines fought the British and prepared to take on the Chileans, Peruvians clashed with Ecuadorians twice, Central Americans became intimately involved in each others' civil wars, and even the long-standing democracies of Colombia and Venezuela mobilized their border troops. The U.S. invaded Grenada and Panama, threatened Cuba, and stoked the Central American conflicts with military maneuvers, material, and rhetoric. One study of Latin American conflicts found more than thirty "conflict situations" arising out of territorial, ideological, power projection, resource, and refugee disputes.[1]

What makes this period so interesting, apart from its human drama, is that since the 1930s Latin America had not known such intense interstate conflict. This chapter uses an empirical analysis of Latin America's history of militarized interstate disputes to address three questions arising from the experience of the 1980s. What changed to produce such a deterioration in regional civility? What does this experience portend for the future? How might the regional security order be better managed?

Contrary to common belief, the use of force in Latin American relations has occurred throughout the region's history. Hence we must understand those factors that lead states to resort to force more and less often in order to appropriately structure conflict management and resolution schemes. The answers we provide emphasize the importance of the failure of diplomacy, shifts in local

balances of power, and economic and political underdevelopment as cata-
lysts to the militarization of conflict, even among democracies.

For intra–Latin American conflict, the failure of diplomacy to prevent or
resolve long-standing issues keeps the potential for military conflict in the
region high. A deterioration of the local military balance produces conditions under which even democrats fear that long-standing issues may be ripe
for sudden and violent resolution. In addition, both democratic and authoritarian leaders facing domestic challenges arising from the condition of economic and political underdevelopment feed the search for foreign scape-
goats.

This chapter has two sections. The first analyzes past patterns of regional
conflict. There are many misunderstandings and misconceptions concerning
Latin American interstate conflict that have hindered both analysis and policy. Chief among these is the myth of a peaceful region. This section both de-
stroys that myth and suggests why militarized conflicts occurred. A second
section offers suggestions for more peaceful resolution of regional disagreements.

Explaining Past Patterns

Latin America has been relatively peaceful by international standards.
Controlling for both the number of states and political regime years in a region, Latin America is second only to Africa in terms of fewest militarized interstate disputes (MIDs).[2] Nonetheless, military force has consistently been
utilized in the foreign policies of Latin American countries and has experienced an upturn since the late 1970s.

The twentieth century has seen more than two hundred instances in
which Latin American states either threatened or used military force or were
the subject of such threats or force by non–Latin American countries.
Democracies have shot at each other, a country with no army was invaded
twice by its neighbor (Costa Rica by Nicaragua under Somoza in the 1950s),
and eight wars meet the one thousand battlefield deaths standard, with an
additional one producing over eight hundred deaths.[3] In the 1970s Peru and
Chile engaged in an arms race, and in 1995 the Peruvian president admitted
that his country had prepared for a war with Chile at that time. In 1978 war
between Chile and Argentina was averted at literally the last minute.[4] Clearly,
these states have not formed a security community in which war among
members is unthinkable.

In one sense Latin America has made important progress in controlling
violent conflict. The wars of the nineteenth century, unlike twentieth-centu-
ry disputes, were drawn-out affairs, which spread beyond two parties to in-

clude other neighboring states and had dramatic consequences in lives lost and the amount of territory that changed hands. The human and economic costs of militarized disputes in the twentieth century, nevertheless, require that we focus on how to lower the absolute number of such disputes in the region, rather than being self-congratulatory about the region's relative international peacefulness.

The use of force within the region is not limited to Latin American countries. The United States, whose security interest in the Americas begins with the presidency of Thomas Jefferson and not that of James Monroe,[5] participated in this general pattern of militarized hemispheric relations. According to the MID data base the United States has overtly used or threatened to use military force against Latin American countries thirty-four times in the twentieth century. If we include the covert use of military force (which the MID set does not), the United States was even more willing to utilize military force in its interstate disputes.

We start our analysis after the wars of independence and the subsequent wars among the former colonies to establish national identities and core boundaries. South America largely achieved its modern characteristics by 1884, and by 1907 the idea that war could recreate the United Provinces of Central America was finally discredited. Hence our analysis starts in 1884 for South America (the end of the War of the Pacific), 1907 for Central America and Mexico (the last war fought to reunite Central America), 1902 for Cuba (the United States formally recognized Cuban independence after Cuba accepted the Platt Amendment, which gave the United States the right to intervene in Cuban affairs), and 1904 for Haiti and the Dominican Republic (when the Roosevelt Corollary to the Monroe Doctrine was adopted. Data extend through 1993).

Table 2-1 analyzes the relevant MID data.[6] The data are analyzed in terms of five categories: total MIDs; average number of years between militarized disputes; the escalation of MIDs to war; total participants; and whether force is used by the initiator of the conflict. Data limitations precluded analyzing the behavior of the target countries in a MID.

From table 2-1 we can see that MIDs occur on average every year (averaging one every 0.87 years in South America, every 0.79 years in Central America). Disputes tend to begin with the overt use of force, rather than merely a threat: 62 percent in South America and 70 percent in Central America. Unfortunately, we do not have sufficient data to evaluate the response of the target of such threats. Although disputes do escalate and become militarized, it is extremely rare that they develop into war (1,000 battlefield deaths): only around 2.4 percent for South America and 2.8 percent in Central America. These data support the claims of other analysts that Latin

Table 2-1   Latin American Militarized Interstate Disputes After the National Period

	Total MIDs		
	Total MIDs[a]	Years per Dispute	War/ MID
South America 1884–1993	127	110/127 0.87	3/127 0.024
Central America[c] 1907–1993	110	87/110 0.79	3/110 0.027

	Participation Characteristics		
	Total Participants	Force[b] by Initiators	Force[b] by Targets
South America 1884–1993	290	91/147 0.62	—[c]
Central America[d] 1907–1993	170	51/73 0.70	—[c]

Source: MID data set.
   a. Excluding WWI, WWII and Korea. See explanation in text.
   b. Force is defined as having a hostility level of 4 or greater in the MID data set (using rather than merely threatening or displaying force).
   c. Includes Central America, Panama, Mexico, Cuba, Haiti, and the Dominican Republic.
   d. Data has too many missing force values to be meaningful.

American states militarize issues for diplomatic and domestic purposes, rather than in preparation for war.[7]

We performed correlational analyses and also ran probit models to infer causal patterns in this history. Data limitations on the military variables prior to 1948 made extending the probit analysis to the earlier period inappropriate; consequently, these models cover the period 1948 to 1993. Since analysis of the causes of a militarized dispute needs to take into consideration its nonoccurrence, we include years when no dispute occurred in the data set. The data points in the probit models are dyadic units in a pooled time series analysis. Thus the Argentina-Chile dyad constitutes forty-six data points (1948–93), Argentina-Brazil another forty-six, Guatemala-Honduras forty-six, and so on. Given the conventional power projection capabilities of the United States we considered it to be contiguous to each Latin American state. We were also interested in the behavior of Latin American states among themselves so we ran the same models excluding the United States. This procedure gives us more than 11,200 observations for analysis when the United

States is included in the analysis and over ten thousand when discussing intra–Latin American relations.

The Independent Variables

The literature offers a number of causal variables for the propensity of states to engage in militarized interstate disputes. We examined the three most often cited: hegemonic policing, military imbalances, and democracy. Given the rarity of war, we could not test for the factors that distinguished militarization of a dispute and war (1,000 battlefield deaths).[8]

Hegemony. Most analysts of interstate conflict in Latin America claim that the United States performs a policing function in the region that severely limits the possibility of Latin Americans using force against each other, though not of the United States using force against regional states.[9] The tools with which the United States allegedly manages hemispheric international relations include diplomatic, economic, and military sanctions. Because of U.S. preponderance, interstate conflict is alleged to have declined, leading one analyst to argue that Latin America had no security concerns![10]

So much good and bad has been attributed to U.S. hegemony in Latin America that if we are to use the concept analytically we must clarify what we mean by it and the logic of its expected impact. Hegemony does not imply empire, with a concomitant ability to effectively control all actions of subordinate states. But it should mean that major irritants, such as those involving the "unauthorized" use of military force in interstate relations within the hegemonic zone, would not occur.

U.S. preponderance in South America dates from the end of World War I (1918). The British withdrew their South American fleet and the United States began to consolidate the significant advances in economic penetration gained at the expense of Europe during the war. We date U.S. hegemony over Cuba in 1898, the island of Hispaniola in 1904, and Central America by 1907.[11] However, the dates for Central America and the Caribbean are too close to independence or the end of the wars for national identity to allow us to make meaningful distinctions about pre-hegemonic and hegemonic period behavior. The MID data base clearly indicates that the hegemony established over Central America and the Caribbean did not mean interstate peace, but we cannot know if international relations in these geographic areas were more or less peaceful than they would have been in the absence of hegemony. Consequently, we can examine the hegemony issue for South America only.

Table 2-2 demonstrates that hegemony itself is insufficient to explain the use of force in South American foreign policies. During the prehegemonic

Table 2-2   U.S. Hegemony and Militarized Interstate Dispute
Behavior in South America

Hegemonic Characteristics	MID Characteristics			
	Total MIDs	Year/ MIDs	Force by Side A	Force by Side B
NO (1884–1917)	47	34/47	22/32	—[a]
		0.72	69%	
YES (1918–1993)	80	76/80	69/115	—[a]
		0.95	60%	

Source: MID data set.
   a. Data has too many missing force values to be meaningful.

period South Americans engaged in militarized disputes less often on average than in the hegemonic period (every 0.72 as opposed to every 0.95 years).
The use of force by initiators of the MIDs did decrease by 9 percent but it was
still 60 percent, a figure too high to argue for the hegemon's significant impact on the decision to utilize force in an interstate dispute.

    Table 2-2 uses an "objective" measure of hegemony, but perhaps the ques-
tion is not one of position, but of will. One author explained the increased
level of violent intra–South American conflict in the 1930s largely as a result
of the U.S. reticence to discipline those who would misbehave in the hemisphere.[12] It would be difficult to cut up the entire data by periods of political
will but the contemporary period gives us a convenient test for this proposition. The United States clearly demonstrated a willingness to act during
1989–93 by invading Panama, preparing to invade Haiti, and imposing sanctions against Peru after President Fujimori's self-coup in 1992 and again during Guatemala's short-lived coup in 1993. Nevertheless, there were five MIDs
in those four years, including among the democratic dyads of Colombia-
Venezuela, Honduras-Nicaragua, and Ecuador-Peru; and in 1995 Ecuador
and Peru went to war. In short, the credibility of the hegemon to sanction
does not appear to be a powerful determinant of whether regional states will
engage in a MID.

Democracy. Democracy is a controversial variable, as is evident in the redemocratization literature on Latin America.[13] The basic question is whether
one should utilize a dichotomous or continuous measure of democracy; if
the latter, which components should be evaluated and what weight should
one assign each in the overall evaluation? Fortunately, for our purposes, a dichotomous measure is appropriate for a number of reasons.

The theoretical foundations of the democratic peace thesis do not postulate degrees of democracy as an important consideration.[14] There are also methodological reasons for sticking with a dichotomous approach. The major data set ranking "democraticness" on a 0–10 scale classifies Latin American democracies in a fashion that few regional specialists can accept. For example, Chile in the 1960s, at a time when peasants and workers are being mobilized to an unprecedented degree by competition among three major parties and which had had competitive elections since the 1930s, is given a democracy value of only a 6! And finally, policy makers and diplomats do not make such distinctions in discussing inter-American relations and the association between democracy and peace. Instead, the focus is primarily on whether competitive elections occur in accordance with constitutional provisions.

For both policy and scholarly reasons, our democracy variable is thus dichotomized as either yes or no. A country is considered to be democratic for the year if it scored a 6 or better on the Polity II data set, the leading statistical compilation of the political characteristics of nations. Using this measure, of the total regime years in the period examined (1,883, including South America 1884–1993 and Central America 1907–93), 23 percent (433) are considered to be democratic. (This includes 274 in South America and 159 in Central America.)

Table 2-3 presents two different cuts on the issue of democracies and the use of military force in interstate disputes. The democratic peace literature claims that democracies will not use force in their relations with each other but will defend themselves in the face of "aggression." Because the international system has many nondemocracies, democratic states may sometimes seek to be pacific but not have the luxury of *being* pacifist. Hence the fact that democratic states at times use military force is explained within the democratic peace argument. Section A of the table examines participation in MIDs without regard to the democratic nature of an opponent, while section B looks at the use of military force in dyads in which both sides are democratic. If the democratic thesis is a sufficient explanation of the use of military force, we should see democracies using force in section A and not militarizing their disputes in section B.

The monadic analysis in table 2-3 supports the notion that democracies are not pacifist. Democracies do participate in militarized interstate disputes in Latin America, both as defenders and challengers of the status quo. As noted above, democratic peace advocates would not have a problem with this finding, given the existence of nondemocratic regimes in Latin America. The dyadic analysis in table 2-3, however, suggests that neither are democracies notably pacific with respect to each other.[15] In United States–Latin

Table 2-3   The Participation of Democracies in Latin American MIDs
After the National Period

	A. Monadic Analysis	
	Revisionists	Nonrevisionists
Democratic Participants	131	211

	B. Dyadic Analysis		
	Total Dyads	MID	Percent of Total
Democratic	1,699	19*	1.12
Nondemocratic	13,217	157	1.19
Mixed	8.082	154	1.91

Source: MID data set, plus revisions noted.

Note: South America 1884–1993 and Central America 1907–1993, dyads include the U.S., but not European states for the relevant time period. For a discussion, see text.

* Includes five Ecuador-Peru MIDs not recorded in the MID data base. Carlos E. Scheggia Flores, *Origen del Pueblo Ecuatoriano y Sus Infundadas Pretensiones Amazónicas* (Lima: Talleres de Línea, 1992), 61, reports a MID in 1983; Ministry of Foreign Affairs, Government of Ecuador, *Hacia la Solución del Problema Territorial con el Perú* (Quito, 1992), reports MIDs in January and April 1985, and April 1988 and 1989.

American and intra–Latin American dyads democracies are virtually just as likely to engage in militarized disputes with each other as are nondemocratic dyads (in 1.12 percent compared with 1.19 percent of all dyad years, respectively).

Clearly, democracies in Latin America use force in interstate disputes and suffer from its use. A quick response by democratic peace advocates would look to the degree of influence by the military over elected civilian officials. Some analysts believe that in democracies in which the military is not subordinate to civilian control, conflict, both domestic and international, will more likely become militarized as the military is relatively more able to impose its preferred policies upon the government. In South America in particular, the greater degree of military autonomy and prerogatives in Chile makes some of her neighbors uneasy.

But the logic of this argument is not self-evident. When a military is equipped and trained to deal with domestic dissidents, they may not be prepared to engage in military conflict with other militaries. Hence governments with such militaries are hypothesized by some analysts to be peaceful, not only refraining from initiating a militarized dispute but also from responding with force if provoked because of fear that the dispute could escalate.[16] We also know that professionalized militaries are reluctant to utilize military force in interstate crises unless military solutions appear viable; it is civilian leaders who often push the military into acting.[17] Even in domestic crises, military officers are often reluctant to be called in to settle conflict.[18]

Consequently, the proposition that the military's domination of a polity or organizational autonomy makes the militarization of foreign policy more likely should be subjected to rigorous empirical testing. Such testing is problematic. The Polity II data set attempted to categorize military domination of a political regime (dictators might have effective control over the military, so this is not just a question of concern to democracies). Because investigators were unable to agree on a measure for a very large number of cases, however, this variable was rendered useless for our study. The analytical problem is exemplified in Peru today: some analysts believe Fujimori is using the military while others see in the situation just the opposite.[19]

Once again, a univariable explanation of the use of military force in Latin American disputes is inadequate. Yet democracy may make a difference when we hold other factors constant. Thus we will carry out a multivariate probit analysis incorporating the democratic character of a dyad (DEMDYAD) as an explanatory variable.

Dyadic Balance Of Power. Latin American countries have very little offensive capacity. Geography makes offense difficult on most of the disputed borders: ice fields and narrow sea passages separate Argentina and Chile in the south, the Andes Mountains keep them, as well as Chile and Bolivia, apart, the Atacama Desert allows Chile to mine the frontier with Peru, and the Amazon jungle makes sustained large-scale action difficult among Peru, Ecuador, Colombia, Venezuela, Guyana, and Brazil. Of course, geography alone is not enough to guarantee security, since one side may believe that the other will be unprepared because of its expected geographic advantages. Hannibal's unexpected invasion of Rome from the north is but one example of strategic surprise.[20]

The offensive capabilities of Latin American militaries themselves are very limited. Only Argentina, Venezuela, and Peru have bomber forces,[21] but these are mainly old, slow, and vulnerable Canberras. Fighter-bombers in Argentina, Brazil, and Chile do not have the ability to carry a sufficient number of bombs to do significant damage to each other and return home. Even the Mirages of the region's strongest air force, Argentina, could not use their afterburners in combat over the Falkland/Malvinas region and return to base.[22] None of the armies has prepared the logistical support to sustain a modern army in enemy territory.

But geography that makes attack difficult and limited offensive capabilities are not enough to provide a reasonable level of security in Latin America. In the 1930s, Peru unsuccessfully invaded the Colombian Amazonian territory of Leticia and thereafter successfully took the Amazonian territory claimed by Ecuador. One factor in the latter victory was Peru's ability to utilize paratroopers, the first instance of such use in Latin America.[23] Chile got around the Atacama Desert in 1881 by using its navy to transport the troops who captured Peru's capital, Lima.[24] The two poorest countries in South America slaughtered each other for three years over a barren piece of land (Bolivia and Paraguay in the Chaco War, 1932–35). In 1978 Argentina purportedly believed that it would surprise the Chilean navy by attacking in the southern waterways and across the northern Andes but called it off when it was clear that the Chileans were ready.[25] The Argentines also did not believe that the British were militarily or politically capable of wresting the Falklands from the occupying Argentine forces.[26]

Low absolute levels of military expenditures or arms arsenals are not in and of themselves sufficient to keep disputes from militarizing. Power is relative and what may matter is the balance of military power between two potential disputants. Balance does not imply equality, but rather that the benefits of utilizing military force are outweighed by the ability of a target to use its own military force to exact costs beyond what a potential initiator is willing to pay. According to this line of reasoning, the absence of a MID is partly the result of a potential initiator being deterred by the existing balance of power between herself and the potential target. When that balance is upset, the party benefiting from the shift is more likely to respond to a dispute by threatening or using military force, *all other things being equal.*

The empirical fact of sporadic aggression in Latin America, despite geographic and offensive disadvantages, strongly suggests a need to examine possible deterrent effects of local balances of power. We operationalized the military relationship of the dyad in two different ways. The first, MILITARY, utilized measures of military expenditures as coded in the National Capabilities Database.[27] Specifically, for any dyad the change (over the previous year) in military expenditures for side A was divided by the change (over the previous year) in military expenditures for side B. This variable was designed to capture any change in the relative military capabilities in a dyad. In order to overcome distortions that resulted from ratios with extreme values over 1 (over a 100-percent change in the capabilities ratios) these extreme values were coded as 1. Likewise, those with ratios less than -1 were coded as -1. While the 1, -1 cutoffs for the ratios are somewhat arbitrary, we felt that coding a large change in the military ratio this way would provide sufficient indication of a significant change in relative military capabilities.

The variable LGMILLD is identical to MILITARY except that it captures the change in relative military capabilities in the year prior to the year analyzed for the occurrence of a MID. We believe that this variable may more accurately capture the dynamics of military imbalances that produce a militarization of a dispute in the short term.

The Model

Our first model specified MID behavior as a function of changes in the military balance both in the year of the MID and in the prior year as well as the democraticness of the dyad. The results were disappointing (see table 2-4).

The hypothesized causal variables in Model 1 were well above the standard cutoff for statistical significance (0.05), and thus the results could have happened by simple chance more often than is acceptable for analysts to be comfortable in proposing policy guidelines from this model. The results of the model suggest that either we measured the variables poorly or the hypothesized impact is incorrect. There is a good likelihood that the MILITARY (statistically significant at the 0.14 level) and LGMILLD (significance of 0.37) variables are measured inappropriately. Our colleagues in this project suggested that military expenditure data for Latin America are both inaccurately reported and do not account for cross country differences in the maintenance of military equipment. Limiting the study to the post-1947 period was intended to minimize those data problems. In light of the statistical and theoretical significance of this variable in other studies of militarization of conflict, as well as the military buildup in Ecuador before the recent border confrontation with Peru, it is reasonable to presume that the variable as measured is problematic.

The democraticness of the dyad variable was also statistically insignificant at 0.12. We utilized a standard definition for democraticness (Gurr's 0–10 point scale) and dichotomized the variable at 6 to include Chilean and other Latin American democracies. Other studies utilizing the Polity II data base find 6 to be a very low cutoff point. To evaluate whether too low a cutoff score was the problem in Model 1, we ran Model 2 (see table 2-5), with the same military variables and a new democratic variable, consisting of countries scoring 7 or better on the Polity II and III scales. The results were more encouraging, though still inadequate.

The military variables remain statistically insignificant but the democracy variable now approaches an acceptable level of statistical significance. We ran another model with democracy levels raised to 8, but significance fell dramatically to 0.21. This outcome may be the result of having an inadequate number of democracies in Latin America that reached this level. Since the

Table 2-4   Model 1 of MID Behavior: U.S. and Latin America, 1948–1993

Variable	Coefficient	Standard Error	Significance
Constant	-2.282	0.037	—
MILITARY	0.069	0.047	0.14
LGMILLD	-0.040	0.045	0.37
DEMDYAD	-0.185	0.118	0.12

Source: Analysis carried out using MID *National Capabilities Database* and Polity II data.

Table 2-5   Model 2 of MID Behavior: U.S. and Intra–Latin America, 1948–1993

Variable	Coefficient	Standard Error	Significance
Constant	-2.284	0.037	—
MILITARY	0.070	0.047	0.13
LGMILLD	-0.041	0.045	0.36
DEMOC7	-0.289	0.159	0.07

Source: Analysis using MID *National Capabilities Database* and Polity II data.

Table 2-6   Model 3 of MID Behavior: U.S. and Intra–Latin America, 1948–1993

Variable	Coefficient	Standard Error	Significance
Constant	-2.406	0.044	—
MILITARY	0.078	0.055	0.16
LGMILLD	-0.025	0.053	0.64
DEMDYAD(6)	-0.038	0.134	0.77

Source: Analysis using MID *National Capabilities Database* and Polity II data.

finding supported by Model 2 was sensitive to a change in level of democracy, we wondered whether the results were sensitive to the fact that the United States scored a 10 throughout the period and did not overtly use military force against a Latin American country scoring 7 or better. We thus ran models excluding the United States from the sample (see table 2-6).

Democracy defined by level 6 was dramatically insignificant in intra–Latin American relations, falling below that for our military variable when lagged one year. As the insignificance corresponds to that found for United States and Latin American dyads at the 6 level, we ran another model with democracy at 7 and then 8. In both cases the level of statistical significance remained abysmally low: Democracy 7 (coefficient -0.044; standard error 0.167; statistical significance 0.79) and Democracy 8 (coefficient 0.068; standard error 0.172; statistical significance 0.69).

The democracy variable in the intra–Latin American models is highly insignificant, meaning that *democracies in Latin America are unaffected in their decision to utilize force in their foreign policy by whether or not the country with which they have a dispute is democratic.* This result has serious implications for the contemporary inter-American approach to security in the hemisphere, which assumes that democracies are inherently peaceful.

Policy Implications

In the wake of the recent experience of militarized disputes in Latin America, discussion of new management schemes for regional security is widespread within diplomatic and academic circles.[28] Many policy makers and analysts believe that redemocratization, economic restructuring, and the end of the cold war represent a watershed in the security environment of Latin America and will be sufficient to produce peace. Historical review and contemporary crises clearly demonstrate, however, that the use of force in Latin America's interstate relations will not be banished so easily. In Latin America, the reality is that democracies and liberalizing states continue to see the use of force as a legitimate diplomatic tool. Prudence and cautious optimism in devising conflict management schemes, rather than euphoric idealism, promise to deliver more security to Latin America.

The following recommendations echo some currently being pursued in the United Nations (UN), Organization of American States (OAS), and elsewhere but also propose addressing some issues that diplomats, particularly in an inter-American forum, often find difficult. Conflict management in the region would benefit from (1) an active preventive diplomacy; (2) community demands that states abide by the fruits of diplomatic negotiations; and (3) progress on conventional arms control, including types of weapons and expenditures.

Of fundamental importance is the need to recognize the legitimate role of the Latin American military in performing traditional security functions and equipping them to do so. A tendency to presume the illegitimacy of military force condemns the entire military establishment without recognizing its appropriate and legitimate sphere and weakens deterrence.

Active Preventive Diplomacy in Trouble Spots

By preventive diplomacy we mean recognizing the disagreement and its potential for escalation and undertaking diplomatic efforts to deal with it before it escalates to military threats or action. The efficacy of preventive diplomacy is the sign of a mature security community. Because disagreements are inherent in all relationships, preventive diplomacy is an important mechanism in all communities, but especially so in those with multiple outstanding issues. In Latin America, borders, migration, smuggling, and drug issues that have escalated into armed clashes in the past and are likely do so in future are chronic concerns.

Historically it has been very difficult for Latin America and the United States to countenance multilateral participation in disputes before they escalated. Mandatory arbitration was widely rejected during the days of the Pan American Union.[29] The dispute resolution apparatus of the OAS was limited to cases in which both sides agreed to its intervention. The United States itself is not blameless. President Carter's willingness to allow the OAS to determine how the United States should respond to the rebellion against Somoza in Nicaragua was not emulated by his successors and was quickly abandoned in the restructuring of the Carter administration's aid to Central America after the Sandinista victory.[30]

The traditional approach to conflict management in the Americas kept serious disputes as bilateral issues so long as active fighting did not occur. After the 1981 Ecuador-Peru mini-war there were other mobilizations and threats, but the larger communities of states (whether subregional [Rio Group], regional [OAS], or global [UN]) were content to ignore the issue that had given rise to the dispute and focus instead on restraining the actual use of military force. Following the 1995 border war between the two Andean countries, U.S. special envoy Luigi Einaudi recognized the mistake of focusing only on the symptoms of the disagreement.[31] Yet the error is being repeated in the Venezuela-Colombia dispute. In early 1995 Caracas newspapers were filled with stories concerning the human and economic costs of violations of sovereignty by Colombian guerrillas, drug producers and runners, and smugglers. Colombian territorial claims in the Gulf of Venezuela were also highlighted. The general level of tension was such that an eminent Venezuelan historian warned that the two countries were spiraling toward war. Despite the fact that the two countries had already engaged in at least five MIDs between 1982 and 1993, the international community remained silent.

Other potential hot spots remain. Argentine President Carlos Menem, an advocate of international peacekeeping, has helped keep the Falkland/Malvinas issue alive by promising on Argentine TV that by the year 2000 the islands will be Argentine. Though he stipulates peaceful means, the British disinclination to relinquish the islands, for which they recently fought a war, makes the Argentine president's statement inflammatory. In another chronic sore spot, Bolivia remains unsatisfied with Chilean proposals for settling the outlet to the sea issue. Again, the international community remains silent.

While the Rio Treaty has largely fallen into disrepute among Latin American analysts, the OAS has recently been active in attempting to construct an effective inter-American security system. The 1991 Santiago meeting produced a resolution on "Cooperation for Hemispheric Security" and, subsequently, a Special Commission on Hemispheric Security. The commission is focused on trying to prevent conflict and not just manage it. It has discussed confidence- and security-building measures, the creation of a Conflict Prevention Center, and linking the regional system to the United Nations efforts in the area of preventive diplomacy, peacemaking, and peacekeeping.[32]

However, the Haitian case demonstrates clearly that the United States and Latin America continue to be far apart on the question of whether military force should be utilized when diplomacy bogs down. As soon as the United States began discussing the possibility of using force to overthrow the dictatorship in Haiti, Latin American as well as Canadian diplomats objected.[33] Even after the United Nations approved the use of force, major Latin American states continued to object and Canada refused to be part of the invasion force. For an inter-American conflict management system to work best preventive diplomacy must remain diplomatic and limit itself to the use of non-military sanctions. The United States (and increasingly Argentina[34]) needs to understand that militarizing conflict management will work to undermine the new OAS in the same way that the Rio Treaty was marginalized.

Willingness to Abide by Diplomatic Resolutions

The problem is not limited to convincing countries to actively negotiate solutions to interstate problems. Once negotiated those agreements need to be accepted and respected. Latin American MIDs occur even when diplomatic settlements appear to have been reached.

Binding arbitration by eminent personalities and institutions was popular among many countries at the turn of the century, leading to numerous settlements. But after 1910 states, including the United States, became more unwilling to abide by such decisions and arbitrations declined.[35] The political negotiations and bargaining that accompany the mediation approach to dispute resolution also has a long history in the region.[36] The Pope successfully mediated the Beagle dispute between Chile and Argentina after 1978.[37] Four Latin American countries (Mexico, Venezuela, Colombia, and Panama) attempted to negotiate a resolution to the 1980s crisis in Central America (the "Contadora Initiative"). They were later joined by a "support group" of four other South American countries. Although the final resolution of the Central American crisis did not follow their lead, the experience was promising enough that the eight merged into the "Rio Group."[38] The actual negotiated settlements to the Central American conflict were the result of diplomatic negotiations among the parties themselves (the Esquipulas, or Arias, negotiations).

Unfortunately, these diplomatic solutions may be ignored or rejected if one of the parties disagrees with the outcome. Willingness to abide by diplomatic resolutions is not a function of democraticness. In the contemporary period, Colombia has proposed to arbitrate its border dispute with Venezuela, but the latter refuses, partly because it lost a considerable amount of territory through previous arbitrations. Ecuador, even since redemocratization in 1979, did not accept the Protocol of Rio ending the 1941 war until 1995. The Guatemala-Belize and El Salvador-Honduras territorial settlements have become stalled in the legislatures. This behavior by both established and new democracies undermines confidence in the diplomatic path to conflict resolution and feeds back into the reticence to depend upon multilateral conflict management schemes for security.

Arms Control: Types, Expenditures, and Confidence-Building Measures

The purpose of arms control is twofold: to mitigate the security dilemma and to limit damage if an armed confrontation should occur. The underlying assumption is that disarmament is not feasible, at least not in the short term,[39] and that there is a likelihood that states will utilize their military force against each other, either purposefully or inadvertently.

Arms control is not a new subject in Latin America. At the turn of the century the British helped broker a naval arms agreement between Argentina and Chile.[40] More recently, the treaty of Tlatelolco seeks to keep nuclear arms out of the region.[41] Negotiated force levels in Central America have helped diffuse the level of tension there. A ban on bombers was discussed in the 1970s, but Peru's opposition apparently killed it, although Ecuador disposed of its small (three planes) bomber force. Diplomacy has also been used to develop confidence-building measures among militaries by increasing contact among them.[42] At the extreme, diplomacy has also been used to advocate disarmament itself. After achieving parity with Chile for the first time in one hundred years, Peru called for regional disarmament in 1975, but no one seems to have taken the proposal seriously.[43] The Andean Group presidents renounced weapons of mass destruction in December 1991 (Declaration of

Cartagena). The OAS is currently attempting to both institutionalize and stimulate the arms control process.

Arms control and confidence-building measures (CBMs) are not simple issues, dependent solely upon political will and an unmitigated good. Rather they are complex, with potential spillovers that are not often considered. OAS resolutions frequently refer to "legitimate defense requirements" when discussing curbing arms proliferation, but what does the phrase mean in practice? Arms registries in principle contribute to confidence building, but are less meaningful in the absence of agreement on what constitutes stable force levels. We also need to think about how modernization and professionalization fit into arms control in the Latin American context. Finally, the impact of arms control on civil-military relations in a domestic context of redemocratization should also concern us.

Many analysts believe that the path of nonoffensive defense provides the starting point for fruitfully resolving these issues. Nonoffensive defense appears ideal in that if everyone had strictly defensive capabilities, offense would be impossible. But geography (as in the case of the long narrow terrain of Chile) and technology can facilitate turning a defensive capability into an offensive one with a shift in military doctrine.[44] For example, Ecuador's increased defensive capabilities gave it an ability to militarily contest its border with Peru, resulting in the recent border skirmish. Thus legitimate defense requirements need to be directly linked to the types of threats perceived by the potential disputants if significant and stable progress on arms control is to be achieved.

There is plenty of evidence that expectations of conflict lead to arms buildups in Latin America. Common opinion erroneously attributes increased arms expenditures to the assumption of power by the military. Arms proliferation followed rightist military coups in neighboring Bolivia and Chile, and subsequently in Argentina.[45] The left-leaning Peruvian military took power in 1968 but did not embark on a major arms push for five years. Yet Colombia and Ecuador both increased the size of their armed forces although their democratic rivals took a different path: Venezuela increased defense expenditures slightly and ended with roughly the same size, while Peru decreased its armed forces significantly. Differences in internal threats are not sufficient to explain this contrasting behavior. Peru faced dramatically increased guerrilla activity from Sendero Luminoso in this period but still steadily decreased its armed forces by almost 50 percent (from 8.9 per 1,000 inhabitants to 4.8). Ecuador had no internal guerrilla threat yet increased its military personnel. Colombia faced an internal threat but also began its military buildup in 1987, when the Caldas incident with Venezuela precipitated putting its military forces on alert.[46]

Latin American leaders also do not feel secure with a unilaterally and significantly diminished military presence, even in the absence of immediate security threats. Contemporary Argentina, democratic for ten years and with clear civilian control of a dramatically and politically weakened military, argues that the level of air power attained by the military government before the Malvinas fiasco is the norm to which it must rebuild to be secure.[47] In fact, Argentina has significantly increased its radar capabilities in the most recent purchases, even threatening to buy the radar from Israel if the United States continues to respect British desires for a weakened Argentine air force.[48] Although Chile does not perceive an immediate threat from Peru, it is also upgrading its air force with purchases of Mirages that will be renovated to be, as the air force commander in chief said, on a par with the Peruvian air fleet.[49] The performance of Ecuador's SAMs against Peruvian fighter bombers and helicopters will also fuel the perception across Latin American that future defense tasks will require more sophisticated equipment on both the ground and in the air.

It is important to note that the need for a deterrent military force is not simply a perception of the military and political leadership in Latin America. In a recent public opinion survey in Argentina and Chile, over 25 percent of respondents believed the other country could attack, despite the democratic systems reigning in both.[50] The nationalist rhetoric in both Ecuador and Peru during the recent border war was very high and acrimonious.[51]

The question of force structure not only affects international relations but has an impact on the domestic civil-military relationship, particularly in redemocratizing countries. The challenge for these countries is to shift military interests from managing domestic conflict to defending the nation from external military aggression. This is part of what we mean by the professionalization of the armed forces. But professionalization also requires that they be respected in this mission and that implies that they be given the tools with which to carry out this function efficiently and effectively. This means force modernization in the Latin American context, because much of their equipment is not only technologically old but also deteriorating because of age and lack of maintenance as a result of the economic crises of the 1980s. Professionalization thus will require, in the short to medium term, increased military budgets and the acquisition of new and more modern equipment.

If arms control efforts seriously hamper this process of military professionalization it may inadvertently undermine the consolidation of democracy. Without resources professionalization is impossible because the military will understand that civilian politicians are asking them to do a job without providing them with the means to carry it out. Civilian politicians will thus be perceived by the military and its civilian allies as either seeking to undermine the military or incompetent. In addition, if the pace of forced modernization varies dramatically within conflictual dyads, the military wishing to professionalize but not getting many resources will also perceive civilian policies as increasing the vulnerability of the nation and hence to be both traitorous and dangerous.

Distinguishing Between Legitimate and Illegitimate Uses of Military Force

Is there a legitimate role for the use of military force in Latin America? What are the implications of recognizing that military forces have a legitimate role to play in Latin America? And what is that role? These questions continue to bedevil U.S.–Latin American relations as well as intra–Latin American relations.

Wars of conquest are clearly inappropriate uses of military force in today's world. But the use of force in Latin America is not about conquest or war. Diplomacy does not always bring satisfactory results (this is as true for Ecuador vis-à-vis Peru as for the United States vis-à-vis Panama or Haiti). One party may decide to open or reopen negotiations to achieve something it currently does not have, but the other party may want to preserve the status quo. How then does one reopen the issue? As long as the costs of creating a crisis are not outweighed by the benefits of forcing negotiations or imposing a solution, militarization of these disputes promise to occur. And as long as militarization of conflicts accomplishes desired ends, it sends the message that militarizing a conflict is a legitimate use of a state's military apparatus. If we want to avoid militarized interstate disputes (MIDs), and we assume that we do, the international community has to weigh in to raise the costs and decrease the benefits of militarization.

❀ Part I

The Transformation of Interstate Relations in Southern South America

How have Argentina, Brazil, and Chile transformed their interstate relations since the late 1970s and, especially, during the 1990s? The three chapters that follow demonstrate the considerable convergence in the foreign policies of these major Southern Cone countries while also highlighting important differences that persist in their approach toward the international system and each other.

Carlos Escudé and Andrés Fontana demonstrate the extraordinary transformation in Argentina's foreign policy. Argentina has downsized its armed forces, dismantled military-run state enterprises, abandoned its attempt to develop a ballistic missile system, and imposed constraints on its capacity to wage war. It has also sought to deepen cooperative ties with its neighbors, with the United States, and even with the United Kingdom, with which it fought a war in 1982. The authors argue that Argentina has come to resemble a peaceful "trading state."

Francisco Rojas characterizes the intertwining of Chile's civil-military relations and external policies. Democratic Chilean governments seek to establish proper civilian control over the armed forces, despite constitutional and legal provisions that make it difficult. These governments have also fashioned a foreign and security policy above partisanship. Chilean civilian leaders, from government and opposition, and military officers have worked jointly to identify and implement a "state policy" that represents the nation's interests.

Mônica Hirst identifies the complex features of relations among Argentina, Brazil, and Chile. She highlights the gradual process of change and accommodation in their relations, which took them from the brink of war toward more constructive relations. She focuses on Brazil's stable approach to foreign policy, contrasting it with the much sharper swings in Argentine foreign policy. Brazil's policies show consistency on such topics as U.S. relations, nuclear energy, relations with neighbors, and international institutions.

Chapter 3

Argentina's Security Policies
Their Rationale and Regional Context

Carlos Escudé and Andrés Fontana

Introduction

With the advent of the Menem administration, Argentina's foreign and security policies underwent a dramatic change. Indeed, until President Menem took over the presidency in 1989, and ever since 1889 (when the first Pan American Conference was held in Washington D.C.) Argentina and the United States had relations that, with few exceptions, were less than friendly and were usually rather tense. Argentina systematically antagonized the United States in diplomatic fora, rejected the Monroe Doctrine, was neutral during both world wars, championed a so-called "Third Position" after 1945, and later joined the Non-Aligned Movement. Concomitantly, under successive governments (and regardless of the type of domestic regime) the Argentine state refused to sign the Non-Proliferation Treaty (NPT), refused to ratify the Tlatelolco Treaty for the prohibition of nuclear weapons in Latin America, devoted its scarce resources to the successful enrichment of uranium (which its reactors, that ran on natural uranium, did not need), and already under the democratic administration of Alfonsín (1983–89) undertook a joint venture with Egypt, Iraq, and Libya for the development of an intermediate-range guided missile, the Cóndor II. On the other hand, until 1979[1] relations with Brazil, which included a nuclear race, were very tense, while war almost broke out with Chile in 1978. Furthermore, in 1982 Argentina invaded the disputed Falkland/Malvinas Islands, which had been under British rule since

1833; in so doing, the Argentine state found itself in a losing war against the United Kingdom in which the United States sided, expectably, with the latter.[2]

This track record was unique in Latin America and was the product of several factors that fed into each other, among them:

1. Argentina's past prosperity (from approximately 1880 to 1942), which had generated expectations of future world power status. This prosperity was the product of a dependent development symbiotically tied to the British economy, but was not in any way (until the Second World War) dependent on the United States.[3]

2. Argentina's geographical isolation, that made it possible to nurture inflated ideas of Argentine development and power.

3. The contents of Argentina's educational system, that encouraged exaggerated perceptions of Argentine splendor and future possibilities.[4]

4. Last but not least, an eclectic ideology of international relations that was influenced by several distinct traditions of thought, some imported and some indigenous.

Like many other states worldwide, until the advent of the Menem administration and at least since the 1940s Argentina subordinated citizen welfare to the quest for regional power, sometimes under the delusion that it would be able to compete in a grander global game. However, the need for a "developmentalist" approach to Argentina's foreign and security policies became increasingly clear as the failure and counterproductive consequences of policies inspired by prestige and power-oriented objectives became more dramatically clear. For some small intellectual circles, this became obvious when in the late 1970s U.S. and British archival material regarding U.S.-Argentine relations during the 1940s was declassified, and it became possible to actually quantify the losses generated by Argentina's challenge of U.S. hegemony, and to identify the devastating consequences of the United States' economic boycott and political destabilization of Argentina, undertaken from 1942 to 1949.[5]

Notwithstanding, this was not enough to convince a wider public or to influence policy. The Falkland/Malvinas War of 1982, however, provided much more dramatic arguments for the need to refocus Argentina's foreign and security policies with a citizen-centric approach.[6] The never fully measured developmental costs of that unnecessary war were enormous: it jeopardized economic relations with the European Economic Community, alienated investments, contributed to raise the country risk index to astronomical levels, and so on. An increasingly intense intellectual debate emerged, based mainly in two institutions, Instituto Torcuato Di Tella and FLACSO Buenos Aires.[7]

Although Argentina has a long tradition of strategic thought based in research institutions, universities, and military colleges, and in this respect the debate was not a novelty (Raúl Prebisch, the father of the ECLA center-periphery approach, was, after all, an Argentine), what was now beginning to be questioned were the premises of the previously dominant paradigms. The latter were based on the (Latin American) dependency, (Anglo-American) realist, and (German) geopolitical schools, and as mentioned above, they had generated an eclectic ideology that was partly imported and partly indigenous, which emphasized the importance of territory, military balances, state power, and "autonomy" as the ultimate goals of a country's foreign and security policies. For many decades, these premises appealed to both the Left and the Right, although there existed differences in the specific ideological "mix" adopted by different ideological forces.[8] After the Falkland/Malvinas War, all of these previously hegemonic values began to be questioned increasingly from liberal quarters, both academic and political.

The time, however, was not yet ripe for the impact of new ideas on policy.[9] The Alfonsín administration, which faced the difficult task of Argentina's transition to democracy, limited its foreign and security policy innovations to the consolidation of cooperative relations with Brazil, beginning the long road toward economic integration, and to putting an end to tensions with Chile, solving a territorial dispute and setting the bases for future cooperation. These were important steps forward, to be sure, but Argentina's policies in the realm of nuclear safeguards and missile development remained unchanged, while the Alfonsín administration concomitantly refused to reestablish relations with the United Kingdom and undertook an aggressive policy against Britain in the South Atlantic, remaining essentially anti-Western in terms of the Argentine state's voting profile in international fora. Such a foreign policy fell very short of what the advocates of a foreign policy inspired in the need for growth and development desired, but they were still a small minority.

The crucial point in which these tables turned was probably the hyperinflation suffered in Argentina in 1989 and, once again, in 1990. Hyperinflation—an economic phenomenon—made political elites and people in general even more aware of their pocketbooks than is usually—and universally—the case. Hyperinflation meant the death of the Alfonsín government, which had to resign months ahead of time to the new president-elect. Hyperinflation brought the country back to its senses, both economically and with respect to foreign and security policies: it obsessed leaders and ordinary citizens alike with a desire for monetary stability and no-nonsense foreign and security policies that would keep the country out of trouble and would be functional to the state's economic goals. It is not a coincidence that President Menem's first foreign minister, Domingo Cavallo, was an economist, and that when Cavallo took charge of the ministry of the economy the new foreign minister, Guido Di Tella, should also have been an economist. Moreover, the ministers of defense have not been drawn from the ranks of the military.

Under the tenures of Cavallo and Di Tella, Argentina's foreign and security policies underwent a dramatic change. The Argentine state explicitly aligned itself with the West, abandoned the nonaligned movement, and completely changed its voting profile in international fora, adopting a clearly pro-Western policy. It reestablished cooperative and indeed friendly relations with Britain. It scrapped the Cóndor II missile project, ratified the Tlatelolco Treaty for the prohibition of nuclear weapons in Latin America, signed a separate nuclear safeguards agreement with Brazil and the International Atomic Energy Agency (IAEA), and subscribed to the Non-Proliferation Treaty (NPT). Additionally, it bandwagoned with the United States, achieving the country's first successful insertion in world military affairs, intervening in the Gulf War, in Haiti, and in several peace missions under United Nations sponsorship. Last but not least, it continued with Alfonsín's policy of political rapprochement with Chile, further advancing in the demarcation of the boundary (the problem that had brought both countries to the brink of war in 1978), and it deepened the process of economic integration with Brazil through the creation of the quadripartite Southern-Cone Common Market (MERCOSUR). Paradoxically—as seen below—a serious challenge to Argentina's new alignment with the West emerged precisely from its growing economic and political interdependence with Brazil.

On the other hand, as can be demonstrated by several press articles published by Foreign Minister Di Tella,[10] the policy change implemented by the Menem administration emerged from a rationale based on the following assumptions:

1. In a liberal democracy, and in the circumstances described above, the principal function of foreign policy should be to serve the individual citizens, and this can be done principally by facilitating economic development;[11]

2. Hence, economic development is the very definition of the "national" interest, especially in the case of a developing country which, like Argentina, faces no credible external threats, and

3. The United States is the single most important external constraint to foreign policy in the Latin American region, and it is therefore in the best interests of a country like Argentina to have good relations with that power, *so long as these good relations are not at the expense of the material interests of Argentina.*

From this set of assumptions, and from a reading of the historical record, it was inferred that any challenge to U.S. leadership not connected to devel-

opment is detrimental to development insofar as it breeds negative perceptions among potential investors and moneylenders, increasing the country
risk index: from a citizen-centric perspective it is all loss and no gain. This is
not to say that the Argentine state has ceased all attempts to have an influence on the international agenda (which it has always attempted to exercise,
as have the other two major Southern Cone countries, contrariwise to, for
example, some of the small Central American and Caribbean states), but
only that its leaders have come to the conclusion that the only way to do this
successfully in the long term (and without hurting the interests of Argentina's citizens) is to adopt a developmentalist strategy and an explicit alignment, as (for example) did the two German states and Japan after their defeat
at war.

This was a part of the rationale for Argentina's abandonment of the Non-
aligned Movement under President Menem: membership carried no practical benefits, while it concomitantly generated dysfunctional perceptions in
the world's most important financial communities. As such, membership
was contrary to the interests of the Argentine people. This was as well a major reason for acquiescing with such U.S. demands[12] as accepting nuclear
safeguards and deactivating the Cóndor II. This was also the primary rationale for satisfying Western expectations with respect to a cooperative policy
in the South Atlantic, leading to the reestablishment of relations with the
United Kingdom despite the Falkland/Malvinas dispute. In terms of this rationale, challenges of U.S. leadership, as well as other direct or indirect confrontations with great powers, are justified only when they are connected directly to factors that impinge on economic growth and development, in
which case they are a calculated risk justifiable from the point of view of future citizen welfare or the long-term construction of state power with a solid
economic base.

On the other hand, bandwagoning with the United States and with the
United Nations Security Council in operations like the Gulf War, the restora-
tion of democracy in Haiti, and the deployment of peacekeeping troops in
diverse scenarios worldwide, as performed by Argentina under the Menem
administration, is not tantamount to independent power politics but, on the
contrary, is a calculated acquiescence to the political needs of the United
States and other Western powers, in which Argentina's material interests are
not jeopardized while the operations involved can plausibly be argued to be
good causes. As such, these operations are perceived as functional to the generation of positive perceptions among financiers and potential investors,
while they are concomitantly perceived not to alienate influential segments
of world public opinion. To this rationale, Argentine officials add that the
consolidation of a world order, of stability and peace, is in the interests of Ar-

gentina herself, and that it therefore makes good sense to participate in these operations. Furthermore, the perception in Argentine government circles is that this policy cannot sensibly be construed, by Argentina's neighbors, to contribute to an Argentine military threat (through the acquisition of military know-how and expertise), inasmuch as they not only come together with the dismantlement of a ballistic missile project and with the unambiguous acceptance of nuclear safeguards, but also with: (1) a reduction of the military budget, (2) the elimination of the draft, (3) the virtual dismantlement of Argentina's arms industry (which was chronically in the red financially, but which produced, among other weapons, fairly efficient armored battle tanks[13]), and (4) a consistent effort to institutionalize confidence-building measures (CBMs) and cooperative security mechanisms in the hemisphere, region, and subregion.

Hence, Argentine involvement abroad as undertaken under Menem is not perceived as being in contradiction with the policies expectable from what Richard Rosecrance calls "trading states."[14]

Argentina's Global Security Policies Under Menem

With respect to global security, the Argentine government states that the main focus of its policies lies in the support of the United Nations and, most especially, of the Security Council, while it is explicitly aligned with the West. As a temporary member of the Security Council (which it was until December 1995) Argentina had a relatively independent policy, having more agreements therein with Great Britain, France, and Japan than with the United States. During its tenure in the council, Argentina became a member of the secretary-general's consulting committee on peace operations. Argentina participated in the Gulf War and became a pioneer in intense Latin American presence and participation in peacekeeping operations.[15]

According to the government's discourse, the participation in peacekeeping and democracy-restoration missions projects an image of Argentina as a credit-worthy state committed to international peace and security. This assumption appears empirically convalidated by an increasing number of positive reactions from the military establishments of North Atlantic Treaty Organization (NATO) members. The government's discourse also acknowledges that the country's participation in these operations contributes to the know-how and professional training of members of its armed forces, and that to some degree this training is acquired at the expense of the United Nations, so it is a good deal whatever the perspective of its evaluation may be. Finally, it is also a part of the rationale for this policy that participation in United Nations peacekeeping operations helps to consolidate democracy through the gradual transformation of the role of the Argentine armed forces, which ever since the collapse of the last military dictatorship have suffered from a sort of existential crisis.

In this context, the Argentine government has held a keen interest in changes within NATO. According to the former, NATO's transformation, which began in 1990, has led the organization to an increasing commitment with the United Nations Security Council. Argentina has established contacts with NATO and has undertaken intense political, military, and academic exchanges both with it and its member states.[16] At an earlier stage of the Menem administration Argentine officials nourished the illusion of eventually being accepted as a member to NATO. Notwithstanding, mild disappointment with the prospects of these expectations has generated a greater realism, and at the present time government discourse emphasizes that its aim is not to join NATO but to cooperate with it. Furthermore, in the Clinton-Menem meeting of December 1996 it was accorded that the White House would study the possibility of formally awarding Argentina the status of extra-Nato ally, a category that very few states (such as Japan, Israel, Australia, New Zealand, and most recently Jordan) enjoy and that must be approved by Congress.

On the other hand, and as stated in the introduction, Argentina has substantively modified its policies in the field of nonproliferation, deactivating the Cóndor II missile and becoming a member of the Missile Technology Control Regime (MTCR), the Australian Group, and the Group of Nuclear Exporters. The sum of these commitments, plus Tlatelolco and NPT, subject Argentina to the strictest nonproliferation constraints accepted by any member of the international community.

Furthermore, Argentina and Brazil have signed and implemented a number of agreements in relation to the peaceful use of nuclear energy that have led to reciprocal inspections of their nuclear programs, to the creation of a bilateral system of accountability and control, and to the inception of a bilateral agency (ABACC) dedicated to the administration of this system. The process of nuclear rapprochement and increased transparency reached its culmination with the signature of a quadrilateral safeguards agreement with the IAEA, in force since March 1994. Parties to the agreement with IAEA are the two states plus ABACC, which has incipient supranational functions.

On the other hand, since 1991 Argentina, Brazil, and Chile have jointly promoted a series of reforms to the Tlatelolco Treaty for the Prohibition of Nuclear Weapons in Latin America in order to update it and to put it in force in the entire region. These amendments were approved and signed by the member states in Mexico City on August 26, 1992, and were later ratified by the legislatures of the three countries. Furthermore, Argentina has initiated formal contacts with the successor agency of the Coordinating Committee on Export Controls (COCOM), which favors greater intrusive powers for the IAEA and promotes greater cooperation between the latter and the Security Council. Last, but not least, Argentina not only has adhered to the Non-Proliferation Treaty but also encourages its neighbors to do the same. It also supported the U.S. position in favor of an unlimited renewal of the NPT, playing a leading role in the April 1995 NPT Conference.

In the field of chemical and bacteriological weapons, Argentina, Brazil, and Chile signed the Declaration of Mendoza in September 1991, which was subsequently adhered to by Bolivia, Ecuador, Paraguay, and Uruguay. Through this accord, the signatory parties have agreed not to develop, store, or use chemical or biological weapons and to be among the original parties to the Convention on Chemical Weapons. Argentina, Brazil, and Chile are among the first states in the world to commit themselves to this multilateral agreement. Argentina's attitude in the United Nations Conference on Disarmament was consistent with these policies, pushing for a rapid agreement on the Convention on Chemical Weapons, which was subscribed by Argentina in Paris in January 1993. Finally, Argentina has abandoned the UN Conference on Disarmament's Group of 21, to formally become a member of the Western Group in January 1995.

Argentina's Regional Security Policies Under Menem

In the field of regional security the policy implemented by the Argentine government has several dimensions. In the first place, it has seconded the pleas of Secretary General Boutros Boutros-Ghali (included in chapters 2 and 7 of his 1992 "Agenda for Peace") with respect to preventive diplomacy and to the support of the United Nations by regional agencies and mechanisms. The Argentine government understands that the system of collective security requires the support of regional mechanisms in order to effectively contain the many challenges to peace and international security. Concomitantly, it understands that regional mechanisms and agencies require the legitimization that can only be provided by a strong link to the United Nations.

Notwithstanding, it is not easy to implement these policies successfully in a regional context where military interests and geopolitical conceptions still have prestige and influence, this being the case, in varying degrees, of Brazil and Chile.

Indeed, as we see below, the ongoing influence of military interests and geopolitical conceptions in neighboring countries has been an obstacle to the implementation of Argentina's developmentalist security policies all across the board (even if, with the advent of the administration of Fernando

Henrique Cardoso in Brazil, some of the latter's security policies have begun to converge with Argentina's). The Argentine government is particularly interested in developing a new concept of regional security that privileges transparency, cooperation, and the abandonment of arms races of all sorts. Toward this end, the Argentine government is interested in the analysis and discussion, in the region, of the Western European postwar security experience. It is interested in fully implementing the concept of cooperative security and in modifying accordingly the system of collective security, thus overcoming the older conceptions of security based on the defensive capabilities of states and power-balancing alliances.

The Argentine government's efforts in this score have focused on preaching the need for changes in the context of the Organization of American States (OAS), and bilaterally to the Brazilian and Chilean governments. Moreover, Argentina has had an active role in the initiatives tending to update the structure and functions of the OAS in everything pertaining to security. The OAS can and to a modest degree has begun to play a relevant role in preventive diplomacy, in the administration of crises, and in joint and complementary activities with the United Nations.

It is with this aim that Argentina has actively supported the Special Committee on Hemispheric Security in relation to measures for confidence-building and for the prevention of conflicts. This purpose was reflected in the meeting of experts on CBMs and security mechanisms, held in Buenos Aires in March 1994; in the conference of ministers of defense held in Williamsburg, Virginia, in July 1995; in the first meeting (on CBMs) of the European Union–Group of Río Dialogue, held in Punta del Este in October 1995; in the regional conference on regional security and CBMs, held in Chile in November 1995; in the second meeting of the European Union–Group of Río Dialogue (on security issues), held in Quito in November 1996; and in the meeting of ministers of defense held in Bariloche, Argentina, in October 1996. The Declaration of Santiago on Security and Confidence-Building Measures, of November 9, 1995, recommends a number of mechanisms that, if formally adopted as binding, would radically change the security climate in the hemisphere.[17]

In the same field, the Argentine government promotes changes in the functions and structures of the Inter-American Defense Board. Until recently, the latter's functions had been dictated by an outdated cold war rationale. Although this problem has been overcome, some of the region's more influential military establishments continue to oppose a subordination of the board to the OAS. Contrariwise, the Argentine government desires to see it integrated into the structure of the OAS in order to make it a useful tool for peace and security, in the context of the board's political subordination to democratic governments and their policies. In other words, the Argentine government feels that the board should no longer be conceived as an exercise in military diplomacy relatively isolated from the other dimensions of diplomacy.

Furthermore, the Argentine government promotes regionwide exchanges between legislatures and their defense and foreign policy committees, as well as periodical meetings of ministers of defense or their equivalents, in order to generate politico-technical fora for the analysis of the region's security problematique. Although little has been achieved with the legislatures, from 1995 to the present two ministerial meetings at the hemispheric level have been held (the already mentioned conferences of Williamsburg, Virginia, and Bariloche, Argentina). An interim meeting is planned for 1997, and yet another ministerial conference is to be held in 1998. Notwithstanding, there is an ongoing debate on whether these meetings should be institutionalized (Argentina's position) or held merely on an ad hoc basis.

Until recently, the Argentine government had seen the absence of a ministry of defense in Brazil (where there is a separate ministry for each of the three armed services) as an obstacle to cooperation and coordination in the field of security. It also perceived this institutional framework as a mechanism that helped the Brazilian military partially to escape civilian control. However, there have been some very encouraging recent developments. Cardoso's administration has upgraded the Brazilian government's Secretariat for Strategic Affairs, an agency that depends directly on the presidency, and has appointed a very prestigious diplomat as its head. Furthermore, it has given policy formulation powers to the Casa Militar, a subagency itself a part of the presidency. More recently, it has created a "Committee for Foreign Relations and Defense of the Presidency of the Republic," which has policy-making powers. Thus, civilian control of the military and the strategic coordination between the three services have been enhanced, and regional cooperation in security affairs has been facilitated. Nonetheless, it can still be stated that too much depends on the political will (and the power) of President Cardoso, and that the centralization of Brazilian military policy still requires a more solid institutionalization.

In the bilateral sphere, Argentina has developed fluid contacts with Brazil and Chile and has proposed periodical meetings for the treatment of security issues of common interest. Cooperation in security affairs has advanced much more with the former than with the latter. Substantive exchanges and military cooperation with Brazil date back at least a decade, when the first joint Army General Staff meetings began to be held. Paraguay, Uruguay, and recently Chile, have been more lately included in these meetings.

In September 1996, for the first time in history, the armies of Argentina and Brazil undertook a joint exercise in the Argentine province of Corrientes. This exercise, titled "Operation Southern Cross," focused on planning and executing a peacekeeping mission under UN mandate, with the participation of approximately 1,300 personnel of both armies. The two countries have agreed to repeat this annually, taking turns in the use of each other's territory.

At the beginning of November 1996, the new defense policy of Brazil was made public. This is the first defense policy to have been coined fully under Brazil's relatively new democracy. The Committee for Foreign Relations and Defense of the Presidency of the Republic drafted the new policy, which eliminates conflict hypotheses with Argentina and foresees the transfer to the Amazon of the Brazilian troops stationed in the south of the country. Immediately afterward, the Argentine vice foreign minister, Andrés Cisneros, asserted that in the near future joint Argentine-Brazilian forces might have a single command, in the framework of subregional military integration. This statement was soon seconded by the chief of the Casa Militar of the Brazilian presidency, who said that it is very possible that agreements might soon be reached for formal military integration in the South American continent. One possibility for the further development of cooperation in this field lies in the coordination of both countries' contributions to peacekeeping forces, which could generate joint routines and operation procedures whose use could later be expanded into other military activities.

The navies of Argentina and Brazil also cooperate in a wide range of activities, including joint exercises for the control of the South Atlantic area (Operativo CAMAS), joint aeronaval exercises using the Brazilian aircraft carrier (Operativo Araex, undertaken on an annual basis), and Operativo Fraterno and Operativo ATLASUR (both of which involve joint maneuvers at sea). Cooperation between the two air forces is less intense and tends to be limited to officer and student exchanges.

Regrettably, nothing comparable to Argentine-Brazilian military cooperation has been achieved in Argentina's bilateral security relations with Chile. In this case, cooperation has been limited to officer exchanges, to coordinated action in the case of accidents and natural catastrophes (search and rescue), to annual joint meetings of the naval authorities of both countries' southern regions, to a recent (and first ever) joint Naval General Staff meeting, and to a system of permanent communication between air force bases in the extreme south for the purpose of air traffic control. On November 8, 1995, a memorandum of understanding for the strengthening of bilateral cooperation in security issues of mutual interest was signed in Santiago. A committee was then created, which met twice during 1996.

On the other hand, Argentina has also strengthened its security links with the United States and Canada. It has participated in a trilateral naval game with the United States and Canada (focused on the exchange of information on military organization and doctrine), and it has established annual bilateral working groups with both these countries, with the participation of representatives of their foreign ministries, defense ministries, and armed forces. In 1995, Argentina and the United States jointly undertook a "peace-force exercise." Furthermore, the navies of both countries undertake biannual meetings for a strategic dialogue (at the staff general level), and annual meetings of their naval committees for surface, aviation, and infantry operations. Combined exercises are quite frequent, the most important of which are the Fleetex (with units of both fleets), the IMARA-USMC (with regiments of both marine corps), and the GRINGO-GAUCHO (with aircrafts of both countries, using U.S. aircraft carriers when they are transiting the region). In the case of the armies and air forces, cooperation is more narrow, limited to the exchange of officers and to graduate courses at the U.S. Air War College and the U.S. Air Command.

Finally, another important regional security policy that the Menem government has pursued and that is consistent with its quest for development and peace has been the normalization of relations with the United Kingdom. The lack of a solution to the Falkland/Malvinas dispute has not prevented the initiation of a constructive dialogue on the South Atlantic nor the development of CBMs between Argentina and Britain. A system of bilateral military consultations has been operating since 1993, which holds two yearly meetings and which includes not only military officers but also civilian officials from both the defense and foreign ministries.[18] Every available opportunity for cooperation (such as joint participation in UN peacekeeping operations) is used to build closer military links. In November 1996, General Martín Balza, head of the Argentine Army, accepted an official invitation of the British Army with very promising results. Notwithstanding, Britain's arms embargo against Argentina continues, making it more difficult for the Southern Cone country to maintain a safe regional arms balance. Repair parts for British-made Argentine equipment are not made available to Argentina even if their need has been generated by the equipment's use in United Nations operations, and despite the very modest present-day level of Argentine military expenditures. In this respect, the United States has at times cooperated with Argentina, moderating British pressures to deprive Argentina of armament. Notwithstanding, the United States is sometimes a party to the embargo and until August 1997 refused to supply state-of-the-art radars to Argentina, at Britain's request. The problems posed by the British arms embargo, as well as by Chile's arms buildup, have been the focus of several bilateral U.S.-Argentine conversations at the ministerial level. Needless to say, the enactment in 1994 of a constitutional clause whereby the recovery of Falkland/Malvinas (through "peaceful means") is a mandatory policy for any Argentine government has not made the solution of this problem any easier.

Alleged Subregional Military Imbalances

Surprisingly enough for a country with its history of military coups and involvement in politics, Argentina has become a successfully demilitarized state to a considerably greater degree than any other in South America. Its military expenses relative to the gross domestic product have decreased enormously since the advent of the Menem administration, reaching 3.8 percent in 1985 (under the democratic administration of President Alfonsín), 3.5 percent in 1989 (Menem was inaugurated in the course of that year), and 1.9 percent in 1991. Subsequently, the military budget continued to suffer reductions. These figures compare with 3.4 percent of GDP for Chile in 1991.[19] In 1994 the obligatory military service was abolished by law, and in 1995 the measure was already implemented. In late 1996 its total armed forces include approximately 75,000 active personnel, vis-à-vis Chile's 93,000, despite that country's smaller population (Brazil's total active men being approximately 300,000).[20] The deactivation of the Cóndor II missile was a unilateral measure of disarmament not comparable to any measures undertaken by the Brazilian or Chilean governments (and indeed, almost unique anywhere, even if we consider that U.S. pressures and Argentine financial vulnerability were the most important factors conditioning it).

Needless to say, although the military have been thoroughly neutralized as a political factor in Argentina, they have not been happy with the decrease of Argentine military power.[21] There was headstrong opposition to the deactivation of the Cóndor II, and in this they were supported both by Alfonsín's Radical Party (the former president having signed the secret accord with Iraq and Egypt)[22] and, paradoxically, by the political Left. As the measures of demilitarization accumulated, the military, some of their allies in the political Right, and the left-of-center Radical Party as well were able to mount a relatively successful campaign that claims that the country has become defenseless vis-à-vis Chile's allegedly ongoing territorial expansionism.[23]

It is difficult to appraise this claim. On the surface it appears to be groundless, but published statistics often conceal more than what they reveal. Without question, in the last few years Argentina has undergone a process of unilateral disarmament, but it is a relative one. Military expenditures have been cut down drastically, military personnel have been reduced, and the military have lost all of their former (and once considerable) local prestige. Notwithstanding, during the military dictatorship Argentina had so overspent in arms that if one were to take the statistics of the International Institute for Strategic Affairs at face value one would come to the conclusion that its hardware is still superior to Chile's. Apparently, Argentina still has considerably more combat aircraft and heavy and light tanks than does Chile.[24] It is of course impossible to know from published sources how many of these are out of service; it may well be that Chile's equipment is more modern, and it is rumored that Chile has a far greater stock of ammunition than does Argentina.

Indeed, when interviewed on the issue of Southern Cone military imbalances, high-ranking Argentine military officers emphatically point out that published statistics do not reflect the state of the matériel. To do this it would be necessary to compare the portion of the military budget dedicated to maintenance during a period of at least five years. In Argentina, during the past five years expenditures on the salaries and pensions of personnel have represented between 70 and 80 percent of the budget of each of the armed services.[25] The rest (which in absolute figures amounts to 120 million U.S. dollars for the army, 80 million for the navy, and 64 million for the air force) is applied to operational expenses, there being at present practically no expenditures in maintenance, which has been the main adjustment variable in each of the successive budget reductions. Argentine officers also claim that their operational budget is so low that while the Brazilian Navy sails an average of 150 days per year, the average for Argentine units is only thirty days, that is, five times less.[26]

The Argentines argue as well that the military statistics that are published do not fully take into account the degree of modernization and investment that has been added on to hardware after their original purchase, and in this they feel that they are very much behind Chile. For example, if a fighter aircraft can be refueled in the air, and if an air force has airplanes for the refueling of fighter aircraft, then a fighter plane (which presumably is a defense weapon) becomes an attack plane. Chile is preparing four Boeing 707s for refueling operations, and according to Argentine military sources the F-16s that Chile is in the process of acquiring will be prepared for refueling.

Similarly, Chile's British-made County class destroyers, which were originally designed to serve as the command unit for an antisubmarine surface group, have been later equipped with MM-38 Exocet missiles that enable them to sink destroyers (42-km. range); with radar-guided Sea Slug MK2 surface-to-air missiles (45-km. range, used successfully by the British in the Falkland/Malvinas War); with radar and optically guided surface-to-air Sea Cat MK2 missiles (5-km. range); with last-generation radar-guided surface-to-air Barak missiles (12–18-km. range); with 115-millimeter Vickers MK6 and MK22 surface-to-surface and surface-to-air dual use cannons; with 20-

millimeter Oerlikon MK9 surface-to-air cannons (800 shots per minute); with 324-millimeter MK32 torpedoes; and with NAS 332 Super Puma/Cougar helicopters capable of firing MM-39 Exocet missiles, which multiply the offensive power of these destroyers. These warships have also been equipped with Chaff systems that allow them to interfere and divert possible air, surface, and submarine attacks, as well as with the Chilean-British SISDEF system of control and command. Equipped with these additional weapons and electronic systems, these warships are now much more powerful than the original County class destroyers were, and they cannot be compared to Argentine destroyers, which statistically appear as the same thing. On the other hand, most of the modernization processes were undertaken by the Chilean ASMAR shipyards, a fact that gives Chile an additional comparative advantage. A similar case can be built for Chile's Leander class frigates, which have likewise been made into much more powerful units than they were when originally purchased and are no longer the standard antisubmarine frigates they purport to be. In the imbalance thus generated the British arms embargo against Argentina, and Britain's continued supply to Chile, weighs heavily.

Whatever the case may be, the prevailing perception both in Argentine military and journalistic circles is that there is a serious and growing military imbalance in Chile's favor. This perception is functional to the interests of the military, but this fact does not invalidate the claims, much less the relevance of the perception itself. The perception, on the other hand, is strengthened by the fact that both the Chilean and the Brazilian governments appear to be less committed to the formal control of conventional weapons and to CBMs in this field than is the Argentine government.

The Divergence in Argentine and Chilean Strategic Thinking

Indeed, although great breakthroughs have been made in the regional control and banning of nuclear, chemical, and bacteriological weapons, there is great resistance in the region to the control of conventional weapons. The Chilean Constitution even establishes a fixed level of military expenditures, while the Brazilian government is extremely jealous of its autonomy in this score.

Ultimately, the differences that set Argentina, Brazil, and Chile apart in this field and in the wider realm of strategic conceptions would appear to emerge from the differences in the processes of redemocratization of these Southern Cone countries. In Argentina transition to democracy took place in the context of defeat at war and severe economic crisis, and it generated a total collapse of military prestige and of the domestic political power of the military. Although former president Alfonsín was only partially successful in

the neutralization of the military, the Menem government managed to totally wipe them out of the domestic political scene through a pragmatic mixture of symbolic concessions and budget cuts, whereby (to put it simply) in
exchange for the presidential pardon for human rights abuses, many military
officers are today reduced to moonshining as taxi drivers.

Nothing of the sort happened in Chile and Brazil. In Chile the military
were not defeated at war, were relatively successful in their economic administration of the country, and retained an enormous amount of power when
they handed the government to democratically elected civilian authorities.
Something similar happened in Brazil: the military did not suffer a collapse,
but simply stepped aside. In Chile the ruling party is historically inimical to
the military, but the latter retain a virtual veto power against any action of
the civilian government that affects their interests. In Brazil the situation is
different inasmuch as there is not even such animosity, and the government
and diplomatic establishment can be described as the loyal partners of the
local military-industrial complex. From this perspective, there is more in
common between the Argentine and Chilean civilian governments than between the Brazilian government and the other two, but the Chilean government does not have the domestic power necessary to translate this into a regional security policy more in tune with civilian, citizen-centric interests.[27]

To further complicate things, the Chilean center and left-of-center political elite is currently attempting to generate what they call "state policies" (in
opposition to shorter-term "government policies") in several fields, especially
in the realm of foreign and defense affairs. It is their understanding that this
can be achieved only through the generation of a civilian-military consensus,
which in turn requires a quid pro quo with their domestically powerful military establishment. This quid pro quo would consist of getting the military to
accept democracy and subordination to civilian power, while the civilian political elite accepts the military's geopolitical theories and policies, especially
vis-à-vis Argentina. Thus, center and left-of-center Chilean officials and intellectuals tend to justify their country's arms buildup, pointing out that:

1. If Argentina has been a danger to them in 1978, it could conceivably become a danger again. Confidence building between Chile and Argentina can
only take place very gradually.[28]

2. Chile's military capabilities must be measured not only in terms of a
potential Argentine threat, but also vis-à-vis Peru and Bolivia, countries
where anti-Chilean irredentist attitudes stemming from territorial losses in
the late nineteenth century still linger on. If a limited war took place between
Peru and Ecuador in 1995, it is clear that Chile cannot afford to downsize its
military.

Thus, center and left-of-center Chilean officials and intellectuals tend to side with their military when it comes to evaluating Argentine policies, and they interpret even the most pacifist Argentine undertaking with suspicion. For example, the elimination of the draft in Argentina was interpreted as a potentially dangerous move toward the professionalization of the rank and file. When it was pointed out to them that this measure must be interpreted in a general context of Argentine disarmament (acceptance of nuclear safeguards, deactivation of the Cóndor II, reduction of the military budget, dismantlement of the arms industry, etc.), they countered with the argument that the very justification of the Argentine measure, as presented by President Menem in the decree published by the *Boletín Oficial*, explicitly says that its objective is to professionalize the armed forces. When it was argued back that surely they must understand that the president was forced to use an argument palatable to a military establishment that did not like a measure that objectively made it weaker, not stronger, they retorted that they and their own military cannot be expected to buy the idea that the Argentine president lies when he says that it is his intention to strengthen the Argentine military. Similarly, Argentine participation in UN peacekeeping operations is interpreted as leading to a potentially dangerous acquisition of military expertise.[29] To be sure, the security-related ideas of the Chilean Center and Left have become heavily militarized, and this spells bad omens for Argentina's citizen-centric policies. Seen from Argentina, the bottom line is that the abolition of the draft and the attainment of military expertise through participation in UN peacekeeping operations cannot honestly be perceived as threatening if these measures have come together with the dismantlement of the arms industry, huge military budget cuts, the abortion of the Cóndor II missile, and the most complete nonproliferation commitment in force in the international community.

This situation is made more serious by the minute yet passion-ridden territorial dispute that still sours Argentine-Chilean relations. A lot of ground has been covered in putting an end to these disputes since the redemocratization of Argentina. The Beagle Channel dispute was solved with the 1985 Treaty of Peace and Friendship, and during the Menem administration twenty-three out of the twenty-four remaining disputes (all of them insignificant in size) were solved in direct negotiations. One of the last remaining disputes, that of Laguna del Desierto, was definitively solved with the ratification of the sentence favorable to Argentina, announced by the court of arbitration in October 1995. Notwithstanding, the situation could be soured if the Argentine Congress should refuse to ratify the agreement reached between the two governments regarding the last of the unresolved disputes, that of Hielos Continentales. Some Chilean sectors argue that the acceptance of some of the previous demarcation agreements is conditioned to the definitive solution of the Hielos controversy: that they all came in a package, so to speak. For the time being, these ghosts of the past are a source of embarrassment to both governments and fuel the corporate interests of both military establishments.

The Hielos Continentales dispute requires legislative sanction because the boundary under the glacier could not be demarcated without straying from the actual wording of the treaty in force, and in Argentina the opposition has thus far made it impossible to ratify the agreement reached between both governments. Although this result can be basically attributed to opposition politics, the entire array of territorial myths and paranoid geopolitical hypotheses was put to use, frustrating ratification because even some Justicialist legislators sided against the agreement. At the time, Chilean officials stated that they were very concerned about Argentine congressional action, it being understood that they would have no problems achieving the ratification from their own legislature if the Argentine Congress ratified it. However, after the Argentine government's failure to attain ratification in 1992 and once again in 1996, doubts have been raised regarding the mood of the Chilean Congress, which might no longer be as disposed to ratification as before. Should the domestic balance of forces in Argentina change and ratification be achieved, this alleged Chilean shift could generate new and previously unexpected frustrations.

Paradoxically, the unratified agreement is in line with the treaty negotiated by Alfonsín and former foreign minister Dante Caputo during the previous administration, and as such it was at first welcomed by some prominent Radical Party legislators. However, the Radical Party leadership decided that the government should be made to pay a political price for the agreement, and these legislators were forced to back down from their initial support.[30] Legislative opposition fed back into strong grassroots feelings in the province affected by the agreement, where it was almost unanimously held that Santa Cruz was being deprived of part of its glacier by Chilean expansionism. This feedback between nationalist passions and political opportunism is what made it impossible to achieve ratification in 1992. At the last minute, when defeat was certain, the government chose to postpone legislative action and wait for a better opportunity, but it once again failed in 1996 and in 1997. Although the government will insist, no further efforts for ratification will be undertaken until after the congressional elections of October 1997, due to the political losses that would ensue if the government were to insist in an unpopular cause. Clearly, the case shows how societal forces sometimes escape the control of the governments that attempt to manage them. Due to deeply rooted cultural factors, Argentine-Chilean relations cannot be subject to a full and "rational" management by the two states.[31] As long as the present situation is not fully solved, there is a potential for a deterioration of relations and for a new arms buildup.

This potential is to a great extent neutralized, one hopes, by growing commercial interdependence and physical integration. In the last four years, bilateral trade has grown 500 percent, new roads have connected the two countries, sizeable Chilean investments (almost six billion dollars) have been made in Argentina, a pipeline project will make Chile dependent on Argentine gas, and there are plans for joint mining projects in the Andes region. However, the strategic visions dominant in both countries are very different. The Chileans, who have been very successful integrating themselves into the world economy through their export trade, have nonetheless chosen a relatively isolationist course in political affairs that is quite the opposite of Argentine protagonism. Underlying this policy is the Chilean state's unwillingness to take any steps that might eventually deprive its armed forces of some of their autonomy. This is especially clear in discussions about the eventual transformation of the hemisphere's collective security system, which the Chilean government refuses to link to discussions about its own defense system. Not only are the Chilean government and armed forces very clearly against the unofficial Argentine suggestion that a bilateral (Argentine-Chilean) or trilateral (Argentine-Brazilian-Chilean) brigade (such as the Franco-German force) be established; they are also basically against their own participation in international missions.

Nonetheless, some progress is apparently being made inasmuch as notice is beginning to be taken, by Chilean military officers, of the example set by the most recent developments in Argentine-Brazilian military cooperation. An illustration of this is what took place at the November 1996 Quito meeting, where a uniformed Argentine military officer first made a description of the Argentine-Brazilian joint peacekeeping maneuvers. He was followed by a uniformed Chilean officer who had been an observer to the exercise, and who stated that he considered it one of the most important events he had ever witnessed in the field of regional security. He added that he would make a personal recommendation to his superiors, advising that this sort of cooperation be closely studied by the Chilean government. This positive attitude was in marked contrast with what happened in 1995 at a trilateral meeting previous to the joint Argentine-Brazilian exercises, where both the Brazilian and the Chilean officers had scoffed at a video showing some operations of the Franco-German brigade, claiming that it was inapplicable to South America. Notwithstanding, this changing attitude has still to be translated into a change in Chilean policy, which is not yet in sight. Although in mid-1997 an agreement for joint military maneuvers was reached at the political level, Chilean military sources immediately denied that they would involve troop deployments, limiting them to an indoor war game.

Thus, despite their success as a trading state, the Chilean leaders still seem to perceive their country as an actor in a world where interstate relations are best described by the assumptions of the realist model. Contrariwise, Argentina has been quite unsuccessful thus far as a trading state, yet in the political sphere its government has opted for policies that clearly correspond to Rosecrance's ideal type.

Divergences Between Argentine and Brazilian Strategic Thinking

On the other hand, the ideology that predominates among the government, diplomatic, and military establishments in Brazil could hardly be more different from that prevailing in the Argentine government. Indeed, the striking contrast between Argentine and Brazilian strategic thinking has led to strong Brazilian attempts to indoctrinate Argentine officials with what for them is the "good doctrine." Because of a degree of cultural affinity, of the growing economic and political importance of MERCOSUR, and of Brazilian military cooperation with Argentina, the Brazilians find fertile soil for their message in significant segments of Argentina's society and bureaucracy.

Indeed, several Brazilian delegations travelled to Buenos Aires with this objective in mind. Basically, their message was that:

1. There is no longer any reason to harbor fears of a danger to security stemming from neighboring countries (in this the Argentine government agrees),

2. Therefore, there is no need for further advances in terms of the control of conventional weapons (in this the Argentine government disagrees), and

3. The real security problem for the Southern Cone countries stems from the United States (in this, the Argentine government could not disagree more strongly).

Indeed, and as an illustrative example, in the seminar entitled "Fuerzas Armadas 2000" held on June 28, 1994, and attended by distinguished members of the Brazilian Institute of Strategic Issues (IBAE) such as General Manuel Texeira, Admiral José do Amaral de Oliveira, Colonel Morgado, and Dr. Antonio Carlos Pereyra, it was clearly pointed out that the most important problems faced by the countries of the region came from both underdevelopment and the hegemonic policy of the United States. It was stated that this hegemonic policy took place in a context of economic globalization and of a widening of the differences between rich and poor countries, and that among other mechanisms to maintain the status quo, the United States operates to obstruct the acquisition of high technology by countries like Argentina and Brazil. Furthermore, it was alleged that the military aspect of this policy is the concept of cooperative security, which crystallizes the hegemony of the United States and advances toward the dissolution of state sovereignties, which are already adversely affected by the process of economic globalization. Therefore, they are against any proposal for the construction of a more integrated hemispheric system of interstate security. In their opinion the countries affected by such hegemonic attempts must unite in order to be in a better position to pressure the powerful; they must resist all attempts to subordinate or weaken their military institutions; they must keep their national identities clearly differentiated, and most especially, they must obtain access to the high technology that is denied to them.

More specifically, the presentation submitted by Dr. Liveiro Ferreira, president of IBAE,[32] pointed out the danger of erosion of national sovereignties; there exists, he said, a contradiction between economic globalization and national security, adding that the role that the countries of the region will allow the United States to perform has not been sufficiently discussed. He emphasized the hegemonic attempts of the United States and said that there clearly exists a potential confrontation between "the Plata (basin) and the North."

In turn, Admiral Amaral (former chief of the Brazilian Navy) emphasized U.S. hegemonic policies and implicitly questioned the wisdom of Argentina playing up to a Pax Americana, to U.S. hegemony, and to an allegedly projected system of (U.S.-led) interstate security. On the other hand, Colonel Morgado (an active officer) emphasized the dangers of globalization and sovereignty erosion, while General Texeira (former army chief of planning) emphasized that the dangers to security are not endogenous to the region but come from outside. Finally, Dr. Pereyra (a specialized journalist and former director of a Brazilian journal on strategy and politics) stated very emphatically that the concept of cooperative security can only be implemented when one country hegemonizes all the others, and that it is therefore extremely dangerous, leading inevitably to the dissolution of state sovereignty.

It is very clear that in the bottom line this ideology assumes that the accumulation of state power is the ultimate goal of states, and as such it is quite at odds with Argentina's citizen-centric ideology, which subordinates state sovereignty to citizen welfare, freedom, and democracy.

Very similar conclusions regarding the ideology that (to some extent) inspires Brazilian security policies stem from the talk given by former minister of technology Helio Jaguaribe (a prominent Brazilian political scientist and man of affairs), in the Argentine Foreign Ministry on September 7, 1994. In this academic session Jaguaribe praised MERCOSUR because, he claimed, it will give Southern Cone countries a greater "retaliation capability" and "temporary self-sufficiency" vis-à-vis the policies of great powers. Moreover, and specifically regarding international security, he said that "weak countries such as ours" need a military safeguard against the growing trend toward intervention. He said that it is necessary to possess a capability to inflict considerable damage to whatever great power might desire to intervene in the Southern Cone. Jaguaribe stated that for this reason he is "a firm defender of the development of a Brazilian nuclear submarine" and that he believed Argentina ought to develop its own as well. He also stated that MERCOSUR must have a defense plan, which should include the deployment of a number of missiles in its perimeter.

Although there is no doubt that President Cardoso has moderated the influence of these extremist views within the Brazilian government, the opinions just cited clearly illustrate that the security and foreign policy ideology that inspires the Brazilian security establishment is at odds with that espoused by the Argentine government. Needless to say, there is a security dimension to citizen welfare, and the fact that the Argentine government is aware of it is illustrated by its concern with the Chilean arms buildup, which apparently is not yet alarming but is an issue that requires attention. In contrast to a state-centric approach, the citizen-centric policies of a developing country will shy away from such unproductive investments as building nuclear submarines, not to say placing missiles in their perimeter.

Indeed, the dismantlement of the Cóndor II is the best illustration of Argentina's citizen-centric approach: it was scrapped because its proliferation threat was inevitably going to be sanctioned by the United States at a great cost to the welfare of the average Argentine, while its further development would only benefit the vanity of military officers and other elites. In sharp contrast to the spirit of this Argentine policy is the opinion of high-ranking Brazilian diplomats, who in November 1994 told the authors of this paper that the scrapping of the Cóndor II had been totally gratuitous, and that Brazil was not going to do a stupid thing like that. This statement became especially meaningful when in June 1995 the White House confirmed that Russia sold sophisticated missile technology to Brazil, which it fears will be used for the missile development program initiated in 1992.[33] Furthermore, in late 1996 it was officially announced that Brazil would engage in the development, production, and sale of satellite-launching vehicles, which means that it plans to produce full-fledged intercontinental ballistic missiles.

Although the Brazilians do not always express themselves in such extreme terms as the ones cited above when they go to Buenos Aires to speak about foreign and security policies, it is nevertheless always clear that there is a strong divergence in the strategic thinking prevalent in both countries. For example, during the meeting on Southern Cone security held on September 11, 1994, under the auspices of FLACSO and FOROSUR, the Brazilian repre-

sentatives made it clear that in their opinion the acquisition of greater powers of intervention by multilateral agencies such as the United Nations or the
Organization of American States, as implemented in, for example, Haiti, was
not advisable, and that the Security Council should not be given so much
power. Contrariwise, Argentina has been a major supporter of and a party to
precisely the Haitian operation, and as a matter of principle it supports the
strengthening of the Security Council. The Brazilians tended to underestimate potential intra–Latin American conflicts, underlining that it was unfair
to call for arms reductions, which would only play up to the interests of the
great powers. Although they are perceived to be sincere when they claim that
there is little or no reason to fear that a major South American state will attack another, they are clearly advocates of an accumulation of state power
and of as absolute a concept of sovereignty as is feasible in the present world.
Rhetorically at least, they (as well as the Chileans) are against the full implementation of the concept of cooperative security, which would imply confidence-building measures such as conventional arms reductions and institutionalized inspections: they consider this a European model that cannot and
should not be transplanted to South America. They most especially object to
the institutionalization of CBMs. Basically, what this means is that a guarantee for long-term stability cannot be achieved for the time being. But ad hoc
measures devoid of a contractual obligation for the future are, on the contrary, the order of the day in the relations between the Argentine and Brazilian military.

Indeed, when it comes to official conversations between the military of
the two countries the Brazilians (in contrast to the Chileans) are remarkably
open and transparent about defense issues. They show an excellent disposition to clear whatever doubts might emerge among the Argentine military,
they generously show their facilities, and (as mentioned before) they take cooperation to the point of letting Argentine aircraft operate, under an Argentine commanding officer, from the Brazilian aircraft carrier. However, when
it is suggested that this type of CBM should be incorporated into a formal,
long-term agreement between both governments, they immediately express
doubts. They are reluctant to carry them from a strictly military-to-military
level to a political one. Although they are willing to be transparent, they do
not want to contract the obligation, and when this is proposed they revert
to the argument that since there are no security problems among us, there
really is no need for CBMs, and that moreover to demand the generation of
confidence when in actual fact there is confidence is really to destroy that
confidence. In this context what repeatedly comes up is a warning and a precondition to cooperation: that the Yanks be kept as far away as possible. They

even objected to a projected U.S. force of 120 men in Paraguay for assistance in the control of drug trafficking.[34]

Finally, another Brazilian argument against the institutionalization of solid CBMs is that, given the "defense deficit" that has in fact developed in Argentina vis-à-vis both Brazil and Chile, why should Brazil be interested in trusting Argentina? Furthermore, they argue that Argentina's defense deficit is contrary to the interests of the Brazilian military and could lead to a deterioration of the relations between both military establishments, because it is a model that could be picked up by sectors of the Brazilian political leadership, or used domestically within Brazil to demand concessions from the military.[35]

Our hypothesis—surely made more solid by this evidence that amounts to a confession—is that CBMs and arms reductions are basically perceived by both Brazilians and Chileans as threats to the interests of their military-industrial complexes. There is of course an important difference between the Brazilians and the Chileans, because in the Chilean case this is coupled to pending territorial disputes with all of its immediate neighbors, whereas Brazil has no such disputes. The Argentine military, in turn, attempts to use the Brazilian argument to serve its own corporate interest, pointing out that an asymmetrical military development is an obstacle to real CBMs, and that a certain degree of symmetry is a precondition to cooperative security.

However, it would be an oversimplification to reduce the Brazilian attitude regarding CBMs to the defense of narrow corporate interests. It is probably also conditioned by ongoing delusions of future world power status, not unlike those suffered by Argentina in a previous period of its history. Indeed, despite the fact that the sum total of MERCOSUR plus Chile and Bolivia represents less than 5 percent of the world's gross production and total trade, former Brazilian finance minister Ricupero publicly stated that MERCOSUR should become one of the power poles of a multipolar world.[36] Indeed, in significant segments of Brazilian society, including the military and the political leadership, the notion that Brazil has a manifest destiny as a world power is still alive. When it suits them, they bring MERCOSUR into the picture to make the prospect more appealing to immediate neighbors.

Naturally, we are aware that the divergent strategic perspectives of the Argentine and Brazilian militaries and governments are to some extent conditioned by the different circumstances facing both states. Among these we can include:

1. Argentina's greater financial vulnerability.

2. Brazil's important arms industry, whose exports to many a pariah state it seeks to defend and promote. In this respect, Brazil has a conflict of interest with the United States (and, objectively, with most of the interstate commu-

nity). This is one important reason for Brazil's opposition to the internationalization of armed forces and defense systems, as well as a source of sensitivity to the erosion of state sovereignty.

3. Brazil's opposition to the efforts of the interstate community to monitor the conservation of its rain forests, which also generates a special sensitivity to sovereignty erosion.

4. Brazil's interest in becoming a permanent member of the United Nations' Security Council. Contrariwise, the Argentine government considers that it is counterproductive for the governability of the interstate order to foster the expansion of the oligopolic group of permanent members beyond those countries that are truly great powers.[37]

Notwithstanding, it is clear that President Cardoso has shown an extra quota of goodwill toward Argentina, as is illustrated by Brazil's new (late 1996) defense policy, which as was said was drafted directly by the presidency's new committee on foreign and defense policy. Nevertheless, Brazil's 1996 military and strategic policy toward Argentina (which has pleasantly surprised everyone inasmuch as it includes the possibility of military integration) is not tantamount to its drawing strategically closer to the West: on the contrary, the 1996 defense policy can be construed as a means to draw Argentina away from the United States. This is in fact what it has achieved with leaders of the Argentine opposition, who now have an additional justification to protest against Argentina's alignment with the United States, inasmuch as they claim that this alignment risks the alienation of the only country that they perceive as willing to be a real guarantor for Argentine security vis-à-vis the danger of Chilean aggression: Brazil.

The case for this rationale of the Argentine opposition is stronger[38] inasmuch as Brazilian apprehensions of the United States remain strong, and they come together with objections to the role that Argentine policy allows the United States to play in the hemisphere. Indeed, although it was warmly welcomed by the Argentine government, Brazil's 1996 defense policy in no way changed the Argentine government's staunch strategic alignment with the United States. On the contrary: it was after the announcement of the 1996 Brazilian defense plan that President Menem travelled to the United States, met with President Clinton, announced that Argentina aspired to the official status of extra-NATO ally of the United States, and acquiesced to U.S. demands to give the Argentine armed forces an important role in the struggle against drug trafficking. These announcements generated misgivings in Brazil, where there is headstrong opposition to the intervention of the armed forces in the war against drugs (and most especially against the possibility of multilateral military operations in foreign soil, which they perceive as a dangerous precedent for eventual U.S. attempts to intervene in the Amazon).

Furthermore, there is no sympathy in Brazil for Argentina's attempt to band-wagon ever more closely with the United States as an extra-NATO ally: this is probably something that the 1996 Brazilian defense plan set out to prevent. As its missile policy under President Cardoso clearly illustrates, Brazil is not a trading state with a citizen-centric foreign policy that is devoid of aspirations in terms of politico-military power. On the contrary, it aspires to regional (and even global) power status.

This being the case, objective factors and structural differences that have already been mentioned determine a divergence of strategic interests be-tween Argentina and Brazil. On the other hand, due to several causes that have also been dealt with above, Argentina has undergone a process of uni-lateral disarmament and has adopted a very liberal attitude with respect to issues such as the erosion of sovereignty and the weakening of the traditional nation-state. To some extent, Argentina is materially beyond the point of no return: not only has it opted for a citizen-centric approach, but its disarma-ment is such that it can no longer compete for military power with its neigh-bors, even if a government of the future should choose to do so. But precise-ly because of the objective divergence of interests and structural realities, this relative impotency does not necessarily mean that (as the Brazilians would wish) the Argentine government will put itself at the service of Brazil and its state-centric policies. On the contrary, so long as the United States adopts an encouraging policy, the present Argentine government is likely to continue to wager its strategic chips on the side of the West.

On the other hand, the Brazilian elites govern a country that: (1) is less democratic politically than Argentina (insofar as its military establishment retains much more domestic political power), and (2) is also considerably less democratic socially than Argentina (inasmuch as it harbors a dual social structure with far greater concentrations of both wealth and poverty, and a proportionately smaller middle class).

Brazilian elites have therefore more domestic power than Argentine elites. For this reason, the former will not be prone to renouncing the accumula-tion of state power as the primary goal of their state, and they will not be prone to elevating citizen welfare to priority status. Argentina's foreign and security policies are based on a citizen-centric approach that the Brazilian government neither can nor wants to imitate, precisely because it rules a country that is essentially more oligarchic. This being the case, the strategic perspectives prevailing in the Brazilian government will probably diverge with Argentina's, for so long as the latter's citizen-centric policies can be maintained.

Conclusions

Although Argentina faces no direct and immediate threat to its security from neighboring states, the continuity of its pro-West, trading-state foreign and security policies has been challenged by Chile's arms buildup, Brazilian attempts to put Argentina under its orbit politically, and ideological conflicts within Argentina itself.

The resistance found in the region to Argentina's proposals relative to cooperative security at a hemispheric, regional, and subregional level have given place to a disequilibrium between, on the one hand, Argentina's achievements in the field of global security, its support for the decisions of the Security Council, its approximation to NATO, its participation in diverse nonproliferation regimes, and the emerging affinity and increasing cooperation in security affairs with the West, and on the other hand its much more limited advances in the field of regional security.

Although (as stated) Argentina's security is not presently endangered by its neighbors, a country's security is to a great extent defined by its specific regional entourage. The limited advances in this field are not only a problem for Argentina, but they are first and foremost an objective limitation to the creation of conditions of long-term stability in the subregion. Lack of advance in this ground has also generated an asymmetry between the progresses of economic integration and political cooperation, on the one hand, and the management of Southern Cone security affairs on the other (especially as regards Chile).

It must be emphasized that with the advent of President Cardoso's administration there has been a very positive evolution in the Brazilian attitude toward cooperative security, CBMs, and some sort of eventual military integration. Indeed, the changes that have taken place between the writing of the first and final drafts of this chapter have been momentous and introduce a significant degree of hope for the future of long-term security guarantees, in what is clearly a very dynamic process. However, attention must be drawn to the fact that what has evolved significantly is Brazil's attitude toward Argentina but not its quest for a grander role in world politics. It can be reasonably conjectured that Cardoso is leading the country into acknowledging that it is presently very costly and difficult to completely refuse to accept international demands for transparency in security affairs, and that Brazil has therefore opted to offer transparency at a subhemispheric level, that is, with the exclusion of the United States, in a limited geographic area in which it can aspire to hegemony without any real loss of autonomy vis-à-vis the United States or other great powers, which is what it really wishes to avoid.

On the other hand, before putting an end to this discussion it must be pointed out that the most important immediate challenge and threat to Argentina's security does not stem from neighboring states at all, but from terrorism. Indeed, Argentina has not been the victim of interstate aggression since at least 1865.[39] In contrast, leftist terrorism and state terrorism produced a heavy toll in the 1970s. And much more recently, in 1992 and again in 1994, downtown Buenos Aires was the victim of major bombings against the Israeli embassy first and then against local Jewish institutions. The second bombing killed nearly ninety and wounded more than three hundred.

Islamic fundamentalists are the foremost suspects for these unresolved cases, at least in terms of their inspiration and financing. Hezbollah cells have been identified within Argentina, as well as in Brazilian and Paraguayan territory close to the Argentine border. However, although the Brazilian government has given assurances that as far as its responsibilities are concerned Argentina's security is well attended to, it has refused to accept a multilateral scheme to monitor Islamic fundamentalist activities, which would have included Argentina, Brazil, and Paraguay, as well as the United States, whose know-how and human resources for the combat against this type of terrorism are essential to the possibility of success (the Southern Cone intelligence services, for example, lack a capability for the infiltration of Hezbollah cells, and they could not possibly acquire it in less than a decade). Nonetheless, the agreement reached by the presidents of Argentina, Brazil, and Paraguay during the Iberian–Latin American summit of October 1995, regarding the eventual implementation of measures to coordinate security in the trilateral boundary region, raises hopes that significant achievements might be made in a not distant future.

This limitation in the capacity for the control of terrorism is aggravated by yet another factor, which is purely domestic. Bombings such as those perpetrated in Buenos Aires, although probably inspired and funded by Islamic fundamentalists, almost certainly required the complicity of local mercenaries, who probably were in charge of the logistics and did all of the groundwork previous to the bombing itself, for which local people are much more useful than exotic, foreign-born Middle Easterners who probably would not go by unnoticed in the vicinity of Jewish institutions. Although there are no precedents of bombings of such magnitude perpetrated by the Argentine extreme Right, it could well be that members of that segment of Argentine society, who are as anti-Semitic as are Islamic fundamentalists, were recruited for the groundwork and logistics by fundamentalist terrorists.

Finally, yet another security problem is exclusively of Argentina's creation and stems from the ongoing claim to Falkland/Malvinas, whose recovery through peaceful means has been incorporated as a mandate into the Argentine Constitution in 1994. Despite the inclusion of the caveat about peaceful means, after the 1982 war this claim is perceived by the Falkland Islanders as a threat to their own security, and they have become the lobbyists in Britain for the continuation of the arms embargo against Argentina. The Argentine government appears to be trapped into this irredentist policy by domestic political factors that are culturally conditioned, illustrating once again how society places limits to governability. Inasmuch as the embargo is combined with British arms sales to Chile, Argentina is itself the creator of a part of the incipiently unfavorable military imbalances that may in due time threaten its security. Notwithstanding, pragmatic agreements, such as the one reached with the United Kingdom in October 1995 regarding the exploration and exploitation of oil resources in the waters of Falkland/Malvinas, raise hopes that this problem too will soon be solved.

Chapter 4

Transition and Civil-Military Relations in Chile

Contributions in a New International Framework

Francisco Rojas Aravena

Introduction

Democracy is the great post–cold war change in the Western Hemisphere. It expresses a community of values. It constitutes a strategic change for the Latin American region and its states. Nevertheless, the mere existence of democracy does not guarantee the creation, makeup, and development of a hemispheric security system.

The end of the cold war has not had a substantive effect on the perceptions of threat in Latin America. The definitions and ideas of defense that emerge from these perceptions are constructed on the basis of neighbor-related factors and border issues. Many of these issues have not varied and, in fact, exhibit a great continuity regardless of official discourse. It is necessary, therefore, to act on these issues. Thus, reaffirming the regional determination to seek peaceful solutions to controversies is a fundamental step, especially given the open confrontation in the Condor Mountain Range between Ecuador and Peru in 1995. At the same time, it is necessary to resolve the issues stemming from the colonial legacy, namely, border demarcation.

The lack of a common military enemy in the hemisphere does not translate, to this date, into a tendency toward the reduction of forces or the prevention of arms races. The lack of effective security institutions and efficient mechanisms for conflict resolution in the region make it difficult to make substantial progress in the development of international regimes centered around the concept of cooperative security.

The processes of integration, complementation, and political dialogue require a hemispheric response in the area of defense as well. The key is to build a higher level of trust and to develop effective mechanisms for its implementation and verification. This will allow for the consolidation and transformation of the process of association, complementation, and opening in the economic realm into a network of interdependent relations. Only in this way will it be possible to achieve the goal, set at the Miami Summit, of establishing a free trade zone by the year 2010.

Parallel to the construction of a hemispheric security system, it is necessary for the countries of the region to generate civilian leadership in the area of defense. The absence of such leadership dramatically illustrates the levels of functional and even legal autonomy enjoyed by the armed forces, which stand as a contradiction to the process of redemocratization. This issue is especially relevant in the Chilean case.

This essay analyzes the space that the topic of defense occupies within the context of the transition and modernization taking place in Chile. It examines the issues of international insertion as well as the way in which the principal strategic positions, civil-military relations, and defense-related objectives have been defined within this context.

In Chile, as in the rest of Latin America, only the consolidation of democracy will permit economic growth and development with a sense of equity and social justice. However, the mere existence of political opening, expressed through regular elections and economic growth, ensures neither the governability nor the international stability of our countries. The challenge of our countries and our hemisphere is to build and consolidate democratic regimes in the domestic arena and to structure a system of cooperative security in the hemisphere.

Latin America and Global Changes

Latin America is at a stage of reaccommodation as it confronts the new international situation. Simultaneously, a process of democratic consolidation and change in the prevailing economic model has occurred. This has meant some positive effects such as the legitimization of democracy, the expansion of respect for human rights, and a tendency toward economic growth in conjunction with a process of regional integration that is globally and hemispherically oriented. At the same time, one can observe negative signs such as the fragility of democratic processes, the persistence of situations of violence and terrorism, growing governability difficulties, and instability in the model of global economic and financial insertion. Even more significant is the persistence of traditional perceptions of interstate threat.

This regional transition is being shaped by several changes: the end of the cold war and the disappearance of the Soviet bloc; regional diversity, expressed through various groupings and forms of concertation; regional unipolarism and the greater weight of the U.S. as a hegemonic power, but with fewer power resources; regional redemocratization; the difficulties in applying the economic adjustments called for by global tendencies; and the lack of effective hemispheric proposals for rendering cooperation in security a viable option.

Two central elements deserve closer analysis: regional diversity, and the processes of redemocratization and economic opening. With the disappearance of the framework of bipolar conflict, and taking into account the Latin American region as a whole, it is evident that there is no inclusive regime. Latin America emerges as a heterogenous region. This hinders the formulation of general policies capable of encompassing the interests of all the actors of the region. Trade linkages and cooperation have increased,[1] but at the same time, border-related conflicts have picked up steam.[2] The negative burdens of the colonial legacy of the nineteenth century in the region have yet to be overcome. The strong increase toward integrationist tendencies in the early 1990s did not eliminate the perception of a Latin America divided into several regions. Changes affect the two large areas—the Caribbean Basin and South America—in different ways. Each of these areas, in turn, proposes different forms of linkage and concertation.

We are facing a growing structural diversity. In spite of efforts to bring about integrationist practices, the region has failed to arrive at a homogeneous position. Recent history depicts this diversity. Taking into account parameters such as development, economic stability and growth, internal conflicts, and forms of national reconciliation that affect subsequent processes of governability, we find very different models in each area or subregion. Differences are further evident if we take into account aspects such as the type and form of involvement in new global issues: the environment, migrations, and transnational crime.

The very idea of Latin America, which conveys a sense of unity and common destiny, is in crisis.[3] To reconstitute the region as an actor presupposes as a key element the search for regional cooperation. This should correspond to a political decision, beginning with the recognition of the variety of situations and interests reflected. Acknowledging diversity enables actors to benefit from the gains that can be obtained from a mutually beneficial process that overcomes conflicts by means of association and interest aggregation and not through confrontation. Overcoming border issues is a basic condition for this.[4]

The second element refers to the economic adjustment that has taken place and that coincides with the regional tendency in favor of democratization. The central process in recent years in Latin America has been to establish several types of democratic transitions: different nations adopted different modes of transition. In Central America, the transitions consisted of moving from civil wars to open political forms by means of peace accords that entail a democratic option. In the Andean region, in particular Peru and Colombia, the essential institutional setting of the processes of democracy and opening persists in the midst of important armed conflicts, which shape the margins of democratic action and participation. In three countries in particular (Grenada, Panama, and Haiti), the democratization process has been the result of U.S. military action, namely, democratization through intervention. The Southern Cone countries (Brazil, Chile, Paraguay, and Uruguay) have witnessed concerted transitions. Argentina is a special case. It is similar to the latter, but its democratization was rooted in its 1982 military defeat in the South Atlantic: redemocratization through political-military collapse.

In the Southern Cone countries, the confluence of domestic and international political factors induced changes in the political system. This led to complex processes of concertation and the establishment of accords and pacts between military and civilian political forces. One consequence of this process is a new type of link and equilibrium in the relations between the state and society, between economic and political forces, and between the armed forces and the civil authorities.

There is no political alternative to democracy in South America. In spite of its transition-based constraints, the threats from terrorist forces and drug trafficking mafia, and the authoritarian remnants, there is no other viable alternative today capable of generating confidence, obedience, and governability with local support and international recognition. This broadens the range of options for establishing sectoral policies of coordination. The extent and duration of these processes is something new in the region.[5] Democracy is the Western Hemisphere's great change in the post–cold war period.

In the economic arena, processes of structural adjustment linked to processes of insertion into the international economic and financial system have been pursued throughout all countries in the region. In the majority of cases, firm support from international financial organizations has been available. These processes of opening constitute a new consensus regarding the options and opportunities available to the economies of the region. However, given the inequities of the economic system, the effects of insertion into the international market through a process of "structural adjustment" devoid of mechanisms of compensation or cushioning for the most vulnerable sectors create serious governability problems that in many cases can damage the precarious economic and political stability.

Chile: Transition and Modernization

Chile was the last South American country to initiate a process of redemocratization. In 1990, a long authoritarian period came to an end, together with an even longer period of instability and search for political projects among polarizing alternatives. Between the end of the 1950s and the October 1988 plebiscite and Patricio Aylwin's March 1990 taking of office, the country lacked a shared project for the future on key issues such as the type of political system and economic development. With redemocratization, a period of consistent search for consensus and national accords on central issues of national development was born.

In this new stage of Chilean political development, the search for consensus has taken precedence. The Chilean case presents two special features: first, it is a case in which the essential components of the economic model were designed under military authoritarianism.[6] Second, the application of the model had to confront the uncertainty of change in the political system. Almost a decade later, the balance is surely positive, although some misgivings are emerging, especially regarding institutional-political factors. Today, constitutional shortcomings are conspiring against the possibility of developing consensus. The authoritarian legacy carries an inherent ideological weight, which, in moments of tension, curtails the country's democratic alternatives. Contextualizing the "Chilean model of transition" necessarily implies evaluating the most significant contributions and features of the period of political transition.[7] Undoubtedly, it also implies discussing civil-military relations and the prospects for the future of the ongoing process.[8] We examine two central aspects of the Chilean case. The first is related to the strategy of international insertion chosen by Chile; the second is related to defense policy formulation within a framework of international change.

Contributions of the Transition

For more than three decades, Chile was polarized by alternative, opposing, and dissimilar projects in three vital areas: the political system, the model of economic development, and civil-military relations. Since the 1960s until the return of democracy in 1990, no consensus existed among the country's main political and social forces with regard to these three areas. These circumstances have changed drastically. Transition and consensus building are both part of the very same process. National reconciliation in the Chilean case took the form of an informal pact of governability—pacted democracy—expressed through the building of basic consensus.

The experience of recent years indicates that the prospects for the country to move toward sustainable development could not be better. A process that initiated as a polarized situation gave way to a concerted transition. This has permitted the construction of a political system that has sought, in the midst of the transition, to move beyond differences and incorporate all significant actors and agents in the task of designing major pathways for the nation. This has injected significant stability into the transition process since 1990. A transfer and continuity of tasks has occurred from the first concertation government (P. Aylwin, 1990–94) to the second (E. Frei, 1994–2000).[9]

Three organizing principles shape this dynamic process: democracy, free markets, and concerted development. Democracy is embraced as the political system that is capable of ensuring stability and promoting prosperity in the country. Market economies, in conjunction with a more effective democratic system, provide the most efficient way of allocating resources and the best possibility for generating a framework of equity. The third feature of the process of transition is the consolidation of a democratic pact of governability. The need to formulate and pursue policies of consensus and concertation define this pact.[10]

Differences exist regarding the specific modes of application of each aspect of consensus, but not with respect to their organizational axes. Thus, regarding democracy, the debate focuses on the questions of what is the best form of representation—a proportional system or a binomial system—and on how to eliminate authoritarian enclaves. In the economic arena, differences center on neither trade opening nor full international insertion, but rather on the instruments for applying these policies. Debates also occur regarding international accords, or the place and role of the state within the free-market system. In the defense area, there has been an effort to establish a linking process that would pave the way for a new type of civil-military relations, free from the noncommunication and mutual distrust that prevailed in the past. Focusing on professional issues makes possible the construction of a promising space for interaction.[11]

Avoiding polarization and broadening the possibilities for arenas of consensus constitute the distinctive seal that the central actors and agents have imprinted on the political process in recent years. The goal of modernizing the country is premised on the country's stability. Modernization and efficiency make possible the resolution of major national problems.[12] This rep-

resents a great change in Chilean politics and society. As we have seen, this
change came about in parallel fashion to transcendental changes in the international system. At the outset of the democratic opening process, the international system was still characterized by the East-West confrontation. The
transition broke out when the cold war was ending. The very process of transition contributed to the termination of ideological conflict. By making the
reuniversalization of diplomatic relations less dramatic, the end of the cold
war, in turn, facilitated Chile's international reinsertion.

The Chilean transition was based in part on the acceptance of a concerted
transition. This meant that the regime would not be overthrown, but rather,
the political process would become increasingly democratic. From polar
views of the present, past, and future, the country moved toward a pact regarding the present and the future. Between 1985 and 1990 opponents and
rulers gradually yielded their positions, allowing for a peaceful evolution and
dodging positions that could lead to conflict.

The above led to a situation of significant mistrust during this period and
throughout the transition. In fact, moments of great tension in the political
and institutional system have occurred. This process, however, did not escalate into polar and antagonistic alternatives that could jeopardize stability.
During the transition process, there has been progress toward the emergence
of areas of consensus. Since 1990, routine interactions under the rule of law
have contributed to the progress that has been made in the creation of increasingly reliable and predictable spaces regarding central political issues.

The constitutional attributions that the military government modified
before leaving office are an example of the above. These attributions sanctioned the institutional autonomy of the armed forces.[13] The ruling parties
grouped under the Concertation find such norms unacceptable. For them,
such norms fail to sufficiently safeguard the concept of armed forces subordination to civil authorities. Another sector, comprising the armed forces
themselves and the parties of the Right, considers the autonomy of the
armed forces from civil authority to be important. The Concertation lacks a
constitutional majority in Parliament to reform such norms. As a result, the
Concertation accepts this condition—albeit in disagreement. The most notorious although not the most important issue about these norms is the irremovability of the military high command. The political tensions that surfaced around the compliance with the Supreme Court ruling that convicted
the director of intelligence of the military government, Manuel Contreras,
are part of this framework.

The debate generated by this event revealed the shortcomings of the institutional political framework. These shortcomings are expressed in important
areas: appointed senators, the electoral system, the irremovability of the com-

manders in chief of the armed forces, the composition of the constitutional tribunal. The government has clearly shown the need to carry out reforms in the political system.[14] This call for reform is much wider today and is embraced by more than just the ruling coalition.[15]

The consolidation of a governability agreement became more explicit in the course of various reforms in the political and institutional systems. Topics were and continue to be treated in such a way so as to not hurt the basic condition for governability. On this point, "democratic pragmatism" and the "ethic of responsibility are united."[16] This has permitted social actors to coexist in areas where different views prevail and to acknowledge such differences without straining the political or social conditions to the point of making the country ungovernable.

One example of this is the capacity of Chilean society to live with at least two central views with respect to the past, specifically, contrasting images of the previous military government, its causes, and its development.[17] The armed forces and some political sectors have their own view regarding the previous democratic system, the causes of its rupture, and the contribution of the military government; whereas the center-left ruling coalition and those nonparliamentarian parties of the Left, together with other organizations (such as those for human rights) share another, completely different perception.

These counterpoints are neatly expressed when it comes to the issue of human rights violations under the military government. In other areas, such as the economy, there are also different views of the past (the social debt and its cost, the process of reconversion, the modes of privatization, the degree of economic concentration). Nevertheless, there are common goals,[18] which are expressed in areas where there is a strong convergence. This should permit the formulation of policies with a high level of social support. Although the issue of different memories remains unresolved, both views continue to coexist. The "Contreras case," however, has greatly strained this coexistence. Whether the actors agree with it or not, this issue is strongly symbolic for everyone and illustrates the lingering weight that ideologies have for each side.

International Insertion. Chile is located in the Southern Cone of Latin America and occupies a long (more than 4,000 km.) and narrow (average width, 200 km.) strip of land, encompassing a total of 756,252 square kilometers. The size of the national surface area increases considerably when the Antarctic territory and marine areas are included. These geographic features provide three identities for Chile: it is a Latin American country, an Antarctic country, and a Pacific Basin country.

Because of both its topography and physical shape, Chile confronts a complex situation of security vis-à-vis its neighbors. For that reason, Chile has developed a significant tradition of strategic policies. It was one of the first Latin American countries to create a well-defined state apparatus, which included armed forces at the national level. Chile has not had international wars in more than a century. It has had to overcome situations of significant tension and crisis, but it has always found diplomatic rather than military solutions. This reaffirms a traditional defense doctrine that is based on self-defense and deterrence.

The international borders of the country were drawn fundamentally at the end of the last century and at the beginning of the current one. By means of a treaty in 1881, Argentina recognized Chile's jurisdiction over the Straits of Magellan and the southernmost islands. Almost a century later, the Papal Treaties of 1984 reconfirmed the nation's positions in the southernmost area. After the War of the Pacific in 1883, the Treaty of Ancón established the border with Peru. The status of Tacna and Arica remained pending until 1929. The 1904 Treaty of Peace and Friendship with Bolivia established the border between the two countries.

The 1970s were marked by significant border tensions. The most significant occurred following Argentina's declaration of nullification of the arbitrated decision regarding the Beagle and the military mobilization that accompanied this act. The international isolation of the Chilean military junta made matters worse. This isolation was evident from the recurrent condemnations by the United Nations and other international organizations. It was a period in which trade opening did not come with corresponding political linkages. Only the reinstatement of the democratic system made it possible to reverse this situation.

The principal foreign policy goal of Patricio Aylwin's government was to reinsert Chile into the international system. This policy produced its intended results.[19] In a short period of time, the country began to occupy a significant space in international fora and was able to regain its status in the international community. The mode of reinsertion in the international system in the 1990s is very different from the traditional one. Numerous global changes play a role, but in a very significant way so does the new economic insertion of the country.[20] From the point of view of strategic-military perceptions and linkages, traditional factors still exercise a strong influence, especially considerations about neighboring countries.

One of the main activities of Chile's democratic governments has been the search for a definitive solution to the pending issues of border demarcation.[21] This constitutes the axis of Chile's policy toward neighboring countries. Economic opening and complementation, as well as the country's image, could eventually be put at risk if border tensions resurface. Insofar as the problems that stem from our colonial heritage are resolved, complementation and integration can acquire a lasting profile.

Relations with Argentina made a qualitative jump. This was due to four principal issues: (1) the endorsement of the Border Agreement; (2) the parallel endorsement of an Agreement for Economic Complementation; (3) the results of Argentina's macroeconomic policies; and (4) the increase in Chilean businesses and investments in Argentina and vice versa.

On August 2, 1991, both countries approved a historic agreement, thereby completing the demarcation of the 5,300 kilometers of border between the countries. The "Presidential Declaration on Limits" sought to eliminate all territory-based conflicts, including all differences regarding the demarcation of the extensive border that divides the two states. The agreements signed on the same occasion demonstrate the growing convergence and collaboration and the important level of rapprochement achieved by both countries. It is important to highlight the accords that refer to economic complementation and additional protocols; the treaty on the environment and complementary instruments; the treaty of reciprocal promotion and protection of investments; the memorandum of understanding to facilitate the transit of persons, and the accords of cooperation between the border patrols of Chile *(carabineros)* and Argentina *(gendarmería)*.

During the process of negotiation, opponents of the border delimitation accords surfaced on both sides of the mountain range. They expressed their dissent in different ways. However, the process of negotiation came to a successful end. The joint efforts of the binational commissions, the political will of both governments, and the process of consultation that took place in both states made possible the resolution of all twenty-four points of dispute. Twenty-two points were resolved in direct negotiations. One meant signing a border treaty for a specific area, and another was resolved in Argentina's favor by the arbitration tribunal that considered the case.

The 1984 Papal Treaties open up the possibility of utilizing a broad set of means, ranging from direct negotiations to resorting to the International Court of Justice.[22] The 1991 accords used direct means as well as arbitration. Chile's commitment to peace has been forcefully demonstrated in its permanent search for peaceful means of settling disputes. It was also demonstrated during the period of military government, especially during the conflict with Argentina regarding the latter's rejection of the ruling on the Beagle Channel.

The dispute over the Laguna del Desierto was taken before a Latin American arbitration tribunal, which carried out its duties in the seat of the Inter-American Council of Jurists in Rio de Janeiro. The initial decision, handed down in 1994, was adverse to the Chilean position. Pressured by the opposition, the government, while accepting the decision, made use of some legal recourses to obtain a revision and clarification of the ruling. The final decision, handed down in October 1995, confirmed the previous result. Laguna del Desierto remained under Argentine sovereignty.

In the case of the zone of Campo de Hielos Sur, the drafted treaty awaits ratification by the congresses of both countries. In September 1997, both governments urged the acceleration of this process.

Relations with Peru have advanced toward greater rapprochement. This process was interrupted in 1992 because of the political vicissitudes inside Peru. A resurgence of intensive diplomatic activity took place in 1993. The Chilean government's desire to settle all border negotiations propelled the country to devote special attention to resolving the pending border-related items vis-à-vis Peru. This occurred parallel to an intensification of trade and Chilean capital flows into Peru. Such was the context that gave rise to the Negotiating Commission for the pending issues from the Treaty of 1929, which established the agenda and the procedure for addressing them. An agreement was reached in Lima in May 1993, hence its name, the Lima Convention. The main disagreement that hindered the resolution of the pending items, addressed in the Lima Convention, concerns the different interpretations of the phrase *for the service of Peru*. This phrase appears in the part of the text that states that Chile would build a docking facility, a railway terminal for trains going to Tacna, and a customs office in Arica. At the end of 1996, the issue remained unresolved.

Chile does not have pending demarcation issues with Bolivia. What exists is a Bolivian claim for passage to the ocean. This issue is repeatedly raised. Bolivia's communications to the Pacific will be enhanced through economic integration and the improvement of road infrastructure. From a Chilean perspective, this is a bilateral issue and not a multilateral one. However, the possibility of a "corridor" was sealed off in 1978 when Peru objected to the existence of such a corridor along its border. Any other alternative is not viable since it would divide the Chilean territory. The 1993 Agreement on Economic Complementation has brought a great increase of trade and business investment opportunities in both countries.

Chile is in the midst of a process of multiple and multilevel negotiations. It signed agreements of trade liberalization with the Southern Cone Common Market (MERCOSUR) and the European Union (EU) and actively participates in the Asia-Pacific Economic Council (APEC). With regard to the countries of the North American continent, Chile signed a trade liberalizing agreement with Canada and expects to sign agreements with the United States and enter into the North American Free Trade Agreement (NAFTA).

In terms of international security, Chile has supported the main initiatives in the area of arms control and limitation. Chile promoted the Mendoza Declaration, which bans chemical weapons. It was already a participant in the Tlatelolco Agreement, which transformed the region into a nuclear-free zone. In parallel fashion to the development of the United Nations Conference to extend the Non-Proliferation Treaty, the Chilean Senate ratified the treaty.[23] Chile's international responsibilities increased significantly in 1996 upon its assumption of a nonpermanent seat on the Security Council of the United Nations.

Chile has taken a case-by-case approach regarding peacekeeping operations. In this area, the government's policy is adverse to placing a contingent under the UN command as part of a rapid-deployment multilateral force. In this period of political system transition, Chile has continued to participate in two traditional and long-standing United Nations observation operations in India-Pakistan and Palestine. It has also participated in peace monitoring on the Iraq-Kuwait border and in Cambodia. Border patrol troops are part of United Nations operations (ONUSAL) in El Salvador. In the Central American region, army officials have collaborated with the Organization of American States (OAS) in the de-mining of Nicaragua.

In the regional arena, Chile has lent its strongest collaboration to the de-activation of the conflict between Ecuador and Peru. Its activities in this area are part of the responsibilities accorded to Guarantor Countries of the Rio de Janeiro Protocol, signed by Ecuador and Peru. As part of the support to the generation of trust-building measures in Latin America,[24] Santiago was the site for the OAS Conference on this issue at the end of 1995.

Civil-Military Relations in Transition. For the sake of governability and stability in the country, the democratic movement that won the 1988 plebiscite accepted a series of "structures" inherited from the military government. These are mentioned in the 1980 Political Constitution itself; they include a binomial electoral system that curtails the real possibilities for democratization, the acceptance of appointed senators, the irremovability of the commanders in chief of the armed forces, and a series of specific norms within several spheres. This situation has special significance for the role of the armed forces and their position within the institutional setting. It acts as a constraint in the framework of civil-military relations.[25] A historical overview of Hispanic America reveals that the armed forces have enjoyed a high level of autonomy and preestablished prerogatives even prior to the formation of national states in Latin America.[26]

In Chile, the first four years of the redemocratization period—the 1990–94 government of Patricio Aylwin—represented a period of constant learning for all political forces, even the armed forces themselves: how to coexist with each other in spite of disagreements and, at the same time, work toward reaching accords. The main issue in the area of civil-military relations concerned the constitutional attributions of the armed forces and the topic of human rights. The former referred to the constant debates and even conflicts about the powers of civil authorities in the area of defense. The latter had to do with investigations about human rights abuses and the decision of the government to create a Commission on the Truth and Reconciliation to examine the cases of human rights violations that resulted in death. Even five years after the end of the military government the issues of roles or attributions and human rights remained the main elements of distrust and tension in the political system.[27]

The differences in all areas, and especially in the areas mentioned, do not manifest themselves as a civil-military divide, but rather as a division between programmatic coalitions that reflect civil and military interests. The principal debate emerged between the executive, represented by the Ministry of Defense, and the army in particular. Since the navy and the air force were less involved in the military government and had fewer cases of human rights violations, they were excluded in large measure from the debate on this topic.

Nonetheless, the Argentine experience shows that, in a universal context in which human rights and democracy are reevaluated, passing moral and historical-institutional judgments on human rights violations is inevitable. This had to be recognized by the highest military authorities.[28] This is what the Latin American experience shows.[29] Several perspectives on history—concerning the facts and their causes—can coexist on this topic. However, a diversity of moral and ethical evaluations concerning human rights violations cannot exist.

Changing the axis of civil-military relations toward professional issues might be the only way to achieve a forward-looking dialogue. This requires resolving human rights issues in a positive way, and with a strong ethical, not ideological, orientation. The issue of autonomy will find its true place whenever it is cast in terms of professional issues and civil leadership prevails in the defense sector. How to visualize and construe civil "control" of the armed forces is an increasingly global issue.[30]

Modernization and Defense Policy

The second Concertation government (1994–2000) marks a change in the axis of the discussion. An effort is being made to move from transition to the process of modernization. Political authorities believe that, without disregarding the issue of constitutional attributions, the political priority of the government should be the modernization of the country. This implies generating conditions for harmonious development to guarantee equity and, at the same time, generating a qualitative change in prevailing economic conditions. Bilateral as well as subregional economic agreements are further pursued. At the same time, incentives are offered to stimulate private initiative in order to leap toward a second phase in the export-oriented model. All of this would make possible the consolidation and deepening of democracy, and concomitantly, of policies of consensus.

One of the most conflictive areas within this framework continued to be the defense sector. The consensus among the political, civil, and military elites and the analyses offered by civil and military academic centers were in favor of addressing the professional issues of the armed forces and making them the axis of the modernization process within this sector.[31]

In the case of the Ministry of Defense, modernization would be expressed through the explicit formulation of a defense policy for the sector.[32] This policy would seek to make objectives explicit, identify specific modernization efforts that are appropriate for the sector, and move forward in the area of civil-military relations. The change of axis entailed an easing of government–armed forces relations.[33] However, the conflict about the functional autonomy of the armed forces persists. This conflict manifests itself as bureaucratic infighting within the state apparatus. In short, the issue is: how can the democratic civil leadership develop policies in an institutional framework in which the armed forces have autonomy to develop their own specific policies?

The persistence of human rights issues has tended to focus the debate on "political topics." The reactions and "demonstrations" of the armed forces are responses to this situation and not to the issue of professional development, which was a characteristic feature of the previous democratic system. Focusing on political issues leads the military to search for a way to preserve higher levels of the institutional and functional autonomy granted by the constitution. At the same time, an ideology-based debate is resurfacing, which resonates with the past and has little to do with real issues of defense, democracy, and the development of the country.

Preconditions for Civil-Military Relations. There are three prerequisites for the type of civil-military relations taking place in Chile. These have served as precedents for the performance of the democratic process, especially in the defense sector, which ultimately provides the framework for the definition of military policy. First, there is a tradition of professionalism in the armed forces.[34] This professionalism resulted in the institutions of the armed forces refraining from participating in political debates during the democratic years prior to the military government. Afterward, during the military government, although the armed forces did adopt political decisions, they did not participate in the political system as such. Among those in uniform, there was a very clear differentiation between those who performed government-related jobs and those who continued to fulfill military roles per se. After the military government, even though the affinity between the sectors of the Right and the armed forces was obvious, there has been no evidence of military participation—along partisan lines and in an institutionalized manner—in party politics. In Chile, the tradition of delinking party politics from the armed forces is thus evident. This facilitates centering civil-military relations around professional issues.

This tradition of institutional professionalism is related to a certain vision and development of a long-term strategic perception on the part of the national political leadership. This has led to a certain view of the world and the national spaces for action. A series of traditions that signal a sense of continuity, which goes beyond the debate of the moment, has been consolidated throughout this century.[35] A strong juridical emphasis stands out among these traditions. This emphasis tends to assign a greater weight to the diplomatic and peaceful resolution of differences. All of this occurs within a framework in which military doctrine has a defensive-deterrence orientation. The facilities and development of the small domestic weapons industry[36] exist to ensure the supply of basic defense-related inputs.

Some of the main factors that condition this strategic vision include self-perceptions about the type and degree of isolation of the country, i.e., its insularity in strategic terms (the lack of depth and the length of the territory). Together with these decidedly geographic elements, there is a view about the institutional weight and firmness of the state. Common sense would reaffirm the perception that a superior institutional setting and state role exist, which from a strategic perspective was consolidated at critical moments. This perception is culturally associated with the building of the national state.

A second prerequisite, which became evident during the military government, was the presence of a hierarchical structure surrounding military roles. The commander in chief of the institution sits at the top of the pyramid. Unlike in other Latin American cases, the Chilean armed forces have maintained—even today—a high degree of institutional discipline, precisely as a result of this hierarchical tradition. No internal dissidence, power struggles, or threats of rebellion inside the military institutions have arisen, precisely as a result of this hierarchical tradition. For the civil authorities, this has served as a guarantee of stability and a key element for the capacity to govern the country. The result of the Letelier case and the respect for its meaning, especially the jail sentence for the highest authorities of the main organ of repression of the military government, put the respect for this hierarchy to a test. Respect for this tradition has been upheld, however, in spite of the strong tensions that human rights issues provoked in the first half of 1995.

Respect for hierarchies and authority is directly linked to the definition and perception of the strategic context and perceptions of threats that derive from it.[37] At the same time, it is also linked to the military traditions that developed throughout military history. The German advisory mission during the final years of the last century played an important role in this military history.

Finally, a third prerequisite came from the civil arena. It translated into a growing interest, especially among the Concertation partisans, in addressing the defense issue in a more systematic way. The academic world contributed significantly to the examination of civil-military relations, defense-related issues, and overall topics of regional and international strategy. Such a tradition did not exist prior to 1973. Since 1990, there has been a higher-quality debate resulting from a better understanding of the issue of the armed forces, its reinsertion into society, and all its ramifications. It was also recognized by those in uniform that an important group of civilians had accumulated a significant body of knowledge. Research networks and specialized publications have articulated a basic critical mass on strategic and military issues.

We should not disregard the fact that different views persist regarding the proper role and functions of the defense sector. While some favor maintaining the concept of the armed forces as guarantors of the democratic process, others prefer maintaining a purely professional role of external defense, and still others insist on engaging the armed forces in the country's development efforts, thereby broadening their roles to include nonmilitary functions. Therefore, several views regarding these longer-term definitions coexist. But as indicated at the beginning, this has not hindered the opening of spaces for discussion and debate of defense-related issues. It is in this view that the prerequisites we pointed out—professionalism, respect for institutional hierarchy, and civilian learning—have been crucial factors for making progress on professional issues within a general framework of civil-military discussion. This is the basis for an effective national, not ideological, state policy.

Defense Policy Objectives. As it became evident that very little substantial progress on the issue of defense was made during the first Concertation government, the second government decided to adopt a different strategy. Professional factors were reevaluated, and the need to come forward with an explicit suprapartisan and consensual defense policy was proposed. The authorities began with the premise that in Chile it was necessary to study, at the highest level, how to formulate a long-term defense policy that would transcend the government of the moment. This is the organizing principle for definitions on international security, military spending, civil-military relations, international cooperation, banning and control of weapons of mass destruction, regional trust-enhancing mechanisms, and so on.

The process of definition making is occurring in a context of democratic consolidation. The second Concertation government undertook from the beginning this objective as part of an effort to restore civilian leadership on defense-related issues. The issues of the transition, which previously were scrutinized through the prism of the different views held by "civilians" and the "military," have begun to be replaced by a technical and professional debate on the contents of defense policy. Consequently, the topic now falls outside of the pending agenda of the transition. Those elements that refer to the authoritarian enclaves within the institutional setting constitute the eminently political issues on the agenda. The president and the minister of defense have upheld and ratified the priorities of the governmental and political alliance. Nevertheless, the authorities in these branches have indicated that they will not risk straining the delicate political system, which is still in the process of consolidation, by developing a testimonial policy, that is, a policy unable to produce programmatic changes because it lacks the necessary legal instruments. Government authorities have sought to establish clear distinctions between political and defense-related issues. They intend to uphold this distinction even though there is a mutual or overlapping presence of actors in both spheres. Given its ideological baggage and pragmatic repercussions, the Contreras case showed the practical difficulty of making such a distinction. Once the case was resolved, with Contreras's jailing at the end of October 1995, it became possible again to accord priority to policies focused on professional issues.

The minister of defense, Edmundo Pérez Yoma, in a speech at the Armed Forces Academy, described Chile's position this way:

The central definitions of Chile's international positioning in the area of defense begin by acknowledging a new international reality. A different world exists today. Chile consistently seeks to build a context of peace and stability for the region. However, it recognizes that, in the region, threats continue to play an important role in the definitions of the state.

The threats that hang over Chile, as well as over every state, are the result of neither capricious nor anachronistic thought processes. The history that we share with our neighbors generates constraining factors, for better or for worse. We sincerely hope to cultivate the good factors and definitively overcome the bad ones, because we want to continue to enjoy this peace that permits us to prosper jointly. Chile is respectful of this peace and the law that helps to sustain it. Chile is in favor of a growing certainty of peace and collaboration with our neighbors, while maintaining, at the same time, an exact sense of reality and a profound commitment to the defense of the fatherland.[38]

The search for professionalism and efficiency in the process of the modernization of defense, which is part of a more general process of state modernization, is framed on this basis.

Contributing to regional stability and to the strengthening of the right to peace that all nations have is one of the driving ideas that guides Chile's actions within the framework of its role as a guarantor country in the Peru-Ecuador case. Likewise, we can also point to the peace observation missions in which the country has participated.

The principal official definitions on this issue point toward four main themes. First, there are no alternatives to globalization. National self-sufficiency is not an option. Global, hemispheric, and regional integration is the main tendency. Autarchy leads to marginalization and an increase in vulnerability. Second, the distinction between domestic and international arenas is increasingly more diffuse. Domestic issues are shaped in a decisive way by international events. International phenomena are transformed into domestic agenda issues. This leads to a growing search for international solutions to transnational problems. Third, the international agenda is more complex, diversified, and interdependent. The expressions of vulnerability and strength vary considerably, depending on how each issue is posed. Fourth, the nation-state will continue to be the key actor. One can confirm the existence of a high level of international constraints, the development of a power network of important nongovernmental actors, and the formation of blocs and conglomerates of state actors. Nevertheless, the state will continue to be the essential unit of the system.

From an institutional perspective, Chile seeks to fortify hemispheric institutionality and redefine hemispheric security. Toward this end, Chile proposed at the Meeting of the Ministers of Defense of the Americas that a special meeting of the OAS be held to analyze the issue. It has reiterated this position in the context of the studies by the Commission on Hemispheric Security in preparation for the meeting on mutual trust-enhancing measures. In the realm of security, Chile supports the proposal of granting the Inter-American Defense Board (IADB) the status of "entity" subordinate to the OAS. The goal is for the IADB to function as a specialized consulting body in the inter-American system. This change also means recognizing the need for a common definition in the hemisphere on the issue of security. This definition should be mindful of the region's heterogeneity and the great differences of power among the participating states. Consensus building in this sphere is fundamental for shaping a context of regional and neighboring peace and stability throughout the hemisphere.

The definition of an explicit defense policy is linked to the general goal of making progress in the modernization of the country, investing in people, and generating favorable conditions for a sustainable process of development. The consolidation of the democratic process requires a policy in this area, which, in turn, requires a prior public debate on the issue. This places the issue of defense in Chile on a new stage, in which a broad plurality of actors work cooperatively toward the realization of peace, democracy, and development. This would not only fortify the process of national democratization but also promote the concerted construction of an international security regime.

Contributions, Shortcomings, and Challenges for Chile in the International Defense Agenda. The Chilean model of transition carries with it a series of contributions, shortcomings, and challenges that have been suggested throughout this chapter. Undoubtedly, the main contribution has been the generation of a domestic consensus that allowed for a peaceful, successful, and reliable transition. Within a new international framework, Chile was one of the last countries of the region to become democratic. Although dissimilar views existed regarding the form and content of the transition, they all yielded in favor of an understanding that privileged stability over other issues on the national agenda. The political—and certainly the military—elite knew that the model of restricted democracy implied accepting a well-balanced functioning of state powers. Breaking this consensus would generate international discredit and national mistrust.

The main contribution was to think of governability as a way of contributing to regional peace. Linked to this reasoning, the transition did not imply the total and absolute redefinition of the prevailing economic model. The successes of the past were accepted, even though criticisms were raised regarding the imbalance that was emerging between those who had access to modernization and those who remained excluded from its benefits. No attempt was made to refound the model but rather to enrich it through concepts such as equity, redistribution of benefits, and a regulatory state. Simultaneously, the economic model implied the strengthening of the notion of internationalization of the economy, in different realms and regions and with different actors. By not discarding associations with different blocs (NAFTA, APEC, EU, MERCOSUR) and by pursuing bilateral agreements with countries that share certain economic criteria (Mexico, Venezuela, Costa Rica, Colombia, Argentina), the Chilean insertion into the international sphere has reinforced the concept of open regionalism.

Nevertheless, there are particular shortcomings inherent to this type of transition and to the subregional framework in which Chile's international policy operates. Among them are the different views that national actors have regarding the evolution of the international system, the persistence of perceptions of threat at the subregional level, and the evident inertia among the actors of the subregion who favor balance-of-power notions over the creation of new formulas for conducting relations among neighbors.

As a participant in a world in transition, Chile has had to face new challenges, looking out for its interests and formulating imaginative and integrated policies in the different areas of its activities. Six strategic issues in some way are affecting and even shaping Chile's actions at the local level.[39]

The first issue concerns resource delivery conditionalities. The current tendencies toward disarmament and arms control have led the superpowers and international financial organizations to favor the delivery of resources to underdeveloped countries on the condition that they reduce military expenditures.[40] In spite of the well-intentioned effort to redirect military spending toward social areas, different positions exist that speak about the need for obtaining effective conditions before reducing such spending. In this way, pending border problems, historic revindications, drug trafficking, poverty, and underdevelopment are insecurity-generating elements. The challenge for Latin America is to seek ways to stimulate security and trust and to generate hemispheric agreements banning certain types of arms; ultimately, the challenge is to cooperate for peace.

The second factor is the new role of the United Nations. From a military point of view, the new role of the United Nations and the proposals on the issue that are being offered should also be part of national discussions. In effect, the changes in the new organization of international security that are now becoming evident pose questions about state sovereignty and the use of resources of force for the benefit of certain powers. At the national level, experience with peacekeeping will, in the future, make it necessary to evaluate whether it is appropriate or not to prepare special contingents for such missions. This could lead to a rethinking of missions and reallocation of human and material resources, depending on the case.

The third issue is the role of the United States in the region.[41] The United States is assuming a strategic unipolarism in the new international context. This has immediate effects on hemispheric relations, even more so given the existence of conflicting interests between Latin America and the United States. The need to seek agreements on areas of shared interests is the first step for establishing a relationship that, although asymmetric, is not detrimental to the development prospects in the region. Since there are no serious tensions in the hemisphere, a new dialogue could be institutionalized that would be equitable between North and South and conducive for the emergence of effective cooperation mechanisms for the region.[42] "Maybe the greatest challenge that international organizations face today is to facilitate and put this dialogue into practice."[43]

The possibility, then, is being created for strengthening the systems of military interaction through a reflection on the future of inter-American security. This would entail a review of the link between the Inter-American Defense Board and the OAS. It would also imply a review of new alternatives regarding a new system of hemispheric security that might be proposed in the Inter-American Defense College or in the periodic meetings of the commanders in chief of the armed forces of the Americas.

The fourth factor is access to technology and markets—a key difficulty that Third World countries face. Diversification of markets, bilateral agreements of coproduction with various military powers, and the dual use of the military industry have permitted Chile to preserve its independence and simultaneously keep open different options abroad. This policy is as valid for the military industry as it is for academic-military exchange, joint exercises, scientific projects, and the like. Current technological developments preclude the possibility of obtaining total autarchy in the military industry. One adequate state policy should be, then, to harmonize national technological development through the implementation of specific (state and private) programs on the issue. It should simultaneously provide incentives for industrial complementation in the external sphere as well as for the export of national outputs, always respecting the pertinent international treaties.

The fifth factor, which is domestic but is beginning to be an issue of great importance, is the coordination of foreign policy and defense policy. There is consensus on the need to coordinate these policies. What is required, therefore, is a broad structure that will allow for daily relations between both sectors. One possibility is the strengthening of the already existing fora within the High Command for National Defense. With the cooperation of different sectors—including the armed forces—it is possible to arrive at a redefinition of the following policy areas: the Antarctic policy, projection toward the Pacific, the integration projects with Argentina, the settling of border disputes, the development of a military industry, participation in international fora seeking to define new concepts of hemispheric security and arms limitation and control, and so on.

Finally, one issue that encompasses the aforementioned points is the need to modernize the state. The observed tendency in favor of broadening relations in the field of defense to include other nontraditional areas (Asia, Europe, the Middle East) is part of a more complex process regarding the growing internationalization and interdependence of states. This new situation requires a multisectoral (state, business leaders, workers) and interministerial (Defense, Foreign Relations, Finance, Economy, etc.) vision. These actors must operate in a coordinated fashion and through debureaucratized and efficient channels. That is, there is a need to modernize the capacity of the state to function. This will enable the incorporation of the country into a dynamic world, which, paradoxically, is becoming more accustomed to change.

Only the consolidation of democracy will enable Chile to fulfill its expectations of economic growth and stability with equity and social justice. The prospects are optimal. However, to transform them into actions and accomplished facts, the democratic governability pact should be permanently guaranteed. One of the pillars of this pact is the establishment of a new form and a new plan of action in defense-related issues. This will make it possible to consolidate the trilogy of peace, democracy, and development into effective policies. The modernization of the nation demands it.

Security Policies, Democratization, and Regional Integration in the Southern Cone

Mônica Hirst

Introduction

In the last fifteen years, changes in security concepts and practices within and between states in the Southern Cone have been strongly influenced by the wave of democratization since the early 1980s. Sharing common political values and bearing similar economic challenges contributed to downgrade previous rivalries and disputes that in the past had hampered cooperative initiatives in this region. In fact, expectations held that security cooperation, together with economic integration and political coordination, would become an irreversible process. In this context, it became appropriate to make use of Kant's interdemocratic peace approach to explain cooperative enterprises in the region, particularly those initiated between Argentina and Brazil.[1]

Though these prospects have not suffered a complete reversal, expectations regarding the "dovish" vocations of the newborn democracies of the Southern Cone have diminished. Pessimistic predictions have suggested that democratic consolidation in this subregion could signify a movement back to a classic security dilemma environment.[2] To understand this sort of projection it is necessary to review the role of democratization for interstate relations in the Southern Cone. Furthermore, the new realities of intraregional relations require the consideration of other developments in this area besides the change of political regimes.

In the past, regional conflictive hypotheses were a substantial part of security doctrines that justified the expansion of military expenditures and the maintenance of political prerogatives by the armed forces in this region. In the last fifteen years, democratization has constrained the political prominence of the military in most countries and such doctrines have been gradually deactivated. The political culture behind conflictive hypotheses, though not completely eliminated, has adjusted to new domestic pressures and international circumstances. As Russett has stated, "Governments and political institutions can change rapidly after a revolution, but norms take time to develop. Laws can change faster than the practices in which norms are embedded."[3]

Certainly, interdemocratic peace is an ambiguous concept in the Southern Cone. To start, major intraregional negotiations in which strategic interests and territorial disputes were at stake had been concluded during periods of military rule. The most outstanding examples are the Itaipú-Corpus Treaty in 1979 and the Argentina-Chile Peace and Friendship Treaty in 1985.[4] Second, there has been a connection between the reduction of military expenditures and the thorough economic constraints of the eighties, which precipitated budget restrictions and downsizing state policies.[5] Naturally, democratic transition and consolidation have favored these cutbacks, yet the principal motive was economic. Third, the link between security cooperation and democratization cannot be understood apart from the recent developments in subregional economic integration. In the mid-eighties, security cooperation initiatives were a "spill-around" effect of closer Argentine-Brazilian economic ties.[6] They belonged to a comprehensive package of agreements in which managed trade and technological cooperation became part of a single strategy.[7] Hence, economic integration arrangements contributed to legitimize security cooperation policies. This process has been deepened even more with the Asunción Treaty (1990), which speeded economic integration by creating an automatic mechanism for the lifting of intraregional trade barriers.[8]

Besides aspects connected to domestic and regional developments it is also important to consider this area's strategic irrelevance in global affairs. Compared with other subregions in the world and even those of Latin America, the Southern Cone does not confront regional or extraregional security menaces. The Southern Cone occupies a marginal spot in the world strategic agenda. Fortunately, it bears none of the ethnic disputes of other recently democratized subregions—as in Eastern Europe—or the religious conflicts in many Third World areas. Also, this area has long been on the low priority list of great powers—especially that of the United States—and in all likelihood will continue to keep this position. Although strategic marginalization has brought undeniable economic costs to South American countries, it has also reduced the importance of intraregional differences on security policies.

To understand the underlying currents of Southern Cone security policies it is important to consider shaping factors as well as shaping actors at three different dimensions: domestic, international, and regional. At a domestic level it is necessary to reflect on the different patterns of postauthoritarian civil-military relations that have taken place in the Southern Cone. At an international level, circumstances have had a major impact on foreign policy options. Finally, regional politics, though influenced by both previous dimensions, has assumed a specific dynamic, influenced by present and past intergovernmental and intersocietal relations.

The Domestic Level

At the domestic level, the periods of transition to and consolidation of democracy are examined in light of emerging security concerns.

Transition

Civil-military relations initiated during democratic transition have had a direct impact on the changes and continuities of defense policies in the area. Despite the fact that all countries in the Southern Cone have experienced democratic transition and consolidation processes, civil-military relations have evolved differently in each case. Postauthoritarian autonomy and the political power of the armed forces in Argentina, Brazil, Chile, Uruguay, and Paraguay have not been uniform, either because previous military prerogatives were preserved or new internal security concepts have been enforced. The unique nature of each case is related to domestic negotiations and the nature of international pressures that took place during the democratic transition and consolidation. These differences contribute to elucidate present foreign policy distinctions, particularly those between Argentina and Brazil, and are even more important in understanding politicization trends in regional politics.

In the case of Argentina, the sudden end of an authoritarian regime, caused by the defeat of the Falklands/Malvinas War, together with a disastrous economic policy, made military politics particularly turbulent during the democratic transition period. Moreover, it delayed effective domestic negotiations regarding the role of the armed forces in a pluralistic environment. During this phase (1983–89), prior Argentine defense policy was partly preserved, though adjusted to the foreign policy premises of the Alfonsín government. Since technological autonomy was perceived as a priority for the new democratic government, the common interests shared by civil and military authorities regarding the need to maintain the weapons industry and sensitive technology programs helped to legitimize such an influence.

Nevertheless, as macroeconomic hardships increased, military armament projects were severely affected and forced to decrease production or even postpone much activity.[9]

Considered by many an "incomplete" transition process, the political system inaugurated with the Aylwin government in Chile (1990) was one of the less successful in the region in subordinating military power to civil authority.[10] In the case of Chile, the armed forces' full control of defense policy was part of a formal negotiation with the civil society as one among many preconditions to initiate democratic transition.[11] Strengthened by a successful macroeconomic performance, the Chilean military managed to retain a broad range of political prerogatives and economic advantages that dramatically curtailed the power of civil authorities. Chilean armed forces dominion of defense policy involved the continuity of a prosperous and diversified weapons industry.

Contrary to the Argentine case, Brazil underwent the longest democratic transition in the Southern Cone. In this case, democratization proved a painless process for the armed forces as they preserved significant prerogatives regarding domestic politics and defense policy.[12] Stimulated by a successful export policy, the Brazilian military enhanced a significant weapons industry, which placed it among the top ten exporters in the international arms market in the mid-eighties. In the case of Brazil, the buildup of a civil-military consensus about the country's economic model survived the change of political regime. This sense of continuity helps to explain why Brazilian foreign policy changes at the time were less significant than those experienced by other Southern Cone neighbors, particularly Argentina and Uruguay.

During the Sarney government (1985–90) military submission to civil authorities increased very gradually in Brazil and a new constitution determined the limits of this subordination.[13] The formal presence of military authorities in the government continued untouched, while they maintained an implicit veto power. In this context, the costs for the Brazilian armed forces of the new rules of the game imposed by a democratic system were quite low. With respect to foreign policy matters, innovations were carefully negotiated between the Foreign Ministry and the military authorities.[14] The Brazilian armed forces also defended capably their interests in other governmental agencies. In the newly created Science and Technology Ministry, common concerns shared by the military and the scientific community regarding technological autonomy were vigorously protected.[15] Similarly, the military was successful in expanding its presence in the Amazon, an area that became a growing concern for the Brazilian Army.

Furthermore, the Brazilian military learned to lobby in Brazil's Congress and to identify allies within political parties when defense policies needed legislative approval. Though Itamaraty (the name of Brazil's foreign ministry) was concerned in preserving the essence of Brazil's previous foreign policy, it assumed the role of a mediator between domestic and international pressures in the decisions concerning international security and high technology. Examples were the domestic negotiations regarding the dispute with the United States over computer hardware and software and the deepening of nuclear cooperation with Argentina.[16] In both cases the foreign ministry's principal aim in domestic politics was to soften the nationalistic stances defended by the Brazilian military.

Although Uruguay and Paraguay play minor roles in Southern Cone security politics, it is important to underline certain aspects regarding developments of civil-military relations within these two countries. Uruguay became the most successful case of fast and nontraumatic military adherence to democracy, as the armed forces have managed to preserve an institutional function with a very limited interference in domestic politics.[17] In the case of Paraguay, however, civil-military relations remained tense and uncertain since democratic values were notoriously limited when democratic transition first initiated.[18]

Consolidation

The consolidation of democratic institutions proved to be as difficult or perhaps even more challenging than the replacement of military governments by civilian regimes.[19] In Argentina and Brazil, democratic consolidation was a costly political achievement that had different—but equally important—effects on the civil-military relations of these countries. In Argentina, the failed antidemocratic military rebellions contributed to deepen the armed forces' demoralization vis-à-vis civil society and offered the Menem government the political conditions to complete the process of military subordination to civil authority.[20] In return, a controversial amnesty law granted forgiveness to previous military authorities for past human rights abuses.

This process deepened as it became directly connected to the broad process of privatization and state downsizing policies that justified the elimination of most military technology programs that had survived during the Alfonsín government. Furthermore, President Menem's audacious military policy became a critical part of his new foreign policy. By abandoning previous military technology programs and adopting new positions on international security, Argentina was also taking important steps toward a closer relationship with the United States.

In fact, Argentina provides the most outstanding example of military subordination to civil control during democratic consolidation. This process has been benefited by a combination of three major factors: one, the positive results of a full-scale stabilization program; two, strong presidential leadership; and three, explicit support given by the United States. For certain military segments, the main consequence of these decisions has been a de facto renunciation of a national defense policy.

In Chile and Brazil, civil-military relations present more complex realities than in Argentina. In the case of Chile, while institutional and economic stability have not been endangered, civil-military relations have improved very slowly. Regarding domestic politics, the renunciation of previous prerogatives has been greatly resisted by the Chilean military, who vindicate the maintenance of the compromises negotiated in 1989 with the political forces. These compromises, supported by a strong rightist coalition, are perceived by the armed forces as part of a long-term agreement rather than a set of transitional conditions.

Overall the Chilean military has managed to preserve considerable political autonomy, due to two critical factors: first, the economic autonomy granted to the armed forces by the Copper Law, and second, the explicit support given by powerful segments of civil society.[21] During the Frei government (1994–2000), initial progress was made in reviewing past human rights abuses, but political conditions have been far from conducive to reconciliation. On the very contrary, Chilean armed forces have been deeply reluctant to support the constitutional reforms proposed by the government and have made explicit their reluctance to deal with a pluralistic political society.[22]

Brazil provides neither an example of dramatic change as in Argentina nor one of continuity as in the case of Chile. As a strong corporation, the Brazilian military adjusted its political practices to the current democratic rules of the game.[23] In doing so, the armed forces of Brazil have become a relevant shaping actor of national and foreign policies when they perceive their political or institutional interests are involved. Initially, Brazilian democratic consolidation brought about the expectation that military subordination to civil authorities would be more effective. Among the goals of the Collor de Mello government (1990–92), three plans of action would be enforced to meet such expectations: the dramatic curtailment and civil control of military technology programs, the adherence of Brazil to all international nonproliferation regimes, and the integration of the three preexisting military ministries into one Defense Ministry headed by a civil authority. These innovations aimed to improve the transparency of military technology programs vis-à-vis Brazilian civil society and to diminish Brazil's exposure to international—particularly U.S.—nonproliferation pressures. In interbureaucratic politics it was expected that the changes in Brazil's international security would be conducted by the foreign ministry, which was expected to experience a dramatic change of its belief system. Also, like Argentina, the new Brazilian security objectives were part of a shift in political and economic policies on both domestic and international levels.

Soon Brazilian reality revealed how fragile the domestic grounds were to enforce all the changes announced by the new government. The resistance of political and economic elites to neoliberal reforms, together with a general repugnance on the part of political movements toward the power abuses of the new president and his closest collaborators, led to Collor de Mello's impeachment. As Vice President Itamar Franco assumed the presidency, Brazil faced a dramatic governability crisis dominated by general macroeconomic disorder, in which the Congress became a major political actor. Interestingly, as Brazil muddled through a serious and unpredictable institutional crisis, the armed forces kept a distance from domestic politics, acting as defendants of the continuity of the democratic order.

Once the Itamar Franco government stabilized, domestic politics in Brazil revealed a peculiar dynamic in which tendencies toward continuity and change were simultaneously set in motion. On the one side, Brazilian politics became an ambiguous setting where pre-Collor interests mixed with an invigorated civil society. On the other, economic policies initiated a phase of gradual rationalization, which sought to end recurrent high inflation rates. Although this process included an important set of neoliberal policies, it no longer involved the broad ideological commitments that would necessarily lead to major domestic and foreign policy changes. In this context, the Brazilian armed forces were granted a legitimate part in the country's democratic consolidation process, while managing to retain a significant influence on defense policy premises and practices.

Though the Cardoso government (1995–99) was not expected to implement significant changes in Brazilian civil-military relations, adjustments have occurred. The idea of creating a Defense Ministry was revived in a context of broad negotiations in which bureaucratic rationalization and the improvement of Brazil's international image became the most important motives (rather than civil-military subordination). The Brazilian armed forces also improved their leverage concerning military salaries and managed to voice their opinions and concerns in all foreign policy matters related to defense policies. The connection between international politics and security interests has been the main function of the secretary of strategic affairs, an agency that has expanded its functions in the Cardoso government.

Civil-military relations in Uruguay and Paraguay maintained more or less the same profile as in the early phase of democratization. In Uruguay, the main problem faced by the military became their limited economic resources to consolidate an institutional mission. Since the Lacalle government (1990–95), budget restrictions seriously reduced the activities of all sectors of Uruguayan armed forces, imposing major reductions of high-rank personnel and the acquisition of new equipment.[24] To compensate, Uruguay's government expanded the country's participation in UN peacekeeping missions, which led to the creation in 1993 of a Peacekeeping Training Academy.[25] In Paraguay, little improvement was reached in curtailing the influence of previous military prerogatives and political power.[26] President Wasmosy (1993–98) became reluctant to accept opposition pressures to disconnect partisan politics (the Colorado Party) from military affairs, thus perpetuating the idea that the strengthening of civil power institutions could lead to a military coup. Moreover, corruption in the Paraguayan military and its growing involvement with drug trafficking remain untouched.

In all the cases described above, defense policies derived from a specific combination of civil-military relations and foreign policy. In each case, however, international politics influenced security policies differently, according to the foreign policy premises and practices that accompanied the democratization process.

International Politics

Security policies have been directly linked to the foreign policies of Southern Cone countries. The end of the cold war has introduced major changes in this connection for Argentina and Brazil, and to a lesser degree for Chile. In Uruguay and Paraguay, though global political changes have been fully acknowledged in foreign policy premises and practices, their effect on international security policy has been less relevant for regional politics.

While the disappearance of East-West ideological constraints has been a positive trend shared by all democratization processes in the area, it has not led to an identical interpretation of the new international order. Since 1989, the change in the structure of world politics has produced differing perceptions regarding the costs and benefits of the post–cold war order, which generated a new source of tension in intraregional relations.

It proves appropriate to use the "qualitative-quantitative" distinction applied to interpret the new world order.[27] Argentina, and Chile to a certain degree, have changed their foreign policy based on the perception of a dramatically transformed post–cold war world and have become strong supporters of globally oriented regional governance initiatives. These initiatives, furthered in the name of multilateral institutionalism, are in fact bandwagoning demonstrations aimed to strengthen political ties with the United States. Brazil, on the other hand, recognizes but deemphasizes the importance of cold war qualitative changes and is more concerned with power distribution at global and regional levels. This position has led to a recurrent resistance to globally oriented reforms of regional institutions, particularly the Organization of American States (OAS), which could menace the classical concept of sovereignty.

Foreign policy in Argentina has followed very different premises during the periods of democratic transition and consolidation. As addressed by Escudé and Fontana, the end of a bipolar confrontation was perceived by Menem's government as an opportunity to redefine international objectives and to consider a close relationship with the United States a top priority for Argentina. Decisions regarding international security have been entirely influenced by this premise. Argentina has supported the United States by complying with its expectations in multilateral and unilateral initiatives.[28]

In the case of Chile, there has been an obvious division between foreign policy and international security policies that derives from the tensions in civil-military relations. While the Foreign Ministry supports all initiatives that aim to strengthen global governance regimes and institutions, military authorities defend a prudent posture vis-à-vis world politics in which autonomous projects are to be preserved. The nation-state is still, in this case, a core concept, and international security is directly connected to national defense policies. Whereas Chile has participated in regional nonproliferation regimes, it has resisted adhering to the Non-Proliferation Treaty (NPT) and has barely participated in United Nations peacekeeping missions. On the other hand, Chile's foreign policy has fully embraced a globalist perception regarding nonmilitary threats, and Chilean diplomacy has been particularly active in the defense of the abandonment of the national sovereignty principle when democracy and human rights are found to be threatened.

In Brazil, foreign policy and international security concepts and practices have developed quite differently than in Argentina. Brazilian international affairs have been more the outcome of a complex interaction between external conditions and domestic interests and perceptions than the result of a straightforward political shift. Also, the Foreign Ministry (Itamaraty) has managed to preserve its influence and legitimacy as the main shaping actor of all foreign policy decisions. Itamaraty's protagonism has been sustained by a belief system that had been responsible for Brazil's foreign policy guidelines since the mid-seventies.[29]

During the Collor government, Itamaraty's belief system was shattered because the first steps undertaken to inaugurate a cooperative relationship with the United States included major changes in international security policies.[30] Under these circumstances, unprecedented nonproliferation commitments were reached that had an extraordinary impact on regional politics.[31] At the same time, the changes put forward during the Collor government stimulated an unusual debate among Brazilian diplomats, which revealed that Itamaraty was no longer an encapsulated entity separated from domestic politics.[32]

During the Itamar Franco government Brazil's foreign policy went through a process of adjustment, influenced by two factors: first, the growing positive impact of economic stabilization measures on the country's international affairs; second, a revival of the belief that continuity and consensus were essential for international credibility. Outstanding priorities in Brazilian foreign policy were active participation in the Southern Cone Common Market (MERCOSUR), the creation of a South American Free Trade Area (SAFTA), close relations with other regional powers (China, India, and Russia), and a less conflictive relationship with the United States.

The Cardoso government has demonstrated its intention to maintain Itamaraty's ascendance in the formulation and implementation of Brazil's foreign policy. Furthermore, President Cardoso has added his personal leadership to Brazil's foreign affairs, aiming to strengthen its domestic and international support.

Though admitting major changes have taken place in the international system, Brazil's foreign policy practitioners have been reluctant to adhere to a globalist perception of world politics. Some Brazilian diplomats argue that this is not a global era but an era of exclusion and of concentration of power, with growing tensions between the North and the South.[33] Nevertheless there is a relevant sector in Itamaraty that believes Brazil must replace its defensive posture with a positive offense, in which the promotion of a broad reform of the world's global institutions has become a priority. In this same direction this country has softened its official discourse about North-South tensions, meriting its role as a "consensus builder"[34] between both extremes in the international community. This is the platform from which Brazil has been mounting its campaign for a permanent seat at the UN Security Council. Brazilian candidacy has been based on the idea that the UN Security Council must reflect a more equitable representation of the North and the South in order to enhance its legitimacy and efficacy in world affairs.

The gradual adjustment of Brazil's foreign policy premises has involved international security policies. After having expanded its regional commitments on nonproliferation regimes, Brazil has approved a bill that controls sensitive technology exports and has adhered to the Missile Technology Control Regime (MTCR) and to the Non-Proliferation Treaty (NPT). All these decisions followed the negotiation of the Nuclear Quadripartite Treaty signed with Argentina and the International Atomic Energy Agency (IAEA) in 1990.

On the domestic front, Brazil's international security policies face the pressures and interests of the military. Nationalism continues to be an important source of cohesion within the Brazilian armed forces, who strongly appraise the country's geostrategic attributes and fear the expansion of the U.S. military presence in South America. This kind of awareness has been stimulated by the increase of U.S. military operations in South America as well as U.S. antidrug activities and radar base operations in other Amazon countries. According to the Brazilian military, whereas power asymmetry and different threat perceptions have affected relations with the United States, history and tradition impose a modus vivendi with the "giant from the north."[35] With respect to global affairs, particular concern exists regarding the difficulties imposed on access to high technology by the core countries, which leads to the idea that these have created a "knowledge cartel" in world politics.[36] This kind of perception, however, has not kept the Brazilian armed forces from expanding their participation in UN peacekeeping missions.[37] The presence of Brazilian officers has become particularly important in Portuguese-speaking African countries (Angola and Mozambique) where cultural and linguistic familiarity together with a previous diplomatic presence have been relevant incentives.

In Brazilian military circles international environmental politics has become the most pressing concern in the new global security agenda. While this is an area in which Itamaraty has become particularly involved, it has also developed into a central worry for the armed forces. These tend to interpret global environmental approaches focused upon the Amazon as an attempt to curtail Brazil's sovereignty over its Amazonian territory. After an unsuccessful program (Calha Norte) installed by the armed forces in the mid-eighties in order to expand the military presence in this area, the military are setting up a huge communication and monitoring system that includes a significant number of radar devices, satellites, and aircrafts. Labeled as the SIVAM (Amazonian Watch System), this program has been considered a reaction against the idea of an "internationalization" of the Amazon. It aims to control drug trafficking and border smuggling activities, supervise the safety of indigenous populations, preserve environmental resources, and assure a more effective presence in an area of five million kilometers of open frontier.[38] For Itamaraty the growing importance of the Amazon area in domestic politics has been an important motivation to deepen political and economic ties with other Amazonian neighbors, particularly in the context of Brazil's increasing commercial presence in the region.

Regional Politics

The combination of civil-military relations with foreign policy options and premises is crucial in understanding developments in Southern Cone regional security politics. Though democratization has been a shared experience in the area, it has not led to the buildup of a pluralistic security community.[39] Important cooperative initiatives have been carried forward, improving peace and security conditions of the region, yet these have not led to a process of security integration. In this context, regional security cooperation has become a spill-around effect of the expansion of economic ties among Southern Cone countries. Hence, intraregional integration arrangements have given place to a new chapter in regional security politics, which are part of the externalities produced by the expansion of cross-border economic relations. These are the security externalities of MERCOSUR. The differences previously mentioned regarding domestic and international politics shaped a process of politicization in which the link between power and economics has become a central issue. Though a fragmenting symptom that can bother the associative environment, this politicization cannot affect the peace and stability of conditions in the Southern Cone. In this case democratic regimes and economic regionalization together represent an element powerful enough to neutralize anarchic developments.

Whereas there has been a growing convergence among Southern Cone countries regarding economic policies, differences have persisted with respect to defense and security policies. A myriad of issues and concerns feed politicization in Southern Cone countries regarding regional security. Two kinds of matters emerge in this case; one is related to the implications of nation-state security policies, and the other to recent regional developments.

In the small Southern Cone states this calls attention to the contrasting role each one plays in regional security politics. On the one side, Paraguay has been a permanent source of concern for Argentina and Brazil. First, because of the overwhelming presence of the military in domestic politics and, second, on account of the involvement of the Paraguayan armed forces with drug-trafficking activities. On the other hand, Uruguay has offered no sort of threat to its neighbors in security matters because of its political stability and the low profile of its armed forces in domestic politics.

Argentina has been the country in the area most concerned with the need to link economic integration with regional security. Since the early nineties the idea of creating a security system for the Southern Cone has been defended in Argentine academic, military, and diplomatic circles. According to certain proposals this system would include the formation of a center responsible for avoiding subregional conflicts, a strategic data center, military technical exchange, armament industry cooperation, and cooperation for civil protection.[40] Yet as this kind of project did not mature, concerns in Argentina increased regarding the perspectives of a growing military imbalance between this country and its neighbors. Particular apprehension existed regarding Chile, because of its continuous military acquisitions and production policy and the maintenance of an active defense policy. In the case of Brazil, it became consensual that a conflictive hypothesis no longer existed on either side and that a strategic alliance would be gradually built up. Yet this process from an Argentine perspective ought to include a balanced reduction of conventional armaments as well as a mechanism of permanent information exchange on space and missile projects. The fact that this kind of commitment did not advance on the part of the Brazilian armed forces did not keep the Argentine military from fostering the continuity of cooperative programs aimed at the consolidation of security ties with Brazil. Though the present imbalance with Brazil is recognized as a second-best situation, the motives behind Brazilian security policies are considered legitimate and are not perceived as threats per se to Argentina. In this context joint military operations were initiated at the Argentine-Brazilian border aiming to recreate situations similar to those faced in peace operations.

Chilean military have been quite less enthusiastic about regional integration and its spill-around effects on security affairs. The dominant perception among the military in Chile is that states have different interests that limit regional complementation and cooperation.[41] Accordingly, closer security relations with other neighbors will have to be subordinated to national defense policies. Paradoxically, these nation-state dogmas coexist with Chilean foreign policy stances strongly in favor of hemispheric cooperative security policies.

For Brazil, though the Southern Cone has a particular significance for this country's strategic design, this area is part of a broader regional and global security agenda. Argentina has become Brazil's most important partner for bilateral security cooperation. This cooperation has enhanced peace and stability conditions in South America and has been crucial for Brazil's credibility in the international community. Secondly, it has become increasingly important for Brazil to consolidate a peaceful environment in its southern borders even more in the face of the security predicaments developing along the northern borders of the country.[42] Local turbulence in the Amazon together with the concerns brought about by the new environmental global approaches have displaced Brazilian military concerns from South to North.

Notwithstanding this new reality, the implications of Argentina-Brazil foreign and security policy differences have introduced a new element of concern within the diplomatic and military circles of Brazil. Uneasiness has emanated that Argentina could be taking its policy of unilateral disarmament too far, generating an inconvenient situation of disequilibrium in the area. While it is true that Argentina's defeat in the Falklands/Malvinas War provided a motive for explicit solidarity on the part of Brazil, it was also a source of relief as it affected Argentina's general offensive capability. At the time, Argentina's bellicosity had become a source of concern to all its neighbors in the Southern Cone. Undoubtedly the end of Argentina's militaristic and geopolitically biased policies in the region has contributed to enhance peace conditions in the area.[43] Yet, certain military and diplomatic sectors in Brazil are concerned about Argentina's 180-degree turn, either because of the risks of abrupt changes in security policies or of its connection with this country's strategic alliance with the United States. Neither Chileans nor Brazilians welcomed the announcement of an extra-NATO agreement negotiated between the United States and Argentina.

It can be interesting in this case to refer to an aspect of the imaginary realm of Argentina-Brazil relations. Within the Brazilian-Argentine relationship it has been recurrent that segments in the political and economic elites identify themselves with governmental or societal preferences that are more influential in the other country than in their own. Cross-border worldviews have been a historic source of intergovernmental and intersocietal interaction between both countries.[44] Presently, this phenomenon occurs in Argentina regarding the economic and international security options of Brazil. One reason why segments in the Argentine government and society approve closer economic relations with Brazil relates to the recognition of the importance of Brazilian industrial policies, which in turn could legitimate the same kind of policies in their country.[45] In security policy, one reason why political and military segments support closer relations with Brazil is linked to domestic postures that would prefer the continuity of military technology programs and would adopt a more independent international security policy vis-à-vis the United States.[46] In this case, security cooperation with Brazil could play an important role in diminishing the impact of the dramatic curtailment of military-technology programs.

The Brazilian military recognize that a "cautious" increase of security cooperation will be a natural and necessary consequence of regional economic integration.[47] Furthermore, there is a perception in Brazil that foreign policy differences with Argentina must be de-dramatized and gradually replaced by a positive agenda that goes beyond economic integration initiatives. This perception is linked to Brazil's broader ambitions in international affairs, which have been driving this country to a new posture at a regional and global level.

To a certain point, the discussion of whether or not Brazil could assume the status of a regional power has become intertwined with the differences between Argentine and Brazilian foreign policy. While acknowledging its regional importance, Brazil has explicitly renounced any kind of hegemonic pretension.[48] Yet its expanded economic and diplomatic presence in South America, together with positive outcomes in important international negotiations—particularly that of a permanent seat at the UN Security Council—would have an inevitable repercussion for regional power politics. For Brazil, a major challenge will be to avoid a negative politicization in South America, particularly in Argentina.

As long-term planning strategies are developed in Brazil, relations with Argentina and with the United States are to become challenging subjects. In order to progress in both directions it has become important to detriangulate Argentina-Brazil-United States relations. This task has been eased by the improvement of the relations between Brazil and the United States ever since the inauguration of the Cardoso government. In the security realm, the fact that the Ministers of Defense Meeting on Hemispheric Security did not generate new obstacles in this direction became a positive development. Previous expectations of creating a hemispheric security regime and collective action commitments have gradually diminished, while confidence-building measures and cooperation initiatives will be carried forward more loosely than had been at first suggested by the U.S. government—with support from Argentina. Simultaneously, Brazil has become more cooperative in other issues of the inter-American agenda, especially those related to human rights and the betterment of social and political conditions of democracy.

Final Remarks

Has the time become ripe in the Southern Cone for the creation of a pluralistic security community?

Though deescalation of conflictive strategies has clearly improved in the last fifteen years and intergovernmental and intersocietal interaction has reached an unprecedented level, there is still a long road ahead to achieve security integration in this area. Paved by centripetal and centrifugal forces, this will be a bumpy road depending on domestic, international, and regional developments. Democratization is an important but insufficient condition to intensify security cooperation in the Southern Cone. The different patterns of civil-military relations that have sustained democratic consolidation have contributed neither to build up a common identity nor a shared mission within the armed forces of the region. Post–cold war foreign policies have also been an element of differentiation among these countries, generating the idea that commonalities in international affairs are no longer a given condition.

Yet being a "no-war" zone and a marginal strategic area in global affairs reduces the effects of foreign policy differences for regional security.[49] Neither the Southern Cone nor South America could remotely become a turbulent region exposed to increasing ethnic, religious, and political fragmentation. Furthermore, confidence-building measures have been enforced with the purpose of consolidating grounds for interstate peace and stability in the Southern Cone.[50] In particular, the Argentina-Brazil nuclear negotiations initiated in the mid-eighties have led to a cumulative process of nonproliferation negotiations nowadays considered an archetype for nuclear weapon–free zones. Democratization has enhanced the use of peaceful settlement mechanisms, strengthening the basis of this region's culture of legalism. In fact, though security cooperation and democratization have not led to security integration they have been effective in diminishing previous mistrust and animosity among Southern Cone societies and states—especially between Argentina and Brazil.

As foreign policy convergences have decreased, economic factors have become the most important source for the identification of common interests in this area. A new economic realm has built up in this region in which the combination of unilateral liberal-oriented reforms with multilateral negotiations have started a process of deep subregional integration. Shared values and common interest have intensified intraregional trade and investment flows, generating unprecedented cross-border interactions. MERCOSUR, as a free-trade area and an incomplete customs union, has expanded the economic interdependence of its member states, giving special impulse to their departure from previous defensive economic strategies. Moreover, the economic international visibility of MERCOSUR has led to a myriad of new regional and extraregional negotiations. Chile has also intensified economic linkages with all countries in this area as it has become more attracted to nearby markets. However, Chilean policy has been cautious vis-à-vis MERCOSUR and it has given less importance to negotiations with Southern Cone countries than to those with the United States, hoping to be next in line in free-trade negotiations with the United States.[51] In fact a parallel can be traced between the fragmenting vocations revealed by both Chilean defense and economic strategies in the region.

In Argentine and Brazilian diplomatic and military circles there is a shared consensus that bilateral political differences do not affect regional integration. Yet it does contaminate the political environment and can be manipulated by anti-integration forces generating a negative politicization when difficult bargaining situations are faced. Since MERCOSUR lacks strong institutions, such circumstances could generate a notion of rivalry not based on concrete disputes as in the past but rooted on the deficit of reciprocal tolerance and on a negative linkage between power and economics.

The lack of mutual tolerance could hurt the essence of interdemocratic relations and could affect the credibility of any sort of post–cold war foreign policy. Political maturity to deal with the particularism of history, culture, and domestic realities is a sine qua non condition for a successful regional integration process. Hence, since nonconvergent worldviews will probably persist, a political and strategic cooperative agenda based on positive coexistence could become in the near future a second-best solution. In this case, the security externalities of MERCOSUR could gradually move from sterile politicization to the set-up of a cooperative agenda, which in the long run would lead to a regional security community.

✿ Part II

The Impact on Latin American Countries of Participation in UN Missions

What is the impact on Latin American countries of their participation in United Nations international peacekeeping missions? The three chapters in this section focus on contrasting outcomes: successful in Argentina and unsuccessful in Venezuela.

Ricardo Lagorio shows how there has been a close correspondence between changes in Argentina's domestic political regime, its foreign policy, and its military and security policies. Argentina fashioned its security policies to consolidate the democratic system at home and claim a significant international role; its internationalist security policies have been driven by domestic factors. Lagorio also shows that Argentine security policies are consistent with the new security policies of North American and Western European countries.

Antonio Pala indicates that Argentina has contributed over half of all UN peacekeepers from Latin America. Large-scale Argentine participation in UN missions, though recent, has already had an impact on military self-esteem and professionalism. Participation in UN missions enhanced the competence of Argentine military officers and connected them to U.S. and European armed forces. Pala argues that this participation is likely to improve Argentine relations with its neighbors and consolidate civilian control over its armed forces.

Carlos Romero traces Venezuela's activist foreign policy with special attention to policies toward Central America's civil and international wars of the late 1970s and 1980s. Venezuelan presidents developed a costly activist policy with weak political and military support. The escalation of Venezuelan participation in UN missions in the early 1990s was ill-planned; soldiers were badly equipped. Venezuelan military officers deployed to a UN mission in Nicaragua later formed part of coup plots to overthrow Venezuela's democratic system.

Chapter 6

Institutionalization, Cooperative Security, and Peacekeeping Operations

The Argentine Experience

Ricardo E. Lagorio

> There is a soldier who is more noble and beautiful than the soldier of war: he is the soldier of peace. I would say he is the only dignified and glorious soldier. If the beautiful and loved illusion of the noble hearts and of perpetual peace would become a reality, the soldier's condition would be exactly that of the soldier of peace.
>
> —Juan Bautista Alberdi, *The Crime of War*

> Will it take even longer for Europeans to understand that they have traded a world with threats but without risks, for a world without threats but with risks?
>
> —Alain Minc, *The New Middle Ages*

The decade of the 1980s ended with the fall of the Berlin wall and thus on an optimistic note, very much influenced by Francis Fukuyama's "endism" theory,[1] as well as by the United Nations' effective and positive results in dealing with major conflicts. In this respect, the UN coalition's important military and political victory in the Gulf War, led by the United States, was perceived as a watershed. The international community was seeking a new paradigm for dealing with aggression, and it was understood that international organizations, particularly the United Nations, had a major role to play in this area.[2] The "rapprochement" between the United States and Russia, presumed to be instrumental in installing this new international system, never entirely worked because of the lack of consensus between the two major superpowers. The wave of optimism that had engulfed the world in 1989 just as suddenly faded.[3]

The end of the cold war meant the vanishing of a "stable" bipolar military landscape in the strategic field, but it did not provide the world with an equally viable alternative scenario.[4] The strategic rationale of the cold war decades, although not exempt from danger, produced a predictable macro-level order. But the concept of collective security embodied in the UN Charter has proved to be an imperfect mechanism for effectively dealing with international crises emerging in the post–cold war era.[5] Peacekeeping has shown itself to be effective when dealing with conflicts between nations, but it is yet to be demonstrated whether the international community can produce similarly successful results in situations characterized by internal conflicts.

Despite important outcomes in conflicts such as Namibia, El Salvador, and Cambodia, in the 1990s we have witnessed an explosion of regional conflicts. Some of these are limited or restrained (such as those in Rwanda, Somalia, Liberia, and Peru/Ecuador), while others, like the one engulfing former Yugoslavia, contain a dangerous potential for spreading beyond their original boundaries. This situation has been characterized as "the crisis in UN peacekeeping." It reflects the new "international mood." A more realistic and traditional view has replaced the early wave of optimism.[6] But the problem does not lie only in the UN's ability to manage and solve international problems and conflicts. We face major systemic changes. One analyst notes:

Not only the configuration of great powers and their alliances but the very structure of political history has changed. . . . The very sovereignty and cohesion of states, the authority and efficacy of the governments are not what they were. Are we going to see ever larger and larger political units? . . . Or are we more likely going to see the break up of several states into smaller ones? Are we going to see a large-scale migration of millions of peoples, something that has not happened since the last century of the Roman Empire? This is at least possible. The very texture of history is changing before our very eyes.[7]

What is to be done? Alexis de Tocqueville wrote: "Among the laws that rule human societies, there is one which seems to be more precise and clear than all others. If men are to remain civilized or to become so, the art of associating together must grow and improve in the same ratio in which the equality of condition is increased."[8] Echoing this sentiment, Samuel P. Huntington has argued: "In much of the world today, equality of political participation is growing much more rapidly than is the 'art of associating together.' The rates of mobilization and participation are high: the rates of organization and institutionalization are low."[9]

These ideas apply to the current situation. As already mentioned, the end of the cold war did not mean the end of conflicts. It did, however, signal a shift from the macro-systemic level (a war between the two superpowers) to a micro-regional level. We witness, therefore, the mobilization of new state and nonstate actors who were demobilized during the cold war, pressuring the international system (inputs) although the system lacks the capacity to react through institutions (outputs). Many of the issues of the so-called new agenda—environment, drug trafficking, migration, fundamentalism, international violence, nationalism—display a mixture of state and nonstate actors, both public and private; this can be seen as part of a process of mobilization.

Argentina's New Foreign and Defense Policies

Argentina's decision makers have grasped these systemic changes. This new perception underlies the country's major shift in foreign and defense policies undertaken at the beginning of the 1990s. Argentina's increasing involvement in the United Nations peacekeeping operations (PKO) has had two dimensions. The first relates to the new perceptions regarding the evolution of the international scenario; the second stems from necessities emerging from its process of redemocratization—mainly the need to rebuild civil-military relations and to reinstitutionalize the armed forces. In this chapter, I present Argentina's participation in PKO as a contribution both to international peace and security and to furthering the process of institutionalization inside the country and abroad.

Argentina has recognized that, albeit indirectly, its security is very much linked to the general situation of the international system or to the "health" of the international environment. In a world of growing interdependence, Argentina has recognized that there are systemic and subsystemic consequences to whatever happens in any region of the world.

Argentina assumes the responsibilities that pertain to it as a founding member of the United Nations, and in particular those described in para. 5, article 2 of the UN Charter: "All members shall give the United Nations every assistance in any action it takes in accordance with the present Charter, and shall refrain from giving assistance to any state against which the United Nations is taking preventive or enforcement action." Under this rationale, we believe that we have—along with all of the members of the organization—an objective responsibility for the maintenance of peace and security throughout the world.

Argentina has been very much aware that we live in a turbulent world and that, as Joseph S. Nye has written, "(T)he world after the cold war is *sui* generis, and we overly constrain our understanding by trying to force it into the Procrustean bed of traditional metaphors with their mechanical polarities. Power is becoming more multidimensional, structures more complex, and states themselves more permeable. This added complexity means that world order rests on more than the traditional military balance of power alone."[10] Our military's professionalism, as well as their acceptance of new roles and missions, feed our foreign policy and allow our diplomacy to have an additional tool for acting in world affairs.

The Gulf War of 1990 was a watershed for Argentina's foreign policy because the decision taken by the government to send two naval warships—the only Latin American country to participate in the coalition—reflected a new perception of the international system, and a kind of "new thinking" on issues related to international security. For several decades Argentina's foreign policy had been characterized by a narrow horizon and thus had been limited to advance certain particular national interests such as the Malvinas issue. However, Argentina's[11] decision to intervene in the Persian Gulf reflected its willingness to be an active partner in the international arena: an investor in international peace and security. However, this decision was not taken in a vacuum nor isolated from internal considerations.

By 1990, Argentina had installed its second democratically elected government. Foreign policy was dramatically shifting from a nonaligned and Third World–oriented focus to a western and democratic orientation. A new system of alliances was emerging, emphasizing trends of collaboration and cooperation as well as the values of democracy, markets, and collective security. MERCOSUR, the process of economic integration with Brazil, Uruguay, and Paraguay, was advancing. Most importantly, Argentina and Brazil reached a historic agreement on their nuclear power policies, which allowed both to deescalate what was perceived to be the principal potential source of conflict between the two major Latin American countries. And with Chile, all but one of the border issues were solved.

Political control over the armed forces was being strengthened and the military was furthering its process of institutionalization and cultural adaptation to the new realities. Thus, as a corollary of a new direction in its foreign policy, the country was well placed to start using its military instrument as an effective and efficient tool of its foreign policy.

In 1992, Argentina made a major commitment to UN peacekeeping. In accordance with Security Council Resolution 743 (1992), the country pledged a nine-hundred-man battalion to be part of the newly established United Nations Protection Force (UNPROFOR) in Croatia. Near the end of 1993, Argentina agreed to participate in the United Nations Peacekeeping Force in Cyprus (UNFICYP); we deployed a 392-member contingent in Cyprus, with military elements of the three armed forces (army, marines, and air force helicopters). We also deployed UN observers under the United Nations Truce Supervision Organization (UNTSO); the United Nations Iraq-Kuwait Observation Mission (UNIKOM); the United Nations Angola Verification Mission II (UNAVEM II); the United Nations Mission for the Referendum in Western Sahara (MINURSO); and the United Nations Assistance Mission for Rwanda (UNAMIR). We posted several military officers and noncommissioned officers to work at the UN headquarters in New York. Until the end of 1994, we also had a mobile air force hospital in the United Nations Operation in Mozambique (ONUMOZ). After participating in UN embargoes against the Haitian military government, in 1995 Argentina participated with a one-hundred-man contingent of civilian police *(gendarmerie)* in the UN mission in Haiti.

In all, in the mid-1990s Argentina contributed to the United Nations peacekeeping operations some 1,500 military men but, considering that there was a semestral rotation of personnel, Argentina annually sent 3,000 men abroad. With the ending of the UNPROFOR mission, in 1997 Argentine deployments to United Nations missions were about five hundred men per semester.

This massive involvement was possible because, among other things, the armed forces has changed culturally. Consider the statement of the chief of the Argentine Army, Lt. General Martín Antonio Balza, who, at a November 5, 1993, conference in the Argentine Council on Foreign Relations (CARI) said:[12]

According to what we have heard yesterday, we can conclude that the advancement of peace and global security constitutes, without any doubt, a major objective of Argentine foreign policy. The challenge lying ahead is to identify the alternatives that the emerging international order gives us. We are convinced that this is the framework where the traditional mission of the Armed Forces can find its raison d'être, which is the defense of the interests of the nation. But we are also aware that in this new order new missions have appeared for the armies: secondary or subsidiary missions. Without any doubt we also believe that armies constitute an effective instrument to collaborate in the construction of the international order by complying with these new roles. The Argentine army is behind the objective to further peace as an instrument of the foreign policy of Argentina.

Unthinkable some years ago, the statement reflects a different culture. It indicates a substantive change that has taken place in the Argentine armed forces. Although I quote only the Argentine Army commander, speeches by the heads of the other two services, Admiral Enrique Molina Pico and Brigadier Juan Paulik, showed the same thrust.

To illustrate this dramatic change, consider the evolution of the participation of the Argentine Army, which represents the bulk of the Argentine PKO. In 1958, the army had four military observers. In the period 1967–87, fifty-eight military observers were assigned to PKO. In 1988, twelve; in 1989, seventeen; in 1990, fifteen; in 1991, twenty-seven; in 1992, 1,796; in 1993, 2,139; in 1994, 2,367; and 2,371 were supposed to participate in 1995.[13] Thus some nine thousand men and women participated in PKO under the auspices of the UN from 1992 to 1995. Approximately 30 percent of the members of the Argentine Army—only officers and noncommissioned officers have participated—worked in a UN mission! In 1995, the Argentine Army stopped being an army of conscripts to become a volunteer army; thus in coming years it may also be possible to send privates to participate in PKO missions.

New Concepts for Argentina's Armed Forces

Argentina's participation in PKO has had positive consequences for the country as well as for its civil society and armed forces, including civil-military relations. There is an important institutional objective and impact in the armed forces' participation in PKO. Since the end of the cold war, military establishments have reassessed and reevaluated their objectives, missions, and goals. The most important task has been the need to rethink the armed forces in terms of the new domestic and international realities.

The post–cold war era poses new challenges and new opportunities, obliging us to think of a new paradigm for security. In this sense, the concept of cooperative security (or preventive defense), developed by former U.S. Secretary of Defense William J. Perry, and the ideas developed by then UN Secretary-General Boutros Boutros-Ghali in his 1992 Program For Peace constitute important and complementary intellectual contributions.

Carter, Perry, and Steinbruner's "A New Concept of Cooperative Security"[14] has been incorporated into Argentina's foreign policy conceptual baggage. Although it has not permeated the conceptual framework of discussion at the hemispheric level—neither at the OAS, nor was the concept explicitly mentioned at the Williamsburg Meeting of Defense Ministers—we believe that it has merit. As stated by the authors:

The central purpose of cooperative security arrangements is to prevent war, and to do so primarily by preventing the means for successful aggression from being assembled, thus also obviating the need for states so threatened to make their own counter preparations. Cooperative security thus displaces the centerpiece of security planning from preparing to counter threats to preventing such threats from arising.[15]

This concept is very much related to Boutros-Ghali's ideas in his Program for Peace. He had also emphasized preventive actions, giving weight to the importance of PKO mechanisms as tools for avoiding the escalation of conflicts or, in the best case, for preventing their explosion. Although in his document of January 3, 1995, "Supplement to 'A Program For Peace'"[16] the secretary-general made a fresh assessment of the situation and of the capacities of the UN to deal with the proliferation of conflicts, his core arguments remained valid. The organization as such did not fail; the lack of willingness from its members to engage themselves in institutional arrangements did hurt.

States are still the main actors in the international system, although they have lost the monopoly of international relations; thus the armed forces, as a natural part of the state, have a key role to play. And as Vice President Albert Gore said when addressing the Hemispheric Defense Ministerial on July 25, 1995: "And let us begin by acknowledging the eternal and most fundamental element of national security: the defense of borders." The raison d'être of the armed forces lies not in conflict but in the very existence of the state. It is necessary to remember that war is a political decision, made by an authority who decides to use its military instrument for a political goal.

We can no longer design our defense and foreign policies just in terms of conflicts or potential conflicts with our neighbors. We live on a continent that is slowly but firmly making its way through democratically elected governments and with political authorities who have strengthened their control over the military. We are also immersed in positive processes of integration throughout the region. And almost all Argentine territorial and boundary disputes have been settled, thus greatly limiting the possibility that a border dispute might degenerate into a wider military conflict.

Lessons from Argentina's Experience in Peacekeeping Operations

I do not pretend to present Argentina as a leading case of civil-military relations in the region, or as a paradigm with regard to the maintenance of international peace and security. However, some conclusions and experiences could help other nations in the hemisphere in the process of reassessing their foreign policy as well as their defense policy.

First, Argentina believes, as discussed and agreed at the Williamsburg Meeting of Ministers of Defense, that the modern nation needs a ministry in charge of defense affairs (MOD). Our experience of having civilians serving as defense ministers since 1984 has been extremely positive. However, this does not necessarily preclude other variants. The very fact that modern armed forces are composed of highly trained personnel obliges the state to have a unique agency in charge of managing civil-military affairs in all its dimensions. The defense ministry must have effective control over the military in professional, administrative, fiscal, political, and strategic functions. It is of paramount importance that the MOD should have a civilian bureaucracy to be able to control all the nerves of power and to centralize the functions and responsibilities that otherwise are divided between several noncivilian actors.

Second, the participation of armed forces in PKO or in multinational forces, under the auspices of the UN, has two positive effects. Internally, it helps to democratize and institutionalize the services and gives them an alternative role beyond the traditional one of defending national and vital interests. It also has a cultural impact on the officers and noncommissioned officers; its side effects are teaching new skills such as language-learning, history, geography, politics, and economics as well as all other relevant topics needed to accomplish their tasks as peacekeepers.

One important byproduct of Argentina's participation in PKO was the inauguration, in June 1995, of the Argentine PKO Center in Campo de Mayo. The center was the first to be established in this region and one of the very few existing in the world. It has three main areas: academic, operational, and physical training. It is supposed to evolve as the focal point not only for all of our PKO activities but also for those of our neighbors. In the future, we hope for a Scandinavian type of center, whereby different countries share various aspects of peacekeeper training and formation. The center should be seen both as a place for training future peacekeepers as well as a potential seed for future collaboration and cooperation with other services of the hemisphere.

Third, peacekeeping enhances interoperability with the services of other countries, which is important for integration and cooperation. It is an indisputable precondition for joint international missions, mainly under UN auspices. This idea of enhancing interoperability with other nations should not be seen as a negative feature or perceived to enhance the professionalism of our armed forces with an aggressive intention.

Under a democratic government and with political control of the armed forces by president and Congress, the military instrument is largely neutralized. Its engagement and the decision to employ it is not autonomous; it is the ultimate decision of the executive and legislative branches of the government. To consider that interoperability with other countries improves the professionalism of the armed forces against a particular country is to think strategically solely in terms of traditional conflicts, and to ignore the positive impacts of processes such as regional integration. In Argentina's case, MERCOSUR (with Brazil, Uruguay, and Paraguay, and subsequently expanding to include Bolivia and Chile) and the process of physical, political, and economic integration with Chile have dramatically altered the strategic landscape of the southern half of the hemisphere. Moreover, participation in PKO implies spending large sums of money every year, thus diminishing resources that otherwise would have been allocated for other defense necessities. A similar diversion of resources toward PKO missions overseas is evident in the realms of logistics and personnel.

Conclusion

Argentina's firm commitment to United Nations peacekeeping operations has been demonstrated by its increasing participation in missions all around the world. It has also been instrumental in furthering the process of democratization and institutionalization of Argentina's armed forces. A feedback process nourishes Argentina's policies.

I started this chapter quoting Juan Bautista Alberdi, one of Argentina's founding fathers, who more than a century ago very precisely described the true nature of a military man. We are well aware that we have to educate our military in the art of preserving an endangered peace, threatened by old types of conflicts as well as by what are called the conflicts of the new agenda. The fact that we, in this hemisphere, can be proud of not facing the prospect of suffering from such conflicts does not mean that we can feel secure. It is very difficult to divide international peace and security and to confine it to certain areas. Interdependence, a key feature of our modern times, also means that peace and security affect all of us.

A key feature of Argentina's new approach to international matters is to invest in processes of institutionalization. We believe that there are no "black holes" or grey areas in security; the challenges to stability that we witness in the 1990s have the potential for escalation because they usually arise independently. States might feel that they have greater autonomy to act in international relations because of the dissolution of the rational strategy that once limited and contained conflicts during the cold war. This is why we believe that the UN has to be empowered not only with legitimacy to act but also with the necessary and effective tools to intervene in those conflicts that cannot be solved unilaterally. For the United Nations to be able to do so, all of its members must be fully committed to support it politically and economically.

Chapter 7

Peacekeeping and Its Effects on Civil-Military Relations

The Argentine Experience

Antonio L. Palá

Introduction

What is the future of civil-military relations in Latin America? Will the democratic ideals exhibited in the Organization of American States' (OAS) commitment to democracy be interrupted by a new surge in military interventionism? What opportunities exist to improve the future of civil-military relations in the Western Hemisphere? One of the greatest challenges to the consolidation of democratic governance in the hemisphere continues to be the incorporation and accommodation of the armed forces within the democratic equation. The establishment of civilian rule over the armed forces is critical in order for regional security issues as well as economic integration to be consolidated. The problem is devising a model to accommodate the needs and wants of all the parties concerned.

The definition of roles and missions for the armed forces is an important factor in the relationship between the government and its military services. It is not a problem unique to Latin America and is one that is exacerbated by the turbulence in the new international order. The United States is currently struggling with these very issues as it looks at the future commitments of its armed forces, particularly their ongoing participation in peacekeeping. This chapter proposes that an effective model for establishing positive civil-military relations in this hemisphere is the integration of the armed forces into social, government, and regional initiatives. It examines the increased and consistent participation of the Argentine military in the United Nations (UN) peacekeeping framework as a model for cooperative civil-military relations. The Argentine experience is similar to that of Spain in the mid-eighties and one that has exhibited the potential for enduring success.

Peacekeeping provides a chance at harmonious civil-military relations, which may yield benefits to both the government and its armed forces. To fully understand the motivations for a Latin American country to incorporate its military into UN peacekeeping, it is imperative to look at two key actors: the civilian government and the armed forces. These two actors may have different, yet not incompatible, motivations for participating within the UN framework. For the civilian authorities the motivations may be of a political nature related to its foreign policy objectives. Peacekeeping may also serve as a carrot to promote harmonious civil-military relations. The armed forces approach the benefits of peacekeeping from an institutional perspective both for its continued survival and its prestige. In any case peacekeeping may provide a valuable opportunity for all parties concerned.

Motivations for Increased Participation with the UN

Both the government and the military have reasons for approving of increased participation with the UN.

Government Motivations for UN Participation

On the domestic front, the government's decision to allow the armed forces to participate with UN missions may be directed at appeasing the military. This decision promotes an "objective" form of control over the armed forces. Peacekeeping—being a valid military mission on a highly visible stage—enhances the professionalism of the armed forces and offers little to challenge their corporate interests. Additionally, the government benefits by providing additional funding to the armed forces at the expense of the UN. The peacekeeping role may help the government define additional roles and missions for the armed forces. Peacekeeping will never become the primary mission of the military services but it increases their value in light of the current international landscape. This study does not intend to promote peacekeeping in order to demilitarize the armed forces but rather to keep them in a professional military environment that can help them serve their society. States are better served by having well-trained soldiers occupied with their profession than by maintaining an ill-equipped, underpaid, and unused military establishment that spends the better part of the day blaming the government for its predicament. It will be essential over the long run for the Latin American governments to determine the size and capabilities of their armed forces.

From a broader point of view, the government may use peacekeeping as a catalyst for greater international exposure. According to some observers President Menem of Argentina has developed a military policy directed at "increased participation in peacekeeping activities and projecting the image of a reliable international partner."[1] As has been pointed out by Carlos Escudé and Andrés Fontana in their section, Argentina has disengaged from its support of the Non-Aligned Movement and its historically antagonistic position vis-à-vis the United States. The Menem administration, under the tutelage of Foreign Ministers Domingo Cavallo and Guido Di Tella, has aligned Argentina's foreign policy with the interests of the United States, the western powers and, in turn, the United Nations Security Council. President Menem has expended considerable effort to ensure that Argentina becomes a reliable and participating member of the international community and peacekeeping is a critical component of this policy. Menem's decision to send Argentine naval ships to the Gulf War was not popular, either with the public (nearly 70 percent opposed it in February 1991) or the opposition parties.[2] The international benefit of making such a decision must have outweighed the domestic political gamble, and it is a clear indication of Menem's desire to integrate his country into the world community.

Peacekeeping and increased participation with international organizations provide opportunities for smaller states to project themselves on a global stage. Canada, India, and several Scandinavian countries—among others—have enjoyed a mutually beneficial relationship with the UN for many years. This increased exposure is not only of a military nature with the troops on the UN mission but a governmental exposure as well. Participating nations provide a number of diplomats and civilian functionaries to support the military contingents and the UN in its mediating efforts. The primary beneficiary of this increased political presence is the Cancilleria (Foreign Ministry), which provides the majority of the civilians required. Argentina also proposed to the UN the creation of a "White Helmet" force that would be manned by civilian specialists to help during humanitarian crises. UN Secretary-General Boutros-Ghali, while visiting Argentina in 1994, praised the Argentine sense of volunteerism toward the UN, particularly its role in peace operations.[3]

Argentina is not the only Latin American country that has recently used peacekeepers to enhance its foreign policy objectives. Carlos Romero in his chapter outlines the evolution of Venezuela's foreign policy, particularly its role in the Central American peace process and the Venezuelan participation in the UN mission to Central America (ONUCA). The decision by President Carlos Andres Perez in 1990 to commit a Venezuelan battalion to ONUCA was part of a greater Venezuelan activism in foreign policy and regional issues. The ONUCA battalion was the first major Venezuelan deployment of military units outside of its borders. Venezuela also offered troops for the UN deployment to Namibia (UNTAG) and gradually increased the number of military observers in other UN missions. This Venezuelan policy coincided with the rapid increase in UN activity resulting from the end of the cold war and the presence of a Venezuelan diplomat in the UN Security Council. The UN secretary-general praised the Venezuelans' participation, stating that they had served "with great distinction."[4] Unfortunately, as Carlos Romero highlights, the Venezuelan military was not as pleased with its participation as was the secretary-general.

With the demise of the cold war the United Nations has been able to increase its contribution to international security, with peace operations being its most visible role. By December 1996 the UN was operating fourteen different missions. In contrast, between 1947 and 1989 the UN was only able to muster thirteen missions.[5] The void created by the absence of superpower competition has permitted the world organization to face the challenges of the new international order. In addition to its surge in the number of operations, the UN has expanded its roles from the traditional peacekeeping and military observer missions to nation building, humanitarian intervention, preventive deployment, and peace enforcement. This increased activism in conjunction with the expansion of its roles forces the UN to seek greater cooperation from its member states to provide the troops required to man these operations.

In light of these changes in the international order several Latin American countries have incorporated their armed forces into the UN peace operations. This chapter does not propose that peacekeeping is a new role for the Latin American armed forces but that the systematic incorporation of peacekeeping doctrine and deployments on the part of the Argentine military is a new trend. Latin American troops have been employed by the United Nations since its first peacekeeping mission in 1948. Latin American officers served as military observers in 1948 with the UN Truce Supervision Organization (UNTSO) and in 1949 in the India-Pakistan Observer Mission.[6] Brazilian and Colombian infantry battalions were incorporated into the UN Emergency Force (UNEF I) in 1956 and on two occasions UNEF I was commanded by a Brazilian general. In 1960, the Argentine Air Force deployed air crews to operate DC-3 aircraft in the UN mission in the Congo (ONUC). The Argentine crews flew in excess of two hundred missions—many in combat conditions—providing transport of personnel and equipment as well as humanitarian relief.[7] In 1974, Peru provided infantry troops in support of the UN Disengagement Observer Force (UNDOF) in the Golan Heights, with a Peruvian general serving as the UNDOF interim commander for six months. These contributions have all been significant and have played a role in the development of these armed forces, but in general they have been isolated and ad hoc.

Since the end of the cold war there has been a sharp increase in multilateral participation on the part of several Latin American states (see table 7-1). The Venezuelan deployment of combat troops to support ONUCA is one of numerous examples of this increased participation. Uruguay's contribution of an infantry battalion to the UN Transitional Authority in Cambodia (UNTAC) was instrumental in the success of that mission. Uruguay is the largest (per capita) contributor to the UN from Latin America, with a consistent participation of over nine hundred troops. The Uruguayan armed forces maintain a peacekeeping training center to prepare troops for future deployments and have promoted regional efforts in multilateral cooperation.[8]

In 1994, Brazil contributed 264 troops to the UN Operation to Mozambique (ONUMOZ), constituting the first deployment of Brazilian combat troops to a foreign country since the 1965 US/OAS intervention in the Dominican Republic. Brazil greatly increased its peacekeeping participation and by late 1995 had increased its contingents to nearly 1,200 men. At the end of the Gulf War, the Chilean Air Force provided a helicopter squadron to monitor the UN-imposed buffer zone between Iraq and Kuwait. In 1995, Guatemala and Honduras each deployed over one hundred men in support of the UN mission in Haiti (UNMIH). Additionally, military and police contingents from Latin America and the Caribbean have been instrumental in Haiti's effort to consolidate their newly restored democratic government.

Clearly, with the increase in UN multilateral operations the possibilities for the incorporation of Latin American armed forces are enhanced. The UN is not the only alternative for multilateralism; Colombia and Uruguay have maintained forces in the Multi-National Force (MNF) in the Sinai, which consolidated the Camp David Accords; and the four guarantor states—Argentina, Brazil, Chile, and the United States—have maintained a military observer presence on the Ecuador-Peru border since their recent conflict. Additionally, Latin American states have routinely contributed to OAS efforts in fact-finding missions and as observers. The international system of the post–cold war may afford even greater possibilities for the Latin American armed forces to serve in a multinational capacity.

In addition to the international exposure, active participation with the UN can offer the government a degree of leverage in the international arena.

Table 7-1 Latin American Participation with the UN

Mission	Civilian Police	Military Troops	Military Observation	Total
Brazil	4	945	29	978
Uruguay	14	856	42	912
Argentina	69	514	12	595
Honduras			12	12
Chile			8	8
Cuba			4	4
Venezuela			2	2
El Salvador			2	2
Total Participation	87	2,315	111	2,513

Source: UN Military Staff Committee, 31 December 1996

This can include offering the cooperation of armed forces in exchange for political or economic concessions from the world community. One concession obtained by Argentina, despite opposition from the British, was the addition of radar to the A4M Skyhawk fighters recently purchased from the United States. A statement by U.S. Embassy officials in Buenos Aires confirmed that Argentina's participation in peacekeeping and its commitment to regional arms control agreements were some of the contributing factors to the sale of the upgraded A4M aircraft.[9] Additionally, the Argentine Army recently obtained surplus OV-1D Mohawk light observation aircraft from the U.S. Army. The OV-1D is equipped with side-looking radar and a variety of cameras.[10] Regional experts argue that Argentina's increasing participation in peacekeeping is part of a broader foreign policy strategy intended to gain economic, commercial, and political concessions from the United States. These concessions may include favorable debt renegotiation arrangements, a free-trade agreement, or even additional military assistance or training. Argentina, in particular, has enjoyed an increase in civilian as well as military staff positions with the UN in addition to being the only Latin American country holding membership in the secretary-general's permanent committee on peace operations. Additionally, Argentina held one of the temporary seats on the Security Council, coincidentally during a period of increased Argentine activism in the UN.

The incorporation of the armed forces into the foreign policy objectives of the state creates linkages between key governmental institutions. These linkages can be instrumental for democratic consolidation. UN missions provide these armed forces with a new role that requires obedience to civilian authority as a condition for inclusion. During a briefing to the Argentine

Army War College in 1994, Ambassador Eduardo Airaldi, who is responsible for dealing with international organizations, stressed that the decision making for participation in peacekeeping was a joint military-civilian process. Airaldi also believes that the peacekeeping role "increases the level of sophistication of the armed forces and for the first time *Cancilleria* and the armed forces share a joint mission."[11] For the government, peacekeeping has afforded a cooperative arena in which to work with its armed forces. This has facilitated the use of the military as a tool of foreign policy, which traditionally has been a trait of only the more powerful states. The armed forces can also benefit from this relationship but perhaps not in the same manner.

Military Interests in UN Peacekeeping

Military motivations for participation in peacekeeping operations are significantly different from those of the government. With the worldwide reduction in military spending as a result of the end of the cold war, institutional survival may appear as the primary motivation for increased participation. This is not to say that peacekeeping has become the raison d'être for the armed forces, but in Argentina's case it has become a significant mission. All three of the Argentine military services list participation in international peace operations as their most significant secondary role, with their primary mission being defense of the homeland.

As highlighted by Escudé and Fontana in their chapter, the Argentine military establishment has undergone serious budgetary cuts, particularly in its military-industrial complex. Peacekeeping offers the armed forces an ongoing role, which is likely to be funded in light of Argentina's increased internationalism. Additionally, a cooperative environment has emerged between the defense and foreign ministries as it relates to funding additional UN missions. Funding from the foreign ministry assisted in preparing two air force helicopters for deployment to Cyprus. This relationship between the military and other government agencies is a new phenomenon in Argentine politics. Ricardo Lagorio, the undersecretary for policy and strategy and one of the Argentine diplomats most closely tied to the peacekeeping efforts, described past relationships as "feudalistic" or of a zero-sum nature, stressing that this current trend is more in line with a "bureaucratic cooperation" model present in most advanced states.[12] This increased cooperation is important for the armed forces since they had suffered greatly in monetary as well as political terms since their withdrawal from power.[13]

The diminishing defense budgets, the dismantling of Argentina's vast military industrial complex, and the neoliberal economic policies implemented by the Menem administration have all greatly affected the morale and operational budgets of the armed forces. The opportunity to deploy large numbers of troops that are partially paid by the UN offers both the military and the government an economic incentive for cooperation. The UN does offer reimbursement to contributing states, but this is generally slow in arriving and does not cover the actual costs of the deployment. Units deployed on peacekeeping missions enjoy the advantage of being well-funded with regard to fuel and spares. The UN outlines minimum requirements from participating members in a Memorandum of Understanding (MOU) for each particular deployment. The MOU spells out what the UN expects the armed forces to accomplish, such as the minimum number of operational vehicles, manhours for observation duties, or aircraft sorties. These are funded by the UN logistics network and also from domestic budgets. A former commanding officer of the Argentine Task Force (Fuerza de Trabajo Argentina, FTA) in Cyprus characterized this point by stating, "We are used to doing a lot with very little at home, the UN provides adequate resources for the accomplishment of the mission."[14] This element is highlighted by nearly all officers returning from peacekeeping operations.

In addition to providing the budgetary benefits, participation in peacekeeping offers an operational environment for the armed forces. Peace operations—for the most part—are conducted in hostile field conditions that in some cases approximate actual combat. The Argentine battalion in Croatia (Batallón del Ejército Argentino, BEA) was certainly exposed to warlike conditions and participated in several skirmishes. Interviews with four hundred Argentine military officers reveal that nearly 86 percent believe that peacekeeping is a valuable role; if only officers with peacekeeping experience are counted, the approval rate increases to 94 percent. Sixty percent of the officers with peacekeeping experience stated that they would be willing to make a permanent career of UN peacekeeping. Younger officers—captains and below—responded favorably at 67 percent to following a UN career. Less than 28 percent of the officers that had not participated in a multilateral operation expressed an interest in a career with UN peacekeeping. In personal interviews with former peacekeepers the value of their operational experience is always an important point, and to a man all would be willing to serve again in a UN mission. Without a doubt peacekeeping is providing a valuable experience for the Argentine armed forces and the acceptance of this mission is increasing as more officers return from their UN deployments. An Argentine lieutenant who had served in Croatia described his peacekeeping experience:

In Croatia I would set out on a morning patrol in command of several armored vehicles which were fully operational with excellent communications equipment. I was responsible for a sector of 100 square kilometers and the welfare of my unit. Here at home we hardly have any fuel for training and many of our vehicles lack spare parts.

Additionally, many of our men have to be released early in the day because they hold a second job in order to provide for their families. If anyone tells you that peacekeeping is not favorable for our army, it is because they have not experienced it.[15]

A retired air force general who had participated earlier in his career as a UN observer in the Golan Heights explained that the techniques that he had learned for building fortifications with the UN in the Middle East proved very valuable when he later commanded the besieged Argentine airfield on the island during the Falkland/Malvinas War. He commented on the similarity between the terrain on the islands and in the Golan Heights. By constructing the same type of shelters he was able to save many lives during the numerous bombardments endured in the conflict. Similar operational experiences are related by the Argentine pilots who participated in the ONUC mission in the Congo. The Congo veterans were always held in high esteem during their military careers because of the harrowing experiences that they faced in ONUC.[16] Peacekeeping provides a field exercise for leadership, military tactics, logistics, and numerous other military functions within a framework that requires obedience to civilian authority.

United Nations pay supplements also offer an important benefit to these armed forces. The average supplement for a member of a unit on a UN deployment is over $980 (U.S.) per month. Specialists within the unit receive an additional 25 percent pay hike. Officers assigned on UN observer missions receive a per-diem rate that varies from $85–$120 (U.S.), depending on the particular operation. When one considers that an Argentine captain's salary is roughly $1,500 (U.S.) per month, these pay supplements are of considerable consequence. A sergeant in the Argentine military is paid roughly $760 (U.S.) per month. While on a UN mission the same sergeant can more than double his income because of the per diem. Defense cuts and low salaries are affecting morale and readiness throughout the Latin American forces. Peacekeeping can help alleviate these ailments by providing both additional pay and reimbursement for operational costs incurred in the missions. Additionally, the Argentine armed forces are using the lure of participating in UN missions as a recruiting tool for their newly established all-volunteer force.

In conjunction with the operational and economic benefits outlined, several of the Latin American armed forces active in peacekeeping have derived additional benefits that appear linked to their UN commitment. Argentina and Uruguay obtained several surplus C-130 transports from the U.S. Air Force. The Argentine Navy acquired two frigates and the Chilean Air Force received additional helicopters and spare parts to support its deployment to Kuwait. In addition to the hardware, the Latin American contingents assigned to the former Yugoslavia have received North Atlantic Treaty Organization (NATO) training and doctrine, to facilitate communication with NATO aircraft enforcing the no-fly zone.

Participation in UN peacekeeping offers these militaries an opportunity to improve their image and prestige at home and abroad. The protection of innocent civilians in the former Yugoslavia, the clearing of mine fields in Kuwait, enforcing the UN mandate in Cyprus, and the operation of a hospital in Mozambique can only enhance their profile at the national and international levels. These new roles cannot erase past mistakes but can offer the prospect for a better partnership with civilian authorities and society. As Deborah Norden observes, "the military's participation in peacekeeping allowed the armed forces to become a valuable player in the government's foreign policy, bringing praise and recognition, where they had previously found disdain."[17] During a visit to Argentina, Vice President Al Gore recognized Argentine peacekeepers at a special ceremony:

The troops assembled here today, veteran United Nations peacekeepers, are proof of their nation's commitment to such noble endeavors. They are the ones who risked and sometimes, sadly, gave their lives for the sake of others. . . . they are the ones who returned full of pride, able to report to their countrymen, Argentina was present— mission accomplished. . . . To these brave soldiers who will carry forever in their hearts the honor symbolized by the blue berets they were privileged to wear, we give our thanks![18]

Military motivations for participation with the UN may have been self-serving but the unintended consequences appear to promote democratic consolidation, foster cooperation with civilian institutions, and increase military professionalism and willingness to subordinate to civilian rule. For the armed forces, participation in UN peacekeeping serves political, institutional, and operational objectives. Argentine Army General Carlos Maria Zabala, a former UN sector commander in Croatia, summarized the advantages of peacekeeping for his army:

On a professional level, it is an occasion to operate in a complex operational environment. You have the opportunity to work with other armies and appreciate their capabilities as well as your own. It provides first hand knowledge of the effects of war, allowing our troops to appreciate the importance of the UN and its peace operations. On a personal level, it lends opportunity for travel to foreign locations and exposure to other cultures and customs. Additionally, it allows the troops to feel as representatives of their country in an important mission abroad.[19]

Clearly peacekeeping appears to provide a win-win situation for both the government and its armed forces. In a recent interview, Sir Brian Urquhart, former UN undersecretary, praised the important and varied contribution of Argentina to peacekeeping: "Argentina has provided hospitals, troops, engi-

neers, police, and electoral observers. I wish that all countries would participate at this level and diversity."[20] Peacekeeping participation enhances national prestige in the international arena, it provides funding for the armed
forces, and it involves them in a valuable role that appears to promote respect
for civilian authority. The Argentine government has been very particular in
the type of missions that it chooses and has incorporated the armed forces in
the decision-making process for peacekeeping participation.

Argentine Military Participation in Peacekeeping

Argentina is consistently one of the most active Latin American countries
within the UN framework. The number of Argentines deployed with the UN
increased over 400 percent since the end of the cold war, from twenty observers in 1988 to over 1,440 troops in 1995.[21] By June of 1995 there were 860
Argentines in the UN Force in Croatia (UNCRO) in the former Yugoslavia
and over 500 others stationed in seven other UN missions.[22] If the 1995 Argentine troop rotation pattern continues, it is expected that by 1999 better
than 50 percent of the military's permanent personnel will have served with
the UN.[23] (For deployments by the end of 1996, see table 7-2.) In recent years
more than half a dozen Argentines have lost their lives in the service of the
UN and several others have been injured or held prisoner. Argentina has
clearly stated that it will cooperate with the UN Security Council in any mission of a peacekeeping nature, but the Menem administration has been re-
served about peace enforcement or peacemaking initiatives.

The Argentine military has been influential in the selection of the missions in which it will participate. The three services have each established a
peacekeeping office within their respective headquarters as well as a joint
office in the Estado Mayor Conjunto (Joint Command). The Argentine military has sought involvement in missions that include a higher degree of military expertise or offer the opportunity to participate with more advanced
military forces. This has not always been possible, but the main objective has
been to obtain a positive operational experience for participating troops. Argentina has filled a broad variety of roles within the peacekeeping framework.

The Menem administration took its first major step in its internationalist
foreign policy during the Gulf War. The Argentine Navy deployed a destroyer
and frigate to the Persian Gulf early during the Desert Shield operation. This
deployment—to a theater of operations eleven thousand nautical miles from
its home bases—was a major logistical accomplishment for the Argentine
Navy, particularly in light of the fact that the navy did not possess the support ships to facilitate the cruise. Once on station, the Argentine ships partic-

Table 7-2   Argentine Participation with the UN in 1996

Mission	Civilian Police	Military Troops	Military Observation	Total
UNTSO (Middle East)			3	3
UNFICYP (Cyprus)		390		390
UNIKOM (Iraq-Kuwait)		50	4	54
MINURSO (Western Sahara)			1	1
UNTAES (Eastern Slovonia)	30	74	2	106
UNMIBH (Bosnia-Herzegovina)	39			39
UNPREDEP (Macedonia)			1	1
UNMOP (Previaka, former Yugoslavia)			1	1
Total Participation	69	514	12	595

Source: UN Military Staff Committee, 31 December 1996

ipated in escort duty and in the enforcement of the economic embargo against Iraq. During the period of November 15, 1990, to January 15, 1991, the Argentine naval contingent assisted in the interception and inspection of nearly six hundred merchant ships.[24] The Argentine ships were assigned under the control of the Canadian Task Group commander. During Desert Storm the Argentine Task Group was incorporated into the Combat Logistics Force providing escort to the allied logistics effort. The chief of staff of the Argentine Navy has stated that the Gulf War experience boosted the confidence and interoperability of the navy. The Argentine Air Force also played an active role providing transport aircraft during the Gulf War. The first UN delegation that flew into Baghdad to negotiate the terms of the peace agreement was transported by an Argentine Air Force Boeing 707 deployed in the region.

Argentine forces have maintained a presence in the Persian Gulf region since the end of the Gulf War. Numerous officers have served in staff as well as observer positions with the UN mission monitoring the Iraq-Kuwait border (UNIKOM). In addition to the observers the Argentine Army deployed a fifty-man combat engineering detachment in mid-1993. Their mission is to remove the thousands of land mines and booby traps laid down by the Iraqi forces in anticipation of the coalition invasion. The unit clears roads and passages through the extensive minefields still present in the region. This is probably the most hazardous duty faced by Argentine peacekeepers, not only because of the inherent dangers of handling explosives but also due to the harsh terrain and climate of the fields of operations. In an interview, a former commander of the engineers stated that this command was the most fulfilling experience of his military career. He related that he receives daily phone calls from his former noncommissioned officers asking how they could be reassigned to UNIKOM. He feels that the increased level of responsibility with UNIKOM in addition to the assets at his disposal were the key factors in forming his opinion. The tasks being performed by the Argentine unit in UNIKOM are directly related to their military mission and a valuable training scenario.

Argentina played a very active role in the promotion of the Central American Peace Process, which eventually led to the establishment of various UN missions in that troubled region. The Argentine Navy performed a significant role in the UN Mission in Central America (ONUCA). Four Argentine Navy fast attack boats (FTB) were deployed to the Gulf of Fonseca to monitor the movement of weapons and irregular forces in the region. The Argentine Navy FTBs were the first naval assets ever enlisted by the UN for a peace operation. The ONUCA naval component faced operational as well as logistical challenges because of the remote locations in which it was based. Additionally, the logistical line of support from Argentina was very limited, which required the FTB commanders to procure all necessary foodstuffs and other needs from local sources.

The largest peacekeeping contribution by Argentina was the Argentine Army battalion (BEA) deployed to the former Yugoslavia with the UN Protection Force (UNPROFOR) and later the UN Mission in Croatia (UNCRO). The BEA first deployed to that troubled region in mid-1992, with nearly nine hundred men and over one hundred vehicles.[25] The BEA personnel rotated every six months; eight rotations of the battalion were completed until its withdrawal in mid-1995. The BEA was responsible for manning checkpoints and observation posts, conducting patrols, disarming mines, escorting relief convoys, assisting refugees, and numerous other tasks. In addition to the BEA, there were usually at least a dozen Argentine officers in staff positions at UNPROFOR Headquarters. Additionally, Argentine Brigadier General Carlos Maria Zabala held command of one of the four UNPROFOR sectors for one year. In this position he commanded not only the Argentine battalion but numerous foreign units as well, for which he received high praise from the UN and the Argentine government. By mid-1995 the BEA mission was withdrawn with the reduction of the UN presence in the region. One year later, in May 1996, the Argentine military deployed a seventy-three-man reinforced company to the UN Transitional Administration for Eastern Slavonia (UNTAES) Mission; over one hundred Argentines continued to serve in the former Yugoslavia by January 1997.

The Argentine Task Force (Fuerza de Trabajo Argentina, FTA) with the UN Mission in Cyprus (UNFICYP) became the most numerous Argentine deployment with the UN reductions in the former Yugoslavia. The FTA encompasses nearly four hundred men from all three services, making it a joint military operation. The FTA is composed of an army unit of 265 men, a marine deployment of 103 men, and an air force detachment that operates two Hughes 500 helicopters.[26] The Argentine Air Force contingent replaced a British helicopter unit that had been assigned to Cyprus since the beginning of the mission. In addition to the troops in the field, officers from all branches serve in the UNFICYP Headquarters. The mandate of UNFICYP is the traditional peacekeeping mission of providing a neutral force to ensure compliance with an agreement. The primary responsibilities of the FTA is to man observation posts, report any clashes between Turkish and Greek Cypriots, and uphold the UN mandate. The FTA shares these responsibilities with contingents from Austria, Canada, Finland, Great Britain, and Ireland. A former FTA commander stated that one of the best experiences with the UN is gained from operating and socializing with the other national units.[27] These experiences foster cooperation and bolster the confidence level of the military as it relates to its ability to operate with other armed forces. In Cyprus this cooperation has additional significance since it has provided an opportunity for Argentine troops to work side by side with British forces, their recent enemy in the 1982 Falkland/Malvinas War. It is interesting to note that a British noncommissioned officer that had fought in that conflict ran into one of his former prisoners, an Argentine Army sergeant that was serving in Cyprus. Both men had the opportunity to exchange old war stories and celebrated their reunion with other members of their respective units. This new cooperation between British and Argentine troops is very positive; on several occasions British commanders have extended letters of condolence to their Argentine counterparts when Argentine peacekeepers lost their lives in the line of duty.

Another contribution demonstrating the diversity of Argentine military cooperation with the UN is the Argentine Air Force field hospital deployed with the ONUMOZ mission in Mozambique. The field hospital, which served from June 1993 to early 1995, included an operating room, emergency room, laboratory, and numerous other medical functions. The primary responsibility of the field hospital was to provide care to the 3,500 UN peacekeepers stationed in ONUMOZ. These included troops from India, Japan, Portugal, Uruguay, and Zambia. The hospital was transported to Mozambique by ship and with the support of three Argentine Air Force C-130 transport aircraft.[28] Additionally, the hospital personnel provided emergency care and humanitarian assistance to the local populace. Within the first twelve months the ONUMOZ hospital treated thousands of cases, mostly dealing with malaria, typhoid fever, and numerous other ailments common to the region.[29] Additionally, the Argentine medical personnel treated numerous UN troops that were deployed in ONUMOZ that were infected with the AIDS virus. The air force medical personnel deployed to Mozambique gained vast amounts of operational experience, as well as living and functioning under harsh field conditions during their six-month tenure. The Argentine high command offered to redeploy the hospital to the UN mission in Haiti but the UN was unable to fund the deployment.

Perhaps one of the most controversial steps taken by the Menem administration—particularly as it relates to its neighbors—was the Argentine support of the proposed invasion of Haiti to reinstate President Aristide. Argentina stood alone among Latin American states in offering its support to such an invasion. Additionally, Argentina provided ships to enforce the UN naval blockade of Haiti, drawing criticism from many neighbors. Argentina had over one hundred men deployed in the UN mission in Haiti (UNMIH), which were for the most part forces from the *gendarmeria* (police) and an aviation unit that operated an Air Force Fokker-27 transport aircraft. The Fokker-27 was assigned to CANARGUS, the joint Canadian, United States, and Argentine flying unit. Unfortunately, the Argentine aircraft was destroyed while attempting to land at a remote field in Jeremy (the air crew and passengers were not injured); the aircraft was never replaced. Argentine peacekeepers and police remained in Haiti until December 1995.

The Argentine commitment to UN peacekeeping has been consistent since the initial deployment during the Gulf War. Multilateral peace operations have become a significant mission within the Argentine military establishment. Additionally, the types of forces deployed by the Argentines have received valuable training and operational experience. These missions are increasingly more popular with the military due to their increased exposure, interoperability with modern armed forces, and other benefits mentioned above. Peacekeeping is offering a viable alternative mission to a military that has seen drastic reductions in recent years. Due to the nature and requirements of peace operations not all branches of service benefit equally (see table 7-3).

Peace operations are generally manpower-intensive endeavors. For this reason, the army has been the primary beneficiary of the UN participation. During interviews with officers from other branches of the military the army predominance in peace operations has been a constant point of criticism. The air force is the service that provides the smallest contribution to the international missions. The UN generally leases aircraft for its airlift or solicits support from member states as required. Few UN missions have a constant aeronautical presence. The Argentine Air Force volunteered to replace the departing British helicopter unit in Cyprus and deployed its ill-fated Fokker-

Table 7-3   Argentine UN Participation by Branch of Service

Branch of Service	Army	Navy	Air Force	Civilian Police
Participating troops	1,173	114	44	110
Percent of total participation	81.4	7.9	3.1	7.6

Source: Revista del Suboficial

27 in Haiti. The air force has offered placing aircraft in Aviano air base in Italy to support the Sarajevo airlift and the NATO Implementation Force Mission. Negotiations also took place to deploy Argentine aircraft to Angola, Georgia, and the Middle East, but none of these proposals ever came to fruition. The deployment of the field hospital in Mozambique increased the air force contribution, but only for its medical personnel.

Similarly, the Argentine Navy maintains a small presence with the UN, mostly as ground forces from the Infantería de Marina (Marine Corps) with the FTA in Cyprus. As previously mentioned, Argentine ships were present in the Gulf War, Central America, and the Haitian blockade. Additionally, the Argentine Navy takes great pride in its humanitarian assistance during the Spanish Civil War in 1936 and in the blockade of Cuba during the Missile Crisis of 1962. The navy benefits from other international ventures as well, including numerous multinational exercises such as UNITAS with the U.S. Navy, IBERIA with the Spanish Navy, and other exercises with Brazil, Uruguay, and Paraguay.

Clearly, peacekeeping offers benefits to the armed forces. Additionally, peacekeeping has established important links and cooperation between the military and their civilian counterparts. The Argentine government has enjoyed an increased level of international exposure and diplomatic presence. The Cancilleria has also benefited from the armed forces' contributions to the UN by providing a diplomatic network in support of these operations. These missions are having a positive impact within Argentina, but how is this activism viewed by Argentina's neighbors and allies?

Regional and International Implications of UN Peacekeeping

Latin America faces its own geopolitical challenges and historical antecedents. A proposal that Argentina will become the peacekeeping equivalent of Canada in the Southern Cone is not realistic. Canada does not share borders with countries that pose a military threat—real or perceived. A large part of the Argentine military establishment still lives with the constant preoccupation of threat hypotheses rooted in geopolitical thought and the fear of neighbors closing in on their territory. Equally important is the perception on the part of Argentina's neighbors of the impact that peacekeeping is having on the Argentine military. Do they perceive Argentina's peacekeeping experiences as just another mission, or as a threatening increase in its military capabilities? Does active participation with the UN create a security dilemma?

Although much of the discussion concerning participation in peacekeeping has been of a favorable nature, some negative aspects are present. One of these is what can be labeled a peacekeeping dilemma between neighboring states. The additional training, funding, and operational experience may provide an edge to the UN participant that could yield benefits in a potential conflict with a neighbor. The experience gained by Argentine officers with the UNCRO mission, in the hostile environment of the former Yugoslavia, could be perceived by a neighboring military officer as a threat. As valid as this argument may appear, it is one that holds little water, but perceptions are often more dangerous than reality.

Peacekeeping possesses many of the inherent characteristics of a collective (or public) good, primarily "non-exclusiveness" and "non-rivalness" (jointness).[30] Peacekeeping is nonexclusive in the sense that, while actors pursue their interests independently, they provide benefits for actors that are not participating. States that do not participate with the UN peacekeeping missions benefit from the stability (in most cases) that these missions may provide. For instance, several Latin American states may have been trading with Central America during the tenure of ONUCA in the region but have not participated with the UN mission. The nonrival character of peacekeeping implies that one individual state's participation in peacekeeping does not necessarily diminish the ability of others states to do so. The UN requires that states voluntarily participate in peacekeeping and does not discriminate in the selection of member states as long as they are in good standing. States choose to participate in peacekeeping as easily as they can choose not to. To view your neighbor's participation with the UN as a threat to your security is not very valid, since the opportunity is open to your armed forces as well. The question should not be, "Does peacekeeping improve my neighbor's war-fighting capabilities?" but rather, "If peacekeeping is such a good deal, why aren't we doing it?"

Peacekeeping is a military mission, but one that places considerable limits on the use of force. The complexity of the UN missions in the post–cold war environment has required the deployment of heavier weaponry to ensure the protection of UN forces, but in general they do not employ or even display their destructive capabilities—even while operating in dangerous surroundings. Additionally, peacekeeping is a very transparent process; the number of troops, their mandates, after-action reports, and training are a matter of public record, which allows states to monitor their neighbor's participation. Furthermore, peacekeeping provides a setting for military officers from neighboring states to cooperate toward a common mission. These officers share experiences and can compare capabilities, which should improve the security equation rather than complicate it.

States can take additional measures to reduce a negative perception of their peacekeeping participation. These measures can include the incorporation of neighboring forces—even if only as observers—into their peacekeeping deployments, the promotion of regional peacekeeping or humanitarian exercises, and hosting conferences on the benefits and lessons learned in peacekeeping, along with a myriad of other confidence-building efforts. Argentina and Brazil have exchanged observers in several peacekeeping missions and participate in regional exercises. It is equally important not to isolate a state that elects not to participate in multilateral missions or to give the appearance of developing security ties with other states that participate with the UN. Extensive participation in peacekeeping is a new phenomena for Latin America; states will have to accommodate to different levels of commitment to international participation and their possible consequences.

Regional Cooperation and Integration

Participation (preferably cooperation) in peace operations, whether under the auspices of the UN or OAS, can only improve regional security. The outlook for a security framework based on the OAS is not positive. The OAS is a remnant of the post–World War II security mentality of limiting foreign intervention within the hemisphere. The Rio Treaty and the Charter of the OAS are ill-equipped to handle regional security issues in the current international setting. Additionally, the OAS-sanctioned Inter-American Peace Force (IAPF), created to alleviate the Dominican crisis of 1965, was seen by many member states as a cover for a U.S. unilateral intervention.

The OAS is taking steps to improve its capabilities in the field of security. In 1992 it established the Special Committee on Hemispheric Security, headed by Hernan Patiño Mayer, Argentine ambassador to the OAS.[31] This OAS committee has been very concerned with the promotion of confidence-building measures (CBMs) in the hemisphere. The UN appears to provide more hope as an interlocutor of security concerns and peace operations within the Latin American system. In a survey of four hundred Argentine officers, nearly 76 percent of them believed that the UN should increase its role in international security, while less than 37 percent felt that the OAS was capable of handling security problems.[32] Many expressed that the OAS could easily be manipulated by the United States, whereas the Security Council of the UN could counter U.S. influence because of the veto power of the other four permanent members.

During the Summit of the Americas, President Clinton and his thirty-three counterparts committed themselves to the establishment of a hemispheric free trade zone by the year 2005. Additionally, the Common Market of South America (Mercado Común del Sur, MERCOSUR) encompassing Argentina, Brazil, Paraguay, and Uruguay has been progressing since 1993, and its member states have begun to address the role of the armed forces within the member states and possible limits on defense expenditures.[33] Proposals for the establishment of a collective security regime within MERCOSUR are also being considered.[34] Additionally, Argentina, Brazil, and Uruguay have been the most significant Latin American contributors to UN peacekeeping since 1994. By December 1996 these three MERCOSUR members accounted for nearly 10 percent of the total of UN peacekeeping troops. Interstate economic and security issues are currently being addressed by civilian and military leaders throughout the hemisphere. The positive increase in the establishment of CBMs in the region has improved the security outlook. Jack Child states that "CBMs have had the greatest impact on the so called 'ABC' countries of the Southern Cone (Argentina, Brazil, and Chile) and have been linked to attempts at economic integration in the same area (MERCOSUR)."[35] Argentina's recent commitment to nuclear nonproliferation and its dismantlement of the Cóndor II missile program are positive indicators for the region. The establishment of an OAS commission to address CBMs and the recent surge in civil-military dialogue in this field are promising omens for the hemisphere.

International Implications

There are natural advantages to the UN's seeking large-scale cooperation from Latin American armed forces. They not only offer an abundant pool of troops and a diversity in national participation, but these armed forces should be well suited—due to their language and culture—to serve in peacekeeping missions in Latin America and parts of Africa.[36] The increased number of Spanish-speaking forces participating with the UN has prompted Argentina and the UN to open a peacekeeping training facility in Buenos Aires.[37] This base provides training for civilian and military personnel destined for UN missions. Symbolically, perhaps, the site of the UN facility is the "Campo de Mayo" army base, where in 1987 rogue military officers attempted a coup against the democratically elected government of President Raul Alfonsín. The peacekeeping center opened in mid-1995, with the hopes of training future UN troops from throughout the region.

Skepticism about peacekeeping still remains in several countries—particularly in the Third World—because some UN troops come from countries with a long history of imperialism. Major powers carry the historical baggage of their colonial or imperial past, making their presence unwelcome and counterproductive in many countries. The difficulties faced by U.S. and Italian contingents in Somalia and by French peacekeepers in Cambodia demonstrate the dilemma faced by a former colonialist power in the delicate world of peacekeeping.[38] An important benefit for the UN and its peacekeeping missions is that Latin American militaries do not have an imperial history in the global arena. By contrast, countries with smaller military forces not associated with unilateral foreign intervention appear to provide less of a threat to countries hosting UN missions. This situation enhances the probability of success. French troops assigned to the UN mission in Cambodia (UNTAG) failed to gain the confidence of the populace and were constantly harassed, probably due to France's long imperial history in Southeast Asia. The French unit was replaced by Uruguayan troops, who proved to be considerably more successful in fulfilling the UN mandate.[39] The importance of impartiality for UN troops was recently illustrated by Canadian Prime Minister Chretien who stated that "as a medium sized country, Canada has always been able to play roles in peacekeeping, because very often we are more acceptable—just because we're small and nobody is afraid of us."[40] If this assumption is true for Canada—a medium military power and NATO member—what threat can a Latin American force pose?

Conclusion

Without a doubt peacekeeping offers a very valuable secondary role for the Latin American armed forces, since it is a military mission that enhances technical skills in a cooperative environment. Peacekeeping fosters cooperation with civilian authorities and develops linkages with other governmental institutions. Additionally, multinational participation enhances the image of the armed forces at home and abroad, as they are contributing in humanitarian as well as peace operations.

Argentina, Brazil, and Uruguay may be setting a trend for future civil-military relations in Latin America. Virtually every European state contributes troops to the United Nations and considers peacekeeping as an important part of its foreign and defense policy. Skepticism may still exist on the part of many Latin American states on the merits, or actual motivations, of increased participation in UN operations. This may be just another growing pain for the region in light of the new international order. Latin America is no longer a battleground for competing superpower ideologies. The regional armed forces must adapt to the increased cooperation in the international arena and realize that their internal security role must be part of a democratic equation. Peacekeeping enhances the value of the military and helps incorporate military personnel into the society they are intended to serve.

Chapter 8

Exporting Peace by Other Means

Venezuela

Carlos A. Romero

Introduction

The Venezuelan government's decision to support the observer missions sent to Nicaragua in 1990 and El Salvador in 1991, better known as United Nations Observer Group in Central America (ONUCA) and in El Salvador (ONUSAL), to supervise the agreements reached between the Nicaraguan and Salvadoran governments and the guerrillas, was a landmark in the country's international actions.[1]

Venezuela has maintained a peaceful stance throughout this century and has not been involved in any international, regional, or bilateral war. Its military have not played a significant role in shaping foreign policy or making decisions that bear on it, with one exception: the military have had a role with regard to land and sea border problems.[2] Venezuela continues to have two active boundary problems with its neighbors. On the one hand, there is a territorial dispute with Colombia, based on the Colombian claim to delimit an area in the northwest of the Venezuelan Sea according to the Law of the Sea jurisprudence; there are other boundary problems such as illegal trade, guerrilla attacks to military posts, and drug traffic sanctuaries. On the other, Venezuela claims part of Guyana's territory. In both cases, the majority of the Venezuelan military personnel have refused to support any diplomatic agreement that could result in a "loss" of Venezuelan territory; this matter is a taboo among Venezuela's officers.

In general, however, the international actions of Venezuela's democratic governments have been peaceful, promoting democracy by civilian means, that is, by fostering democratic leadership, backing democratic endeavors, and rejecting militarism and war as a method for settling conflicts between governments and internal groups. At the same time, the prestige of the Venezuelan democratic system and the power of oil enabled the country to carry on an active foreign policy of backing governments threatened by military or revolutionary outbreaks.

During this century the various Venezuelan governments have neither become involved in any outside armed conflicts, nor sent troops to take part in military operations—whether with the United Nations, the Inter-American Treaty for Reciprocal Assistance (TIAR), or the Organization of American States (OAS)—nor as part of multinational or unilateral operations (as in the case of Grenada or Panama). On the contrary, they have rejected military solutions as a means of achieving external or internal stability. Civilian politicians from the political parties and the diplomatic bureaucracy make most foreign policy decisions, except for intelligence and counterintelligence work in border areas.

This chapter analyzes the role played by the Venezuelan battalion sent to Central America as part of a United Nations mission: ONUCA. There is a special emphasis on the effectiveness and extent of the commitments assumed by a foreign policy that sectors within the military, the foreign service, and even public opinion considered to be overextended. At one point, Venezuelan officers and troops were part of the missions in Nicaragua, Honduras, and El Salvador; this fact fed—but was not the original cause of—growing criticism of Venezuelan activism within the military. The criticism focused not only on professional aspects (logistics, movement of troops, civilian origin of the decision) but also on the nature of the mission (the support of the governments headed by Presidents Violeta Chamorro in Nicaragua and Alfredo Cristiani in El Salvador).

Venezuela and Central America

In the following section, the historical background of this regional policy is summarized. The development of peace is discussed below, and UN participation in Central America and Venezuela is described, along with Venezuelan participation in ONUCA.

Historical Background

Venezuelan presence and activism was most strongly felt in Central America. Ever since the beginning of Venezuela's democratic system in 1958, this subregion was considered to be of interest to Venezuela. One goal was to avoid "a progressive escalation that could turn the entire region into a theater of operations in the east-west [confrontation]."[3] Geopolitical goals generally prevailed over economic or commercial goals. During the 1960s, the governments headed by Presidents Rómulo Betancourt (1959–64) and Raúl Leoni (1964–69) followed an antidictatorial policy, based on the Betancourt Doctrine, which held that Venezuela would not recognize any governments taking power by means of coups d'etat that overthrew democratically elected presidents.[4] The government also adopted a policy to contain the Cuban-Soviet influence in the subregion.

Under the government headed by Rafael Caldera (1969–74), the country's foreign policy became less regionalist, taking on a more bilateral stance. There was also a merger of state interests and the interests of the political parties; ties developed between Acción Democrática (Social Democratic Party) and COPEI (Christian Democratic Party) and their counterpart leaders in Central America. The end result was increased Venezuelan political intervention under Caldera and his successor, Carlos Andrés Pérez (1974–79), in the internal affairs of the Central American countries.[5]

With the reduced danger of subversion in Venezuela and the consolidation of its democracy, the problems of security and defense in Central America and Venezuela's offers of political and economic assistance became more significant during the presidency of Luis Herrera Campíns (1979–84). Within the framework of Central America's "heated" political climate, with the Sandinistas' rise to power in Nicaragua and the progress made by the insurgents in El Salvador, the Herrera administration developed what it called "Projection Diplomacy," aimed at fostering a democratic solution to the Central American crisis, avoiding unilateral military intervention by the United States, and backing democratic sectors from middle-of-the-road Christian Democrat and Social Democrat parties in the region.[6] This was the beginning of spiraling Venezuelan political interventionism, based on political and financial assistance to governments, parties, and individuals. Venezuela backed regional peace initiatives, spoke out against Cuban-Soviet interference, and even strongly criticized possible U.S. military actions.[7]

Venezuelan foreign policy toward Central America took a new turn in 1982 with the creation of the Contadora Group. From 1978 to 1982, Venezuelan initiatives had been unilateral and were harshly criticized in the region and in the hemisphere. By the time the Contadora Group was created, Venezuela had reduced its direct presence and begun taking part in multilateral schemes, such as the San José Agreement (signed in 1980) to provide petroleum at a discount to the Central American countries. After joining the Contadora Group, Venezuela participated in other multilateral negotiations, such as Esquipulas I and II during Jaime Lusinchi's government (1984–89). It would also join the Group of Eight (1986), supporting OAS and SELA (Latin American Economic System) resolutions concerning Central America. It took part in the creation of the Group of Three (1989) with Colombia and Mexico, and throughout those years it fostered peace talks and informal meetings between adversaries as part of secret presidential initiatives. This activity peaked during Carlos Andrés Pérez's second term (1989–93).[8] His personal diplomacy, directed from the president's office, caused great displeasure not only within the Ministry of Foreign Affairs but also among parts of the general public and the armed forces.

Venezuelan activism in Central America (as well as in the Caribbean and, to a lesser extent, in South America) was based on the country's active foreign policy during the first thirty years of democracy. As the years went by, what had begun as a strategy aimed at fighting insurrection in Venezuela and attracting U.S. support to political solutions turned into an overall strategy aimed at making Venezuela's presence felt. While seeking to prevent a war from breaking out in Central America and mushrooming into a worldwide conflict, Venezuela became interventionist on different levels, ranging from financial assistance to intelligence work. Despite the strategic importance of this presence and its consequences, nonetheless the process remained under civilian control and was firmly tied to commitments with Social Democrat or Christian Democrat organizations and leaders and, in any case, non-Marxists. This network of commitments, however, was the subject of a great deal of controversy in Venezuela. Many observers asked whether this overweening foreign policy was appropriate.[9]

Peace in Central America

The creation in 1983 of the Contadora Group (Mexico, Venezuela, Colombia, and Panama) and the implementation of a hemispheric support policy seeking a peaceful solution for Central America's problems was an important turning point for the political prospects of most of the Central American countries, which had been facing deep-seated domestic and external challenges. At the time of its founding, the Contadora Group members were genuinely worried about possible U.S. military intervention in Nicaragua and the chance that it might lead to an indirect superpower confrontation in the region. Contadora Group members provided the foundation for agreement among the contending forces; in due course, the group's efforts would help to reduce the risk of a regional war and military escalation.

The Contadora process featured lengthy consultations and negotiations among the governments of the Central American countries, the United States, the Contadora Group, the Contadora Support Group (created in 1985 by Argentina, Brazil, Peru, and Uruguay), and representatives of the irregular groups operating in the region. On January 12, 1986, the ministers of foreign affairs of the Contadora Group and the Support Group countries met in Caraballeda, Venezuela. They issued a "Message for Peace, Security, and Democracy in Central America."[10] This declaration was backed by the secretaries-general of the United Nations (UN) and the OAS, who offered to work together in favor of the peace process, and by the Central American presidents meeting in San José, Costa Rica, in February 1987.[11] The creation of the Río Group in 1986 (combining the Contadora Group and the Contadora Support Group), the Caraballeda declaration, the offer of support from the UN and the OAS, and work for peace of the Central American presidents turned Central America's political climate toward peace.[12]

The second stage of the peace process began in 1986. The Contadora Group no longer played a starring role; the Central American governments themselves did. The president of Costa Rica, Oscar Arias, put forth a draft plan (called the "Arias Plan") in February 1987 and a final draft in August 1987. It was unanimously approved by his Central American colleagues and backed by the Río Group, the Contadora Group, the Support Group, the UN, the OAS, and other countries. (President Arias was awarded the Nobel Peace Prize in December 1987).[13]

The Arias Plan called for an agreement to achieve regional security and reduce local conflicts. It was significant because it was a regional initiative and also because it included a commitment to begin talks with the guerrillas and other armed groups in each Central American country within the framework of "regional reconciliation, political amnesty, democratization of the region, and an end to foreign or domestic support for insurgency movements, a call for free elections, and no aggressions by one state against another."[14] The signing of the Arias Plan by the Central American presidents on August 7, 1987, in Esquipulas, Guatemala, ended the second stage of the regional peace process, called Esquipulas II. This also marked the beginning of the third stage.[15]

The CIVS (International Verification and Implementation Commission) was created in Caracas in August 1987; its members were the presidents of Costa Rica, Honduras, Guatemala, El Salvador, and Nicaragua, the ministers of foreign affairs of the Contadora Group and Support Group countries, and the secretaries-general of the United Nations and the OAS. Its purpose was to oversee compliance with the Arias Plan. In January 1988 the CIVS created an Executive Committee, consisting of the ministers of foreign affairs of the Central American countries; in April it created a Technical Advisory Group, whose members were Canada, the Federal Republic of Germany, Spain, and a fourth country (recognized to be Venezuela) plus representatives of the General Secretariats of the UN and the OAS.[16]

The Central American presidents met again from August 5 to August 7, 1989, in Tela, Honduras, a meeting that led to greater UN participation in the peace process. In fact, negotiations seemed to be at a standstill and several of the Central American governments were accusing each other of failure to comply with Esquipulas II and the Peace Plan. At the same time, there was a pressing need to begin the demobilization of the Nicaraguan resistance, active in the border areas of Nicaragua, Honduras, Costa Rica, and El Salvador. The petition that the Central American governments presented at Tela launched the fourth stage of the peace process, headed by the United Nations General Secretariat.[17]

The United Nations in Central America

Together with the secretary-general of the OAS, the secretary-general of the United Nations, Javier Pérez de Cuéllar, visited the five Central American countries in January 1987; they were accompanied by the ministers of foreign affairs of the Contadora Group and Support Group countries. The impact of this visit and the fact that the UN secretary-general was a member of the CIVS led the United Nations to organize a UN Observer Group for the Verification of Elections in Nicaragua (ONUVEN) on August 25, 1989, as well as the International Support and Verification Commission (CIAV) that same month to supervise the plan for the demobilization, repatriation, and reconciliation of the Nicaraguan insurgents. The secretary-general of the United Nations sent an evaluation mission, lasting from September 3 to September 23, 1989, to look into the possibility of sending a military observer mission to Central America. The eighteen-member mission—three of whom were Venezuelans—flew in a Venezuelan Air Force plane.

The report recommended a military mission. The secretary-general asked the UN Security Council to authorize a military-observer mission for Central America. Pérez de Cuéllar stated that "the question of demobilization as such concerns the Security Council particularly since it is an operation of a clearly military nature."[18] This marked the beginning of the fifth stage of the Central American peace process during which the CIAV was replaced by a UN Observer Group for Central America.

On November 7, 1989, the United Nations Security Council passed Resolution 644/89, creating the ONUCA to observe and verify compliance with the Esquipulas II peace agreements and the demobilization and disarming of the Nicaraguan resistance.[19] The enactment of this resolution was a landmark in United Nations participation in Central America. This was the first time that a Military Observer Group operated in the Western Hemisphere and the first time worldwide that such a group was used to demobilize and disarm irregular forces.

ONUCA would go through four operational stages. The first lasted from the date of its creation in November 1989 until March 1990. The Observer Group was formed with officers from Canada, Colombia, Spain, Ireland, and Venezuela; logistics support was provided by Argentina, Canada, and Venezuela.[20] A second stage began in March 1990 when its mandate was extended for another six months and the Venezuelan battalion was added. Stage three began in April 1990 when new goals were added through Resolution 653/90. And stage four started in May 1990 when the term for the mission was extended again.[21]

The United Nations' original goal in Central America changed between 1987 and 1990. It began with an offer of good offices to verify the Esquipulas II agreements and to prepare for elections in Nicaragua (CIVS, ONUVEN, CIAV). It was expanded to create ONUCA as an observer group in November 1989 and to add a peacekeeping force between March and July 1990. ONUCA was to "observe and verify regional peace-making agreements but also to disarm and destroy weapons from the irregular forces operating in Central American countries."[22] Thereafter, it reverted to the original purpose of a military observer mission.

Venezuelan Participation in ONUCA

Before taking part in ONUCA, Venezuela had played a fairly modest role in United Nations and OAS observer missions. In 1957 the OAS sent a Committee of Military Advisors (including two Venezuelan military officers) to supervise the cease-fire between Honduras and Nicaragua. Between September 1965 and March 1966, twelve Venezuelan officers were included in the United Nations India-Pakistan Observation Mission (UNIPOM), created to supervise the cease-fire between India and Pakistan.[23] The Venezuelan government did not take part in the so-called Inter-American Peace Force sent to replace the U.S. troops that had occupied the Dominican Republic in 1965. Caracas, however, did not object to the appointment of a well-known Venezuelan diplomat, José Antonio Mayobre, as personal representative of the secretary-general of the United Nations in that Caribbean nation. Mayobre was to offer his good offices to reestablish internal peace following the coup d'etat against the provisional junta headed by Donald Reid Cabral, the civil war, and the U.S. invasion.[24]

With the expansion of the United Nations' military role in the 1980s and the increasingly activist foreign policy of the second administration of Carlos Andrés Pérez, Venezuela's contributions to UN missions began to grow. When the UNTAG (UN Transition Assistance Group for Namibia) was being formed, Venezuela offered twelve officers (out of a total of three hundred) as military observers, plus two hundred soldiers to help complete three battalions with 850 soldiers each. (In the end only the twelve military observers were sent.)[25]

In April 1991, Venezuela sent seven military observers to join a team of 913 military observers for the first stage of the U.S. Iraq-Kuwait Observation Mission (UNIKOM), created to observe the cease fire and monitor the buffer zone between the two countries. Also in 1991, fifteen Venezuelan officers were part of a group of five hundred military observers and civilian employees in the UN Mission for the Referendum in Western Sahara (MINURSO); the referendum would take place in the territory being fought over by Mauritania, Morocco, and the Polisario Front for the territory's independence.[26] None of these efforts compared, however, to the magnitude of the effort entailed when Venezuela decided to participate in ONUCA in November 1989 and in ONUSAL in May 1991.

The first ONUCA military observers arrived in Tegucigalpa, Honduras, in December 1989 and set up their headquarters in that city. The first group, consisting of 160 observers, included fifty Venezuelans who were spread out among the five Central American capitals, fourteen verification centers, and three operational posts in Honduras and Nicaragua from December 1989 until March 1990.[27]

Based on a report by the secretary-general dated March 1990, the United Nations Security Council passed Resolution 650/90, dated March 27, 1990, in which it "Decides to authorize, on a contingency basis in accordance with that report, an enlargement of the mandate of the United Nations Observer Group in Central America and the addition of armed personnel to its strength, in order to enable it to play a part in the voluntary demobilization of the members of the Nicaraguan resistance." Thus ONUCA grew from 160 to 260 military observers, and an infantry battalion of some eight hundred men was also created.[28]

The government of President Pérez, as part of its policy seeking an active role in the Central American peace process, offered troops and officers for the battalion. A special ad hoc battalion of Venezuelan Army paratroopers, consisting of members of the José Leonardo Chirinos, Antonio Nicolás

Briceño, and García de Sena Battalions, was formed and stationed in the city of Maracay in order to prepare for the mission.[29]

The first 170 Venezuelan soldiers arrived in Tegucigalpa, Honduras, on April 10, 1990, under the command of a Spanish general, Agustín Quesada Gómez.[30] The UN battalion set up its headquarters in Los Trajes, a Honduran town on the border with Nicaragua. By mid-April the mission, which was given the name of "Home Run," included 702 Venezuelan soldiers and was assigned the task of supervising the demobilization and disarming of the Nicaraguan Resistance fighters (better known as the Contras) who were based in Honduras as well as other irregular forces along the Honduras-Nicaragua border area.[31]

The UN battalion immediately faced practical problems. It had to come up with a flexible plan for moving around because the area where it was to operate consisted of mountainous and humid terrain that was inappropriate for setting up permanent observation posts. Furthermore, the Venezuelan group arrived without enough gear and without the transportation equipment that the Venezuelan government had offered. The ONUCA command had to rent buses to take the troops from Tegucigalpa to Los Trajes; Germany and Canada had to handle the logistics. In addition, the Venezuelans also lacked support helicopters and fast motorboats.[32]

The greatest problem, however, was political—the purpose of the mission. Violeta Chamorro won the Nicaraguan presidential elections in February 1990. The Sandinista Army declared a unilateral cease-fire in March. On March 23, 1990, representatives of the president-elect, the Roman Catholic Archbishop Miguel Obando y Bravo, representatives of the departing Sandinista government, and a majority of the guerrilla leaders signed the Toncotín (Honduras) Agreement. As a result, most of the Contras that were in Honduras moved back to Nicaragua.[33]

On April 16, 1990, the Venezuelan troops that were part of the UN mission reached Kiatara, in the northeastern area of the border between Honduras and Nicaragua, and demobilized a group of 260 Contras, most of whom belonged to the Miskitos ethnic group (from the Nicaraguan Atlantic area—the Yatama rebels). On April 18, the troops reached Yamales, the former headquarters of the Contras' so-called Northern Front, where they found just old short-range military matériel and five hundred Contras, most of whom were ill, both adults and adolescents.

"Comandante Franklin," one of the main Contra leaders, refused to sign the Toncotín agreement; the other "comandantes" suspended the previously agreed demobilization and disarmament process. The secretary-general of the United Nations, Javier Pérez de Cuéllar, then addressed a letter to the chairman of the Security Council on April 19, 1990, reporting on the agreement reached in Toncotín and suggesting that, for it to be properly implemented, the objectives of ONUCA would have to be expanded. On April 20, the UN Security Council passed Resolution 653/90 setting new goals for ONUCA: observing the cease-fire, the withdrawal of the Sandinista forces from the security zones established in Nicaraguan territory, and the separation of forces in Nicaraguan territory.

On May 4, 1990, the UN Security Council enacted Resolution 654/90, again extending the ONUCA operation until November 1990. But on May 7, 1990, negotiations and the voluntary demobilization came to an abrupt halt. This stagnation in the peace process was accompanied by heavy rains that immobilized the UN battalion. On May 30, 1990, President Violeta Chamorro and the Contra leaders signed the Managua Protocol. It reactivated the demobilization process; up to that date, only nine hundred Contras had been demobilized. On June 9, a demobilization ceremony at which heavy weapons were surrendered took place in El Almendro, Nicaragua. On June 28, the Contras handed over their main store of weapons and Comandante Franklin accepted the peace plan, once foreign "assistance" had been reduced to a minimum. At that point, there were seven hundred Venezuelan soldiers and twenty military observers; the operation cost nine million U.S. dollars. On July 5, 1990, after spending three months in Central America, the battalion returned to Venezuela and ONUCA reverted to its original purpose. By then, twenty thousand Contras had been demobilized.[34]

The Unwanted Effects Of Exporting Peace

President Carlos Andrés Pérez arrived in Caracas on February 3, 1992, at 10:00 P.M., returning from Switzerland where he had attended an international conference on the world economy in Davos. Early that morning, at approximately 4:00 A.M. on February 3, two battalions of Venezuelan paratroopers—the Antonio Nicolás Briceño and the José Leonardo Chirinos, both stationed in the city of Maracay—had begun to take up arms against the government. A majority of the officers, noncommissioned officers, and enlisted men in the José Leonardo Chirinos and Antonio Nicolás Briceño Battalions, most of whom had been in Honduras and Nicaragua with the ONUCA, seized the city of Maracay by 4:00 P.M. At 9:00 P.M., soldiers from both battalions took off for Caracas in buses, led by Lieutenant Colonel Hugo Chávez Frías. Other army and air force units and, to a lesser extent, the navy and the national guard also began to rebel in various Venezuelan regions at 5:00 P.M. When President Pérez arrived at Simón Bolívar International Airport—the airport serving Caracas—at 10:00 o'clock in the evening on February 3, the minister of defense, who was there to greet him, informed him that there were rumors of an uprising by units in the army. At 11:20 P.M. on February 3, 1992, forces from the José Leonardo Chirinos Battalion took over La Carlota, a civilian-military airport in Caracas, the Museum of Military History at La Planicie, and (for a few hours) the surroundings of the presidential residence, La Casona. At 1:00 A.M. on February 4, 1992, President Pérez, whom the rebels had been unable to capture, escaped miraculously from La Casona and Miraflores (where the presidential offices are located) and spoke on national television accompanied by the minister of defense who, together with the other officers of the Military General Command, remained loyal to the president and the constitutional government. Within a few hours, the uprising failed.[35] The insurgents, however, would go down in history as popular figures, as would their commander, Lieutenant Colonel Hugo Chávez.

Is there a relationship between the Venezuelan battalion's part in an observation and peacekeeping forces mission under United Nations auspices and its role in the coup d'etat of February 1992? This analysis focuses on three explanations:

1. The changes in ONUCA objectives in March and April 1990 and the problems that the Venezuelan officers and soldiers faced in doing their job led to serious objections to Venezuelan foreign policy in Central America and to the Pérez administration in particular.

2. The battalion's role in the attempted coup in 1992 was part of deteriorating relations between many officers in the Venezuelan armed forces and the Pérez administration and, in more general terms, was due to differences of opinion between the political elite and the military regarding Venezuelan foreign policy.

3. The role that Venezuela played in the ONUCA and other United Nations military missions is not directly related to the attempted coup in 1992; the fact that members of the José Leonardo Chirinos and Antonio Nicolás Briceño battalions were involved on both occasions was merely a coincidence.

First Explanation

The changes in ONUCA objectives in March and April 1990 and the problems that the Venezuelan officers and soldiers faced in doing their job led to serious objections to Venezuelan foreign policy in Central America and to the Pérez administration in particular.

Arguments in favor: President Pérez's decision to offer the Venezuelan battalion to ONUCA in March 1990 was a last-minute decision. The battalion's arrival in Honduras was extremely disorganized. There was little activity during the first two months of the campaign. Then, in June 1990 ONUCA pressure on the Contras to surrender and demobilize involved the Venezuelan armed forces in another country's domestic conflict. In addition, some Venezuelan officers, noncommissioned officers, and soldiers felt that what they were doing was fairly pointless and could actually be harmful for their careers.

Arguments against: The Venezuelan mission with ONUCA took place in 1990, two years before the coup. Given the extent of mobilization and rotation of personnel in the Venezuelan armed forces, it is hard to find out who was actually involved. Moreover, Lieutenant Colonel Hugo Chávez Frías, the leader of the uprising on February 4 and commander of the Chirinos Battalion, was not given that command until July 1991 after passing the General Staff course for promotion to lieutenant colonel in 1990–91. Given this timing, the link between the uprising of February 4 and the ONUCA mission is weak.

Second Explanation

The battalion's role in the attempted coup in 1992 was part of deteriorating relations between many officers in the Venezuelan armed forces and the Pérez administration and, in more general terms, was due to differences of opinion between the political elite and the military regarding Venezuelan foreign policy.

Arguments in favor: To attribute the origin of the crisis among the Venezuelan military to the problems the Venezuelan battalion faced in ONUCA alone would ignore important elements such as:

1. The increasing and varied role that Venezuela played in the Central American peace process (bilateral from 1973 to 1983; multilateral [Contadora] from 1983 to 1989; mediator from 1989 to 1992);

2. The possibility of a negative outcome in the bilateral border negotiations with Colombia, and a territorial agreement "unfavorable" for Venezuela from the viewpoint of the military;

3. President Pérez's direct role as a broker between the four Central American governments (El Salvador, Nicaragua, Guatemala, and Honduras) and several insurrectional groups operating in each country contributed to delegitimizing the Venezuelan government and to the movement toward the military uprising.

Carlos Andrés Pérez had been president for the first time in 1974–79. At that time, Venezuela enjoyed international prestige; Pérez himself became one of the most important democratic leaders in the hemisphere during the "golden years" of the Venezuelan political system. However, by the mid-1980s several national and foreign analysts warned that the Venezuelan political system showed signs of running dry. Yet it was not until Pérez's second term that the country definitely felt a turn for the worse.

The drop in the price of oil, the aftershock of "Black Friday" in February 1983 (when the administration of President Luis Herrera Campíns devalued the *bolívar* relative to the dollar), signs of increases in widely varied and costly international commitments within the public sector, and the reality of the public foreign debt all led to a decline in international activism between 1983 and 1988. The reelection of Pérez as president in December 1988 meant the return of activism. "The democratic feast," the swearing-in ceremonies that drew a great many well-known leaders (including Fidel Castro) from around the world to Caracas, sent a favorable message in support of government reform and decentralization. Shortly after the inauguration, the government watched in horror as, on February 27 and 28, 1989, the people rose up against the so-called "Great Turnaround" in economic policy (the shift from a statist toward a market orientation), venting a great many pent-up frustrations exacerbated by the sudden drop in oil prices and the partial breakdown of elite consensus.[36]

The loss of faith in the Great Turnaround did not affect foreign policy during the early years of Pérez's second term. Just as if nothing had occurred on the domestic front, there was a reactivation of Venezuela's international role. The country was active in the Organization of Petroleum Exporting Countries (OPEC), the Movement of Non-aligned Countries, the Río Group, and the Group of Fifteen. It created the Group of Three, expanded relations with Colombia seeking to overcome the effects of the border dispute, and took up a nonpermanent seat on the United Nations Security Council.

Unfortunately for a country reviving its activism, the world had changed. "Third World causes" were no longer as important, international cooperation was being reduced to bilateral or regional arrangements, and unfettered pragmatism was eroding commitments and loyalty. At the same time, Pérez was trying to gain international backing for the Great Turnaround in the midst of a domestic political crisis. Venezuela faced serious difficulties in obtaining more favorable treatment for the foreign debt and in attracting new foreign investment. With the tragic events of the attempted military coup on February 4, 1992, the domestic crisis could no longer be kept hidden from foreign eyes. It was symbolic (whether planned this way or not) that the military uprising occurred the very day that the president returned from a world economic conference in Switzerland. The country's foreign policy and image plummeted and, in fact, it has yet to recover fully.

Understanding that the world had changed from the earlier bipolarity and that Venezuela had lost its international "magic touch" was not enough, however. It was also necessary to reassess the extreme activism that had led the country to get involved and take on costly commitments in uncertain circumstances in Central America and in support of President Jean Bertrand Aristide in Haiti. Instead, Venezuela's ambassador at the United Nations began to promote Venezuela's participation in world affairs, especially in Namibia, Yugoslavia, and Angola. This vast number of aimless commitments and confusion also contributed greatly to the feeling on the part of many people and especially within the armed forces that the foreign policy had lost its legitimacy, and that President Pérez had lost his as a democratic and political leader.

Arguments against: The overextension of Venezuelan foreign policy had begun already in 1970. Although the prospects for a negotiation of the territorial disputes with Colombia to demarcate water and underwater areas had long been much criticized, there had been no previous military coup attempts. Further, Venezuela had already taken part in other United Nations missions and would do so again after 1990.

Third Explanation

The role that Venezuela played in the ONUCA and other United Nations military missions is not directly related to the attempted coup in 1992; the fact that members of the José Leonardo Chirinos and Antonio Nicolás Briceño battalions were involved on both occasions was merely a coincidence.

Arguments in favor: The masterminds of the military uprising on February 4, 1992, were a group within the military who had been extremely critical of the Venezuelan political system and, above all, its civilian leaders since the early 1980s. With regard to foreign policy, even before the ONUCA experience, this group of officers had long been openly critical of Venezuela's alleged weak stance in its negotiations with Colombia, the Pérez administration's rapprochement with Guyana, and the civilian and military involvement in Central America. Therefore, the presence of the Venezuelan battalion in the ONUCA and the active role of army units in the attempted coup on February 4, 1992, is no more than a coincidence.

Arguments against: Although it is true that Lieutenant Colonel Hugo Chávez Frías was not a member of the ONUCA mission, many of the officers, noncommissioned officers, and enlisted men who were sent to Central America were also involved in the coup (including those from the Antonio Nicolás Briceño and José Leonardo Chirinos Battalions); most of them had good professional achievements.

Final Remarks

The elite Venezuelan Paratrooper Battalion returned to Venezuela in July 1990. This left eleven Venezuelan officers as observers with ONUCA and twenty-three observers assigned to ONUSAL (created in May 1991). By July 1992, there were thirty-eight Venezuelan military observers in El Salvador: two colonels of the army, eight lieutenant colonels (of the army, air force, and national guard), along with majors and captains from the four forces.[37] In 1992, following the attempted coup, the commitment to send military observers on United Nations missions (ONUCA, ONUSAL, UNIKOM, and MINURSO) remained, although the number of officers deployed was smaller.

What conclusions can be reached? This study should provide a better understanding about Venezuela's role in the Central American peace process—a role that began in the 1970s and continued thereafter despite the variations between and within administrations (Caldera, Pérez I, Herrera, Lusinchi, Pérez II). The tradition of fostering democracy in the Western Hemisphere, fundamentally in Central America and the Caribbean, is part of the complex world of relations that links the Venezuelan party elites to their kindred Social Democrat and Christian Democrat parties and leaders. Thus, the desire to prevent regional war, intervention from outside the continent, and a confrontation between the two superpowers did indeed motivate the support that Venezuela provided to Central America and the Caribbean.

Changes around the world, however, led to a change in Venezuelan foreign policy. During the first stage of civilian governments (1960–85), fighting Communism and the so-called Cuban-Soviet influence was as important as defending democracy. With the waning of the cold war, Central America ceased to have strategic bipolar significance; beginning approximately in 1986, this worldwide change opened the possibility of a negotiated regional peace agreement. Within this framework, Venezuela began its more multilateral engagement in the region, becoming part of the Contadora Group (1983–87).

With the reelection of Carlos Andrés Pérez as president of Venezuela, the country again became more involved in Central America. President Pérez appointed himself as mediator among the various parties (including the United States) in the peace process. His government took part officially and, at times, behind the scenes in a number of political initiatives. Many of these took the form of personal diplomacy, giving rise on various occasions to bureaucratic infighting among the president's office, the Ministry of Foreign Affairs, the Ministry of Defense, and the Congress.[38] These initiatives, along with the general rapprochement with Colombia, the reactivation of negotiations with Guyana concerning the Venezuelan claim to the Essequibo territory through the offices of the secretary-general of the United Nations, and the activist Caribbean policy produced an overextended foreign policy despite little public support for many of these actions. (Severe problems developed, for example, when Haitian president Jean-Bertrand Aristide was ousted in 1991 and sought refuge in Caracas, fueling rumors of an alleged and unpopular plan for a Venezuelan military invasion of Haiti in support of Aristide.)[39]

It is precisely within this context that one must place the role of Venezuela as part of the United Nations missions in Central America and El Salvador, ONUCA and ONUSAL. The Venezuelan initiative to send military officers and noncommissioned officers and a battalion of army paratroopers was caused by the hyperactivism of Pérez's government and by the dynamics of the United Nations itself, many of whose military operations would have questionable results.

Why did the development of an international military role by Venezuela's armed forces not improve civil-military relations nor redound to the gain of Venezuelan policy? The contrast to Argentina's case during the same years is striking (see the chapters by Escudé, Lagorio, and Palá). In contrast to the Argentine case, President Pérez did not consult or even ask the military about which decisions to make. Nor did Pérez place his country's role in UN peacekeeping forces within a strategic plan or in a new and coherent foreign policy. Last but not least, he acted in bad times and certainly did not build channels of communication between civilians and the military regarding those new Venezuelan international initiatives. Thus Pérez decided to join ONUCA, a mission that, within a few months, grew from being a good-offices activity of the UN secretary-general to an observer mission and then to a peacekeeping force with coercive enforcement tasks.

It is not easy to relate the participation of Venezuelan officers and soldiers in ONUCA and ONUSAL with the military coup attempt in February 1992. None of the three explanations outlined above provides a satisfactory answer. However, the second one comes closer to a sustainable argument. The role that Venezuela played in Central America and the policy of "exporting peace" probably contributed to heating up its foreign policy. Subsequently, there developed growing feeling among many groups in the country, the military among them, that something was turning wrong in Venezuelan political life.

✿ Part III

New and Nontraditional Security Threats in Central America and the Anglophone Caribbean

How and why has the concept of *security threat* expanded in the Western Hemisphere? The following four chapters explore traditional and especially nontraditional security issues, notably those concerned with the growth of violence related to drug trafficking and with the demobilization of armies and guerrillas in Central America. The chapters focus principally on Central America and the Anglophone Caribbean.

Ivelaw Griffith sheds light on security collaboration and confidence building. He pays special attention to the Caribbean, where these practices have been consolidated. He expands the scope of the analysis of security by focusing also on unconventional security threats, including drug trafficking–related violence. He assesses the significance of the Caribbean's Regional Security System, the evolution of other international security arrangements, and the extent of cooperation between Caribbean countries with the United States.

Anthony Maingot focuses on the illicit drug trade in the Caribbean. He calls attention to the region's role in transshipment and money laundering and to the extensive use of drugs by Caribbean peoples. Corruption and violence have ravaged many of these countries and threaten democracy and public order thereby. He assesses the relative commitment of governments to combat this problem and concludes that only Barbados has developed an effective strategy, though other islands could emulate it.

Caesar Sereseres analyzes the change in Central America's security situation. The region has ended its three long-lived simultaneous civil and international wars in Nicaragua, El Salvador, and Guatemala. New problems have emerged with the incomplete absorption of former combatants on both sides into civilian life, however. The armed forces of each country, moreover, have had difficulty finding new proper roles. Sereseres argues that only Guatemala's army has a clear sense of mission and strategy and the means to accomplish its goals.

Fernando Zeledón documents citizen insecurity in Central America. In Nicaragua, Honduras, El Salvador, and Guatemala, there are high levels of poverty, low levels of development, weakly consolidated democratic institutions, high levels of violence and criminality, and very high costs of maintaining military establishments. Various territorial disputes remain unresolved, but the main security challenges stem from social violence, gangs of demobilized soldiers, rising crime, and especially drug trafficking.

🍀 Chapter 9

Security Collaboration and Confidence Building in the Americas

Ivelaw L. Griffith

The aftermath of the cold war has witnessed in various parts of the world a renewed emphasis on multilateralism in many areas of interstate conduct.[1] The security issue area is receiving its share of this emphasis. Needless to say, security collaboration in the Americas is not new, but the December 1994 Summit of the Americas, which gave a fillip to multilateralism in this part of the world, has created a new spirit and expectancy about collaboration, although security was not given special attention at the summit. Where the summit itself failed to offer evidence of a rekindling of the spirit of security collaboration, the July 1995 defense ministerial meeting in Williamsburg, Virginia, one of its outcomes, compensated for this summit deficiency. The thrust of Williamsburg led to the second defense ministerial meeting the following year, in San Carlos de Bariloche, Argentina, in October 1996.

One aspect of this multilateralism focuses on security confidence building, and part of the task here is to identify some challenges to policy makers as the confidence-building agenda is pursued further. Attention to collaboration here is not meant to depreciate the value of unilateral or individual security initiatives. Such initiatives are often necessary, but not sufficient. Many of the critical security challenges are transnational or have transnational consequences, making collaboration necessary and not just desirable. Moreover, collaboration is necessitated by financial, manpower, technical, and other limitations by individual countries. However, before discussing collaboration and confidence building, it is important to offer an assessment of the contemporary security situation in the hemisphere.

Security in the Contemporary Americas

Security has long been a highly contested concept with a multiplicity of definitions and usages, founded mostly on traditional realist theory. Hence the traditional approach to security emphasizes the military variable, focuses on the state as the unit of analysis, and sees states as rational actors pursuing their national interests. Threat orientation is mainly external, and the utility of security countermeasures is measured largely in military terms. Security is considered part of a country's high politics. Although traditional realism has long been challenged, with the end of the cold war scholars are increasingly questioning the validity of the realist conceptualization of international politics generally and of security in particular.[2] Consequently there has developed an advocacy for a postrealist definition of security.

Postrealists believe that nonmilitary developments can pose genuine threats to long-term security and citizens' quality of life; that traditional concepts of sovereignty cannot cope with the torrential transborder flow of narcotics, money, AIDS, arms, and immigrants; that no single country can combat these threats alone; and that new regional and international rules and institutions will be needed to cope with the nonmilitary threats facing most countries.[3] They do not jettison the military variable from the security matrix, but the economic, political, and, for many, the environmental variables are considered as equally important. They posit that internal security issues are important in their own right, complicating, and sometimes aggravating, external ones. Indeed, circumstances often are such that the distinction between internal and external threats and apprehensions is blurred. Moreover, not only are states no longer the only critical actors in the international arena, but nonstate actors abound, and some of them wield considerable power, oftentimes more than some states, as the drug barons demonstrate in some parts of Latin American and the Caribbean.

Two important observations must be made here. First, while it is heartening to know that this new approach to security is endorsed by respected professional military officers[4] and not just reputable security scholars, understandably, security analysts are not all sold on it. Some are not merely skeptical but downright hostile.[5] The second observation is that this "new thinking" does not represent a total debunking of traditional realism, for as Richard Falk has correctly noted, "To challenge the centrality of realism does not imply its total repudiation. States do remain important actors, war does remain profoundly relevant to international relations, and many interna-

tional settings can be better understood as collisions of interests and antagonistic political forces."[6] Although specialists at the United Nations share the
postrealist view of security, seeing it as "an all-encompassing concept that is
not dependent on the absence of violence and the effective prevention or re-
moval of aggression,"[7] they rightly observe: "Notwithstanding recent encouraging trends toward resolving outstanding conflicts through peaceful means,
many states continue to face traditional threats to security. Weapons of mass
destruction still pose a serious threat. In many parts of the world violations
of international law, competing territorial claims, and mutual suspicion of
aggressive intentions remain sources of conflict."[8]

Attention is paid in this hemisphere to threats and apprehensions defined
in both traditional and nontraditional terms. Territorial and border claims,
arms control, and geopolitics are the chief traditional concerns, while instability, migration and refugee issues, environmental matters, and drugs are
the main nontraditional problems. Some issues, such as terrorism and insurgency, have both traditional and nontraditional dimensions.[9] Also important
is the fact that a few traditional issues that were high-priority concerns during the 1970s and 1980s are no longer of great import. The 1994 case of Haiti
notwithstanding, military intervention (outside of territorial conflict) is one
of them. Although attention cannot be paid to all these issues here, it is important to deal briefly with some of them.

The outbreak of hostilities between Peru and Ecuador on January 26,
1995, not only threatened to shatter the Spirit of Miami six weeks after it was
created, but it provided sobering testimony to the continued salience of territorial and border issues. Moreover, while there had been an accentuation of
peace and cooperation even before the Summit of the Americas, among the
collateral consequences of the Peru-Ecuador conflict has been a jolting of
memories about the number of similar disputes in existence and a rekindling
of nationalist sentiments about the prosecution of claims. In the cases involving Colombia, Guyana, and Venezuela, for example, the aftermath of the
Peru-Ecuador war led to apprehension in Colombia and Guyana over troubling signals coming from Venezuela. For instance, in relation to its Guyana
claim, which is for two-thirds of the country, Foreign Minister Miguel Burel-
li Rivas visited Guyana on March 2–3, 1995, and asked for priority attention
to the issue. More troubling, though, is the fact that he called on President
Cheddie Jagan of Guyana to have "a proposal to be pursed in practical terms"
ready for the Cheddie Jagan–Rafael Caldera summit, then planned for some-
time in fall 1995. Guyana flatly refused this diplomatic arm-twisting.[10]

The fairly quick end to the Peru-Ecuador hostilities, itself a reflection of
the Spirit of Miami and the emphasis on peace, justifies the optimism that
territorial conflicts will not erupt throughout the hemisphere. However,

these factors will not eliminate any of the disputes, although they may influence how they are dealt with. Peru-Ecuador apart, significant disputes exist between Argentina and Chile, Argentina and Britain, Bolivia and Chile, Peru and Chile, Guatemala and Belize, Colombia and Venezuela, Guyana and Suriname, and Venezuela and Guyana. These cases differ in the amount of territory involved and in the likelihood of the use of force, but they all have complicated histories, some involving repeated hostilities. Others have been part of geopolitical (not necessarily cold war–related) games and have been used by various political constituencies for their own political ends. Nevertheless, the April 1990 treaty between Venezuela and Trinidad and Tobago over the Gulf of Paria dispute illustrates that disputes are not all beyond peaceful settlement. Still, the incongruity of some claims casts doubt on any possibility of their fulfillment. Guatemala's claim for the entire country of Belize is a case in point. Although Guatemala recognized Belizean sovereignty in August 1991, it has not renounced the claim.

It is partly the existence of territorial disputes and the intractability of some of them that explain the persistence of another traditional security concern: arms control. Two key elements of this issue have been military expenditure and weapons production. A 1995 assessment indicates that while Central American and Caribbean military spending has decreased, spending in South America has remained constant, at about 2 percent of gross domestic product (GDP). Defense spending itself reflects the vicissitudes of domestic politics and the perception of threats, both internal and external, and in both traditional and nontraditional terms.[11]

Examination of weapons production in Argentina, Brazil, and Chile—the countries that account for over 90 percent of Latin America's weapons manufacture—found no correlation between increased democratization and decreased weapons production. The evidence suggests that "the transition to democracy does not necessarily imply peaceful, non-military solutions to international conflicts or a tendency for civilian regimes to reduce the level of military expenditure and limit arms production. Indeed, Argentina initiated the development of a very costly, sophisticated, and threatening weapon of mass destruction (the Cóndor II) as an integral part of the foreign policy of the first post-authoritarian government (Alfonsín's)."[12]

Arms control itself is a manifestation of hemispheric geopolitics. As Jack Child has explained, geopolitical conflicts in the Americas have had two dimensions to them: one with an East-West, cold war element, the other being indigenous to Latin America.[13] Thus, the end of the cold war will not have ended geopolitical conflicts, threats, or apprehensions in the hemisphere. In many respects Central America is still experiencing the effects of cold war geopolitical withdrawal. Partly because of territorial and other interests, and because they have the necessary capability and political will, some Latin American states have pursued both the politics of prestige and the politics of power.

There is thus only limited credence in Augusto Varas's contention that "within Latin America, the only powers capable of possible regional hegemonic projections are Brazil and Mexico."[14] An examination of the broad geopolitical landscape would indicate that vis-à-vis the Caribbean Venezuela has had both the capability for and interest in power projection. Within the Caribbean itself Cuba has pursued both prestige and power agendas, although not militarily in the latter case. In the hemisphere as a whole, although Canada has not projected its power, it certainly has the ability to do so in relation to parts of Latin America and the Caribbean.[15] The United States, of course, has long demonstrated both the capacity and willingness to project its power.

While the 1995 Peru-Ecuador conflict has reminded us of the continued relevance of traditional security concerns, incidents before and after it indicate that there are issues that straddle both the traditional and the nontraditional camps, and others that stand squarely in the nontraditional area. The January 1994 Chiapas uprising is an example of one that straddles the two camps; narcotics falls within the nontraditional one. Of all the nontraditional threat areas, the narcotics issue commands the greatest convergence of threat perception by states in the hemisphere. For a few states it is a latent threat, but for most the threat is manifest; the dangers are real, and clear and present.

In the absence of perception analysis for individual countries, one thing that confirms the importance of drugs is the frequency with which narcotics issues command the attention of hemispheric leaders when they meet and the amount of time they devote to them, as reflected in summit agendas and communiques. For example, drugs have been featured consistently at all the summits of CARICOM (Caribbean Community and Common Market) leaders since 1988. A review of Francisco Rojas's summary of the issues and outcomes of the seven "security summits" of the Rio Group held between 1987 and 1993 shows that drugs featured in all of them and the issue was a priority item in many of them.[16] Moreover, hemispheric leaders have often held summits devoted solely to narcotics, for example: Cartagena (Colombia) in February 1990, San Antonio (Texas) in February 1992, and Belmopan (Belize) in February 1993. CARICOM leaders also held a special drug summit in December 1996 in Barbados.

Contrary to the impression that may be formed by the considerable attention paid to trafficking as compared to other areas, the narcotics issue is not a one-dimensional matter. It is a phenomenon that is multidimensional, both in its main problems and in its consequences. The main problems are production, consumption and abuse, trafficking, and money laundering. There is no uniformity in how the problems or their consequences are manifested. In the production area, for example, Colombia, Bolivia, Peru, Brazil, and Venezuela are the largest cocaine producers, with Colombia alone producing about 80 percent of the world's cocaine (although only some 20 percent of worldwide coca leaf cultivation is done there). No cocaine is produced in the Caribbean, but, along with the United States and Mexico, Caribbean countries are among the largest marijuana producers. In 1994, for example, little St. Vincent and the Grenadines—388 square kilometers with 118,000 people—was the Caribbean's second largest marijuana producer, after Jamaica, with marijuana seizures that year totalling 881 kilos.[17] As regards consumption, the United States has the dubious distinction of being the world's single largest consumer of narcotics. One U.S. official estimated that about three hundred metric tons of the approximately 575 metric tons of cocaine available worldwide in 1994 were consumed in the United States.[18]

The narcotics phenomenon has developed out of—and is still developing—dynamic interrelationships among four factors: drugs, geography, power, and politics. These interrelationships have led to the development of conflict and cooperation among national and international actors, both state and nonstate. The term *geonarcotics* has been used to describe the dynamics of these factors and actions to which they give rise. Geography is a geonarcotics factor because of the global spatial dimensions of drug operations and because the physical and social geography of some areas facilitates certain drug operations. Power is both state and nonstate in origin, and some nonstate power brokers often exercise more power than state agents. Consequently, politics, which determines who gets what, when, and how, becomes perverted and all the more so in places where it already was perverted.[19]

If nothing else, the narcotics phenomenon provides clear evidence that an approach to security that is preoccupied with the military variable is of limited utility in interpreting and acting on the security circumstances of the hemisphere. The nexus between drugs and security lies in the consequences and implications of drug operations for the protection and development of individuals and state and nonstate entities in the hemisphere. The main operations—production, consumption-abuse, trafficking, and money laundering—along with the numerous problems they precipitate show that the phenomenon has implications for all aspects of the postrealist definition of security: military, political, economic, and environmental. Crime, corruption, arms trafficking, resource reallocation, and deforestation are among the most critical consequences.

Thus, the war on drugs is not purely a military matter. Consequently, the utility of some of the most modern weapons for counternarcotics operations will be zero or near zero. Attempts by United States defense officials to commit resources of the Colorado-based North American Aerospace Defense (NORAD) Command to the drug war make this only too clear. First, the NORAD surveillance system, which was designed to identify high-flying Soviet bombers and nuclear-tipped missiles, is blind to aircraft flying below ten thousand feet, the altitude range of most narcotics air trafficking missions. Moreover, not only has NORAD had to ground its sixteen radar-carrying balloons that scan for aircraft below ten thousand feet whenever there is stormy weather, but its fighter jets fly too fast for pilots to see tail numbers on suspicious aircraft.[20]

This is not to suggest that there is no need or room for military capabilities and sophisticated military technology in combatting drugs. Yet, it should be recognized that military assets are sometimes unnecessary and at other times insufficient in coping with the multifaceted nontraditional threats and apprehensions arising from the drug threat. Hence, the tendency in some places to "throw the military at them" reflects (1) (mis)perceptions about the nature, scope, and gravity of the threat(s); (2) a crisis-management approach where the military is considered the institution with the best prospects of countering the threat(s); and (3) underestimation of the difficulty of role adaptation by the military—of mandating an institution largely dedicated to traditional security missions to undertake nontraditional ones.

The result is that many countries have been facing problems relating to jurisdictional conflicts between military and police forces, resource (re)allocation, corruption by the military and in some cases increased and new sources of corruption, training and technology adaptation, and the potential for (re)militarization in some places. In countries where the military have never exercised direct power, like in the Caribbean (except Haiti), many leaders worry that successful or prolonged use of the military in antidrug campaigns might catapult them into the countries' power centers, with the potential for the development of a guardian mentality. If the military comes to be seen—or, worse, if they come to see themselves—as indispensable to this critical aspect of national security, there is every risk of their intrusion into the political arena, with or without force.

Even if front-line use of the military in counternarcotics operations does not lead to the compromising of civilian control, a danger looms in another area. This danger is corruption. In some places in Latin America and the Caribbean this corruption is institutionalized, in other places it is sporadic.[21] In some places where corruption is not a problem, the potential for such certainly exists. The corruption of military and police officials compromises these agents of national security, with the result that their capacity for effective action is undermined, and individuals and groups in society become inclined to resort to vigilante tactics because of that diminished capacity, or a perception of such. With regard to the Caribbean, vigilante operations have long existed in Haiti, Jamaica, and a few other places. However, they are spreading elsewhere, to the extent that the national security minister of Trinidad and Tobago was forced to make a nationwide radio and television broadcast on the subject in June 1993. Among other things, he declared: "I wish to state quite strongly that under no condition will the government condone the formation of vigilante groups [where people] may choose themselves to be unlawfully armed with dangerous weapons on the pretext of protecting the community."[22]

The undermining of effectiveness noted above is partly a function of a loss of public confidence, either in the government as a whole or in certain specific institutions. The October–November 1994 drugs-arms-murder-riot saga in St. Kitts-Nevis, which precipitated the ouster of the ruling party at early elections held in July 1995, reflects the former. An example of the latter was highlighted in a recent study of crime in Jamaica: "The solving of crime depends to a large extent upon information supplied to the police by citizens. However, the breakdown in [that] relationship has made citizens reluctant to give the police information as they no longer regard the police as a friend of the community. The abuse of citizens' rights and the obvious partiality with which the police execute their duty, have given them a corrupt reputation. The link between the police and the criminal element has resulted in a loss of [public] confidence in the police."[23]

Collaboration and Confidence Building

A variety of countermeasures and initiatives have been adopted to meet the challenges mentioned above. Some are adopted unilaterally; others are pursued on the basis of collaboration, both bilateral and multilateral. Collaboration generally is guided by decisions based on two sets of assessments; an assessment of threats, and an assessment of needs and capabilities. The former points to the existence of common (subregional, regional, other) threats, or at least the perception of such by the relevant political and military elites. As regards the latter, the logic is that capability limitations—of money, manpower, weapons, technology, training, and so on—make it infeasible for a single country to deal credibly with the perceived threats. Consequently, collaboration is a function of necessity and not so much desire, although the latter could be of considerable weight in decisions to collaborate.

Collaboration has been varied in geographic, institutional, and functional terms. Some of it has been pan-American, but most of it has been subregional and regional—Rio Group, Andean, CARICOM, Eastern Caribbean, Central American, and so forth. One can find multidimensional collaboration even within a single region in relation to a single set of threats and apprehensions. This is precisely what one finds in the Caribbean in relation to drugs. Collaboration is both bilateral and multilateral. And because of the transnational—and transregional—nature of drug operations, collaboration is both intraregional and extraregional. For instance, Antigua-Barbuda, Jamaica, the Bahamas, the Dominican Republic, Suriname, Trinidad and Tobago, St. Kitts-Nevis, and Grenada are among countries with bilateral Mutual Legal Assistance Treaties with the United States. These deal with intelligence sharing, joint interdiction, training, and material and technical assistance. It is useful to note that although no formal agreement exists between Cuba and the United States, at times there is significant counternarcotics cooperation.

Other bilateral arrangements also exist. There is one between Belize and Mexico, for instance, pertaining to intelligence exchange, rehabilitation, and crop eradication. Agreements are also in place between Suriname and Guyana, Cuba and Guyana, Jamaica and Cuba, Venezuela and Guyana, Suriname and Colombia, and other pairs of countries. As for multilateral arrangements, a treaty is in force among the Bahamas, Britain (for the Turks and Caicos dependency), and the United States for OPBAT—Operation Bahamas and the Turks and Caicos—a joint interdiction and intelligence arrangement. Moreover, in September 1996 Caribbean countries established a Regional Training Center for Drug Law Enforcement in Jamaica.

At the wider hemispheric and international levels, Caribbean countries collaborate on narcotics through the Inter-American Drug Abuse Control Commission (CICAD), the Meeting of Heads of National Law Enforcement Agencies (HONLEA), the Organization of American States (OAS) Money Laundering Experts Group, the United Nations International Drug Control Program (UNDCP), and other agencies. (Although these agencies concentrate on multilateral collaboration, they also facilitate bilateral contacts.) In relation to the United Nations, a Caribbean country—the Bahamas—has the distinction of being the first nation to ratify the 1988 Convention Against Illicit Traffic in Narcotic Drugs and Psychotropic Substances, which provides for collaboration, as well as mandates unilateral action, on a wide range of issues.[24]

Although the aim here is neither to tabulate nor evaluate all the hemisphere's collective endeavors, it is important to observe that the nature, scope, and outcome of collaboration have depended on such factors as the scope, intensity, and proximity of threats, resource availability, geopolitics, domestic politics, and the amount of competition for attention and resources by other policy areas. Because of the salience of both traditional and nontraditional security matters, policy makers have often felt compelled to pursue initiatives that simultaneously address traditional as well as nontraditional threats and apprehensions, and ones that are manifest as well as latent. As a result, although important, some endeavors become half measures. One such endeavor in the Caribbean is the Regional Security System (RSS).

The RSS was established in October 1982 through a memorandum of understanding (MOU) by five Eastern Caribbean countries—Antigua-Barbuda, Barbados, Dominica, St. Lucia, and St. Vincent and the Grenadines. St. Kitts-Nevis joined the following February, and Grenada secured membership in January 1985. Because of concerns about militarization, efforts in 1986 to upgrade the MOU to a security treaty and thereby give the Regional Security System (RSS) international legal personality were futile. However, those efforts were not abandoned. The MOU was revised in 1993, and a treaty was finally signed on March 5, 1996. The treaty comprises thirty-two articles covering a range of operational, organizational, and policy matters. It operates on the basis of collective self-defense and requires the RSS to assist member countries in a variety of security areas, including drug interdiction, search and rescue, customs and immigration control, protection of off-shore installations, and natural disasters.

The structure of the RSS involves a Council of Ministers, comprised of national security ministers, as the central policy-making body. Operational command falls under a regional security coordinator (RSC) who heads a Central Liaison Office (CLO), which is located in Barbados. Barbados also provides the coordinator, currently Brigadier Rudyard Lewis, substantively the chief of staff of the Barbados Defense Force. (Lewis is the founding coordinator.) The CLO plans and coordinates in collaboration with a Joint Coordinating Committee composed of army commanders and police commissioners. Not all RSS member countries have armies; only Antigua-Barbuda, Barbados, and St. Kitts-Nevis do, and the army in the last country was created only in May 1997. A key component of the police forces of the countries without armies is the Special Service Unit (SSU), elite paramilitary police with the equivalent of Special Weapons and Tactics (SWAT) training and weapons. They are designated to deal with crises beyond the capacity of the regular civil police and are the police units that are active in RSS operations.

The RSS gained notoriety in 1983 for its role in the United States intervention in Grenada: mopping up and postinvasion policing, roles that were more politically expedient, given the controversy over the intervention, than militarily necessary.[25] However, the RSS had become involved in Grenada's crisis even before the intervention itself, by conducting intelligence missions and designing plans to rescue Maurice Bishop, all of which became subordinated to U.S. plans once the decision to intervene was made in Washington. Apart from its roles in Grenada and continuous interdiction and other measures, the RSS has deployed forces in Trinidad and Tobago following the coup attempt there in July–August 1990, to support the local military and police forces. Troops and police were also deployed in St. Kitts-Nevis during November 1994 following a mass prison riot that was part of a larger drugs-driven crisis.

RSS forces have been deployed annually since 1985 in military training exercises, in conjunction with forces from other Caribbean countries, the United States, and, at varying times, from Britain, France, and the Netherlands. The first exercise, Operation Exotic Palm, was held in September 1985 and focused on counterinsurgency. The 1995 maneuvers—Tradewinds '95—were held between March and May and dealt with amphibious missions, mainly coast guard search and rescue, oil pollution management, and port management. The 1995 exercises involved all Anglophone Caribbean countries, reflecting the growing participation that began significantly in 1989. In addition to Caribbean and United States forces, French troops also participated, mainly in the St. Kitts-Nevis phase, and on a bilateral basis with St. Kitts-Nevis. Some technical support was granted by Canadian forces and there were Venezuelan and Dutch observers.[26]

The maneuvers themselves reflect one of the dilemmas of the RSS. They are not conceived by the RSS, neither does the CLO control their planning and execution. This was done by the United States Atlantic Command (USACOM) until June 1997, when the Pentagon shifted responsibility for the Caribbean from USACOM to the United States Southern Command (SOUTHCOM). Because of this, RSS (and Caribbean) interests are not always paramount. The dilemma that this reflects is the reliance of the RSS on foreign support. The original foreign benefactors were Britain, Canada, and the United States, operating on a bilateral basis with RSS member countries. But given geopolitical changes, budget pressures, and organizational adaptations, the level of support has diminished, with Britain and Canada making the greatest cutbacks. At the same time, RSS member states have themselves been experiencing economic difficulties, preventing them from fulfilling their financial obligations to the system, thereby aggravating the dependency problem.[27]

It is partly to redress half-measures and boost multilateralism in the security arena that confidence building has again become a key agenda item in the hemisphere. Basically, a confidence-building measure is an act between two or more states that reduces tensions among them and decreases the likelihood of accidental conflict or unintended escalation. Traditionally, it is used to inhibit the use of force for political intimidation, propitiate military-political crisis management, reduce the risk of surprise attacks, and facilitate the termination of armed conflict. A wide range of measures may be adopted to achieve these ends. The measures invariably fall into one or more of the following categories: information, communication, access, notification, and constraint.

Information measures involve the exchange of data on military forces and activities, the idea being to increase transparency and reduce misperception about the capabilities and disposition of other countries. Of course, the danger exists that incorrect data can create a false sense of predictability. Hence, the importance of the ability to check the data. Communications measures are designed to air differences and clarify mutual intentions, while access measures enable parties involved to check the accuracy of data exchanged and the validity of statements provided in the execution of communications measures. Access measures include observation of military exercises, onsite inspections of military activities, and open skies agreements. Notification measures are intended to enhance predictability by requiring states to inform each other about impending military activity, thus avoiding surprise and miscalculation of actions. Constraint measures actually prohibit certain activities and as such are arguably the most difficult to negotiate. Such measures could include agreements on the size, frequency, and or duration of troop movement, restricted activities in specified geographic areas, and time restrictions on certain activities.[28]

Security confidence building is grounded conceptually in collective security, which "displaces the centerpiece of security planning from preparing to counter threats to preventing such threats from arising—from deterring aggression to making preparations for it more difficult."[29] Working with the premise that joint efforts to shared problems are the most effective way to promote security for all the states involved, confidence building requires relationships and links in a variety of military, political, and other areas, and at several levels. As one Canadian specialist has observed, "Dialogue is the very essence of a cooperative security system because it is the discussion, compromise, and cooperation inherent in developing and undertaking this dialogue which permits and promotes transparency, thus building confidence and security."[30]

Analysts generally agree that a cooperative security order need not be reflected in a single all-encompassing regime. More likely are complementary and overlapping agreements. Much hope is placed in collective security as the "new" approach to peace internationally. Many writers share the view expressed in the study by Carter, Perry, and Steinbruner that "Cooperative security is the corresponding principle for international security in the post-cold war era," (cold war principles being deterrence and containment). The subject of confidence building gained most of its prominence in relation to Europe, but it is not new to the Americas. Indeed, it featured prominently in a project directed in the early 1980s by Michael Morris and Victor Millán.[31] However, the pursuit of confidence building now is differentiated from efforts in earlier decades by at least four factors.

The first is the cold war, which contributed to and was used for the generation of mistrust and apprehension in parts of the hemisphere. The end of the cold war therefore offers a new and different environment. Second, states in the hemisphere now seem more disposed to using the OAS as a catalyst for confidence building. Previously, cold war–related factors and hegemonic pursuits and postures by the United States created distrust by states about OAS initiatives and about possible ulterior motives by the United States, especially because the United States was noted for orchestrating OAS pursuits. A third difference relates to the resolution of several conflicts, especially in Central America, many of which saw the application of confidence-building measures. Thus, the hemisphere is less volatile than two decades ago, at least in traditional conflict terms. Finally, unlike earlier times, nontraditional security concerns are pitched in wide regional and hemispheric terms and have an important place on the inter-American security agenda.

The OAS has recently become a prime mover in the area of confidence building. The efforts are spearheaded by its Special Committee on Hemispheric Security, formed in 1992, with Ambassador Hernán Patiño Meyer of Argentina as chairman and Ambassador Patrick A. Lewis of Antigua-Barbuda as vice chairman.[32] Among other things, the committee's mandate is to increase dialogue on and collaboration in security matters, to affirm one of the central purposes of the OAS, which is to prevent conflict and resolve disputes peacefully, and to study the special security problems of small states in the hemisphere, notably their vulnerability to drug trafficking and arms smuggling.[33]

The committee approaches security as a multidimensional matter, but the military area is preeminent. There is concern about both internal and external security. There is also a sense that security is not only about real and tangible threats and apprehensions; it is also a function of perception. This is important because it is perception, or worse, misperception that often guides security policy, sometimes casting security shadows and aggravating situations. Cooperative security is the guiding principle. Patiño Meyer once asserted: "The challenge [today] consists of articulating cooperative security relations which, by their depth and diversity, might not make conflicts impossible, but would put more obstacles in their way and reduce the possibility of widening the conflict in a co-active manner."[34]

At a November 1995 conference in Santiago, Chile, the committee identified some general and specific initiatives to be pursued. According to the Santiago Declaration issued by the meeting,

The governments of the OAS member states, meeting in Santiago, Chile, agree to recommend the application, in the manner that is most suitable, of confidence- and security-building measures, among which the following should be mentioned:

a. Gradual adoption of agreements regarding advance notice of military exercises;

b. Exchange of information and participation of all Member States in the United Nations Register of Conventional Arms and the International Standardized Report on Military Spending;

c. Promote the development and exchange of information concerning defense policies and doctrines;

d. Consideration of a consultation process with a view to proceeding towards limitations and control of conventional weapons;

e. Agreements on invitation of observers to military exercises, visits to military installations, simple arrangements for observing routine operations, and exchange of civilian and military personnel for regular and advanced training;

f. Meetings and activities to prevent incidents and increase security for transport by land, sea, and air;

g. Cooperation programs in the event of natural disasters or to prevent such disasters, based on the request and authorization of the affected states;

h. Development and establishment of communications among civilian or military authorities of neighboring countries in accordance with their border situation;

i. Holding seminars and courses, and studies on mutual confidence-building measures and policies to promote confidence involving the participation of civilians and military personnel, and on the special security concerns of small island states;

j. High-level meetings on the special concerns of small island states; and

k. Education programs for peace.[35]

The mandate and pursuits of the OAS Special Committee have great merit and deserve adequate attention. However, my intention here is not to examine the merits and demerits of specific agenda items but to suggest some challenges of which scholars and policy makers should be mindful as confidence building is pursued on a hemispheric basis. These challenges are not suggested in order to discourage the pursuit of confidence-building agendas, but to inject a cautionary note that might serve to temper the understandably high expectations that may exist over confidence building. These challenges are not presented in any special order of importance. Each is significant, but their combined, interactive importance rises above the import of any single one.[36]

The Conceptualization Challenge

Two related matters are involved here. In the first instance, the confidence-building measures advocated by the Special Committee are essentially military confidence-building measures. This reflects not only the preeminent status of the military aspect of security as viewed by the committee, but also the bias of confidence building as a collective security approach, which is to focus on traditional security concerns. However, as we saw earlier, neither the committee nor the OAS can limit its purview to the traditional area, because of the importance of nontraditional areas generally, and because at least one nontraditional area—drugs—presents the greatest convergence of shared threat perception. And it is partly shared threat perception that motivates collaboration. Put differently, there is a discrepancy between the traditional security cloak in which cooperative security and its progeny, confidence building, are cast conceptually and the exigencies of both traditional and nontraditional security issues confronting actors in the hemisphere.

The second and related aspect of this conceptual challenge pertains to level of analysis and operationalization. The Carter-Perry-Steinbruner study tacitly acknowledges one potentially serious weakness of cooperative security, the foundation of confidence building: "Focused on restraining the organized preparations of established militaries, cooperative security does not address itself directly to substate violence, which is a principal source of chronic conflict and human misery in the world."[37] In essence, the analysis is cast at the systemic level, with the state as the unit of analysis and the threat orientation as external. But as was seen earlier, not only are some of the significant hemispheric threats not presented by state actors, but the level at which threats and apprehensions appear or are perceived is often substate, and they straddle both internal and external areas. There is therefore need for conceptual adaptation of cooperative security, in relation to both core concerns and level of analysis for its meaningful application in the Americas.

The Prioritization Challenge

Prioritization will be necessary for several reasons. First, because of the multidimensionality of security, it stands to reason that confidence may be needed in a variety of military and political, if not economic and environmental, areas. However, all areas cannot be addressed simultaneously. Selectivity will, therefore, be necessary. Among other things, prioritizing will be influenced by the following:

• Definition of the nature and severity of threats or apprehensions;
• Budgetary, technical, manpower, and other resources (and limitations) of states and the OAS;
• Political will.

The endorsement by states of cooperative security and the adoption of confidence-building measures will not eliminate the use of national interest considerations to guide interstate conduct. Such considerations may dictate that countries support or pursue only a select set of confidence-building measures. It is unlikely that all countries will support or pursue the entire menu of mechanisms established by confidence-building regimes. This will be so even for matters, such as narcotics trafficking and crime, where there is a threat shared by many states, and where there is convergence of perception of its nature and gravity. Convergence on the perception of threats is no guarantee of consensus on how to deal with them.

The National Policy Challenge

Confidence building is not merely the creation and maintenance of technical mechanisms; political will is an indispensable feature, as confidence-building endeavors in Europe and within this hemisphere—between Argentina and Chile, for example—attest. Comfort in the fact that precepts and practices of democracy are supported overwhelmingly and are assets to confidence building is justified. But the endorsement of democracy and the maintenance of democratic polities are by themselves no assurance that states will act cooperatively or will demonstrate the political will to join confidence-building regimes.

Political will is largely a function of domestic politics, affected by the regional and international environments. Security policy, foreign policy, and confidence-building pursuits will, therefore, be driven largely by domestic political considerations. These would include the dynamics of party rivalry, the composition and control of executive and legislative branches and of the military, the amount and potency of media and interest group activity, budgetary situations, ideology, the state of the economy, and the nature and severity of any political unrest that may exist. All these considerations may generate actions that appear irrational, parochial, trivial, and even contradictory. And some actions might be many or all of these. Nevertheless, the bottom line is that political considerations constitute the core of what drives national policy.

A test of national policy commitment—and this is linked to domestic politics—will be the extent to which states support the institutionalization of confidence-building regimes, through the elaboration of treaties, conventions, and protocols. Regime institutionalization is necessary not only to give regularity and consistency to regime mechanisms, but also to have the commitment of states secured in a way that is conducive to continuity without having every state's participation constantly jeopardized by the vicissitudes of domestic governmental change. This is not to say, however, that new governments should or can be precluded from (re)evaluating their countries' participation and even delinking from some mechanisms.

Despite the porousness of sovereignty, states guard their sovereignty jealously, especially the small ones whose experience with colonization is still fresh in the national memory, and those that have been victims of intervention. Hence, it is important to be sensitive to concerns about confidence-building regimes with arrangements that facilitate or appear to facilitate intervention. Ultimately, though, the essence of the national policy challenge will be the willingness of states to go beyond paying lip service to confidence building; to act and correct problems and missteps; and not to delink from the process or undermine it whenever their national sensibilities are offended. It must be recognized that confidence-building is a long-term process and project, central to which are progressive, incremental steps.

The Institutionalization Challenge

One test of the commitment of states to support the confidence-building measures that are established will be their willingness to institutionalize the regimes or agreements by incorporating them into national policy. In practical terms this could be judged, among other things, by (1) whether or not states sign, and later ratify, the regime instrument—treaty, convention, memorandum of understanding, etc.; (2) whether they procrastinate on such action or act with deliberate speed; and (3) whether or not they adopt enabling, supporting, or collateral legislation or other domestic policy instruments.

Some countries have a poor record when it comes to sustaining, and sometimes merely launching, initiatives. This is often because of financial, technical, manpower, or other reasons. Often, though, it is due to plain and simple neglect. Hence, once states accept confidence-building mechanisms they should be encouraged and reminded to create the necessary domestic arrangements to give meaning to them. This may entail adapting existing agencies to the confidence-building pursuit, reorganizing governmental agencies to fulfill regime requirements, or creating new units, divisions, and so on for the same purpose. Attention should also be paid to technical and other assistance to states to enable them to do these things.

The Bureaucratic Politics and Coordination Challenge

One of the harsh realities of probably all OAS member states is that bureaucratic politics, jurisdictional disputes, and turf battles abound among services of the military, and between: the military and the police; foreign and defense ministries; those ministries and finance ministries; presidential secretariats and ministries or departments; legislative and executive branch agencies; and traditional law-enforcement agencies and special narcotics agencies; and among various intelligence units.

Of course, the nature and extent of these battles and rivalries vary from place to place. But perhaps more critical than recognition of their existence is awareness that they can frustrate, undermine, and sometimes even precipitate termination of some initiatives and arrangements. This should be kept in mind not because the Special Committee or the OAS in general may be able to end such, but because every effort should be made to mitigate the effects of these on the pursuit of confidence building. In a sense, this is a plea for confidence building within states, but it is no less vital than confidence building among states.

Confidence-building measures will require the involvement of different ministries, departments, bureaus, and services. The absence of coordination among relevant entities can serve to undermine confidence building. As a matter of fact, noncoordination or contradictory actions can lead to misperception by others, triggering acute reaction with considerable fallout and aggravating matters rather than ameliorating them. To use an adage known in many parts of the hemisphere, one hand should know what the other is doing, and the two should work together.

Conclusion

This discussion has suggested that while there are powerful reasons for states in the Americas to collaborate and pursue confidence-building measures, the continuity of traditional threats provides a compelling reason for skepticism about the ability of the end of the cold war and the Spirit of Miami to usher a bright new age of peace and tranquility in the hemisphere. For one, the Peru-Ecuador conflict not only reminded us about the salience of such threats, it also served to reopen several territorial (and other) sores. Indeed, one writer feels that it will trigger some deceleration, if not outright reversal, in the general downward trend in Latin American military spending.[38]

This is a reasonable proposition. Yet the Peru-Ecuador conflict is itself a compelling reason to pursue peaceful measures to prevent the outbreak of war. Given the mistrust generated by the territorial dispute that led to the war, that conflict is also a compelling reason for cooperative security and confidence building. Nevertheless, traditional security concerns are not the only ones that threaten peace, security, and democracy in the hemisphere; nontraditional ones also exist. While their implications are not all military, their dangers are often no less clear and present than some traditional ones. This calls into question the adequacy of applying the conventional approach to cooperative security and confidence building to the hemisphere. Advancing the confidence-building agenda, therefore, presents several challenges to scholars and statesmen in the hemisphere.

Chapter 10

The Illicit Drug Trade In The Caribbean

Use, Transshipment, and Violent Crime

Anthony P. Maingot

The revenue collected by the Cali drug cartel in the United States alone is calculated to be $6 billion. Half is estimated to be laundered through U.S.-based businesses, the other half through third countries. It will come as no surprise that one of those third countries is the island of Aruba.[1]

Even the most jaded student of the Caribbean has to take seriously some of Claire Sterling's revelations, not the least of which is the following startling assertion: "The world's first independent mafia state emerged in 1993. The sovereign island of Aruba . . . proved to belong to the Mafia in fact if not in name. Small islands are not so hard to acquire."[2] Sterling probably overstates the degree of Mafia control and she errs in calling Aruba a sovereign state (its defense and foreign policy are still under control of the Netherlands). Nevertheless, her account of how the Caracas-based Cuntrera brothers had managed to penetrate Aruba and buy everything "from hotels . . . to the prime minister" found partial corroboration in the massive investigation of the Sicilian Mafia launched in Italy in the early 1990s. Just before her book appeared, the Italian Carabinieri took the Cuntrera brothers, Paolo and Pasquale, out of Caracas, in handcuffs, to face an Italian court. Up to that point they had functioned as respectable Venezuelan and Caribbean businessmen.[3]

Claire Sterling has been joined by many others—few, if any, academics[4]—in warning the world about the threat of organized crime and how corruption makes that threat an international issue. Anthony Lake, President William Clinton's first national security advisor, has spoken of the threats stemming from organized crime and a "nefarious nexus of crime, terrorism and the weapons of mass destruction."[5] Even a cursory survey of the literature on the Caribbean Basin in the early to mid 1990s reveals the outlines of a monstrous new menace to the survival of these small states and their larger Latin American neighbors. There are accounts of the corrupt banking practices that stretch throughout the hemisphere[6] as well as detailed accounts of regionwide organizations smuggling drugs, guns, and aliens.[7] Finally, there is the literature that deals specifically with what Sterling calls the Pax Mafiosa: the cross-continental links between the various national criminal cartels that are often beyond the reach and certainly beyond the control of national crime-fighting forces.[8]

No one can fail to be dismayed by the apparent unending litany of stories about the social ravages caused by drug addiction, crime, and the corruption of state officials they engender. This is especially galling when the stories come from societies with scarce resources forced to engage in heavy international borrowing to sustain minimum standards of living. To read of the economic distortions caused by infusions of dirty money and of the levels of illegal capital flight equal or larger than the level of indebtedness, at a time of social and political restructuring with all its strains, is to experience a sense of the absurd but also of the extreme perfidy of this phenomenon. Yet, there are no systematic studies of these crises in the Caribbean.

Part of the problem of studying the effects of the drug trade in the Caribbean is the total absence of figures that speak to the domestic situations. There are sporadic reports but the design of a general situation statement that would include both an overall assessment of the situation as well as estimates of drug use, expenditure on drugs, drug-related arrests, and social costs (criminal and medical) does not exist in the islands. It would be necessary to construct such a statement of the situation for each island before a general assessment can be attempted. As of now, individual governments in the area depend on statistics compiled by U.S. agencies serving U.S. national security ends. Specifically, these governments depend heavily on the various annual Department of State, Bureau for International Narcotics and Law Enforcement Affairs, *International Narcotics Control Strategy Report*. Its 1995 issue caused a small crisis in U.S.-Caribbean relations with its allegation that, "In the Eastern Caribbean, corruption among public officials is rarely met with strong countermeasures" (194). Especially riled was Sir James Mitchell of St. Vincent who felt that his country had been singled out unfairly.[9] (The issue of March 1995 is referred to in this essay as the *1995 Report*.)

The *1995 Report* emphasizes that the U.S. war on drugs focuses on crop eradication and drug traffic interdiction. The Caribbean is not a major producer and, as we observe below, has been displaced by Mexico as the hemisphere's major transshipment point. This explains why the Caribbean receives an extremely small portion of the U.S. budget for narcotics control. Note the request for 1996 in table 10-1:[10]

Table 10-1   U.S. Budget for Narcotics Control, 1996

Bahamas	$700,000
Jamaica	$1,000,000
Venezuela	$500,000

Total for Latin America: $150,600,000 (71% of total budget)

It is a well-known fact among Caribbean scholars that the crackdown in South Florida and the Bahamas in the 1980s led to a shift in cartel tactics. Operations were shifted to Mexico and, in the Caribbean, to Puerto Rico. This involved all aspects of the business: transshipment, money laundering, and criminal enforcement activities, including murder. In the Bahamas, cocaine seizures went from 231,126 pounds in 1987 to 9,921 pounds in 1991, and marijuana seizures from 705,554 to 661 pounds during that same period. Similarly, marijuana seizures in Jamaica went from 705,554 to 94,799 pounds.

Today, the first point of contact for the Puerto Rican operators is the Dominican Republic. Not surprisingly drugs are not the only items involved. The Dominican newspaper, *Ultima Hora,* recently published letters from various Dominican ministries ordering over $100 million worth of machine guns from the Czech Republic. These weapons were clearly destined for use elsewhere.[11] With powerful Dominican drug rings operating in New York, and with no legislation against money laundering, the Dominican drug lords have penetrated their island's banking, business, judiciary, police, and even the Congress. This has occurred virtually unhindered.[12]

The rest of the Caribbean countries play essentially supporting roles to this U.S. (New York, Miami)–Puerto Rico–Dominican Republic axis; which, of course, is not to minimize the damage this role is doing. The problem is that transshipment routes shift, always seeking softer or more porous spots in the region. For instance, three weeks after the new Chilean airline, Ladeco, began a twice-a-week stop in Montego Bay, Jamaica, 814 pounds of cocaine were discovered there.[13] The damage done by the original corruption and initial drug use remains and, because of diversification, it has spread to more islands. Keeping in mind the small size of most of the islands in the Caribbean, one realizes that even the relatively small amounts of drugs (viz., less than 200-kilo packages) being transshipped from Colombia via Venezuela through the Eastern Caribbean have dramatic consequences for each island.

Aside from the domestic impacts, the cartels use the islands for two other well-thought-out purposes. First, this use serves to dilute, if not totally neutralize, counternarcotic activities by multiplying the trouble spots. The fundamental way of assuring this is through the corruption of administrative and police authorities in each island. They have been frightfully successful. The second major function the Caribbean plays for the mafias is the laundering of the proceeds of the drug trade, the bulk of which comes from the United States.[14]

At a "Technical Anti-Drugs Summit" held in Puerto Rico in May 1995, the head of Puerto Rico's Drug Enforcement Administration (DEA) office spoke of the "Colombianization" of the region.[15] He was not the first to so characterize the region and, in my opinion, that characterization is unfortunately all too accurate. The most tragic evidence that this is, indeed, so is the increase in professionally executed murders of those combatting the rot or of those involved and soiled but fallen out of grace.

People in the region are finally realizing that the "drug problem" is no longer "an American problem." It is everyone's problem. In Puerto Rico, the drug wars are so violent that the governor has put certain areas under the authority of the national guard to back up the police; the legislature was rocked by allegations of drug use and collusion with traffickers on the part of senior legislators. Grand juries sit in the U.S. Virgin Islands looking at police corruption and even murder; commissions of enquiry sit in the Bahamas looking at the widespread corruption that has characterized the past two decades. In island after island, the New Scotland Yard, the DEA, and the Federal Bureau of Investigation (FBI) operate. In fact, one can speak of a benign form of "recolonization" of the Caribbean as the United States, the Netherlands, the United Kingdom, and France intensify their surveillance and investigations into the problem.

Consider first Jamaica, which its commissioner of police, Col. Trevor MacMillan, has described as being in a "pre-Colombianization" stage.[16]

Jamaica

The *1995 Report* is quite accurate when it describes Jamaica as a "major producer of marijuana and a *flourishing* transhipment site for South American cocaine."[17] It is less accurate when it maintains that there is no evidence of money laundering, and it makes no mention of drug use. Also questionable are the following figures on drug-related arrests, cited in table 10-2 without commentary:

Table 10-2   Drug-Related Arrests in Jamaica, 1990–1994

Year	Nationals	Foreigners
1990	4,908	524
1994	788	98

The obvious puzzle is: if the trade is "flourishing," why was there such a dramatic drop in arrests? This is certainly not what Jamaican journalists tell us: "Drug Trade Soars," avers the *Jamaican Weekly Gleaner* (June 16–22, 1995). The story notes that US$1.3 billion in crack cocaine was confiscated and 2,400 drug-related arrests were made in the first six months of 1995. One plausible explanation for the disparity is that, because the U.S. government often subordinates drug policy to broader foreign policy concerns, in 1995 U.S. authorities decided to report the views of Jamaica's political class, long sensitive and concerned over national image and any possible damage that could be done to the tourist industry.

There has been a long history of public denial about the drug issue. None of the important politician-writers of Jamaica, or of the Caribbean generally, in the 1960s, 1970s, and even early 1980s ever admitted that the threat to Caribbean security would come largely from drug-traffic-related corruption, internal and external. Even the prolific Michael Manley was totally absorbed by what were termed "North-South" issues. Elected in 1972, he published a book in 1973 advocating national control of the "commanding heights of the economy" plus a "non-aligned" foreign policy, and another book in 1975 that took an even more strident "democratic socialist" stance. In his decade out of power, Manley published an explanation of why his party lost the 1980 elections (U.S. "destabilization" was a major cause), a new call for his idea of "self-reliance" through a New International Economic Order and South-South cooperation,[18] as well as a monumental book on cricket. In none of these works is the issue of drugs and of a criminal threat to Jamaica mentioned. These would not be seriously discussed until Manley's return to government in 1989.

Scholars tended to follow suit; their concern was with issues of "revolution" and dependency. Even one as moderate and well-informed as Carl Stone refused to confront the issue of the international criminal threat. As late as April 1988, Stone wrote that he found it distressing that, in a year when Jamaicans were electing a new government, "we are spending as much time agonizing over petty U.S. gossip about supposed mafia-type links between local politics and drug dons." He called for a discussion of "the real issues."[19] A similar position was taken by the then minister of labor.[20] Exactly one year

later, after Jamaican voters had elected a new government without any serious debate or discussion of the Jamaican drug problem, Stone demonstrated
a dramatically changed perception of the threat. The drug dealers, he wrote,
were "crippling Jamaica . . . the very future and livelihood of this country and
its people are at risk." Such was his sense of threat that he urged that steps be
taken "in a hurry" to stop this trade, including making "any constitutional
changes necessary."[21] What explains such a dramatic switch and what does it
say about the nature of the threat to the security of Caribbean countries? The
answer is that it was a response to some very real challenges to the Jamaican
state's control over its public health and economic activities.

Perhaps most urgent was the realization that what was generally called the
Jamaican "drug culture" was no longer limited to marijuana (ganja). As Stone
himself discovered in his first major foray into drug use on the island, there
had emerged a "syndrome" of multiple drug use at all levels of the society.
The traditional wad of ganja was now a "splif," ganja sprinkled with cocaine.[22]

Then there was the threat to the economy. Between 1987 and 1989 several
major shippers stopped shipping goods out of Jamaica: Evergreen Lines had
already paid US$137 million, and Sea-Land Services US$85 million, in fines to
U.S. customs; the Kirk Line had one of its ships confiscated in Miami (released after the payment of a fine); Air Jamaica was suffering from constant
fines imposed because of drug finds, and the Free Zone manufacturers were
said to be in a "tailspin" because of the use of the port by drug lords. In the
midst of all this, Jamaica was experiencing a flood of imported weapons,
which no doubt heightened the political violence already endemic.

The discovery on January 6, 1989, of a container in the port of Kingston
loaded with US$8 million in arms illustrated that the problem had wider
ramifications. Of West German manufacture, the weapons were shipped
from Portugal on a Panamanian registered ship and were destined for an un-
specified group in Colombia. It took a joint effort of Jamaican, British, U.S.,
and Colombian intelligence to break the Jamaican link of what was called
"an international network of drug traffickers and terrorists." The Panamanian ship was owned by Bluewater Ship Management Inc. of Panama. Both
the company and its British (naturalized Panamanian) president had previously been linked to illegal arms shipments, cocaine distribution, and the
laundering of drug-related monies.

Part of the Jamaican elite's tendency to deny this major problem is the
penchant for sweeping drug-related crimes under the carpet. This has been
quite evident regarding Jamaica's criminal gangs, "posses" or "crews" ("yar-
dies" in the United Kingdom). These gangs have become a major source of
friction between Jamaica, the United States, Canada, and the United Kingdom. Occasionally romanticized in song, film, fiction, or history,[23] it has tak-

en the writings of courageous journalists to fill the void. In October 1994, *Jamaican Gleaner* columnist Dawn Ritch started to reveal the links between crime, drugs, and political protection of the gangs. Despite the well-documented columns, in November 1994 the deputy commissioner of police skirted the issue, claiming not to have seen Dawn Ritch's columns. He gave the following "philosophical" (to use his word) responses to the query, "Why do Jamaicans regard crime as the number one national problem?": "When social conditions exist which do not comfortably accommodate all social classes on an equal level, it is not uncommon for crime to increase."[24]

The redoubtable Ms. Ritch was not about to be silenced. In the face of considerable pressure to keep quiet she published facts taken from police records (see table 10-3). These are the constituencies that Jamaicans call "garrison constituencies" because the gangs exercise such control that the police have to be "garrisoned" in fortified stations. In August 1994, I toured one of these constituencies under the "protection" of the popular local parish priest. The Mercedes Benzs of the drug dons were everywhere in evidence, signs that the drug trade was flourishing. With the police presence limited to single highly protected garrisons, the fear of the residents was palpable.

It is understandable that Jamaicans would want to protect their reputation and that of the all-important tourist industry. Yet, when the island recorded 656 murders in 1993 and 650 in 1994 (nonelection years), crime was hardly under control. The drug-related problems of so much concern in the 1980s were still manifest.

In 1994 the Narcotics Division of Jamaica's Police Services seized and destroyed J$1.3 billion worth of crack cocaine, ganja, and cocaine powder. They arrested 2,400 people. In 1995, according to Jamaican sources, the traffic in drugs increased dramatically. On the upswing, according to Deputy Commissioner of Police Francis Forbes, was the use of small aircraft for airdrops along the coasts. These craft were registered in the Bahamas and owned by Bahamians who were often resident in the United States. Moreover, according to Minister of National Security K. D. Knight, Jamaica was making every effort to contain this trade since it represented a threat to the island's national security: "if the smugglers are successful to any significant degree, there will be no ship willing to transport Jamaican bauxite."[25] And in early June 1995, virtually the complete staff of United Parcel Service (UPS) in Kingston was caught redhanded loading cases of marijuana onto a UPS courier plane; the plane was seized by Jamaican authorities. One week later, a DHL courier service plane was stopped; ganja-laden honey bottles were on board.[26] For an export-driven economy, the involvement of container cargo, small aircraft, and courier services in the drug traffic could eventually prove disastrous.

Table 10-3 Jamaican Garrison Constituencies Compiled from Police Records, July 1994

Member of Parliament	Constituency	Criminal Bases	Criminal Gangs
Marjorie Taylor	Eastern Kingston	Dunkirk	110 Posse
		Dunkirk	Borrows Gang
		Rockfort	East. Kingston
		Dunkirk	Garfield Gang
		Rockfort	Glamour Gang
		Dunkirk	Red Square
Col. Leslie Lloyd	Central Kingston	Tel Aviv	Ankleman Crew
		S. Side Pow Cnr	Chubby Dread Posse
		Tel Aviv	Dessert Posse
		J Lane/Laws St	Devon Crew
		Tel Aviv	Kremlin Posse
		Southside	Raiders
		Tel Aviv	Rapid Posse
		S. Side–Renkas Cnr	Renkas Cre
		Wildman Street	Spoilers
		Top Rd/Sussex Ln	Top
		Allman Town	Tr
		Raetown	U
Dr. Omar Davies	S. St. Andrew	Jones Town	
		Craig Town	
		Concrete Jungle	
		Concrete Jungle	
		Concrete Jungle	ve's Crew
		Maxfield Ave/Sunlight St	ew
		Raphel Ave	. Gang
		Lincoln Crescent	es Crew
		Rema–Wilton Gdns	sse
Harry Douglas	East St. Mary	Annotto Bay	ng
Edward Seaga	Western Kingston	West Street	nter Crew
		Tivoli Gardens	New Kids
		Orange St. Eadic Lane	
		Fletchers Land	Crew
		Fletchers Land	s
		Lower Matches *(sic)* L	Crew
		Tivoli Gardens/May Pe	r Posse
		Matches *(sic)* Lane/Luke	nglers
D. T. Williams	Western St. Andrew	Duhaney Park	Brook Valley Crew
Portia Simpson	South West St. Andrew	Maxfield Avenue	Chi Chi Boy Gang
		Payne Land	Doverman Crew
		Oakland Road	Oakland Road
		Payne Avenue	Payne Avenue

(table continues)

Table 10-3 *(continued)*

Member of Parliament	Constituency	Criminal Basis	Criminal Gangs
Portia Simpson *(continued)*	South West St. Andrew *(continued)*	McKoy Lane Waltham Park Road 8th St./Greenwich Farm 9th St./Central Avenue	McKoy Lane Gang 35 Lane Spratt Gang Stumpy Top
Arnold Nicholson	West Central St. Andrew	Olympic Gardens Waterhouse Waterhouse	Drews Land Crew Tower Hill Crew White Lane Crew
Vernon Robinson	West Rural St. Andrew	Rose Hill/Lawrence Tavern	John Crow Gang
Karlene Robertson	N.E. St. Andrew	Grants Pen Area	Leonard Crew
Karl Samuda	N. Central St. Andrew	Maverly	Maverly Gang
Easton Douglas	S.E. St. Andrew	Nannyville	Nannyville Crew
Fritz A. Jackson	South St. Catherine	Braeton/Scarlett Rd.	Punchun Gang
Bruce Golding	Central St. Catherine	Old Harbour Rd. Area	Saddam Crew

Source: Dawn Ritch, *The Jamaican Weekly Gleaner,* Nov. 25–Dec. 1, 1994, 6.

Contrary to the *1995 Report*'s assertion that no money was being laundered in Jamaica, sources at the central bank (the Bank of Jamaica) reported that "billions" of dollars were being laundered. The *Jamaican Weekly Gleaner* quoted a source in the Bank of Jamaica: "significant deposits of foreign currency were crucial to the stability of the economy, so [the government] decided early not to ask commercial banks to question the source of the incoming funds."[27] It is an extraordinary indication of the importance of this dirty money that a committee established in 1993 to seek to have Jamaicans serving jail sentences in the United States returned to Jamaican jails so that they could be close to their families gave as an ameliorating reason that criminals made a "contribution to the development of the country by providing the much-needed foreign exchange."[28]

Money laundering was difficult to control; not just banks were involved but also remittance companies and "cambios," all more numerous as the Jamaican economy and its migrants integrated into U.S. society. In June 1994 there were eighty "cambios" licensed, all operating without many of the restrictions on banks.[29]

Not just the tourist industry felt threatened. In June 1995 businessmen in downtown Kingston closed their shops for two days after a fellow businessman was murdered. The businessmen asked the government to "call out the army" to put down the armed gangs that so evidently controlled their streets.[30]

Others started to join Dawn Ritch in making public what had previously been left unspoken. A schoolteacher described the nearly open operation of crack houses in Kingston, Montego Bay, and other tourist resort areas. Relating what his students told him, he noted that many of these drug dens were either owned by police or protected by them.[31]

Jamaicans finally began mobilizing to take on what they themselves called the war on drugs. Colonel Trevor MacMillan was seconded from the army to the police to fight this war; constant attention and honors have been bestowed on him. As already noted, MacMillan described Jamaica as being in a "pre-Colombia" stage of drug-related crime and corruption. His first task, he noted, was to "clean house" in the police services. From all appearances, MacMillan has been doing a creditable job. As he collected yet another award, this time in New York, he related how he was changing a police force that he found with low morale and little equipment but, worse, in which "criminality, corruption, and power abuse were prominent features."[32]

Yet it has taken the society a long time to mobilize against what was at last being described as the greatest menace to the Jamaican state and society. No one can minimize the threats to all the island's vital institutions for its development: transportation, banking, tourism and, in general, a good reputation as a decent place to live and to invest in.

Trinidad and Tobago

In late 1994, the editors of the *Trinidad Express* decided to do a special report on the Cali cartel "into whose heinous clutches Trinidad and Tobago so easily succumbed."[33] Using data provided by the U.S. embassy, the *Express* noted that, of the one thousand kilograms of cocaine shipped into and through the island every month, less than one percent was ever interdicted. In fact, the island's counternarcotics efforts generally appeared dead in the water. Whatever the problems were, they certainly could not be attributed to lack of legislation or the absence of international assistance.

In 1992 a special unit, the Office of Strategic Services, was put in charge of the overall counternarcotics effort. In 1994, after much debate, the island's parliament passed a comprehensive Dangerous Drugs (Amendment) Bill. Experts were brought in from the U.K. Customs Financial Investigations Branch, the U.S. DEA and Customs, the Royal Canadian Mounted Police, and the French Technical and International Police. Computer access was given to the U.S. El Paso Intelligence Center (EPIC) and island delegates attended a dozen-odd international conferences on drug abuse, drug interdiction, and money laundering. In January 1993, Trinidad and Tobago signed on as a member of the Inter-American Drug Abuse Control Commission, an organ of the Organization of American States. Despite all this activity, breaking out of the "heinous clutches" of the drug cartels is not going to be easy for this twin island state.

According to the 1995 *Report,* "Trinidad and Tobago is not a major producer, consumer or trafficker of illegal drugs, precursor chemicals or a significant money laundering center."[34] This was correct only as regards production of drugs and precursor chemicals. The country consumed large amounts of cocaine, was a major transshipment center, and was fast becoming a significant center of money laundering. Reflecting all this is the escalating violence and corruption that afflicted the society.

On Thursday, June 22, 1995, former Minister of National Security and Attorney General Selwyn Richardson was assassinated in what can only be called a professional hit. The responses in the region revealed how the situation in Trinidad-Tobago was perceived by those in the Caribbean who followed events closely:

"So they have murdered the Trinidadian politician and lawyer who had so deservingly won the enviable reputation of "Mr. Clean" in a society riddled with 'bobol'—corruption—and where mafia-style killings and shocking violent crimes are reminiscent of the crime scene in Jamaica" (veteran Caribbean journalist Rickey Singh, *Weekend Nation,* June 23, 1995, 9). Sir James Mitchell, prime minister of St. Vincent, was quoted in the *Weekend Nation* of June 23, 1995 (16): "I know he is someone who has stood up vigorously and vehemently against the drugs trade and it looks as though someone like him has to be silenced." The ex-minister of legal affairs of Trinidad-Tobago, Hector McLean, commented, "I'm afraid that the carnage and the assassination will continue. Heaven knows who is going to be next" (*Barbados Advocate,* June 23, 1995, 13).

Contrary to the assertions of U.S. authorities, Trinidad-Tobago was in the grip of a massive drug-related crisis. Even though precise statistics were not available, field research indicated a substantial trade coming from Venezuela via the Gulf of Paria.[35] What did not move up the chain of islands was consumed locally. There was heavy use of crack cocaine among unemployed youth and powdered cocaine among the middle class. With virtually no facilities for rehabilitation, the consequence of the epidemic was crime so rampant that it literally changed the architecture, tempo, and style of the country's social life.

Sources in the banking community, who wished to remain anonymous, have for some time alleged that there was significant money laundering taking place on the island. Only recently did former minister of national security Russell Huggins admit that it was "a very serious problem" especially since the local money launderers have had extensive international links.[36]

While these are the all-too-evident manifestations of the drug trade, potentially the greatest damage was the threat, through drug-related corruption, to the very structures that should be stemming the problem: the security and criminal justice systems. Despite multiple well-documented requests for extradition of alleged major drug kingpins by the United Kingdom and the United States, not a single person had been extradited nor had one single significant drug dealer been convicted in a Trinidad Court. Witness intimidation and even murder are some of the reasons why.

The situation with the security forces is arguably even more threatening. Their corruption, and especially their suspected involvement in the drug trade, had been the subject of an inquiry that produced a report (the Scott Drug Report) submitted to Parliament in 1989. While the report was silent on names of drug dealers, it left no doubt as to the seriousness of the local situation with regard to drug traffic and drug addiction. Fifty-one police officers were suspended and Police Commissioner Randolph ("Rambo") Burroughs resigned after being indicted as a drug dealer; he was acquitted in court. As subsequent events would prove (including the murder of a policeman in a failed illicit drug operation), the situation was worse than what the government revealed. By the early 1990s, the evidence of drug-related criminality and the participation of members of the security forces in it had become so serious and public concern so strongly expressed that the newly elected government of Patrick Manning went abroad for help. The United Kingdom responded to a request from the government of Trinidad-Tobago and sent a high-level investigative team from the New Scotland Yard. The general conclusions of this foreign team were that corruption was evidently widespread within the police force but that a more thorough investigation was not possible for three reasons: (1) after seven four-week tours, the British detectives were still not sure whom they could trust in the Police Service; (2) they had no clout and were given none by the Trinidad-Tobago government and thus could not compel testimony; and (3), worst of all, their work was being actively sabotaged by corrupt higher-ups. "There had been promotions, transfers, and acting appointments," said the foreign investigators, "which have had the effect of giving a clear message to the honest element in the police service that the old and corrupt guard was still very much in control."[37]

Corroboration for the Scotland Yard's assessment came on June 20, 1994, when the minister of national security of Trinidad-Tobago reported to Parliament that major parts of the documentation and evidence collected by the New Scotland Yard had disappeared. His explanation was typical of the political bureaucratese that some officials of democratically elected governments in the region use to explain their incompetence or incapacity in the face of organized crime's growing role: "That [the loss of the Scotland Yard documents] is the kind of problem that I would find it extremely difficult to lay blame at the footsteps of any Government, because the Government does not have control over the police files, the court files, and that sort of thing."[38]

Trinidadians can be excused for being cynical, knowing that none of the over one hundred officers identified as corrupt by the New Scotland Yard Report had been sanctioned even as the attorney general discussed new bills to deal with the nature of bail and one-way mirrors in identification parades. A former minister of national security, George Padmore, commented on the disingenuousness of the government's excuses at a time when the drug problem had taken on "octopus-like proportions" and the police service appeared to have "careened out of control."[39] The assassination of ex-Attorney General Selwyn Richardson was evidence that Padmore had not been off the mark. It also revealed, however, that there had been no decisive actions by the Trinidad government to regain control over law and order, justice, and simple civility.

In July 1995, the leader of the opposition, Basdeo Panday, threatened several times to use Parliament to reveal the names of government ministers who were involved in the drug trade. Hours before his scheduled declaration on July 28, his house was firebombed. Like most others in this society, Panday got the message. "I don't want to be a dead martyr," he told the press, "I have nothing to say about drugs again."[40]

While the government—and the society generally—appear immobilized, the strains on that historically divided multiethnic society intensify as each ethnic group accuses the other of being the godfathers of the trade. It is my judgment that elements of all groups are involved: Indian, Black, and Syrian-Lebanese. This is a societywide crisis, not a class or ethnic issue.

Eastern Caribbean and the Bahamas

If Jamaica and Trinidad-Tobago have the size and diversity of resources to provide the wherewithal to a government with the political will to redress the damage from the drug trade, this is less the case with smaller islands. In islands such as Antigua, St. Kitts, St. Lucia, Dominica, St. Vincent, and the Bahamas, the damage can be so massive that a truly monumental effort, political, civic, and economic, is required to wean them back to a healthy state of affairs.

In the few paragraphs dedicated to the Eastern Caribbean, the 1995 Report noted that there had been an increase in drug activity through an "escalation" in air drops off the islands. It also noted that the islands' political stability was menaced because the political parties had become "so vulnerable to corruption."[41] Finally, there was increasing addiction to crack cocaine and, thus, increasing crime, all of which represented a major threat to the main economic enterprise of these islands, tourism. It is generally agreed that the goal of the traffickers is to use these islands as stepping stones toward the booming markets in Puerto Rico and the U.S. Virgin Islands, both designated by the DEA as High Intensity Drug Trafficking Areas (HIDTA).

This analysis starts with St. Kitts–Nevis; its 45,000 people have been the most traumatized. The best way to tell the complicated sequence of events in that nation is to cite seriatim the headlines from the then opposition (since July 1995 the new government) party's newspaper, the *Labour Spokesman* (LS), and other papers. These are some headlines:

June 22, 1994: "Ambassador Herbert, Wife, and Fishing Companions Missing."

July 9, 1994: "US$50,000 Reward Offered for recovery of Herbert."

July 13, 1994: Reprint of a whole page from *Business Week* (May 30, 1994) entitled "Confessions of a Money Launderer." The confessions were of Miami lawyer, Kenneth W. Ryock, arrested for laundering the money of several major Miami drug lords. "The Caribbean and its banks," says Ryock, "constitute a black hole of money laundering." No Caribbean names are listed.

July 23, 1994: "Arrival of Scotland Yard Officials." The *Toronto Star* says this is related to the Herbert disappearance. St. Kitts government denies this. *LS* quotes the *Toronto Star* to the effect that Herbert "had been the target of numerous rumors regarding corruption, money laundering and other activities."

August 6, 1994: "Colombians, Drug Runners, Money Launderers Behind Herbert Disappearance."

August 10, 1994: "Political Interference Frustrates Investigations of Scotland Yard Detectives."

October 8, 1994: "Dark Cloud Bursts Open on St Kitts: Minister's Son, Girlfriend, and Car Disappear Mysteriously."

October 15, 1994: "Jude Matthew [Deputy Commissioner of Police, in charge of drug investigations] Shot Dead."

October 23, 1994: The *Sunday Times* (London) in major story, "Drug Find Sparks Terror on Island," reveals that there were 14 Scotland Yard detectives in St. Kitts, and that Matthews was about to make the link between Herbert's banking activities for the drug lords and his disappearance.

October 29, 1994: *LS* claims that St. Kitts government handed out 100 diplomatic passports to "white collar criminals and drug barons."

November 12, 1994: "Deputy Prime Minister's Sons Arrested on Illegal Guns and Drugs Charges."

202 Anthony P. Maingot

November 19, 1994: "Crime Wave Linked to Several Hundred Kilos of Colombian Cocaine, Says Scotland Yard."

January 29, 1995: The *Sunday Telegraph* (London) publishes lengthy investigative essay, "The Devil in St. Kitts." Describes how Ambassador Herbert was tied to smuggling of arms to IRA in 1986 and since then to money laundering for Colombian and Miami drug lords; Herbert was the Caribbean link, through his bank in Anguilla (Caribbean Commercial Bank), with Miami drug lawyer Kenneth W. Ryock. Herbert's disappearance might have to do with the cartels' anger at his inability to stop Scotland Yard from taking incriminating files out of his bank.

April 22, 1995: "Missing Ambassador Herbert's Son in Custody: Guns, Drugs, Ammunition and Illegal Anguillans the Centre of Investigation."

June 3, 1995: "Thieving and Corruption Gone Mad in Government." *Editorial:* "The criminals all love the PAM [People's Action Movement] because [Prime Minister] Simmonds, as Minister of Home Affairs, has aided and abetted their activities by politicizing and virtually destroying the Police Force."

In June 1995, St. Kitts geared up for elections and, predictably, crime and corruption were the opposition's main themes. Prime Minister Kennedy Simmonds's government pushed themes that had been very effective during the cold war: anticommunism and religious beliefs. To the governing party's paper the *Democrat* (June 24, 1995), the choice in this election was "between democracy and communism." On June 19, the prime minister and his cabinet, the diplomatic corps, and representatives of all religious groups on the island attended a Service of Remembrance for Ambassador William Herbert at the Anglican Cathedral. Ambassador Herbert was eulogized as a fine, upstanding, and pious member of the community. No mention anywhere of his gun-running and money-laundering activities or the fact that his only remaining son seemed to have picked up the business.

Many of the island's elite were sticking their heads in the sand, in total denial of the rot that surrounded them. The most important weapon in society's hands, however, is the vote. On July 2 citizens went to the polls and gave the opposition St. Kitts Labour Party seven out of Parliament's eight seats. After his loss, defeated Prime Minister Simmonds was still unwilling to admit that the people responded against the crime and corruption that so evidently permeated that society. It was a "normal" desire for change, he said.

The Bahamas presents an interesting parallel to St. Kitts–Nevis. Few governments had been more investigated for corruption than Lynden Pindling's in the Bahamas. The various commissions of enquiry never quite found Pindling personally guilty of any specific cases of corruption. They had repeatedly revealed widespread official corruption, however. In the words of a

1984 commission, they were "alarmed by the extent to which persons in the public service have been corrupted by the illegal [drug] trade. . . . Apathy and a weak public opinion have led to the present unhappy and undesirable state of affairs in the nation."[42] The corruption was so palpable, the presence of the Colombian cartels so evident (capo Carlos Lehder "owned" his own island at one point), and U.S. pressure so strong that many outsiders repeatedly expected adverse electoral consequences for Pindling's Progressive Liberal Party, in power since 1973. That was not to be: Pindling won three elections between 1973 and 1992 by comfortable margins despite serious charges of drug trafficking and general malfeasance. He fully expected to be reelected in 1992 but was roundly defeated by a party that promised to call on the FBI, the DEA, the Scotland Yard, and the Canadian Mounted Police to return the nation to "an acceptable level of accountability." They have done a commendable job in one area: transshipment. They have not been able to control another: money laundering.

Antigua-Barbuda

There is a widely held sentiment in the Caribbean that Antigua has been living quite on the margins of the law for some time. Antigua's award-winning muckraking newspaper, the *Outlet,* describes the situation: "Antigua and Barbuda is no longer the laughing stock of the region. It is regarded as the last frontier of the Wild Wild West, where there is neither law, constitution, nor the appearance of fairness" (May 19, 1995, 3). This is not a new situation. Since independence, Antigua and Barbuda have been involved in the most sordid affairs, with few if any negative consequences to its ruling dynasty, the Bird family. It is not the purpose here to detail all the schemes in which the Birds have been involved.[43] I just cite a few specific cases that nearly turned the state into an agent of international terrorism. They reveal the depths to which the links with international drug cartels can take a Caribbean state.

On June 11, 1995, the *New York Times* announced on its front page Cuba's arrest of Robert Vesco, fugitive from U.S. justice. The *Times* revealed what people in Costa Rica, the Bahamas, and Antigua had long known: Vesco had been a major figure in the drug trade and a master at the corruption that invariably accompanied it. Vesco and many others like him have always known just where they would be welcomed.

There had never been anything hidden about their criminal intentions. They invariably attempt to secure some "sovereign" pied á terre from which to conduct their skulduggery with impunity. This was attempted in Anguilla in the early 1970s. Two attempts were made to secure Dominica for the mob;

one was a 1979 attempted invasion of mercenaries led by members of the Ku Klux Klan of Louisiana, including David Duke, erstwhile candidate to the U.S. Senate.

In Antigua, "the Sovereign Order of New Aragón" schemed to establish a "principality" in Barbuda, the sister island of Antigua. The deal collapsed after its front man, the actor Rossano Brazzi, was arrested for smuggling guns for the Italian mob. It is not known what the links between Vesco and the New Aragón group were, but they were in Antigua at the same time and both had schemes for a "sovereign" base in Barbuda.

While these schemes did not come to fruition, the Medellín Cartel did better. This Antigua case—as revealed by the Official Commission of Inquiry—exposes the depth and spread of corruption, indeed, its internationalization.[44] It also clearly reveals the links between internationalized corruption and violence. The charges were that ten tons of arms were bought in Israel, the end user to be the Antigua Defence Force (less than one hundred men, already armed by the U.S. government). The weapons ended up on the farm of Medellín Cartel henchman José Rodríguez Gacha. It was proven that some of the guns were used in the assassination of popular Colombian presidential candidate Luis Carlos Galán. Among the many terrifying details revealed by the Commission of Inquiry are the following:

1. While Antigua had "a heavy moral duty" to Colombia and the world to pursue this matter, its meager diplomatic and police capabilities meant that it could not alone pursue the investigations, which had to cover "over four continents."

2. Despite the wider conclusion that small Caribbean states cannot confront the cartels on their own, "Intellectual collaboration to elicit the truth about Israeli firearms finding their way into the hands of Colombian drug barons was not to be easily achieved" (Blom-Cooper, "Guns for Antigua," 40). "The British government," said Blom-Cooper, "have turned a blind eye" to evidence that their nationals, operating as skilled mercenaries, "turned untrained killers into trained killers" (34).

3. On the central role of the city of Miami: "This conspiracy was, in my judgment, hatched in Miami and developed in that city." (37).

4. On the role of the banks: "I find it wholly unacceptable that banks in America, whose services were used to facilitate what can without exaggeration be described as a crime against humanity, should be permitted through the inaction of the American authorities to hide evidence of that crime behind the cloak of confidentiality" (37).

5. Finally, and critically, the commission called attention to the role of wider, more enduring corrupt relationships between the principals in the scheme and high officials of the Antigua government, which called for "fur-

ther investigation" (83). Two questions in particular required urgent investigation: (a) what, if any, were the roles of Israeli and British mercenaries in establishing a training camp for terrorists in Antigua, and (b) were there plans to train Tamil guerrillas in that camp in exchange for access to the East Asian heroin trade?

These questions were partly answered by an investigation undertaken by the Permanent Subcommittee on Investigations of the U.S. Senate. In a hearing held in February 1991, the subcommittee established conclusively that: (1) British and Israeli mercenaries, under contract to Colombian drug cartels, had been operating in Colombia since 1988; (2) that because of pressure from the Colombian government they decided to shift operations to Antigua; (3) Antigua would serve both as a training base and conduit of guns for the cartel; and (4) that the Antigua deal was only one part of a much deeper and wider operation. As the subcommittee noted: "This transaction provides a case study of the multinational nature of arms trafficking. In this case, we had weapons made in Israel purportedly going to a Caribbean nation which wound up with the drug cartels in Colombia, financed through banks and individuals in Panama, the U.S., Israel, Antigua and, probably, Colombia."

The subcommittee was adamant that efforts against such international networks had to be multinational in scope. By the 1990s few could doubt that the most serious threat to the security of the Caribbean stemmed from the drug trade and its links to violence.

Despite an election in which the corruption of the elder, V. C. Bird, and his oldest son, V. C. Jr., were issues, the new administration of the second son, Lester Bird, has proven to be equally corrupt. The case of the youngest son, Ivor Bird, illustrates it. On May 5, 1995, custom officials arrested Ivor Bird and a courier from Venezuela carrying a bag loaded with cocaine. What surprised Antiguans was that they had been arrested at all; those in the know had been aware of numerous such deliveries in the past to "Mr. Ivor Bird, ZDK radio, St. Johns." Antiguans were not surprised that Ivor would be immediately bailed out by his father, the ex–prime minister. The only question was whether the US$250,000 check used for bail came from the trade union controlled by the Birds. Also curious, though hardly surprising, was the immediate retaining of highly paid British criminal attorney John Platt Mills to represent Ivor Bird.[45]

That this was not some isolated case of individual wrongdoing but rather another in a pattern of hemispherewide drug trafficking activities was made evident by the fact that the courier arrested, Marcus Trotman, is the son of Rufus Trotman, an employee of the Barbadian embassy in Caracas dismissed for his alleged involvement in a drug scandal in 1989. He was accused of using the embassy's diplomatic pouch for transporting drugs.[46]

206 Anthony P. Maingot

Even as this case was unfolding, on June 2, 1995, the *Outlet* reported a find of four hundred kilos of cocaine, dropped at Shell Beach. No arrests were made and worse, there was no apparent or, at least, visible indignation by the society. On May 26, 1995, Tim Hector, editor of the *Outlet,* noted the virtual conspiracy of silence: "In spite [of all the skulduggery], the Bar Association remained with its legal tail between its monied legs; the Police Association was dead silent. The Evangelists directed their attack at "The Communists" and therefore saw nothing and heard nothing. Civil society is in a shambles. . . . Everything is permissible."

Including, it appears, murder. On July 14, 1995, Johnny Barton, brother of Antigua's antidrug task force chief, Charles Barton, was assassinated. Charles Barton was the one who had arrested Ivor Bird for smuggling cocaine. It is not safe to perform one's duties in societies like Trinidad, St. Kitts, and Antigua.

In these cases, corruption at the highest levels has led dangerously close to the collapse of civil society and collective vigilance. As distinct from Jamaica and the Bahamas, where there appears to be some government response to the awakening of public awareness and concern, in these Antiguan cases there has been little if any government response. There is great expectation in St. Kitts that the electoral defeat of the government will turn things around. Whether there can be a complete victory in any single country, without a broader regional victory against drugs, is an open question. The cases of Belize and Barbados illustrate how varied and different Caribbean societies' responses to the drug problem—and to the violence and corruption it spawns—have been.

Tackling Corruption: Belize Versus Barbados

In 1990, the prime minister of Belize, Manuel Esquivel, startled his society by declaring that the drug trade was a greater threat to the nation's security than the long-standing Guatemalan territorial claim. As he began to make the necessary legal and institutional changes to meet the challenge, there was a hue and a cry about this being an American imposition and a threat to civil rights. "It is feared in some quarters," wrote a respected Belizean academic, "that under sanction from the United States, the Belize government may use the enforcement of drug laws to become more repressive toward its citizens." She noted that this sentiment was shared regionwide.[47] Indeed, as already noted, academics in the region have been notoriously slow to recognize the drug menace as an issue not just for the United States but for each and every island.

There is no evidence that the feared erosion of civil rights has materialized in Belize (or elsewhere in the English-speaking Caribbean). Belize succeeded in eradicating much of the marijuana cultivation, but success was not achieved in three other areas of the illicit trade: cocaine transshipment, money laundering, and the sale of passports and visas.

Given its location near Guatemala and Mexico, its two hundred miles of coast, its two hundred cays, its well-established ethnic networks through New Orleans up to Chicago, it was to be expected that Belize would be involved as the trade shifted from the Caribbean to Central America and Mexico. It was also predictable that local drug consumption would rise as the entrepot business increased; crack cocaine became a major social problem. With no criminal laws against money laundering, there has been a sudden boom in companies registering under the archaic International Business Companies Act. This is part of the offshore Caribbeanwide scene and directly related to increased flows of drug monies into and through the region.

Most notorious has been Belize's involvement in one of the most troublesome results of corruption and the trade in drugs, weapons, and illegal aliens: the sale of official documents. According to testimony in April 1995 before the U.S. Senate Subcommittee on Terrorism, Narcotics, and International Operations, Taiwanese criminal organizations operate in various countries including: Dominican Republic, Bahamas, Jamaica, Guatemala, Costa Rica, Honduras, Nicaragua, Panama, Bolivia, Brazil, Paraguay, and Belize. Belize in particular, testified the director of the Center for the Study of Asian Organized Crime, is "owned" by the Guatemala-based Taiwanese syndicates. They have, he said, "literally purchased the country of Belize and its Minister of Immigration."[48] In June 1995, the Belizean government dismissed the director of immigration and began a thorough housecleaning in that office. This effort has been quite insufficient: corruption generally, but especially in transshipment of drugs and money laundering, has yet to be seriously tackled.

Belizeans are quick to ask rhetorically, on just how many fronts can we attack this hydra-headed problem with our limited resources? Sadly, the answer is precisely the one they expect: not many. Even more sadly is that this still leaves the question, can any small state afford not to attack on *all* fronts? The history of the Caribbean demonstrates that it cannot, that the whole society has to be geared to tackling corruption everywhere, since the drug cartels are constantly searching for "soft spots."[49] Barbados stands as testimony that this can be done in the Caribbean.

In May 1995, Prime Minister Owen Arthur's newly elected government confronted its first cabinet crisis: the minister of tourism stood accused of

Table 10-4   Arrests in Barbados, 1990–1995

Year	Arrests	Increase
1990	568	16%
1991	661	
1992	523	18%
1993	617	
1994	838	35.8%
1995 (Jan.–Mar.)	219	15.8%

drawing US$700 per diem on a recent trip abroad, double the official allowance. It was sufficient cause for dismissal. In early June 1995, the Barbadian Commission on Casino Gambling submitted its report and recommendations. By a vote of five to two the commission voted against legalizing casino gambling. According to the local press, the majority report elaborated on the experiences in the rest of the Caribbean: casino gambling, they said, "is associated with increased crime, money laundering, drug trafficking, fraud, prostitution, and violence."[50] Barbados's government led by example in establishing probity and transparency.

Barbados has not escaped the ravages of the drug trade. In August 1994 Barbadian police seized US$2.2 million worth of cocaine destined for New York. Two months later, police arrested two Colombian citizens after they attempted to retrieve US$5 million worth of cocaine dropped offshore. The destination appeared to be Europe. Police figures, as noted in table 10-4, indicate that in 1994 there was a steep rise in crime, increasingly drug-related.[51]

In response, Barbados implemented a new "law and order" program; primarily, it puts more policemen on the beat. In Barbados, the concept of law and order is related to an intrinsic understanding of the nature of the society and the economy: both are increasingly service-based and, thus, "open." The island's leadership is quite aware of the dangers posed by international criminal monies to such openness and are concerned to establish a "real" rather than a "public relations" reputation. "Barbados," said Prime Minister Arthur, "places [a] premium on its reputation as a place where sound and reputable off-shore business is undertaken and will seek to retain its image for total integrity and will continue to be willing to sign exchange of information agreements with other countries."[52]

The Barbadian governing elites have made an explicit decision in favor of strict ethical standards and administrative transparency. In so opting, Barbados bucks the trend in the Caribbean. As Minister of State Phillip Goddard told a Miami gathering, Barbados has no intention of giving safe haven to the criminals of the world, and that includes tax dodgers. Rather than no taxes, Barbados has opted for low taxes; rather than secrecy laws and numbered accounts for faceless clients, Barbados insists on knowing the identity of the client. As its attorney general, David Simmonds, has put it, preventing money laundering and combatting crime serve the "central objective" of promoting economic development and combatting poverty.[53] There is in Barbados a realistic sense of what some of the causes of corruption in the Caribbean are and that they are not themselves immune from these dangers. Attorney General Simmons summed up the situation in three specific points:

1. Barbados, like the rest of the region, needs substantial foreign capital and resources in order to develop.

2. Barbados's capacity, like that of the rest of the region, to check and investigate each source and each applicant is very underdeveloped.

3. Criminals have the advantage of flexibility of maneuver through the various and often contradictory national laws.

If forewarned is forearmed, then it has to be said that Barbados's governing elites have taken care of forearmed. Their actions remain a model of good governance in a region where many states are sinking in the rot brought about by the drug trade.

Conclusion

Despite its relative insignificance to the total scheme of U.S. geopolitical and geoeconomic concerns, the Caribbean retains a certain *droit de regard.* Its location, the shared mutual interests, including the definition of what the threats are, and, thus, its potential for causing either good or great evil, all make it so.

The Caribbean Sea acts both as a barrier and as a bridge. Both functions favor the new internationalization of corruption and violence. By balkanizing the region into relatively weak nation states while at the same time facilitating the flow of international commerce and transnational activities of some of the world's great producers and exporters, this sea leaves many international activities beyond the control of governments. The result is often an asymmetry in maneuvering capabilities between national and international actors. This asymmetry is augmented and perpetuated by the technical and electronic revolution that gives even private parties enormous capacities of communication, including the electronic transfer of capital. The international cartels have also preferential access to human talent; indeed, as ex-President Alfonso López Michelsen of Colombia has noted, the transferability of skills and technology from legitimate industry to the drug trade has made the latter a truly modern transnational industry. The Caribbean provides the bridge between producers and consumers in that industry while its modern banking system provides virtually impenetrable shelter to its profits.

Throughout the region, corruption has engendered violence and uncertainty about the loyalty of forces of law and order. "The most serious implication for the region becoming a major transshipment area," notes one source, "is the corruption of the island nations' political systems."[54] Efforts to deal with the corruption and violence that the drug trade has engendered stumble on a real paradox in the basically conservative societies of the Caribbean. Despite their emphasis on piety, there tends to be a fairly blasé approach to behavior that, if not directly corrupt, is at a minimum conducive to corruption. There might be two sources of this: the admiration for individual efforts and material success stories and the propensity to live and let live. As the cases of the Bahamas, St. Kitts, Antigua, and Trinidad illustrate, it takes a long time for the natural capacity for moral indignation of these societies to express itself and, when it does, it tends to be at the polls. While experience shows that such reactions do eventually occur in these societies, in the interlude the damage being done is great and often hard to reverse. What is called for is not reactive indignation but the kind of ongoing demands for ethical vigilance so evident in Barbados.

In his poignant 1990 book, *Tropical Gangsters,* Robert Klitgaard addressed two fundamental questions: How can one help a "recalcitrant, inefficient, sometimes corrupt" government move forward? And what are the "creative possibilities and the inherent limitations" to outside assistance? The questions are equally applicable to the Caribbean; the answers, however, differ from Klitgaard's, who spoke of "decadence" in the African case. There is no intrinsic or structural decadence among these island societies. There are cases where a *government* with corrupt members survives by co-opting significant elite sectors and through the indifference of the society. The speed and style of public mobilization and moral indignation used in elections to "throw the bums out" varies from one island to the other. It took a long time to occur in the Bahamas and in St. Kitts; it has yet to occur in Antigua.

The whole Caribbean has in Barbados a model of what a Caribbean society can do through the maximal use of its creative possibilities. The days when geopolitical considerations made overlooking maladministration in particular cases a necessity are gone. The threats are different; the strategies to ward them off must be adjusted accordingly. Concerned outside actors should identify good local initiatives, reward them according to a developing standard of good governance, and make sure that they are seen to be so doing.

Chapter 11

Central American Regional Security

Postwar Prospects for Peace and Democracy

Caesar D. Sereseres

After decades of violence and conflict all the Central American wars have finally concluded. Guatemala's was the last to end. On December 29, 1996, after nearly a decade of talking about peace and some five years of actual negotiations between the Guatemalan government and the guerrillas, the Guatemalan National Revolutionary Unity (URNG) officially ended the thirty-five-year war.[1] Beginning with the Guatemalan insurgency of the mid-1960s, until 1996 at least one country has been engaged in an internal war in the Central American region.

The Central American region (Guatemala, Belize, Honduras, El Salvador, Nicaragua, Costa Rica, and Panama) consists of some thirty million inhabitants. The region, its inhabitants, and its governing systems have endured some thirty years of intense, internationalized warfare. The postwar search for an appropriate, democratically based civil-military relationship, with military and police institutions having defined missions, and a national security doctrine supportive of national and regional needs will be one major factor in shaping the democratic future of the region.[2]

From 1979 to 1996, one army (the Panama Defense Forces) was militarily defeated and demobilized by direct U.S. military intervention. A second army (the Nicaraguan National Guard) was defeated on the battlefield by the Sandinista insurrection. El Salvador's military was forced to accept major institutional reforms as part of a peace agreement. During the 1980s, Nicaragua had the largest army (the Sandinista Popular Army). Yet this army, too, was forced to separate from its political parents in the Sandinista National Liberation Front (FSLN) after an unexpected electoral defeat in 1990; in the 1990s, this army was subjected to significant downsizing and role modification in the governing of society as a result of a U.S.-supported insurgency and Sandinista election defeat in 1990.[3] In Guatemala, the army carried out significant internal reforms in anticipation of a peace agreement that would (and did) call for such reforms; in late 1996, the Guatemalan army agreed to a complex peace settlement that created uncertainties about its future after thirty-five years of fighting a guerrilla insurgency. Lastly, a small military force emerged in Belize with the departure of British security forces from the former colony.

Hundreds of thousands of lives were lost in the conflicts of Guatemala, El Salvador, and Nicaragua. Thousands disappeared in these three countries during the three decades. Honduras did not escape the political violence of the region. While the numbers were much lower, battles with Honduran guerrillas took place in the early 1980s, and there were political killings and disappearances. Hundreds of thousands more were displaced within their own countries or fled their homelands as refugees to other Central American countries, Mexico, or the United States.[4] The wars of Central America from the 1960s into the mid-1990s had been internationalized and conducted within the cold war context. Global actors from Asia, Africa, the Middle East, Eastern and Western Europe, and North America participated in the region's conflicts. The cold war reached into the villages of Quiché, Guatemala; Chalatenango, El Salvador; and Quilalí, Nicaragua.

The Honduran armed forces never recovered from the one hundred million dollars in security assistance provided by the United States between 1980–1990. The presence of the Nicaraguan Resistance (so-called Contras), U.S. military forces and operations, and large amounts of U.S. security assistance during the period ended in deprofessionalization and politicization for this army. By the mid-1990s Honduras was receiving token amounts of security and economic assistance from the United States. The Honduran army lay institutionally weakened—barely a shell of an organization in 1997. The end of the Central American wars would find El Salvador, Panama, Costa Rica, Belize, and Nicaragua attempting to establish strong, professional, civil police forces as the primary state institutions responsible for public security.[5] By the mid-1990s, the Central American region had half the number of soldiers that were in uniform at the high point of the wars ten years before; and private police and security personnel outnumbered uniformed civil police in the region.

Several conclusions concerning Central American security issues are suggestive of the organizational and doctrinal challenges facing those who govern in the region—civilian, military, or police officials alike. These conclusions are: (1) military institutions are smaller and have reduced budgets but are expected to be more complex and expand their missions into nontraditional security areas like environment and international crime; (2) there is less state violence but increased common and social crime and violence throughout the region; (3) there is a clear vacuum of authority largely as a result of military withdrawal and insufficient civil police and judicial system capabilities; (4) the socioeconomic conditions that contributed to the wars of Central America since the 1960s are actually as bad if not worse today; (5) the nature, role, and size of the state is undergoing a rigorous debate and restructuring; and (6) the relationships between civilians and the military are evolving as the search for new missions and security doctrines is discussed and debated.

Of significance is the growing complexity of the small military institutions of the region. Complexity is seen in such areas as computerized budgets and personnel pay, higher levels of education for military officers, establishment of civil-military education institutions, military involvement in environmental issues, military ventures into economic enterprises, and the development of elaborate military social security and pension systems.

The Democracy and Security Nexus

All the countries in the region have gone through at least two cycles of democratic elections. The May 1993 *auto-golpe* of President Jorge Serrano in Guatemala failed and he was replaced by Human Rights Ombudsman Ramiro de León Carpio. Elections were held in Guatemala in November 1995 and a second-round election was held in January 1996 to determine the winner between the top two presidential candidates; Alvaro Arzú narrowly defeated Alfonso Portillo, the candidate backed by the former president, General Efraín Ríos Montt. In Nicaragua, elections were held in October 1996 when anti-Sandinista candidate and former mayor of Managua Arnoldo Alemán won an overwhelming victory over the Sandinista candidate Daniel Ortega.

In every country, a civil-military dialogue is under way regarding the roles and missions of the armed forces and civil police. In Belize, Costa Rica, and Panama the focus of attention is how to develop professional police forces capable of securing the nation's borders while also managing public safety. In Guatemala, Honduras, El Salvador, and Nicaragua the relationships between the police and the armed forces are being discussed, debated, and legislated in public. Civil police independence from the military is a prime goal but also slow and expensive and has clearly contributed to a security vacuum throughout the region—opening up these societies and national territories to old-style rural banditry, aggressive urban gangs, and high-technology international crime organizations.

The exponential growth of security vacuums in the Central American region constitutes a multidimensional process that includes: (1) diminished military presence in rural and urban areas; (2) smaller military forces and resources to provide support to police activities; (3) the growth in common crime as urbanization and unemployment increase; and (4) inadequate police and judicial systems to cope with growing population, weak economies, and a less active military institution to provide security.

Guatemala is a good example of this security vacuum. With the peace agreement signed in December 1997, the military institution is less involved in internal security matters and (unless specifically called upon by the president) provides little operational and intelligence support to the police. This is a significant change from the previous three decades during the fight against the URNG guerrillas. The military commissioner system (rural deputies and informants) has been disbanded by presidential order. And, over a period of several years, the self-defense patrols established by the army in the rural areas to fight the guerrillas, and represent law and order in the absence of police, have disappeared. Both systems provided security (some critics argue that the paramilitary groups were as much the sources of insecurity and violence) in the vast areas where neither military nor police forces are to be found. In addition, Guatemala has a civil police force of approximately twelve thousand, of which some eight thousand are assigned to the capital where it is estimated that six to eight thousand gang members known as *maras* are active in a multitude of criminal activities. In Guatemala City, home to nearly two million inhabitants, there are over fifteen thousand armed private policeman who are paid to protect individuals, businesses, residences, vehicles, and goods. Indicative of the inadequacies of the justice system, the majority of those in prison have yet to have the opportunity to go to trial for their alleged crimes.

The discussion among civilians and between civilians and military and police force officials can be found in three related but separate defense-security paradigms: (1) the environmental-ecological-demographic threat; (2) the threat from organized domestic and international crime organizations related to drugs, money laundering, immigration, stolen vehicles from the region and the United States, weapons and ammunition, contraband goods, kidnapping and extortion, and street gangs; and (3) the traditional security threats posed by guerrillas, paramilitary groups, and the potential for territorial and border disputes.[6]

The discussions and debate between civilians and security (civil police and military) officials in these countries are influenced by the focus on one or more of these security paradigms. Even within the officer corps of the region's armed forces, the internal debate over size, role, and missions forces the discussion to move from one paradigm to another. These discussions touch on the relationship between police and military institutions, the nature of the national security threats, and the ability and willingness of governments to provide the appropriate political and budget support for the military and police institutions to assume responsibility for managing, within a democratic setting, the security threats.

As each of the region's wars reached a peace settlement, the discussions in the societies of the region became open, candid, and productive. The core questions that government leaders and the civil societies sought to answer include: (1) the role of civilians in the development of national defense and security doctrines; (2) the development of political and policy mechanisms to manage military and police institutions and operations; (3) the ability and willingness of governments and their respective societies to support the needed military and police budgets to face the spectrum of perceived traditional and nontraditional national threats; and (4) the willingness and ability of the governments in the region to cooperate on military, civil police, and general security matters.[7]

Military Missions and the Institutional Dimension of Security

All the armed forces in the region are seeking ways to modify their missions. Each continues to hold on to its respective constitutional requirements to defend national territory, sovereignty, and the constitution itself. Beyond this constitutional mandate, the armies of Guatemala, Honduras, Nicaragua, and to a lesser extent, El Salvador (where the peace accords dictate in large measure the doctrine, structure, and missions of the armed forces) are seeking a practical accommodation to the challenges of the three security paradigms. For the late 1990s, there are four basic questions that the armed forces must address: (1) the downsizing of their force structure and budget; (2) the defining of postinsurgency and post–cold war threat perceptions and national security doctrines; (3) the domestic role expansion options; and (4) the mission externalization options, i.e., primarily United Nations peacekeeping missions beyond the Western Hemisphere.[8]

The military institutions of the region understand and accept the necessity to downsize in postwar society. The real policy struggle focuses on the need for military institutional stability and legitimacy and defending the military vocation in these societies after decades of war, coups, military governments, human and civil rights abuses, and large defense budgets. Role expansion will largely depend on the civilians. Elected civilian leaders in the executive and legislative branches of these democratic governments must decide if the military is the most appropriate state instrument to protect national treasures and the environment, engage in national socioeconomic development projects in isolated rural areas, and be a vehicle for national service.[9]

Mission externalization is largely a white elephant. While Panama, Costa Rica, and Guatemala have provided military and civilian personnel for peacekeeping operations in the hemisphere, most military and police institutions in Central America (with the exception of Guatemala) have neither the professional competence nor the operational capabilities to successfully engage in peacekeeping missions—especially beyond the Western Hemisphere. The mission externalization option of peacekeeping is not feasible for either civilian governmental leaders or the military and police institutions of Central America.

The institutional dimension of national security is the most interesting, yet the most problematic in the region. Only Guatemala has seriously attempted to establish a national security council and intelligence secretariat directly responsible to the president. Both institutions would be staffed primarily by civilians and headed by a civilian appointed by the president.[10] There is considerable debate both in Guatemala and Washington concerning the appropriateness of such security institutions, with critics arguing that such legislation would make the president a captive of the military intelligence community. However, such a secretariat of the presidency could provide the needed institutional setting to bring civilian professionals (including police and judicial branch officials) into the national security process and into closer dialogue with the military institution.

In other countries of the region, the concept of a national security council exists in name only. There is often little more than infrequent meetings between the president and a few cabinet members to discuss crisis issues with little or no professional support staff. For the most part, in Central America national security doctrine and security and defense policies are discussed and implemented within desperate government institutional settings and tend to be highly personalized.

Conflict Escalation and Conflict Management

There are points of potential conflict throughout Central America.[11] One is the Guatemala-Mexico border, which once provided easy access for Guatemalan guerrillas to establish a strategic rear guard for logistics, communication, and political support. With the war over in Guatemala, the Zapatistas (EZLN) in the southern state of Chiapas have been left alone with their idea of a greater "Mayan" highlands war covering southern Mexico and Guatemala. (The EZLN guerrillas once threatened the Mexican government with the idea of an alliance between themselves and the URNG.) The Mexican and Guatemalan governments, military commands, and intelligence services have been cooperating since the Zapatista army initiated military operations in January 1994. Mexico also played an important role in facilitating negotiations between the Guatemalan government and the URNG guerrillas by acting as the host nation for the peace talks and by supporting the voluntary return of tens of thousands of Guatemalan refugees who chose to return to their homes.

A second troublesome issue is the boundary between El Salvador and Honduras on land and in the Gulf of Fonseca. Demarcations of this boundary have been largely resolved by the International Court at The Hague, but uncertainties remain for Salvadoran citizens living in southern Honduras and for the status of several small islands in the gulf. The two countries are working out the court's judgment on the enclaves along the border and the islands in the Gulf of Fonseca. It has been slow but both sides through bilateral commissions and periodic contact between governments and military institutions have sought to avoid potentially serious military provocations or conflicts. In the long run, the more serious issue is the growing number of Salvadorans who have returned to southern Honduras. For the time being, the Hondurans, especially the military, have decided not to make an issue of this, partly because the presence of Salvadoran workers and business investments are a major factor in the economic health of the southern region of Honduras.

The Guatemala-Belize territorial dispute remains a mild irritant in the bilateral relations between the two countries. It is basically settled, however, and very much part of the region's history, but frustrations and fears continue to exist in both countries over Guatemala's century-old claim to Belize. When Belize gained its independence in 1981, Guatemala was still pressing territorial claims. British military forces were posted in Belize throughout the 1980s. In 1991, during the administration of Jorge Serrano, Guatemala officially recognized the independence of Belize without resolving the territorial claim. After heated debate, both the Constitutional Court and the Guatemalan Congress supported President Serrano's decision to recognize the independence of Belize. Soon after Serrano's fall in May 1993, however, the issue of Guatemala's territorial claim resurfaced. It soon was cast aside again as a nationalist rallying cry through the establishment of a "Belize Commission" made up of prominent Guatemalan lawyers, professionals, and academics to "study" the issue and provide recommendations to the government. In September 1995, after an incident involving the mistreatment of

Guatemalan farmers growing agricultural crops within the Belizean border, Guatemalan and Belizean foreign ministry and military officials met at Caye Caulker to coordinate the needed responses to the illegal farming in Belize, illegal logging, drug trafficking, the trade in Mayan artifacts, and illegal immigration. During the 1995–96 presidential election campaigns, no major presidential candidate or party made Belize a campaign issue.[12]

There are two other potential sources of conflict. The Nicaragua-Colombia dispute over the island of San Andres remains an often heated diplomatic conflict. The Honduras-Guatemala conflict regarding the Rio Montagua is a less significant though recurrent issue.

There are also low-level, sporadic tensions over populations that have moved into neighboring countries: Guatemalans, Hondurans, and Salvadorans into Belize; Salvadorans into southern Guatemala; Guatemalan workers in the southern states of Mexico and Guatemalan immigrants traveling through Mexico on their way to the United States; and Nicaraguans in Costa Rica and Honduras. Reconciliation and resettlement processes still continue in El Salvador, where until 1995 the United Nations had a large peace implementation and monitoring mission; in Nicaragua, where the Organization of American States (OAS) maintained from 1990–97 a verification commission to report on the treatment of some 120,000 former Contra combatants, their families, and supporters; and in Guatemala, where the United Nations Mission-Guatemala (MINUGUA) is responsible for human rights monitoring and peace verification to carry out the December 1996 peace settlement.

In the mid-1990s, there were no significant, provocative military imbalances in the region. International and regional peace and security endeavors have been a feature of Central America for almost fifteen years since the Contadora peace effort began in 1983.[13] The presence of the United Nations in El Salvador and Guatemala and the OAS in Nicaragua and the continued efforts of the Central American Security Commission (CASC) to develop a regional security treaty have proved successful.

Since 1990 the CASC—a regional arms control forum established in San Jose, Costa Rica, by the region's presidents and constituted of the region's foreign ministers—met about a dozen times to develop a comprehensive security agreement. The "Framework Treaty on Democratic Security in Central America" was signed by the Central American presidents (the exception was the signature by Nicaragua's vice president) on December 15, 1995, in San Pedro Sula, Honduras. The treaty, one of a kind in the Western Hemisphere because of its comprehensive nature, consists of approximately twenty pages and seventy-eight articles. It includes language and concepts drawn from the original draft Contadora agreement of the mid-1980s. It calls for the establishment of confidence-building measures, the elaboration of a legal framework of action by the military and police of the region, the eradication of weapons trafficking, the establishment of an arms limitation and control regime, and the creation of a Central American Security Commission and Mechanism of Information and Communication for Security. Like most comprehensive security treaties, the ability to sustain permanent institutions and to properly resource such efforts will ultimately determine its significance and impact. The treaty is a result of thirty years of warfare and some fifteen years of regional peace negotiations involving the Central Americans, the United States, dozens of Latin American and European countries, and the United Nations and the Organization of American States.[14]

In addition, by 1995 the Central American Parliament facilitated several meetings among the defense ministers of Guatemala, Honduras, and El Salvador (with Nicaragua demonstrating a faint desire to participate in the future, if invited) to share information and cooperate on matters of common interests in the peace processes and security concerns of the region.

United States Military and Security Relations in the Central American Region

The United States continues its military presence in Panama and Honduras. The U.S. Southern Command—a joint U.S. Army, Air Force, and Navy command—was headquartered at Quarry Heights, Panama. Joint Task Force-Bravo (JTF-Bravo) is located at Soto Cano air base in Honduras. Southern Command Headquarters moved to Miami, Florida, October 1, 1997.[15] All other U.S. military units will leave and bases will close by December 31, 1999. However, there are talks between the U.S. government and Panama over future base rights (for the purposes of antidrug operations, military training, and humanitarian and disaster relief operations) and the presence of U.S. military personnel.[16] Thus almost one hundred years of a permanent U.S. military presence and operational bases in the region may end on the last day of this century.[17]

U.S. Military Groups and Security Liaison Offices are located in Belize, Guatemala, Honduras, El Salvador, and Costa Rica. They are small but representative of U.S. military and security concerns. Multilateral training exercises are conducted in disaster relief, humanitarian assistance, road construction, and naval and riverine operations. These exercises have been called "Fuertes Caminos," "Fuerzas Unidas," and "Cabanas." The latter are often peacekeeping "table exercises" that include civilians and members of nongovernmental organizations (NGOs), especially human rights organizations.

The U.S. military effort is multilateral, not bilateral. The objectives are to encourage and support the region's governments and security forces to cooperate with each other in peacekeeping operations, disaster relief, and humanitarian assistance. U.S. military personnel also engage in DFT (deployment for training) operations. During the 1994–1995 period, DFTs were conducted in Guatemala, Honduras, El Salvador, and Belize. The policy of the United States is to support military and public security institutions in Central America to develop professional standards for peacekeeping operations, to engage in regional multilateral operations, to promote and improve civil-military relations within a democratic setting, and to build visible contact with Central America's elected civilian leaders.[18]

Supporting the U.S. government effort in the region is the International Military and Education Training (called Expanded IMET), involving Latin American civilians in U.S. military training and educational programs. Other programs include commercial sales, foreign military financing, and antidrug programs. Military sales and financing are virtually down to zero, however. Drug interdiction programs, mainly for civilian police forces, constitute the largest of the programs and efforts carried out by both U.S. civilian and military agencies.[19]

Defense, Security, and Democratic Politics

The consolidation of democratic politics will continue despite the uncertainties posed by the new security threats that have emerged in this region. The armed forces of the region will be responsive to civilian leadership and will participate in the debate with civilians about the future missions and roles of the military. While the civil-military dialogue will enhance better understanding between the two cultures, the institutional dimensions of security will move slowly. The obstacle is to be found in the reluctance of elected civilians to engage the military and civilian police forces in developing a coherent state institutional setting, such as national security councils and civilian national intelligence agencies, for managing and operationalizing the security policies needed to defend and protect the democracies of Central America.

One major danger is that the state, smaller and poorer for the remainder of this decade, may not be able to afford effective and efficient military and police institutions to face the challenge of domestic and international crime organizations, social discontent, and increasingly borderless societies. The threat of organized crime (with domestic and international roots) is serious and with far-reaching implications. These organized crime networks are more mobile in the global community, better armed with modern weapons, computers, aircraft, and communication, and exceedingly well-financed with enormous amounts of available cash. These crime organizations can easily become the principal threat to democratic institutions and civilian rule in the region. The downsizing of the military, the slow development of professional police forces, and an antiquated and inefficient (if not corruptible) judicial system contribute to the steady growth of security vacuums throughout the countryside and urban centers of Central America. The victims are rich and poor alike. However, the ultimate victim could be the health and vitality of democratic society in the region after thirty years of war.

The most serious danger for the future is not military intransigence but the reluctance and inability of the civilians in all the Central American countries to provide leadership and active participation in the development of defense and security doctrines, institutions, and policies. The burden will fall to Central America's civilian leadership and the ability of elected officials, supported by the constructive dialogue of civil society, to reform and restructure the armed forces of the region. At the same time government and society must be willing to invest heavily in the police and judicial system. Lastly, civilians cannot shy away from the responsibilities of engaging and participating (through leadership and involvement) in the working out of security and defense doctrines appropriate for the defined security concerns of Central America and in the management of the professional institutions needed to provide for the public safety and national defense of the society within a democratic setting.[20]

Chapter 12

Security, Agenda, and Military Balance in Central America

Limits to Democratic Consolidation in the 1990s

Fernando Zeledón Torres

Introduction

The process of regional reconstruction that began with the Esquipulas II Accords (1987) has taken a succession of steps forward
and backward, illustrating important limitations and achievements
in the democratization of these societies. More than eight years
after the historic signing, a widespread paradoxical notion has
emerged, which suggests that it was relatively easy to open prisons,
hold free elections, demobilize irregular forces, reduce the "human
size" of the armed forces, and identify those who were responsible
for human rights violations as a daily practice of repression. Today,
what appears to be truly difficult is to develop a mechanism of economic transition that permits the establishment of a legitimate and
credible base to democratization through an adequate distribution
of wealth.[1]

As former Costa Rican President Oscar Arias has pointed out,
with the signing of peace in Central America (and the effort to preserve it), foreign aid vanished just when it was most needed. Explicitly highlighting the contradiction of the ongoing substantial military spending embedded in poor economies of Latin America,
Arias indicates:

if during the Cold War this military spending was justified, if during the
1980s in the Central American war that we experienced in this region we
had to spend what we spent, if the eyes of the world were then on us here

(in the region), well, irony of ironies, today we silenced the weapons and the wealthy world forgot about Central America. But the truth is that what matters is to choose priorities, to define priorities and, if we want to spend more on education, drinkable water, health, local roads, inland roads, etc., we need to choose. . . . what concerns me is that it be clear to us Latin Americans that no area affords us greater savings in order to achieve greater development than military spending.[2]

Many of the causes that produced the armed conflict in this region have been worsening rather than disappearing. Our societies have begun to wonder about the future of a democracy that lacks sustenance, land, economic stability, redistribution of wealth, or political participation. In Tegucigalpa, Honduras, there is graffiti in the street that reads: "So much stability scares me." With the signing of the Esquipulas II Accords, the transition from peace to democracy and from democracy to economic development was thought to consist of short steps; however, recent history shows that the road is much steeper than previously imagined. The countries of the region continue to be heavily indebted and their economies continue to depend on the "export of desserts." These countries also lack the mining resources that other regions enjoy. How are we to finance the type of economic democracy that we intend to have? This is one of the major questions that Central Americans must attempt to answer in this decade.

A study on security and military balance in Central America in the 1990s must attempt to address the following questions:

1. What are the principal variables that define the security agenda for the region today? How is the concept of regional security constructed and which factors influence this redefinition? What are the "new old" problems that pose a real threat to the security of these countries? What can be said about the potential for interstate conflict?

2. What is the current state of the armed forces? What is the size of current military spending in Central America and its relation to the size of the armies? And how is this spending and military capability related to the current perceptions of threat to the security of the region? How should the vicissitudes of the demobilization processes in Nicaragua and El Salvador be characterized? What have been the scope and repercussions of the Organization of American States (OAS) and United Nations (UN) peace missions in Central America?

One of the most important challenges is that civil leaders or professionals play a greater role in the decision-making process of security matters. Initiatives, like the "Agreement of Democratic Security" written by the presidents of the region within the framework of the isthmus integration process, demonstrate that new borders have been created by the democratic process in Central America.[3]

The Pending Security Agenda for the 1990s: Redefinition of a Category

This discussion of Central America's security agenda for the near future addresses the context of an agenda and attempts a redefinition of security.[4]

The Context of an Agenda

In spite of being an isthmus with quite a homogeneous history, Central America exhibits pronounced geopolitical contradictions.

First, the region is located within the zone in the Western Hemisphere that is nearest to the geostrategic influence of the United States. As is well known, this zone is called the Caribbean Basin and involves two important features, which are useful for understanding the security dynamic: the intertwining of insular interests with regional or isthmus interests. This can be seen from the existence of a cultural circle of Afro-Caribbean tradition. This circle is made up of the Caribbean islands and the Caribbean coastline of Central American countries. In terms of security, the particular dynamic of this zone renders it extremely vulnerable to the effects of the new security threats (it is not groundless to think of the Caribbean as a drug-trafficking bridge). The other part of the Caribbean Basin is the cultural strip of Spanish tradition. This strip is made up of five of the seven Central American countries.[5] Although this strip shares key similarities with the previous group of countries and regions, historically it adopts a different behavior in security matters: security problems have regional repercussions.

There is a triangle composed of Guatemala, Honduras, and El Salvador, in which the armed forces have had a historic predominance in making fundamental national decisions, although in the last few years they have withdrawn some of this influence. Nicaragua broke with this tradition with the fall of the Somoza dynasty and the National Guard along with the Sandinista Front for National Liberation's (FSLN) arrival to power in 1979 and its ten years in power coexisting with an internationalized war. Costa Rica has practically discontinued this game of military predominance since the nation-state was constituted at the end of the nineteenth century, and more specifically since 1949, when it adopted the abolition of a permanent army as a constitutional norm.

Toward a Redefinition

The efforts to consolidate democracy in Central America have influenced the redefinition of the concept of security.[6] There is a tendency to broaden the concept of security to include not only issues of national defense (protection of national sovereignty, acquisition of powerful arsenals, and keeping the public order) that are directly related to interstate conflicts (referring to the regional dimension), but also the particular human development shortcomings of these communities and their vulnerability to new threats (referring to the insular dimension).

Gabriel Aguilera understands the breadth of the security category that is emerging in the region:

This formulation encompasses what many have tried to inject into the discussion of this issue since the 1970s—that national security threats should be construed also as stemming from non-military sources. The central argument is that the situation of underdevelopment—rampant poverty and misery, lack of access to education, housing, health, work, etc.—jeopardizes the ability of the state to guarantee its inhabitants a worthy life and project internally and externally the power of the nation. . . . From this perspective, security is understood as the possibility of creating a democratic and socially just political order. Any plot against this goal is a threat that should call for a reaction by the state.[7]

Thus, although many of the historical security threats still linger today (conflicts that stem from ambiguous border demarcations, the existence of offensive arsenals, and pockets of destabilizing irregular forces in specific geographical regions, among others), the particular shortcomings associated with socioeconomic underdevelopment (e.g., the deficiency in basic necessities and social exclusion, criminality, and street and family violence) emerge as other areas of conflict. Three related new threats to security can be added to these factors, namely, the illegal contraband of arms, drug trafficking (with its attendant problems), and the deterioration of the environment.

Furthermore, one still detects yet another destabilizing factor that can be added to these variables: the current situation of increasing distancing of the United States from the region and the erosion of the region's strategic value for this superpower. With the end of the cold war and the disappearance of its ideological enemy in the world, the foreign and security policies of the U.S. toward the region have lost their status. As a result of this indifference (or the shift of interest toward internal problems and conflicts in other regions of the world), a relatively new phenomenon is taking shape that can be called the development of an informal U.S. foreign policy. One can mention, among others, the role played by senators, the policies pursued by corporations with transnational interests, and the threatening actions of the main labor union confederation in the United States, AFL-CIO, against different governments' actions that affect U.S. interests in the region.[8]

For these years, regional and national security should be construed as the framework of reaction vis-à-vis the perception of these categories of threats (defined as critical or dangerous) by the countries of the isthmus.[9]

Pending Issues

The security issues facing Central America can be categorized as interstate conflicts, including border disputes, and socioeconomic development and citizen confidence.

Interstate Conflicts. Among the historical threats that have been mentioned, it is important to highlight border disputes. We should bear in mind the recent events that followed the verdict that was handed down in September 1992 by the International Court of The Hague with respect to the well-known, century-old case of territorial dispute between El Salvador and Honduras (in which, in some way, Nicaragua also takes part). Of less importance, but still worthy of the attention of specialists in preventative diplomacy, are the problems that in 1995 surfaced between Nicaragua and Costa Rica as a result of illegal migration and faulty installation of landmarks on the border dividing the two countries.[10]

After unfruitful mediation efforts by the OAS and other countries of the region, a General Peace Agreement was reached in Lima between Honduras and El Salvador on October 30, 1980. The agreement allowed for the reestablishment of diplomatic relations and the formation of a joint commission to address the problem. In 1985, unable to arrive at an agreement on territorial delimitation, this commission decided to remit the case to the International Court of Justice of The Hague for consideration. On September 12, 1992, the presidents of Honduras and El Salvador, at a point along the border dividing the two nations, received the "final" ruling handed down by the International Court of Justice of The Hague as a solution to the territorial conflict that erupted between the two countries in 1969,[11] with the so-called Soccer War. The territorial dispute was caused by a diffuse demarcation of approximately 419.6 square kilometers[12] of populated areas endowed with significant exploitable natural resources. This territory consists not only of land border points but also of the maritime demarcation of the Fonseca Gulf (Honduras's passageway to the Pacific Ocean) and its interior islands (this directly involved Nicaragua, which also has sea rights in the gulf).

In spite of twenty-four years of mediation efforts (1969–92), serious crises related to border instability and confrontations between the two armies have occurred. However, in the 1980s, at the height of the civil war in El Salvador and the regionalization of the Central American conflict, this dispute acquired new connotations as a result of basically two factors: (a) the armed forces of both nations experienced up to a tenfold expansion (with respect to 1969) in terms of the number of active-duty soldiers and operating capacity; and (b) the Farabundo Martí National Liberation Front (FMLN) was using many of the territories in dispute as its base of insurgency. After the 1992 verdict, the problem of the (dual) nationality of the inhabitants of these territories resurfaced as a pivotal point of discussion among the authorities of both nations.

The ruling of The Hague in all items favors Honduras more than El Salvador because the former was granted the right to two-thirds of the disputed territory. In short, the ruling established the following:

The sentence thereby upheld the rights of Honduras in the 6 "pockets" under litigation: a 100 percent right in the Goascorán "Pocket," 75 percent in Dolores, 86 percent in Naguanterique, 83 percent in Sazalapa, 31 percent in Cayaguanca, and 6 percent in Tepangüicir. Regarding the island territories, the Court upheld the sovereignty of Honduras over El Tigre Island and legitimized the possession of El Salvador over Menguera and Menguarita Islands. With respect to the maritime areas, the Court recognized a three-mile strip for each coastal state, and simultaneously guaranteed Honduras' access to the Pacific Ocean. Regarding the extension of maritime spaces, the justices also reaffirmed the same rights for Honduras that the States of Nicaragua and El Salvador have to territorial sea, the continental shelf and the exclusive economic zone that starts with the line that marks the end of the Fonseca Gulf.[13]

Although officially accepted by both governments, the ruling has failed to lower border tensions. It has also failed to demarcate the border as effectively as originally intended in the ruling. The principal problem is the change of nationality and loss of land that affect thousands of Salvadoran peasants.[14] In September 1994, the peasants of Salvadoran origin living in the zones of Naguanterique and Mesetas denounced the Honduran Army for harassment, which again gave rise to a deployment of troops along the border. These new situations of border tensions lead one to question whether in reality the problems of ambiguous border demarcation in Central America are in the governments' security agenda. Did the decision of The Hague in this case fail to take into account the consequences for rural Salvadorans? It is clear that the issue of territorial sovereignty in the region continues to be a security threat.

Further confirming evidence of this point stems from the diplomatic friction that surfaced in the first half of 1995 between Nicaragua and Costa Rica, as a result of Costa Rica's adjudication of the lands for Costa Rican peasants in Nicaraguan territory. This border problem has origins in illegal migration as a cause of interstate conflict. Migration is a historic problem between these two countries. The domestic conflict in the Nicaragua of the 1980s and, more recently, the poor living and working conditions of Nicaraguans have exacerbated this problem.

The politically based migrations of the last decade have given way in the 1990s to migrations of an economic nature. It is estimated that approximately 14 percent of the population of Costa Rica is of Nicaraguan origin[15] and so is the majority of the rural workforce in the banana, coffee, and sugar cane industries. The current Costa Rican administration (1994–98) has pursued a policy of migratory restructuring, as a result of which, it has "returned" a significant number of *ilegales* (illegal aliens). This has given rise to diplomatic rigidities between both governments.

In this context, in February 1995 a group of peasants from the northern border of Costa Rica decided to carry out an unusual action. They proclaimed Airrecú (friendship, in the Maleku language) a republic and asked the United Nations to establish a protectorate. The territorial base proclaimed as independent is a 213-square-kilometer territorial strip between the boundary landmarks 12 and 14, facing the border towns of Buena Vista and Casa Quemada of the northern Costa Rican canton of Upala. In June, in the face of the insistence of the separatists, the Nicaraguan Army deployed troops to enforce territorial sovereignty over the strip of land.[16]

Although not as significant, this action had the same roots as that of the conflict between El Salvador and Honduras: the loss of Costa Rican nationality and lands suffered by some peasants who, as a result of a correction of border landmarks, ended up in Nicaraguan territory. The characteristics of the group of peasants were similar since all had been relocated by the Institute of Agrarian Development (IDA) to a farm that this institute had acquired in 1982, unaware of the fact that the farm was located on Nicaraguan territory.

For some, this case is insignificant. Nonetheless, although the border conflict has been waning as a result of diplomatic dialogue and the transfer of peasants to other settlements on Costa Rican territory, this incident demonstrates that border problems continue to be potential threats to the security of Central America.

Socioeconomic Development and Citizen Insecurity. Still within the framework of so-called historical threats, it is also fitting to analyze the threats stemming from the poor conditions of socioeconomic development. The point should be stressed continually that these conditions have been the main cause of the domestic struggles of the Central American nations. Rather than disappearing, some indicators point to a further worsening of these conditions.

Poverty is a structural problem in Central American society. However, in the recent history of the region, its sharp and irreversible presence is fertile ground for the growth of criminal delinquency. One of the principal characteristics of the majority of threats to regional security is the emergence of a culture of violence. The 1990s has witnessed the emergence of an unfortunate combination of dissatisfaction of the basic necessities of an increasing number of groups and the resorting to criminality and delinquency for survival. Civic leaders suspect that the "former death squads" have reconverted into criminal gangs with links to drug trafficking. In short, a quite dark panorama stretches over the Central American population. The lack of a police force capable of confronting the underworld effectively seems to exacerbate this phenomenon.

Abelardo Morales's recent study accurately points out the parameters of the region's new degree of political conflict in times of political transition.

The transition of political action away from military fighting toward political-institutional struggles has failed to bestow on Central American societies the means to confront the security consequences of the process of differentiation and socio-economic exclusion. This weakness is manifested in the emergence of an organized and restricted response, which, although not mass-based, carries nonetheless potential anarchic characteristics. These can give rise to other forms of violence that will act as fertile grounds for outbreaks of latent authoritarianism within the armed sectors that resist the processes of institutional transformation. It is a dimension of social violence; it is not an inorganic phenomenon. They are leftovers from former structures, remains of a culture of violence that, in spite of an ideal design, have yet to yield to the trouncing of political institutional modernity.[17]

The poverty indices from the Reports on Human Development of the United Nations Development Program (UNDP) for the first years of the 1990s show that the social problem has worsened. The data appear in table 12-1.

On the other hand, a simultaneous study carried out in Costa Rica, Panama, Honduras, and El Salvador by the firm Gallup-CID (1993) reveals that, after the cost of living and unemployment, the main threat for Central Americans is violence and crime.

The CID-Gallup data indicate that between 20 and 25 percent of Salvadoran families reported having been victims of robbery; in Costa Rica, 25 percent experienced similar ordeals in the last year. Ten percent of the citizens in Honduras and 18 percent of the citizens in Panama said that they were affected by this same type of crime.[18]

To complete this picture, table 12-2 shows how all the countries of the region are recording increasing percentages of crime.

Another security threat that characterizes the postwar period in Central America is related to the illegal trafficking of arms and their widespread uti-

Table 12-1   Profile of Human Deprivation, 1992

Country	Human Development Index	Population* (Millions)	Absolute Poverty (Millions)	Health Spending	Education Spending
				(Percent of GDP in 1990)	
Costa Rica	39	3.2	0.9**	4.6	5.6
Panama	47	2.5	1.1	5.5	—
Belize	88	0.2	—	6.0	2.2
Nicaragua	106	3.9	0.8**	—	6.7
Guatemala	108	10.2	6.9	1.4	2.1
El Salvador	112	5.5	2.8	1.8	2.6
Honduras	115	5.0	2.0	4.6	2.9

Source: United Nations Development Program, *Human Development Report* (México: Fondo de Cultura Económica S.A., 1994).
   * Information on population is from U.S. Arms Control and Disarmament Agency, "World Military Expenditures and Arms Transfers 1993–1994."
   ** There is a doubt about whether the data on absolute poverty is indeed accurate for Costa Rica and Nicaragua, as the numbers supplied do not seem to reflect reality. Contrary to these numbers, Nicaragua does not have less poverty than Costa Rica.

lization in criminal acts. When this threat is combined with the previous one (economic deprivation and high crime indices), an explosive set of variables emerges that can jeopardize the achievement of political stability so necessary for periods of political transition.

One document that reveals more accurately the magnitude of domestic security instability in Central America is the Report of the Joint Group for the Investigation of Illegal Armed Groups, with political motives, published in 1994 concerning El Salvador.

The thesis set forth by the investigative team is that political changes—meaning the transition from war to peace—left "some people who participated in the armed conflict and members of the so-called 'death squads' without any operating space." These groups had to search for other structures and spaces of *modus operandi* to which they could transfer their methods and procedures of the recent past. However, one cannot dismiss the possibility that these highly organized, common-crime-oriented apparati will assume the role of "perpetrators of politically motivated criminal actions in the future."[19]

The main concerns facing the police and military authorities have to do with the growing illegal trafficking of weapons in the region. The black mar-

Table 12-2   Criminality in Central America, 1993

Country	Statistics
Costa Rica	Average growth of criminality in ten years: 12.5%.
Nicaragua	Number of crimes in: 1992: 35,000 1993: 42,394
Guatemala	75% of crimes take place in the capital city; of this percentage, 95.5% of crimes are carried out by youth gangs.
Panama	Criminality grew by 41.2% with respect to 1992. Drug-related cases grew by 300%.

Source: Central American journal, *Hombres de Maíz* 25 (August 1994).

ket that has resulted from the arsenals that eluded confiscation and destruction and the demobilized guerrilla and military personnel fuels this trafficking. This situation has given rise to an important phenomenon for regional security: although the arms race among these countries has decelerated, there has been an increase in the transit or flow of arms (especially small weapons) throughout the entire isthmus. Evidence of these fears are the cases of the Guatemalan National Revolutionary Union (URNG) guerrillas in Guatemala and, more recently, the uprising in Chiapas, Mexico, where the insurgent forces possess arms similar to those used by the irregular forces of the past decade.

At the same time, a situation of great instability has emerged in the northern and southern zones in Nicaragua and in the northern zone of Costa Rica with the uprisings of the *recompas* (former Sandinista troops) and the *recontras* (former anti-Sandinista troops) and the flourishing of gangs of kidnappers, hired guns, and robbers carried out with high-caliber weapons that have become available following the process of demobilization of the guerrillas and the reduction of the armies. On the other hand, there are well-grounded suspicions of the existence of mined zones and of still unlocated arsenal depositories. The case of Nicaragua provides an idea of the magnitude of the problem. In Nicaragua, the "Special Brigades for Disarmament" have achieved the following:

In the first half of 1990, the Sandinista People's Army (EPS) collected all the arms that were distributed for territorial defense during the armed conflict; 50,561 weapons of all types were requisitioned. At a second stage, the National Commission for Disarmament, created by Decree 60–90, managed to confiscate 28,368 weapons. At a third stage, the government created the Special Brigade for Disarmament (BED) in September 1991, made up of 583 active duty soldiers. . . . The BED began operations on January 21, 1992. Its method consisted of buying weapons and ammunition, as well as collecting war material found in reserves and searches. In terms of arms and ammunition collected for destruction, the following results were obtained by 1993: 46,086 rifles, 184 machine guns, 490 rocket launchers, 157 artillery items, 18,880 grenades, 7,000 mines, 5,533.5 kilograms of explosives, 6,623,420 missiles, 5,332 rockets, 57,510 cartridges and 77 pistols. At the same time, a de-mining plan is being carried out with the objective of removing 116,000 mines.[20]

Regarding the case of El Salvador, the total number of weapons destroyed by the United Nations Mission in El Salvador (ONUSAL) is deemed to be satisfactory, although the possibility exists that not all the reports on deposits and transport of war materials by the ex-combatants have been verified. A document sent to the Security Council by the secretary-general of the United Nations reporting on the specific activities of ONUSAL states that:

There is no doubt that, due to the circumstances that characterize a fierce armed conflict like the one that El Salvador experienced for 12 years, the irregular nature of the war and the sense of insecurity inherent to postwar periods in any country, it is probable that for the time being an unknown number of weapons and implements of war will continue to remain in the hands of different people or groups, among them some criminals. According to statements by the FMLN, these cases will be dealt with according to the laws of the country. In addition, it is possible that there continue to be cases of individuals disinclined to turn over their weapons. It is also possible that isolated hiding places for weapons, unknown to the FMLN, that were at some point under the responsibility of people who later lost their lives in the conflict, may be discovered by chance.[21]

Tied to this problem but belonging to the so-called group of new threats, drug trafficking and its consequences emerge as the main security problem for the 1990s. Throughout the 1980s, Central America was considered by drug organizations and its detractors as a bridge for drug trafficking. In the current decade, however, this situation has changed substantially: in addition to being a bridge, Central America as a region has also become a consumer, producer, and creator of local drug cartels. In the region, the problem of drug trafficking and its consequences is only beginning to surface as part of a new dimension of the political struggle. There is no doubt that this threat poses one of the main impediments to democratic consolidation.

The Caribbean coastline of these countries has become a favorite operating site for criminal gangs, fueled by the narcotraffic phenomenon (traffic, laundering, and production influences). In the Atlantic zone of Costa Rica, the entire police delegation of the Judicial Investigation Agency (in charge of intelligence services) was discovered in 1994 to have been corrupted by drug trafficking. Members of this delegation executed one of the local dons linked to drug trafficking. This execution showed all the signs of being the result of problems of bribery and trafficking of influences. Subsequent investigations have revealed the existence of a local drug cartel. The extent of this cartel's military power (utilization of sophisticated weapons) and penetration in the political and police realms has yet to be clearly established.

In the debate over the inability of the police to control this phenomenon, one of the main topics of discussion is whether it is necessary or not for the armed forces to intervene in the actions programmed by the U.S. Drug Enforcement Administration (DEA) and the special police of the region. Some military personnel think that involvement in the struggle against drug trafficking is prejudicial for the armed forces, given the corrupting power that these organizations wield. Others, on the contrary, think that given the profound weaknesses of the national police in the majority of the countries, it is necessary for the army to intervene. In this regard, in 1993 the minister of national defense of Guatemala, Mario René Enríquez, pointed out that

the illegal traffic of drugs, in its different phases (drug production, drug trafficking, local consumption, and money laundering), is the most serious threat that Central America will confront in the short term, given the incredible economic and even military power of the organizations devoted to this activity. Its effect is highly corrupting of governments and of society in general. Because of this, in the majority of cases it is impossible for the public force to control and neutralize drug trafficking without the backing of the armed forces.[22]

Regarding security issues and their connections to the protection of democratic regimes, since the signing of the Esquipulas II Accords there has been a broad and bitter debate between civilians and the military. For the majority of political sectors, the armed forces have acquired too much autonomy as a result of the counterinsurgent and civil wars of the 1980s. Far from remaining a taboo topic, questions about the role and size of the Central American armed forces in times of peace and democratic transition need to be raised again. This is the focus of discussion that follows.

Military Capabilities and Military Budgets

The topic of demilitarization often leads to a dead end—the call for abolition of the army. It seems that some realities related to this topic have been distorted since there is a strong militaristic culture rooted in the people of Central America. There are two clearly defined groups of civilian leaders fighting for radically opposing positions regarding the future of the armed forces: those who advocate the disappearance of the armed forces versus those advocating a redesign of their mission. However, except in the case of Panama, which in September 1994 abolished the army as a permanent institution,[23] in the other countries that have significant armed forces, the discussion has increasingly been centered on the topic of reconversion or redesign of the military.

In spite of this debate, one ought not trivialize the important reductions in the size of the Salvadoran and Nicaraguan armies (approximately 30,000 and 80,000 demobilized soldiers, respectively). However, one also ought not fall into the trap of thinking erroneously that demilitarization is only a matter of numeric reduction. It also entails addressing the reasons for keeping such large-size, heavily armed, and prerogative-laden armies.

In the same way that one should ask what type of army the region needs for democratic consolidation, it is also important to ask how and for what the military budget is spent. This budget continues to consume a significant percentage of the public resources of Central Americans. Tables 12-3 and 12-4 illustrate the state of military capabilities in Central America, comparatively showing the physical and budget characteristics of the armed forces in the region.

Summing the numbers in table 12-4, the countries of the region that have armed forces allocated $301.9 million in 1992 and $344.9 million in 1994. The

Table 12-3   Growth of Armed Forces in Central America, 1970–1988

	70–71	79–80	80–81	81–82	82–83	83–84	84–85	85–86	86–87	87–88
El Salvador										
Population (millions)	3.5	4.6	4.7	4.8	4.8	4.9	5.3	5.5	5.6	5.8
Total A.F.	5,630	6,930	7,750	9,850	15,000	24,560	41,660	41,660	42,640	47,000
Guatemala										
Population (millions)	5.2	6.8	6.8	7.2	7.8	7.8	8.2	8.4	8.6	8.9
Total A.F.	9,000	17,960	14,900	15,050	18,650	21,560	40,000	31,700	32,000	40,200
Honduras										
Population (millions)	2.6	3.6	3.7	3.9	4	4.2	4.3	4.4	4.5	4.7
Total A.F.	4,725	11,300	11,300	11,200	13,000	16,200	17,200	16,600	19,200	16,960
Nicaragua										
Population (millions)	2.0	2.5	2.5	2.6	2.7	2.8	3.2	3.2	3.3	3.4
Total A.F.	7,100	8,300	—	6,700	21,700	48,800	61,800	62,860	72,000	72,000

Source: Hal Klepak, *Verification of a Central American Peace Accord* (Ottawa, Canada: Department of External Affairs, 1989), 6–7.
Note: A.F. = armed forces

Table 12-4   Characteristics of the Police and Armed Forces in
Central America, 1992–94

Country	Military Budget ($ U.S. Millions)	Armed Forces (1994)
Belize	1992: 8 m 1993: 10 m 1994: 11 m	Active: 950 Reserve: 700 militias 400 volunteers
El Salvador	1992: 100 m 1993: 101.9 m 1994: 99.5 m	Active: 30,700 Reserve: ex-soldiers
Guatemala	1992: 109.2 m 1993: 112.6 m 1994: 112.6 m	Active: 44,200 Reserve: 35,200
Honduras	1992: 42.7 m 1993: 45.3 m 1994: 48.9 m	Active: 16,800 Reserve: 60,000
Nicaragua	1992: 42 m* 1994: 72.9 m	Active: 15,200 Reserve: 150,000

Source: The International Institute for Strategic Studies, *The Military Balance
1994–1995.* (London: Brassey's, 1994).
  * This information is from U.S Arms Control and Disarmament Agency,
"World Military Expenditures and Arms Transfers, 1993–1994."

tendency toward growth is uninterrupted during the first five years of the
1990s. If these figures are matched with the size of the active forces of the
armies, it is clear that military spending has not suffered any significant reduction in spite of army personnel reductions in Nicaragua and El Salvador
from 72,000 and 47,000 active-duty soldiers, respectively, for the two-year
period 1987–88, to 15,200 and 30,700, respectively, for 1994.

In the cases of Guatemala and Honduras, rather than shrinking, the size
of the armies has increased in the former and remained unchanged in the
latter. The Guatemalan Army went from 40,200 active-duty soldiers (1987–
88) to 44,200 (1994), although the peace agreement signed in late 1996 con-
tains provisions for close to a 40 percent reduction in the armed forces. The
Honduran Army remained at almost 17,000 active-duty soldiers during these
same years.

In the case of Costa Rica, the figures from the National Budget indicate
that this expenditure in public security amounted to $33,704,404 in 1993 and
$37,067,012 in 1994. For 1995, an increase of approximately $10 million was

estimated, raising the figure to $47,881,615. These data show the paradox[24] that the Central American armed forces experienced their highest level of development at the end of the 1980s, coinciding precisely with the beginning of the peace process in the area. This has meant that the region initiated the processes of political liberation with a heavy military burden on its shoulders.

Notwithstanding this situation, there is no reason to belittle the aforementioned reduction process of the Popular Sandinista Army (EPS) and the Salvadoran Armed Forces (FAS). As can be observed in table 12-3, Nicaragua had the largest and most powerful army, and Guatemala, one of the smallest in the late 1980s. Today, in part due to the particular circumstances of the Nicaraguan demobilization, and in part due to the civil war that lasted in the Guatemalan highlands until the end of 1996, these standings have been inverted—Guatemala now has the largest army, and Nicaragua, the smallest (see table 12-4). It is also necessary to understand that the most likely reason for the eventual long-term decline in military spending is the almost total absence of U.S. foreign military aid to the region already by the mid-1990s.

In spite of these circumstances, several doubts surface regarding the use and abuse of Central American resources for maintaining armies that still possess a significant arsenal and combat weapons that are useful only in times of war. In order to better appreciate the significant disproportion that exists between the capabilities of the armies and their budgetary allocation, one must examine the percentage of military spending in relation to the total national budget. The following list shows military expenditures as a percentage of the national budget in 1993:[25]

Belize	3.2	Honduras	7.6
Nicaragua	N/A	Costa Rica	N/A
Guatemala	9.5	Panama	N/A
El Salvador	10.1		

Although figures are not available[26] to trace the tendencies of these percentages, it is important to reiterate that what is important is not so much the level of expenditures, but rather how this money is spent. That is, as long as the operative capacities in effect (number of active-duty soldiers, combat arsenals, and counterinsurgency training) remain as large and well-supported by the budget as they are now, the processes of democratization will continue to respond to the logic of the "National Security Doctrine" and not to a process of national reconciliation that would enable the stability of the political system through the transference of resources for the purpose of peace, economic progress, and civilian participation in decision making regarding security (defense and civilian).

The Case of the Demobilized: Postwar Vicissitudes

The magnitude of the problem of those who were demobilized and displaced by the war in the region has not been precisely conceptualized in the respective peace accords or negotiations.

This problem, which looms as a new security threat, has evolved concomitantly with the democratization process. It is directly related to the operative capabilities of the armies because of the behavior exhibited by the new sector of the population called "demobilized." What makes this problem controversial is the lack of resources and mechanisms to ensure the socioeconomic reinsertion of thousands of individuals who lived in the turmoil of armed conflict for years.

The reaction to this lack of land and employment has differed from country to country based on the manner in which the soldiers and guerrillas have been demobilized. In the case of Nicaragua, where the conflict was settled through the acceptance of electoral results, the issue of the demobilized became a threat right at the very moment that the electoral decision was being made. It was thought that the mere return to daily life, without indemnification or the possibility of economic development, would be sufficient. However, the phenomenon of the *recompas, realzados,* and *rearmados* (those bearing arms once again) soon emerged as a security threat. The demand of these groups was the same—land for farming.

In the case of El Salvador, where the conflict was resolved by subscribing to a pact or an accord, the issue of the demobilized formed part of the negotiations. Resources were provided to allow for a more orderly process of demobilization than in Nicaragua. In addition, with the establishment of the new Civilian National Police, the decision was made, in part, that a significant group of guerrillas and soldiers would continue to hold security-related jobs. Even so, demonstrations by the demobilized in the capital have been a permanent factor since the process began. On the one hand, the ex-soldiers request greater economic indemnification, while ex-guerrillas seek a resolution to the problems of lack of land and farming resources.

In the Guatemalan case, the question of demobilization has been one of the most critical points in the negotiation since it is particularly linked to the indigenous problem, which applies to the majority of the demobilized, as well as to the disarmament of the Civilian Action Patrols and the displaced population. Guatemala is a clear case of lack of institutional and financial re-

Table 12-5   Demobilizations in Nicaragua, El Salvador, and Guatemala, 1990–93

Country	1990	1991	1992	1993
Nicaragua				
EPS:			71,500	
RN:	23,000			

Total: 94,500
Note: Approx. 95,000 family members and support base to RN returned; program for 23 zones of rural development with an extension of 23,000 sq. km.; compensation of US$5,000 to high-ranking officials of the EPS; 70 salaries for the rest of the lower ranks of the EPS.

El Salvador				
FAS:			10,470	
FMLN:		-		31,362

Total: 41,832
Note: FMLN estimated a program of three years valued at US$142 million; National Reconstruction Plan estimates that each demobilized member of the FMLN costs US$720.18, for each soldier US$14.64; for each inhabitant of an armed conflict zone US$4.51; and for each refugee or displaced person US$4.65; in 1992 the consulting group estimated the minimum budget for the demobilized program at US$800 million.

Total Nicaragua and El Salvador: 136,332

Guatemala*				
Civilian Self-Defense Militias**	500,000 enlisted			
URNG:	There are no exact numbers			
FAG***	50% of enlisted force			

Note: Population directly affected by the armed conflict: 43,000 refugees; 7,700 returned, 200,000 internally displaced, and the poor population of the country marginalized in 9 out of the 22 national departments.

Source: Gabriel Aguilera P., *Seguridad, función militar y democracia.* (Guatemala: FLACSO-Fundación Ebert, 1994).

* These statistics are approximations.

** The Civilian Self-Defense Militias are, mainly, made up of farmers who despite their work patroling the area have not abandoned their productive labor.

*** The URNG has proposed a reduction of the FAG by 50 percent as a point of negotiation. In reality, the FAG is the largest army in Central America with 46,000 enlisted.

Key: EPS: Sandinista People's Army. RN: Nicaraguan Resistance. FAS: Armed Forces of El Salvador. FMLN: Farabundo Martí National Liberation Front. URNG: Guatemala's National Revolutionary Union. FAG: Guatemalan Army.

sources to guarantee the viability and effectiveness of a credible process of demobilization in Central America.

Table 12-5 demonstrates the magnitude of the problem of the demobilized in the region. It reveals the need to adopt more concrete policies to help find a solution to the most immediate needs of these sectors.

Peace Missions in Central America: An Experimental Laboratory?

The region has had broad experience with the intervention of international missions on behalf of peacemaking and peacekeeping as key factors of conflict resolution. Some specialists mark the beginning of these interventions with the so-called Contadora Process and the contributions that this process made in its role as mediator. It is important to highlight this origin because one of the last proposals of the Contadora document included the need for verification and monitoring of political and disarmament accords, through the supervision of a multinational commission sent by the OAS. The supervisory group is called the International Commission of Support and Verification (CIVS). Some of the principal tasks assigned to CIVS include:

• verifying the cease-fire and amnesty;
• promoting commissions for reconciliation, dialogue, and national democratization;
• monitoring security stability by hindering the emergence of irregular forces and discouraging the use of the national territory to attack neighboring states.

In spite of its short life, the CIVS opened the doors for subsequent international peace processes in the region. The following are some of the tasks that this commission was able to carry out:[27] the support of the cease-fire in Nicaragua (1988); the establishment of commitments for the democratization of Nicaragua (1989); and the verification of the withdrawal of Contra forces from the territory of Honduras (1989).

The signing of the Esquipulas II Accords in 1987 constituted a new stage in international participation in support of the recently launched peacemaking process. Esquipulas takes up the mandate of the CIVS-OAS and simultaneously obtained the support of the United Nations in its first peacekeeping mission known as the United Nations Mission in Central America (ONUCA). This stage, which can be labeled "deregionalization of the conflict," began in 1988 with Security Council Resolution 644. This resolution authorized a multinational mission to verify the cessation of aid to irregular forces and insurgent movements and simultaneously to ensure that these groups refrain from using the territory of other countries to carry out their attacks.[28]

ONUVEN (United Nations Observer Group for the Verification of Elections in Nicaragua) is an appendage or extension of ONUCA. In reality, as a mission it has acted as a third party in the technical development, observation, and verification of the validity of the 1990 elections. These elections set the terms of the resolution of the Nicaraguan conflict after the acceptance of

240 Fernando Zeledón Torres

the victory and the defeat. (It is important to point out that, unlike in the Salvadoran case, what finally seemed to resolve the conflict in Nicaragua was the technical reliability and trustworthiness of the elections and not a negotiated agreement). The end of the ONUCA mandate constitutes the beginning of the UN peace mission in El Salvador. Although ONUCA participated in the launch of peace negotiations in El Salvador, its mandate languished as the demobilization of the Contras in Nicaragua was being supported and verified.

The second phase could be thought of as a true experimental laboratory for the United Nations in terms of establishing, maintaining, and strengthening the peace in El Salvador. This initiative represents the most important effort of the UN in the region to try to become directly involved in a peaceful resolution of a conflict. Thus, as the Berlin Wall was falling and the cold war was coming to an end, UN Secretary-General Javier Pérez de Cuéllar commissioned Alvaro de Soto as a mediator between the parties in conflict in El Salvador. De Soto was also asked to promote the resumption of the negotiations, broken off since 1987. Alvaro de Soto's efforts made possible the achievement of the Geneva Accord, which reopened the negotiations and set the stage for the subsequent agenda and calendar agreements of 1990.

The point of departure of this new experience for the UN and its conceptualization as one of largest peace missions carried out since the creation of the UN begins with the achievement of a cease-fire and the establishment of an international commission for the monitoring of human rights violations (known as the Commission on the Truth). After two years of intense negotiations and as a result of the mediating efforts of the UN and the willingness of the parties, the Chapultepec Accords or the Peace Accords of El Salvador were signed on January 16, 1992. As a result of these accords, four entities were created, each with UN involvement: The Observance Mission of the United Nations in El Salvador (ONUSAL); The National Commission for the Consolidation of Peace (COPAZ); The Ad Hoc Commission for the Purging of the Armed Forces; The Commission on the Truth.

The ONUSAL mandate expired in April 1995. During these years the United Nations played an important role in the entire process of peacemaking and peacekeeping, but not in its reinforcement. This became clear with the failure to adhere to the schedule of the peace calendar in El Salvador, evidenced by the delays associated with the demobilization and the unavailability of programs of labor-market reinsertion and land distribution for returning individuals. However, as Abelardo Morales states in his book, the UN has drawn fruitful lessons from the Central American experience.

The transformation of the level of conflict in El Salvador is a fundamental part of the transition of regional and world security systems. From an operational point of view, the United Nations mission was successful given the complexity of the process. However, the true dimension of the change introduced by the peace mission can be measured only when the sociopolitical process in that country is conducted without the dissuasive effect of an intervening organism.[29]

Conclusions

The security problems for Central America in the 1990s point toward the reformulation of the problems inherent in the transition from an authoritarian regime to one that seeks to become consolidated as democratic. These problems have obstructed the advance or initial impulse that emerged in the midst of the euphoria of the basic accords to reorganize institutionally these societies that have lived with extreme violence for decades.

Thus, the region has been a laboratory for international missions of peace and cooperation. Useful conclusions can be drawn from these experiences so as to avoid the same errors elsewhere in the world, such as Africa. Nevertheless, it is necessary to understand that a disequilibrium exists between the achievements related to political liberation and the regressions toward situations of intolerance or violence reconversion.

The problems of tense interstate relations, social exclusion, and illegal arms and drugs trafficking constitute a volatile mix that threatens the very stability of the process of institutional modernization. If one adds to this the fact that important disequilibria exist between military expenditures and budget allocations for health and education, what emerges are societies subsumed in democratic hopelessness, in which the notion of democracy is reduced exclusively to the mere act of designating rulers.

The economic cost of setting up and maintaining a democratic process in underdeveloped circumstances is very high. It is vital that the security and defense corps play the role of stabilizing and controlling agents. The ability to establish a balance between civil control of security and democracy, between coercion and consensus, is the scenario for the region in the present decade.

✿ Part IV

U.S. Foreign and Military Policy and Inter-American Security Issues and Institutions

How does U.S. foreign and military policy affect the international security environment in the Americas? The final two chapters assess the nature of U.S. security interests in the Western Hemisphere and explore the evolution in U.S. strategy, instruments, and experiences as they affect Latin American and Caribbean countries. Special attention is also given to inter-American security institutions that include the United States.

Michael Desch argues that the end of the cold war may lead to a less rational and consistent U.S. foreign policy toward Latin America; the cold war, he suggests, had disciplined U.S. policies. In this unreliable environment, he argues, regional international institutions are unlikely to ensure hemispheric cooperation. He doubts that democratic political systems will ensure peace, and he expects that civil-military relations are likely to be troubled. He proposes ways for Latin America to cope with this new uncertainty.

Paul Buchanan assesses the U.S. role in the changing security environment in Latin America. He demonstrates how the end of the cold war and the demise of the Soviet Union influenced U.S. strategic perceptions and policies toward Latin America. He analyzes the new emphasis of U.S. defense policy in the hemisphere on cooperative security, peacekeeping and peacemaking, reductions in force, and arms control and disarmament. He ponders whether these U.S. policy changes are substantive, merely tactical, or just rhetorical.

Chapter 13

Why Latin America May Miss the Cold War

The United States and the Future of Inter-American Security Relations

Michael C. Desch

Introduction

Will the United States continue to play a consistent role in the post–cold war inter-American security system? If not, will inter-American regional security institutions continue to be effective? Will ongoing regional democratization produce more pacific regional international relations? Finally, will the Western Hemisphere countries continue to have firm civilian control of their militaries in the post–cold war era? In short, will the United States play as central a role in shaping the post–cold war regional security environment as it did in the past and, if not, what will the future hemispheric security environment look like?

The conventional wisdom tends toward qualified optimism. While recognizing that there may be pressures in the opposite direction, Abraham Lowenthal has advanced a compelling set of arguments as to why the United States should remain deeply involved in the Western Hemisphere.[1] Further, even if the United States were to lose interest in managing the Western Hemisphere regional security system, it is possible that the extant regional security institutions, such as the Organization of American States (OAS), could step in to fill the void.[2] Others might argue that the extent of democratization in the Western Hemisphere, and the widely embraced notion that democracies do not go to war with each other, means that the future inter-American security environment will be quite benign even if the United States and the OAS do not play much of a role. Vice Minister of Foreign Affairs Eduardo Ponce Vivanco of Peru optimistically forecasts that Latin America "is a region with its future in cooperation."³ Finally, many might also conclude that widespread peace and democratization mean that the "military moment" has passed in the inter-American system.⁴ In short, there are many reasons for optimism about the future of the inter-American system.

In this chapter I argue that this optimism is misguided. First, I show that expectations for consistent U.S. leadership in the Western Hemisphere in the post–cold war era are likely to be disappointed as long as the international security environment remains fairly benign. Second, I explain why regional security institutions will not be likely to fill the vacuum in regional security management. Third, I call into question the belief that widespread regional democratization will produce perpetual peace in the Western hemisphere. Finally, I lay out an argument as to why even a relatively peaceful Western Hemisphere regional security system might not guarantee stable civil-military relations. In short, I make the seemingly counterintuitive case that Latin Americans may in fact come to regret the passing of the cold war.

I begin by making the argument that states pursue the most rational and consistent policies when they face significant external military threats and illustrate how this has been true of U.S. foreign policy in Latin America. I continue by examining the theoretical arguments that international institutions can play an independent role in managing security relations among states and showing that the main regional security institution of the Western Hemisphere—the OAS—has largely operated as an instrument of U.S. foreign policy. I then question the widely held belief that democracies do not fight each other and consider the extremely pacific history of predemocratic Latin America. I further argue that even if the hemisphere remains peaceful, this will not necessarily ensure reliable civilian control of the military in the future. I conclude with a series of modest policy recommendations based on this pessimistic assessment of the future regional security system.

My bottom line is simple: The end of the cold war may see a less rather than a more consistent U.S. foreign policy toward the region. Regional security institutions will not ensure hemispheric cooperation. Even if widespread democracy survives in Latin America, this will not automatically cause peace. Even if the Western Hemisphere remains peaceful, this will not guarantee that the generally satisfactory civil-military relations of the present will persist in the future. Instead, civilian leaders of the Western Hemisphere nations ought to expect that they will see a less rational and consistent set of policies from the United States than they did during the cold war and that they will not be able to depend on the regional international institutions to fill the void. They would be wise to resist excessive optimism about the link between democracy and peace and seek other means to ensure that their militaries remain subordinate to civilian authority.

Why Latin America Shouldn't Count on the United States After the Cold War

This section begins with a theoretical argument about why states will act more rationally and coherently in a challenging threat environment and less so in a more benign international threat environment. It then illustrates this by looking at how U.S. policies toward Latin America varied in higher and lower threat periods.

The conceptual foundation of this section is the classic argument from group conflict theory in sociology that common threats bring individuals together and make groups more cohesive.[5] In the face of a common threat, it makes sense to talk about a group of individuals acting as a single coherent unit.[6] Further, there is evidence in the international relations literature that large groups of individuals such as states act more rationally in the face of external challenges.[7] In short, there are persuasive theoretical reasons for thinking that states will be more cohesive and act more rationally when faced with an external threat and conversely will be less cohesive and less rational when that threat declines. This is the case for the simple reason that the other issues that might animate individuals in the state besides common security—for example economic interests or ideology—will tend to be more divisive than unifying.

"Rational" action is not synonymous with the adoption of the best policies. Rather, I am using a much narrower definition of rationality. An action is rational if it satisfies three conditions: First, it must be the best action given a certain set of beliefs or desires. Second, those beliefs and desires must be based on the best evidence available. Finally, the right amount of evidence should be collected given those beliefs and desires.[8] The key limitation on rational action explanations for behavior is that rationality is frequently indeterminate.[9] My argument is that high threat environments tend to be more determinant (the stakes are obvious, the options clearer, and the interests of most members of the group are involved) than lower threat environments. Therefore, when I argue that U.S. foreign policy was more rational and consistent during high threat periods than low threat periods, I am not arguing that it was necessarily better for all the states of the Western Hemisphere, only that it was more likely to be consistent with what the United States believed and desired at the time. There is a growing consensus among practitioners that post–cold war U.S. foreign policy has become less rational and consistent.[10] This was clearly the case with U.S. foreign and defense policies toward Latin America in the twentieth century.

It was the conventional wisdom during the cold war in the Western Hemisphere, and especially among many Latin Americanists, that most of what was wrong with U.S. policies toward the region was the result of excessive preoccupation with U.S. national security concerns.[11] The basic argument was that this preoccupation caused the United States to overestimate the importance of regional conflicts for the global cold war rivalry and underestimate the particular regional and domestic dynamics in these cases. While there is certainly a measure of truth in this conventional wisdom, there are nevertheless reasons for thinking that we might look back to the cold war period of U.S. Latin American policies with some nostalgia.

While I would certainly not want to minimize the human costs of the cold war in Latin America, I suggest three reasons for thinking that U.S. cold war foreign policy was not all bad. First, during the cold war—and the other periods of intense international security competition of this century—Latin America was a primary concern of U.S. foreign policy. At present, it is probably secondary or tertiary.[12] Second, U.S. policies had a modicum of rationality and coherence during these high threat periods but were quite incoherent and irrational during lower threat periods. Finally, the other issues in U.S. foreign policy have not produced as coherent a set of U.S. policies toward the region. Let us briefly look at three particular periods.[13]

Consider U.S. policies toward the Mexican Revolution before and during the First World War. From the beginning of the Revolution in 1910 until 1916, U.S. policies toward the region were dominated by economic and ideological considerations. The role of U.S. business interests in shaping—or distorting—U.S. policies toward Mexico are well-documented.[14] When U.S. policies toward Mexico were shaped by the desire to protect the interests of particular U.S. business concerns, U.S. policy was highly controversial, relatively incoherent, and generally counterproductive. The same can be said of U.S. policies animated by moral or ideological concerns. For example, the policies of the early Wilson administration aimed to promote American-style democracy in Mexico and were widely recognized to have been ineffective. I argue that both ideological and economic concerns animated U.S. policies toward the Mexican Revolution from 1910 to 1916 and produced such debacles as the Vera Cruz intervention of 1914 and the Pershing Expedition of 1916. In fact the latter set the stage for what would be the most serious threat to U.S. national security in the Western Hemisphere during the First World War.

The punitive expedition led by General John J. Pershing into Mexico after the raid by Francisco "Pancho" Villa on Columbus, Arizona, on March 10, 1916, very nearly produced an all-out Mexican-American War. With fifteen thousand U.S. troops roaming around northern Mexico chasing Villa's forces, clashes with the forces of the Carranza government were inevitable. When these clashes finally occurred, they led the Germans to believe that the Carranza government might be receptive to an alliance with Imperial Germany and that a large part of the United States Army could be diverted from Europe to Mexico by a U.S.-Mexican war. The result was the infamous Zimmermann Telegram, which offered German military support to Mexico in exchange for a Mexican attack on the United States. British intelligence intercepted the telegram and revealed its contents to the United States, which by 1917 had concluded that its interests lay in joining Britain and France in the war against Germany, and so the United States began to try to finally shape a rational and coherent policy toward revolutionary Mexico. "It comes down to this," noted Secretary of State Robert Lansing: "Our possible relations with Germany must be our first consideration; all our intercourse with Mexico must be regulated accordingly."[15] This meant subordinating all other concerns—both ideological and economic—to preventing Germany from winning World War I. To that end, the United States explicitly linked its policy in Mexico to that of the war effort in general. Specifically, the United States withdrew the Pershing Expedition, recognized the Carranza government, and gave less weight to promoting U.S. economic and ideological interests in Mexico for the duration of the war. In short, from both the Mexican and American perspectives, U.S. policy toward the Mexican Revolution was far more rational and coherent during the period of U.S. participation in the First World War than it was before it.[16]

One could make a similar argument about the period before and during the Second World War. After World War I, in the less intense international security environment of the early interwar period, United States Latin American policies again became dominated by ideological and economic, rather than national security, considerations. The result was a return to a high level of U.S. intervention in the region (for example from 1927 until 1933 the United States occupied Nicaragua) but a less rational and coherent set of policies.[17] There is widespread agreement that the inauguration in 1933 of President Franklin Delano Roosevelt's "Good Neighbor" policy represented one of the high points of U.S. Latin American policy. I would argue that what really led to the full implementation of this policy were concerns for U.S. national security. Consider two important cases:

First, economic concerns had again come to dominate U.S. policy toward Mexico during the interwar period. The culmination of this was the crisis resulting from the decision by the Mexican government to nationalize some of the holdings of the U.S. Standard Oil Company in 1938. Standard Oil pushed hard on the U.S. government to get the latter's support against the nationalization policies of the Cardenas government. Initially, the U.S. government seemed inclined to do so on the grounds of both economic interests and also ideological convictions. However, there was also widespread recognition within the U.S. government that another major war in Europe was approaching and that U.S. policy toward Mexico and the rest of the region had to be considered in the context of the global security environment.[18] When viewed from this perspective, the best course seemed to be not to take a hard line against Cardenas on this issue. Economic considerations led to conflict, and national security considerations led to a more accommodating U.S. policy toward Mexico.

Second, U.S. relations with Argentina throughout the war demonstrated that ideological considerations led to irrational and incoherent U.S. policies. Unlike Mexico and Brazil, which were strategically vital due to their proximity to the United States and its lines of communication with Europe, Argentina's remote location made it less strategically vital and therefore events in that country could present far less of a threat to the U.S. war effort. Nonetheless, during the war, U.S.-Argentine relations were strained as a result of Argentina's neutrality toward the Axis. After Juan Perón came to power in 1944, relations between the two states deteriorated even further. The central problem was that U.S. policy makers—especially Assistant Secretary of State Spruille Braden—came to believe that Perón was an ideologically committed Nazi. The reasons for Argentine neutrality were complex, and Perónism was a populist authoritarian political movement modelled on Italian fascism, but there was little reason to believe that Argentina had become an Axis ally by the end of the Second World War. Rather, given Argentina's remote location, the pressures on the United States to pursue a rational and coherent set of policies based on national security considerations were minimal. The low point in U.S.-Argentine relations ironically came just as the war was winding down. This allowed the United States to pursue a more diffuse set of policies based on Braden's personal dislike for Perón, lingering public resentment of Argentine neutrality, and government misapprehension of the ideological content of Perónism. The result was an irrational and counterproductive policy that, had it been applied earlier and to the rest of the hemisphere, could have been disastrous.[19]

In sum, the Second World War—another period of intense international security competition—saw more rational and consistent U.S. policies than the interwar or postwar eras but only toward those areas of significant strategic value.

One can make a similar argument about U.S. policy toward Cuba during the cold war. As with the previous cases, early U.S. policy toward the Cuban Revolution was heavily influenced by economic and ideological considera-

tions. Castro's seizure of power adversely affected a number of significant
U.S. economic interests, and Castro's vociferous nationalism and increasingly evident leftist ideology also raised the ideological hackles in the American
government. Initial U.S. policy responses were incoherent and contradictory.
On the one hand, under pressure from U.S. business interests and the anticommunist Right, the U.S. government opposed Cuban expropriations of
U.S. economic assets and sought to stem Castro's leftward drift. On the other
hand, the Eisenhower and Kennedy administrations also sought some degree
of normal relations with Castro's Cuba. The fundamental inconsistency of
trying to live with Castro's Cuba while simultaneously trying to overthrow it
did not seem to have become apparent to the U.S. government until the Missile Crisis of 1962. The covert deployment of Soviet Medium and Intermedi-
ate Range Ballistic Missiles (M/IRBMs) with nuclear warheads presented the
United States with a direct threat to its national security by giving the Soviet
Union a robust capacity for targeting the United States with nuclear
weapons. Ironically, this crisis was finally resolved when the Kennedy administration concluded that U.S. national security did not really require a capi-
talist and pro-American regime in Havana; only the evacuation of Soviet
nuclear missiles.[20] Once again, economic and ideological considerations produced an inconsistent and incoherent U.S. policy; national security considerations, in contrast, produced just the opposite.

What are the implications of this for U.S. post–cold war foreign policy toward Latin America? My guess is that if the post–cold war international security environment remains fairly benign, we will again see U.S. policies toward
Latin America that are animated primarily by economic and ideological considerations.[21] These sorts of considerations are less likely to lead to rational
and consistent policies. Therefore, U.S. foreign policy toward the region is
likely to be confused and contradictory. Take a couple of concrete examples:
The debate over the U.S. economic stake in the Mexican financial bailout has
been quite controversial and highly ideological. The Clinton administration
was ultimately forced to adopt second-best measures for financing the move
and was forced to put significant conditions on its aid to Mexico.[22] There was
a similarly bitter and contentious debate over U.S. intervention to restore democracy in Haiti.[23] Finally, there was a major debate about what should be
U.S. post–cold war policy toward Cuba.[24] The acrimonious debates over U.S.
policy toward Mexico, Cuba, and Haiti may be harbingers of future U.S.
Latin American policy. In short, I predict that U.S. policy toward the region
will be far less rational and coherent as long as the security environment remains benign, and therefore the United States is unlikely to play the same
consistent role in the Western Hemisphere in the post–cold war period that it
did in the recent past.[25]

Why Regional Security Institutions Won't Fill the Gap

One might concede that my analysis above is correct yet argue that pessimism is unwarranted since U.S. regional leadership is no longer necessary because there now exist formal and informal regional security institutions that can fill the void. This section considers this argument in depth by first examining the theoretical argument for the importance of international institutions and then briefly assessing the role of Western Hemisphere regional security institutions.

Scholars of international relations vigorously debate whether and how international institutions—sets "of rules that stipulate the ways in which states should cooperate and compete with each other"[26]—can affect state behavior. Basically, Realist scholars argue that international institutions are merely reflections of the underlying balance of power in the international system, while Liberal Institutionalists hold that international institutions can have an independent role in encouraging interstate cooperation because they can change state preferences. This debate, which was first waged about the future of Europe,[27] is also obviously relevant to the post–cold war Western Hemisphere security environment. Therefore, we should consider both the logical consistency of the Liberal Institutionalist arguments as well as the empirical track record of the international institutions of the Western Hemisphere.

As John Mearsheimer makes clear in a widely discussed article in *International Security*, the logical and empirical foundations of Liberal Institutionalist optimism are unwarranted. There are significant logical flaws in the Liberal Institutionalist's causal argument: First, Liberal Institutionalists underplay the central obstacle to cooperation among states in an anarchical environment—relative gains (the concern that even mutually beneficial cooperation may disproportionately benefit a potential adversary).[28] Second, the empirical evidence adduced by Liberal Institutionalists on behalf of their claim that international institutions can play an independent role in fostering cooperation among states is remarkably weak. As Mearsheimer demonstrates, even the most important institutions (the International Energy Agency and the European Community) played remarkably little role in actually changing state preferences and facilitating cooperation during the Energy Crisis or the Falklands War.[29] In short, there is little theoretical reason to be confident that international institutions will play much of an independent role in international relations.

The origins and development of the major regional security institution of the Western Hemisphere provide a good test of these two competing sets of propositions about the role of international institutions. If Liberal Internationalism is correct, then the OAS should have played a relatively independent role (in terms of the distribution of power in the hemisphere) in regional international relations. In contrast, if Realism is correct, then the OAS should merely reflect the preferences of the dominant regional actor—the United States. Further, if Liberal Institutionalism is right, then the OAS ought to continue to play an important role despite a waning in U.S. interest in the Western Hemisphere. In contrast, if Realism is correct, then the effectiveness of the OAS should wane with U.S. interest in regional affairs. While this latter prediction will stand or fall based on future developments, we can make some preliminary judgments about the first proposition based on the history of the OAS to date.

In 1947 the Western Hemisphere states met in Rio de Janeiro to sign the "Inter-American Treaty of Reciprocal Assistance" (the Rio Pact) which established the collective defense foundation of the OAS. The OAS itself was formed in March 1948 to institutionalize the Pan American system. This development occurred within the general context of the establishment of a whole host of international organizations such as the United Nations (UN). Indeed, the UN and the OAS were interconnected by the provisions for collective defense through regional organizations in the UN Charter. But from the very beginning, this institution of Western Hemispheric security cooperation was dominated by the United States. This is clear from the fact that there were two competing visions of what the OAS should focus upon, which reflected very different sets of preferences in Latin America and the United States. Specifically, the Latin Americans saw the primary role of the OAS as fostering regional economic cooperation. In contrast, the United States emphasized its security role.[30] Subsequent history demonstrated that U.S. preferences generally prevailed throughout the cold war.

For example, the United States was able to secure OAS support for the isolation of Jacobo Arbenz's Guatemala in 1954,[31] Fidel Castro's Cuba in 1962,[32] and diplomatic cover for its intervention in the Dominican Republic in 1965.[33] If the OAS had had an independent role in regional international relations, we should have expected that it would have constrained the United States from acting in its own national interests against the wishes of the other members of the Western Hemisphere. In fact, just the opposite occurred: In the Guatemalan and Cuban affairs, the United States clearly violated OAS rules against intervention in the internal affairs of regional states. And in the Dominican case, the United States was able, despite deep reservations from other regional states such as Chile, Mexico, Peru, and Venezuela, to get the OAS to ratify its unilateral intervention ex post facto. I am not interested here in whether the United States was justified in its actions in any of these cases from a national security standpoint. Rather, I point to them merely as evidence that the OAS, the most important regional security institution of the Western Hemisphere, served largely as a vehicle for the promotion of U.S. national interests and policies rather than as an independent set of rules that stipulated how the states of the Western Hemisphere should cooperate with each other.

What this suggests for the future is that the OAS, or any other regional security institution, will not be able to play much of an independent role in facilitating hemispheric cooperation in the future. If the OAS was largely the instrument of U.S. foreign policy during the cold war, and the historical record unfortunately suggests this to have been the case, then there is little reason for thinking that it will play much of an independent role in the post–cold war period. In sum, regional security institutions are not likely to play a greater role in the post–cold war era.

Why Democratization May Not Ensure Peace

One might also concede my argument about the irrelevance of regional security institutions for ensuring the maintenance of peace in the post–cold war era but still be optimistic based on two seemingly incontrovertible facts. First, much of Latin America is democratizing.[34] Second, democratic states rarely, if ever, have gone to war.[35] Unfortunately, both of these arguments are not ultimately compelling. First, while it is true that most of Latin America is moving toward democracy, many of these democracies are far from consolidated.[36] Second, while there are many reasons to think that consolidated democracies are pacific, there are also reasons for thinking that democratizing states are extremely war-prone. Third, there remain significant problems with the theories and evidence that even mature democracies do not go to war. Finally, the historical evidence from the Western Hemisphere suggests that it has been relatively pacific despite the absence of widespread mature democracies. The implication is that other things besides democracy—perhaps the hegemonic role of the United States or defense-dominant technologies and defensible geographic positions—best explain the nearly perpetual peace of the Western Hemisphere.[37]

Since Immanuel Kant's famous essay "The Perpetual Peace," there has been a widespread belief that democratic states behave differently in international relations. The most important manifestation of this is that they seem never to go to war with each other. In the mid-1980s, at the crest of what Samuel Huntington called the Third Wave of global democratization, political theorist Michael Doyle resurrected Kant's argument, looked at some more systematic data, and concluded that the democratic peace had been scientifically established.[38] Since Doyle's articles, the debate has moved from the question of "does democracy cause peace?" to "how does democracy cause peace?" Two sorts of answers have been advanced. Some hold that democracy causes peace because democratic states share liberal norms such as tolerance and accommodation. Others hold that democracy causes peace because the structure of democratic states makes it impossible for leaders to go to war without the consent of the public, which is likely to be reluctant to bear the costs of war in any but the most dire of circumstances.[39] In either case, the shift in the debate from the *does* to the *how* suggests how widespread the democratic peace consensus has become.

This consensus has not gone unchallenged, however. Two articles in *International Security* provide important theoretical and empirical reasons for questioning it. Christopher Layne examines both versions of the democratic peace thesis, applies them to crises among democratic states, and concludes that neither actually explains why the democratic states involved did not go to war. Rather, he shows that Realist explanations such as the balance of interests and the balance of power best account for the maintenance of peace.[40] In an accompanying essay, David Spiro shows how the seemingly impressive statistical evidence upon which much of the current democratic peace consensus rests may in fact be a statistical artifact of how the data is aggregated rather than a real empirical phenomenon.[41] While neither of these studies have definitively disproved the democratic peace argument, they have provided important grounds for skepticism.

A more recent strand of research suggests an even more important refinement of this debate. Jack Snyder and Edward Mansfield have demonstrated that "democratizing" states actually have a very high probability of going to war.[42] Given that most of the states of Latin America would fall under the rubric of "democratizing" rather than "consolidated democracy," this finding is of great relevance for Latin America. For example, the recent border skirmish between Peru and Ecuador, both relatively recent democracies, nicely illustrates this phenomenon.[43] In short, even if consolidated democracies are peaceful (a not uncontested proposition), new democracies certainly are not.

Finally, the Western Hemisphere provides important evidence that democracy may not be the only cause of peace. In a provocatively entitled essay, Stanislaw Andreski argued that nondemocracies—specifically military dictatorships—could also have harmonious relations with each other.[44] This makes sense because, as I argue in the next section, militaries usually only seize power when they perceive a severe domestic threat; once they become politically involved they are usually quite inefficient at waging external war, and therefore clusters of military dictatorships develop quite compatible sets of foreign policy interests. In addition, the empirical evidence clearly demonstrates the relatively low propensity for war in the Western Hemisphere. According to Singer and Small, the Western Hemisphere had the lowest number of wars per year during their sample (0.11) and the lowest battle deaths per year (3,100) of any region of the world. By way of comparison, in this same sample Europe had .22 wars per year and average yearly battle deaths of almost 150,000![45] Clearly the Western Hemisphere has not historically been a very war-prone region even before the recent wave of democratization.

Therefore the democratic peace thesis should not lead us to be overly optimistic about continuing peace and stability in the Western Hemisphere. There are significant logical and empirical problems with the more general democratic peace argument. There are also reasons to believe that even were that literature more robust, it will still not lead to optimism about the Western Hemisphere given recent findings about the war-proneness of democratizing states and the relative immaturity of many Western Hemisphere democracies.

Finally, the historical experience of the Western Hemisphere suggests that it was extremely peaceful even absent democracy and this further confounds the democratic peace argument. Of course this historically low level of war could provide the basis for optimism about the future. However, given the Snyder and Mansfield findings, and the large number of new democracies in the region, this optimism may be misguided. Ironically, the propensity for war in the hemisphere may increase as the process of democratization continues. In addition to the Peru-Ecuador border dispute, there are a number of other unresolved interstate issues in the region.[46]

Why Regional Peace May Not Promote Good Civil-Military Relations

Even if the Western Hemisphere maintains its extremely pacific pattern of international relations, there is scant ground for optimism about the prospects for maintaining firm and reliable civilian control of the militaries of Latin America. This section argues that the key explanation for the pattern of a state's civil-military relations is the international and domestic threat environments those states face. My argument is that states facing a challenging external threat environment will tend to have good civil-military relations while states facing a serious internal threat environment will tend to have poor civil-military relations. Given that the post–cold war international security environment is likely to remain quite benign, and the domestic security environments could easily deteriorate again especially in Latin America, it is not at all certain that good civil-military relations will endure among the states of the Western Hemisphere. This section begins with a conceptual discussion of how different combinations of internal and external threat environments affect civil-military relations. It then proceeds to illustrate this with a consideration of changing patterns of civil-military relations in the United States and the Southern Cone of Latin America. It concludes with an assessment of the future prospects for the maintenance of civilian control in the post–cold war Western Hemisphere.

Most of the literature on civil-military relations looks almost exclusively to domestic factors—such as the structure of the military institution or the state of civilian governmental institutions—to explain various patterns of civil-military relations.[47] Both of these factors are necessary parts of the explanation of a state's pattern of civil-military relations but they are not sufficient because these military and civilian governmental variables are ultimately shaped by the nature of the domestic and international threat environments.

Threats affect both military and civilian institutions. First, the location of the threat orients the military in either an internal or external direction. Second, the intensity of the threat affects the cohesion of both civilian and military institutions.[48] The greater the threat, the more cohesive the institution; the lower the threat, the less cohesive the institution. My primary assumptions are that the less cohesive are civilian institutions, the greater will be the problems of civilian control. Also, the more cohesive the military institution, the greater will be the problems of civilian control. To simplify the argument, there can be four different sorts of threat environments. First, a state might face a high external threat and no internal threat. This should lead to the best pattern of civil-military relations. Both civilian and military institutions will be highly cohesive and the military will be oriented outward. Second, a state might face neither external nor internal threats. This should lead to fair civil-military relations. While the military will probably not be oriented inward, neither the military nor the civilian institutions will be very cohesive and this could lead to low-level civil-military conflict. Third, a state might face an external and an internal threat. This sort of situation could lead to relatively noncohesive military and civilian institutions and may also produce an inwardly oriented military. This could lead to difficult civil-military relations. Finally, a state might face no external but high internal threats. This should lead to the worst pattern of civil-military relations. Civilian institutions will lack cohesion while the military institution will probably be cohesive and they will also be inwardly oriented.[49]

A number of cases nicely illustrate these propositions. First, the best patterns of civil-military relations existed in states facing significant external threats and few internal threats. A clear case in point was the United States during the Second World War and the cold war. In fact the United States was widely regarded as a model of stable civilian control of the military.[50] Second, one might look to the post–cold war United States as an example of a state facing neither external nor internal threats. The current low-level tensions in U.S. civil-military relations can be explained by the changed threat environment. Third, the difficult patterns of civil-military relations in states facing significant external and internal threats are evident historically in the cases of Germany under the Hindenburg-Luddendorf dictatorship during the First World War and France during the Algerian crisis.[51] Finally, good illustrations of the pathologies in civil-military relations faced by states with no external threats but significant internal threats were the military dictatorships of the Southern Cone of Latin America.[52] In short, the structural threat environment facing a state goes some way toward explaining that state's pattern of civil-military relations. Let us consider the Western Hemisphere cases in greater detail.

The cold war United States was a model of stable civilian control over the military. Despite incidents such as the Truman-MacArthur conflict during the Korean War, civilian leaders were generally able to prevail over the military in most major disputes. For instance, President Harry S. Truman overcame fierce military opposition to ending racial segregation in the military and integrated the military well before civilian society was integrated. Similarly, President Dwight Eisenhower was able to impose his strategic and fiscal programs on a reluctant U.S. military throughout the 1950s. President Lyndon Johnson overcame military resistance to limitations on the conduct of the ground and air wars during the Vietnam conflict. In fact, if one considers the aggregate pattern of U.S. civil-military relations during the cold war, one is forced to agree with historian Allan Millet that "one cannot assert that military organizational preferences or the advice of senior military officers have dominated foreign policy decisions, let alone domestic policy. . . . Despite successive buffetings administered by civilian leaders and foreign enemies, the American system of civilian control has shown a resilience and strength that few predicted thirty years ago."[53] A high external and low internal threat environment produced very good civil-military relations in the United States during the cold war.

Unfortunately the same is not true of the post–cold war United States. While discussion of a "crisis" in contemporary U.S. civil-military relations is overdrawn,[54] it is nonetheless true that U.S. civil-military relations are not as stable as they once were. Take a few examples. First, there is widespread agreement that military resistance to intervention in the Yugoslav civil war— manifested most dramatically by the unprecedented public activities of then Chairman of the Joint Chiefs of Staff General Colin Powell[55]—forced the

Bush and Clinton administrations to retreat from playing a larger role in the Balkans. Similarly, the military services were initially resistant to Senator Sam Nunn's efforts to get them to seriously rethink their "roles and missions." Also, the military played a key role in getting the Clinton administration to endorse the standard of two simultaneous military regional conflicts (MRCs) as the benchmark for post–cold war U.S. force posture. In addition, the military made only token concessions to the Clinton administration's efforts to expand the opportunities for women in combat arms and combat support positions. Finally, military resistance completely undermined Clinton's efforts to lift the Department of Defense's exclusionary policies on homosexuals in the services. In the much more benign external threat environment of the post–cold war era, the United States has experienced an increase in low-level civil-military conflict.[56]

To be sure, the United States does not face the sort of extreme breakdowns in civil-military relations experienced by many Third World states. The reason that the United States is unlikely to experience the most extreme manifestations of bad civil-military relations—outright military insubordination or even a military coup—is that the institutions of civilian rule are still fairly robust. In addition, the U.S. military has not yet been asked to take on an extensive internal role.[57] Therefore, my expectations about future U.S. civil-military relations are that they will probably not worsen beyond the low-level conflict we are seeing today. Nonetheless, U.S. post–cold war civil-military relations are not as good as those of the cold war period.

However, I am more pessimistic about stable civil-military relations in Latin America because of the relative weakness of civilian institutions throughout the region and the recent history of extremely bad civil-military relations in a number of Latin American states. Three of the largest and most developed states of Latin America suffered from severe breakdowns in civilian control of the military and even periods of direct military rule in the last thirty years.

In Brazil, for example, as early as the mid-1950s, the military institution began to focus upon internal "threats" such as economic underdevelopment, elite corruption, and leftist subversion. When in 1964 the military came to the conclusion that the Goulart regime was contributing to the growth of an internal threat, they assumed a direct role in Brazilian politics and would remain in power until 1985, by which time they had concluded that the internal threat had been eliminated.[58] Given the continuing weakness of Brazil's civilian institutions and the dramatic increase in internal problems such as crime, who is to say that this sort of civil-military conflict could not reemerge?[59]

A similar pattern was evident in Argentina, especially in the mid-1970s. While the Argentine military had taken power in 1966 and relinquished it again in 1973, the period from 1976 was qualitatively different. Indeed, there was a widespread perception that the Perón regime (1973–76) was hopelessly weak, which in turn undermined the civilian institutions of the Argentine government. Further, the internal threat to Argentine society and the military from the growing urban insurgency of the Montoneros seemed quite significant to most Argentine citizens. This set the stage for another military coup and a much more intensive period of military rule. However, once the Argentine junta had eliminated the Montoneros as a serious internal threat, the unity of the regime began to crumble. This led General Leopoldo Galtierri to try to rally the Argentine military and civilians by invading the British-held Falkland/Malvinas Islands in 1982.[60] But after years of focusing on internal military operations, the Argentine military performed so badly in the war with Britain that they not only lost the war but also political power in Argentina. The Argentine case therefore not only shows how internal threats might lead to worse civil-military relations but also how deep military involvement in politics might make a military organization incapable of fighting a conventional external adversary.

Finally, the Chilean case lends further support to this argument about how internal threats can undermine civil-military relations. Chile had, until the early 1970s, been a model both of civilian democracy and reliable civilian control of the military. In contrast to Brazil and Argentina, which had unfortunate histories of frequent military excursions into politics, Chile had experienced only one previous period of military usurpation of civilian authority. What changed this situation was the breakdown of one of the key civilian institutions in Chile—the Christian Democratic Party[61]—and the growth of a serious internal threat from the militant extremes of the Right and the Left. After the election of Socialist President Salvador Allende in 1970, it was initially the extreme Right that began to use violence to try to destabilize Chilean politics. However, by 1973, the extreme Left also began to adopt violent means to advance its political agenda. In early 1973, in the face of growing social unrest and economic chaos, Allende invited a number of military officers to join his government and assume control of certain ministries. This played a key role in legitimating an internal role for the military in the minds of both the public and the officer corps. Allende himself turned the military inward. By September 1973, the situation had so badly deteriorated that the military overthrew Allende and seized control of the country. Once the internal threat had been eliminated, the grip of the Chilean military on power loosened and the military took a back seat in the personalistic regime of General Augusto Pinochet. Once again, the weakness of internal institutions and the emergence of a serious internal threat made a crisis in Chilean civil-military relations inevitable. It is not clear that stable civil-military relations have been reestablished yet in Chile.[62]

In sum, given the weakness of the civilian institutions of the immature democracies of Latin America, the significant possibility that the internal threat environments in those states might again deteriorate, and the few counterbalancing external threats,[63] the military moment may not in fact be over in the Western Hemisphere. Indeed, the end of the cold war may not witness continuing stable civil-military relations in the Western Hemisphere.[64]

Response to Likely Objections and Qualifications of the Argument

There are at least four possible objections that might be raised to the arguments offered in this chapter. First, one might argue that states can act rationally and coherently in areas outside of national security. Second, one might question whether the end of the cold war really represents the emergence of a less intense international security environment. Third, one might argue that in some cases national security led to irrational and incoherent policies and therefore we should welcome a period in which U.S. foreign policy is driven by other concerns. Finally, one might suggest that other, less formal regional institutions played an important role in facilitating cooperation in the Western Hemisphere. These are all reasonable but not ultimately persuasive objections.

To begin with, national security is what economists characterize as a "public good": It is nonexcludable, and the marginal cost of providing it to additional individuals is quite low. Therefore, national security tends to be a unifying rather than a dividing issue. It makes eminent sense to talk about the state as a rational and coherent actor in national security affairs. In contrast, most economic issues are better characterized as publicly provided "private goods."[65] They are definitely excludable and the cost of providing them often increases as they are provided to additional individuals. While it is conceivable that all individuals within a state may have common economic interests, it is more often the case that they do not. Economic issues often lead to vigorous disagreement within a state. Take, for example, the debate in the United States over the North American Free Trade Agreement (NAFTA). Support or opposition to NAFTA fell along economic interest lines. Support for the agreement was strongest among Republicans and export-oriented business sectors; opposition was strongest among Democrats and organized labor.[66] Clearly, it makes far less sense to talk about states as rational and coherent actors on issues other than national security.[67]

Similarly, while the end of the cold war has not fundamentally eliminated the condition of international anarchy, which Realist scholars identify as the key source of potential conflict and threat in the international system,[68] the current international environment is certainly less threatening. The Soviet Union has fallen apart, the United States is the only remaining superpower,[69] Russia and the United States are eliminating large numbers of nuclear weapons, and the main arena for interstate conflict seems for the moment to have moved to the economic realm. While there will most certainly be future periods of intense international security competition, for the present the Western Hemisphere is in a threat trough and likely to remain there for some time to come.

Third, it is true that irrational and incoherent policies have sometimes been pursued in the name of national security. The classic example was the United States' military involvement in Southeast Asia in the 1960s and early 1970s. One might also argue that the United States pursued an excessively hard line against leftist regimes in Latin America including Arbenz's Guatemala, Castro's Cuba, Allende's Chile, and the Sandinistas' Nicaragua. But those excesses of U.S. security policies in the Western Hemisphere, and indeed throughout the Third World during the cold war, were due not to national security thinking per se but rather to an unnecessarily broad rather than narrow definition of national security.[70] By a broad definition of U.S. national security interests, I refer specifically to the argument made by some U.S. policy makers that U.S. credibility was tied up with developments throughout the world. According to this reasoning, if the United States did not defend its allies in Latin America or allowed the Soviet Union to make inroads in the region, the credibility of the U.S. commitment to its allies elsewhere would be undermined. This thinking was pervasive among U.S. policy makers during the cold war and proved to be both wrong and dangerous.[71] However, a narrower definition of U.S. security interests that focuses on those areas of direct material and military value did not produce overly expansive and ultimately counterproductive U.S. policies. In sum, national security interests, narrowly defined, will produce more rational and coherent U.S. policies.

Finally, it is true that there were less formal regional institutions in the Western Hemisphere besides the OAS. For example, the Esquipulas and Contadora groups played a role in the solution to the Central American crisis of the 1980s, and more recently Caribbean Community and Common Market (CARICOM) has been involved in the Cuban and Haitian crises. The issue is not whether these other regional institutions were involved in these issues but whether they changed the basic preferences of the actors involved or whether the outcome would have been different in their absence. It seems clear in the Esquipulas and Contadora cases that the key to the resolution of those civil wars was the willingness of the parties to finally negotiate rather than fight.[72] Changing U.S. and Soviet perspectives on the strategic importance of those conflicts due to the end of the cold war were also critical. It is true that once the parties to the conflict decided to negotiate rather than fight they did so through these informal institutions. This, however, is not evidence that they really played much of an independent role in the outcomes of these conflicts.[73]

In sum, objections that issues other than national defense will lead to the United States acting rationally and coherently toward other states in the Western Hemisphere, that the international security environment has not become less challenging in the post–cold war era since the anarchical nature of the international system has not changed, that national security considerations are more often the source for irrational and incoherent foreign policies, or that informal regional institutions have been effective actors do not seriously challenge my argument.

Conclusions and Policy Recommendations

My main message in this chapter is one of pessimism: I do not expect the post–cold war United States to behave rationally and coherently in its foreign policy—especially toward Latin America—absent the emergence of a serious national security threat. I see few such threats on the horizon and the other issues in the economic and ideological realms are less conducive to such policies. Nor do I think that extant regional security institutions will be able to play much of a role in facilitating regional cooperation. Contrary to Liberal Institutionalist theory, institutions rarely play much of an independent role in international politics. Therefore I am skeptical that the OAS, or other informal regional institutions, will contribute much to managing the future Western Hemisphere security system. Despite the widespread democratization that has blessed the hemisphere since the early 1980s, I am not confident that this will bring to us the blessing of a perpetual peace in the post–cold war period. Predemocratic Latin America was relatively peaceful and there is solid evidence that democratizing states are in fact quite warlike. Finally, I am not sanguine about the prospects for continued stable civil-military relations in the Western Hemisphere. Ironically, the most desirable patterns of civil-military relations occur in states facing few internal but significant external threats. In contrast, Latin American states face few serious external threats but often many internal ones. While civil-military relations in the region improved in the 1980s, there are scant grounds for confidence that they will remain stable in the future.

Given my bleak prognosis, it may seem a little contradictory to offer policy recommendations. But despite my pessimism, I do think that there is room for constructive policy initiatives in both North and South America. First, U.S. policy makers should recognize that the future issues on the hemispheric agenda are likely to be controversial. The bitter and divisive debates about NAFTA, the Mexican loan bailout, the Haitian intervention, and Cuba policy are harbingers of the future. Therefore, U.S. leaders will have to choose their issues carefully and devote much time and effort to building public consensus for any initiatives launched. U.S. leaders should focus upon those nonsecurity issues that affect the largest numbers of American citizens, such as the promotion of hemispheric free trade and immigration.

Second, Latin American leaders should clearly recognize that the United States will not have as deep an interest in Western Hemisphere affairs as it did during the cold war. Rather, various sectors of the U.S. economy (export versus domestic-oriented sectors) and various regions of the country (Southwest versus Midwest) will have very different interests in developments in the hemisphere.[74] Therefore, they might want to shift their attention from Washington and the U.S. federal government to regional centers such as Miami and Los Angeles and state and local governments and nongovernmental organizations such as business associations and academic centers.

Third, since democratizing states are particularly prone to war, the new democracies of the Western Hemisphere ought not to become overly complacent about the continued prospects for regional peace. Externally, Western Hemisphere states should continue to try to resolve outstanding conflicts such as the Peru-Ecuador border dispute. They should also focus on designing and implementing defensive military doctrines, plans, and force postures. Internally, they should recognize and try to dampen the pressures that lead newly democratizing states to adopt aggressive foreign policies.

Finally, Western Hemisphere civilian leaders should recognize that civil-military relations remain a potential problem area—especially in the less intense international security competition of the cold war era. It is certainly neither desirable nor practical for civilians to try to stir up external conflicts in order to ensure better civil-military relations. Nevertheless, there is a way to reorient the military externally without exacerbating the security dilemma in the hemisphere. A number of scholars are beginning to point to the Argentine military's increasing participation in international peacekeeping as a means to maintain an outward-looking military without provoking their neighbors.[75] Canada also provides another hemispheric model, which even the United States seems to be emulating.

I should emphasize that none of these recommendations will guarantee that the post–cold war Western Hemisphere security system will remain stable nor that the United States will remain attentive to the region or that it will pursue rational and coherent policies. However, they do recognize that the changed international security environment poses new challenges to the Western Hemisphere that demand creative policy responses from Western Hemisphere statesmen.

Chapter 14

Chameleon, Tortoise, or Toad

*The Changing U.S. Security Role
in Contemporary Latin America*

Paul G. Buchanan

Introduction

This chapter assesses the U.S. role in the changing security environment in contemporary Latin America. It begins by offering a brief historical introduction that frames the subsequent discussion in the context of the Rio Pact (1947) and traditional U.S. notions of collective security and the Inter-American Security System. In this regard it highlights the effects of cold war mentalities on both U.S. defense policy makers and their Caribbean and Latin American counterparts and shows how this influenced the role the U.S. defense establishment played in the promotion of regional security networks in the post-World War Two era.

It then moves on to address the impact that regional conflicts have had on the U.S. security perception and role, to include the Cuban and Nicaraguan revolutions, the occupation of the Dominican Republic, and the Falklands War. It also demonstrates how the end of the cold war and the demise of the Soviet Union has influenced U.S. strategic perceptions, and how this has had an impact on U.S.–Latin American security relations. The essay then offers an analysis of current U.S. defense policy in the Western Hemisphere, stressing how the themes of cooperative security, peacekeeping and peacemaking, reductions in force, arms control, and disarmament have been integrated (or not) in the current administration's policy of promoting the democratization of civil-military relations throughout the region. It ponders the question of whether the current U.S. regional security position is merely a doctrinal adaptation to the changing tactical requirements of the regional theater, whether it is merely a rhetorical championing of strategic concepts currently in vogue in the region and elsewhere, or whether it represents a more substantive transformation of the U.S. strategic perspective on the hemisphere. The essay concludes with an assessment of the relative utility of the current U.S. posture.

The modern U.S. defense role in the Western Hemisphere is framed by the terms of the 1947 Rio Treaty, the 1948 Organization of American States (OAS) Charter, and subsequent bi- and multilateral protocols such as that which created the Regional Security System in the Eastern Caribbean in 1982. As parts of an explicitly anticommunist collective security system, the Rio Treaty and its successor documents were established to combat the threat of direct Soviet aggression and Soviet-sponsored Marxist-Leninist infiltration in the region, which remained as the mainstay of the U.S.–Latin American strategic alliance for over forty years. Most importantly, the orientation of the Inter-American Defense System fostered the notion that, within the embrace of the U.S. strategic nuclear and conventional umbrella, military threats to the Western Hemisphere would originate primarily from within, aided and abetted from abroad by the Communist alliance. This belief in and fear of internal enemies became an enduring theme in modern Latin American geopolitical thought, even when sharing space with traditional external defense concerns.[1]

As we see below, it remains, modified for circumstance and context, as the dominant strategic perception on the part of the United States and several of its most important allies (even if their assessments of specific threats—and each other—differ), specifically when addressed to the issue of narcotrafficking and other so-called grey area phenomena. However, the relative lack of U.S. concern with the traditional external defense interests of its neighbors has often led it to overlook or be surprised by interstate conflicts in the region, including the Chilean-Peruvian-Bolivian territorial dispute of the last century, the so-called Soccer War between Honduras and El Salvador in 1969, the Argentine-Chilean dispute over the Beagle Channel islands in 1978, and the undeclared border war between Ecuador and Peru in 1995.

But on other issues, the U.S. strategic perspective has changed dramatically. Spurred by the so-called "Third Wave" or "democratic revolution" of the last two decades (in which both left and right authoritarians were displaced by elected civilian regimes),[2] the United States has (however belatedly) sought to modify its strategic perspective to account for the changed world environment brought about by these transitions. The emphasis is now on nonnuclear regional conflicts; the use of special operations in low-intensity conflict environments; and peacekeeping, peacemaking, nation building, mutual disarmament, and cooperative security. This may be more a product of the perceived need for new missions on the part of an increasingly financially strapped U.S. defense hierarchy rather than a pragmatic assessment of the Latin American and Caribbean strategic context. As a result, the new view has coexisted somewhat uneasily with the traditional strategic perspectives still in vogue in some United States and Latin American military circles. Yet more importantly, it does not necessarily interfere with the tutelar role the United States has traditionally assigned for itself when addressing regional security issues. This may be an important contradiction.

The question is whether the United States is adapting, chameleonlike, to the changed strategic environment, whether it is merely creeping along with the theoretical fetishism currently fashionable in security circles, only to retreat under the carapace of traditional security perspectives when imminent threats appear in the region, or whether it is undergoing a genuine metamorphosis from the security concepts of the cold war to those more appropriate for the new world order. That is, is this adaptive doctrinal change at the tactical level, is it lip service to the strategic concepts currently in vogue, or is it a genuine process of substantive role transformation? If it is the latter, then the metamorphosis is as yet incomplete, but the process of change (if not transformation) is clearly underway. The larger question is whether this has been a useful change, or an exercise in futility.

Revolution, Counterinsurgency, and the National Security Doctrine

The U.S. response to the threat of Marxist incursions in the Western Hemisphere was to actively promote anticommunist counterinsurgency training throughout the region. Formalized with the signing of the Inter-American Defense Treaty (also known as the Rio Pact) in 1947, the thrust of the U.S.-led regional collective security system was to deter and combat Soviet- (and later Chinese-) backed Marxist-Leninist infiltration throughout the Western Hemisphere. In the 1950s, no longer worried about Axis influence in the region and preoccupied with the Korean War and rising tensions with the Soviet Union, the United States adopted a status quo approach: it reaffirmed Latin America as a preferred sphere of influence under the U.S. military/ strategic umbrella. This was underscored by covert interventions in Guatemala in 1954 and in Nicaragua the same year on behalf of conservative economic and political elites and against more popular-oriented politicians.[3]

The Cuban Revolution of 1959 brought home to the U.S. foreign policy elite the threat of Marxist-Leninist subversion in the region, and worse yet, the first Soviet toehold in the Western Hemisphere just ninety miles from Florida. After the failure of the Bay of Pigs covert intervention in 1961, and in parallel to the Alliance for Progress, the United States instituted a military assistance program that was centered on counterinsurgency training and equipment for allied militaries. Trading on the bitter lessons learned in Vietnam, U.S. Special Forces units were deployed throughout the region to begin to professionalize the armed forces of nations that were confronted by insurgencies. As part of this strategy the U.S. Army School of the Americas was created in 1946, located at Ft. Amador, Panama, and later transferred to Ft. Benning, Georgia, in 1984. The Kennedy-Johnson administrations maintained the counterinsurgency assistance program, which was expanded under the Nixon administration with the incorporation of police training and urban counterinsurgency projects jointly administered by U.S. military and FBI personnel.[4]

After the Ford interregnum, the Carter administration withdrew from many of the military assistance agreements entered into during the previous twenty years because of human rights abuses on the part of allied militaries. Partially as a result, several countries saw a flourishing of insurgent challenges, the most successful being the Sandinista National Liberation Front that seized power in Nicaragua in July 1979. In other instances the armed forces merely shifted to alternate suppliers of assistance and material or developed armament and defense-related industries of their own, the most notable examples being in Argentina, Brazil, and Chile. This was accompanied by a reemphasis on indigenous strategic doctrine, as specifically informed by the geopolitical perspectives of the military hierarchies in question.

Ronald Reagan countermanded the Carter approach, downplayed human rights as a criteria for military assistance, and reintroduced and expanded anticommunist counterinsurgency military assistance programs, particularly to "frontline" states such as El Salvador and Guatemala where insurgencies were flourishing. The Nicaraguan Revolution of 1979 also played into this scenario, as the Reagan administration viewed the Sandinista regime as the second Marxist-Leninist beachhead in the region and therefore resolved to remove it one way or another. Thus the rationale for creating, funding, and equipping the counterrevolutionary forces operating from bases in Honduras and Costa Rica.[5] The self-perceived U.S. resolve on combatting Marxism-Leninism was tested again in 1983 in Grenada, where U.S. troops were sent in to remove a Marxist regime that had broken down into violent infighting, and in Panama in 1989, when Manuel Noriega was removed by U.S.

troops as a result of his various anti–United States activities (narcotics trafficking, money laundering, and espionage, specifically).

From then on, the United States returned to a status quo policy toward
the region, even while increasingly emphasizing the fight against narcotrafficking along with its traditional anticommunist concerns. This was most evident in its continued reliance on unilateral U.S. military intervention over
multilateral approaches to collective security.

Justification for U.S. military assistance to conservative anticommunist
regimes was premised on a "lesser evil" approach: better to support procapi-
talist dictators than to confront authoritarian communists, and better to prevent the spread of communism through effective counterinsurgency assistance and training (including covert operations) than have to respond
directly to the possibility of a communist takeover via U.S. military intervention.[6]

Whatever the merits of the U.S. strategic focus on counterinsurgency and
counternarcotics, what it did not take into account were the traditional external security concerns of the region's militaries. This myopia caused the
United States to be surprised and react clumsily (or not at all) to a number of
territorial and political disputes throughout the hemisphere, including the
(as yet ongoing) postcolonial style conflicts between Guatemala and Belize
(where a British garrison is stationed as a safeguard against Guatemalan aggression on behalf of the former colony), and the Argentine-British Falk-
land/Malvinas Islands dispute, which remains unresolved in spite of improved relations between the two countries. Additional situations that the
United States has reacted clumsily to include the border disputes involving Argentina and Chile (most of them recently resolved); Chile, Bolivia,
and Peru (unresolved); Peru and Ecuador (unresolved and recently in
armed conflict); Colombia and Venezuela (unresolved, with occasional
armed conflict); Colombia and Nicaragua; Brazil, Peru, Colombia, Paraguay,
and Uruguay (unresolved, and demonstrating Brazil's focus on its border regions); Venezuela and Guyana (unresolved); Guyana and Suriname (unresolved); El Salvador, Nicaragua, and Honduras (unresolved); and a host of
less significant political conflicts. In fact, the dispute between Cuba and the
United States over the U.S. naval base at Guantanamo Bay can be viewed in
historical perspective as a classic territorial dispute compounded by the ideological conflict of the last three decades.

For its part, what emerged in terms of strategic doctrine throughout the
region was not exactly what the United States may have had in mind when
the Rio Pact first came into existence: the National Security Doctrine (NSD),
which in its various permutations became an enduring cornerstone of Latin

American and Caribbean geopolitical and strategic thought that remains to this day.[7]

The NSD wedded "organic" conceptualizations of society with garrison state mentalities in a geopolitical perspective that was both internally and externally oriented. Internally, it emphasized the need to forcibly extirpate the "malignancies" of Marxist-Leninist subversion. This led to a series of pathologies and aberrations, the most notorious being repeated human rights abuses and the popularization of the concept of the no-rules "dirty war," with its attendant practice of "disappearances."

Externally, the NSD promoted a Darwinian view of the international arena in which nations thrived or perished based upon their ability to secure and defend a self-sustaining "living space."[8] What this made for was systematic repression at home and military aggressiveness abroad, neither of which were the ostensible goals of the U.S. government when it fostered the creation of the Inter-American Defense System. This was glaringly underscored by the Falkland/Malvinas conflict of 1982.

The view of the strategic environment fostered and perpetuated by the NSD is directly at odds with the notions of civil-military democratization, cooperative security, peacekeeping, peacemaking, arms control, and disarmament. All of these concepts involve a surrender of military and national prerogatives, running the gamut from corporate interests to national sovereignty on defense-related issues. For those militaries that see themselves as being successful in applying the NSD to counterinsurgency struggles and national reconstruction (e.g., Chile, El Salvador, Guatemala, and Brazil), or which continue to be confronted by such problems (Colombia, Peru, and most recently Venezuela and Mexico), these new concepts strike at the heart of the military raison d'etre. Absent a more compelling rationale to abandon the NSD (whatever its specific manifestation), it is unlikely that military establishments such as these will wholeheartedly embrace the new strategic concepts currently being promoted by the United States. Only the Argentine military, perhaps more for internal reasons of its own, has shown a willingness to do so.

Thus, on the one hand, in spite of doctrinal shifts in the foreign policy apparatus at specific times, the United States continues to hold the prospect of unilateral military intervention as its threat in reserve, should all else fail. On the other, many Latin American and Caribbean military establishments continue to strategically operate according to various manifestations of the NSD. Whatever the rhetorical championing of alternate security concepts for the region, these are the underlying realities, and it is against this background that the new U.S. military role in the Western Hemisphere is being framed.

Post–Cold War Theater Dynamics in the Western Hemisphere

The demise of Stalinist regimes in Eastern Europe and the Soviet Union removed the primary strategic threat to the continental United States and forced a general reappraisal of U.S. strategy both globally and with regard to the Western Hemisphere.[9] In parallel, the bankruptcy of Marxism-Leninism and Stalinism removed the primary internal ideological threat to the dominant political and economic interests throughout the region, even if the region's militaries did not structure their strategic perspectives exclusively in response to the cold war. In fact, it is worth noting that it was the post-1989 collapse of the Soviet bloc rather than the earlier wave of democratization and diminishing conflicts in the region that brought about the reconsideration of the U.S. security role in this hemisphere. The irony is that for most of the region's militaries, little or nothing had changed in the strategic landscape. The Soviet Union had long abandoned its support for insurgent groups, Cuba had also limited its internationalist ambitions in the wake of the Grenada invasion, and most of the internal threats were almost pure in their domestic origins. So the reappraisal had more to do with the United States's self-defined interests rather than the actual strategic realities of the Latin American and Caribbean context.

Without the long-standing justifications for obsessive anticommunism, the United States and (albeit to a lesser extent) its regional allies have focused their collective (if not cooperative) sights on new roles and missions. This has accompanied a downward trend in military expenditures over the last decade, so that regional military spending dropped from 3.3 percent of the regional gross national product in 1987 to 1.6 percent in 1992, and it has stabilized at the lower level during the last five years. This has left Latin America as one of the least militarized regions in the world.[10]

The question remains, however, whether this relative lack of militarization has translated into a higher degree of peace and stability in the region. If we use as a measure levels of subnational violence, state repression, and low-intensity conflicts between states, the answer is a resounding no. Relative lack of militarization, in other words, does not necessarily correlate with relative peace, something that the U.S. foreign policy elite continues to overlook.

Whatever the case, the United States sees little in the way of direct military threats to U.S. security in the region. This has allowed the United States to direct most of its contingency planning toward other more unsettled regions where U.S. interests are more directly at stake while simultaneously adopting a new and more flexible approach to hemispheric security issues.

The United States has been aided in this endeavor by the acceptance by most of the Latin American Left that the peaceful road to socialism, if in fact socialism is ever to be achieved, is the best strategy in the present context.[11] Most Latin American leftist movements, with notable exceptions such as the Sendero Luminoso revolutionaries in Peru and the Zapatista Liberation Front in Chiapas, Mexico, have adopted a negotiating and electoral-based approach toward national politics. Among other things, this has resulted in the reaching of internationally brokered peace accords between the Farabundo Martí National Liberation Front (FMLN) and the government in El Salvador in 1991, and its establishment as a viable political party shortly thereafter, as well as the incorporation of the M-19 revolutionary movement into the political mainstream in Colombia. In other cases, such as that of the Frente Amplio in Uruguay, this has allowed the Left to play the role of power broker in parliamentary politics as well as occupy important local positions such as the mayorship of the capital city, Montevideo. Even where leftist regimes previously ruled, such as in the case of the Sandinistas in Nicaragua, there has been an acceptance of the electoral road as the preferred method of competing for power.

Without the cold war ideological enemy as a referent, many Latin American militaries have returned to traditional geostrategic concerns such as territorial defense, internal security, and nation building. The U.S. strategic approach has dovetailed with the latter but has been less amenable to the former, primarily because a return to traditional territorial concerns takes away from the emphasis on cooperative security and external peacekeeping functions. Nevertheless, the mutual quest for new roles and missions has opened space for a new dialogue between the United States and its regional military allies on the redefined terms of a renewed alliance system. "Through active participation in regional security dialogues, we can reduce regional tensions, increase transparency in armaments and improve bilateral and multilateral cooperation. By helping to modernize defense capabilities of our friends and demonstrating our commitment to defend common interests, we enhance deterrence, offset downsizing with higher quality, encourage responsibility, decrease the likelihood that U.S. forces will have to be committed later, and raise the odds that U.S. forces will find a relatively favorable situation should a military response be required."[12]

The goal is to encourage greater regional integration that will strengthen the trust, cooperation, peace, and stability among the hemisphere's neighbors. Among other things, this has allowed for the use of regional military forces, particularly Venezuelan and Colombian troops, as peacekeepers under OAS authority in the negotiated processes of disarmament and national reconciliation as yet ongoing in Nicaragua and El Salvador. On the other hand, force modernization has also served to increase the lethality of relatively minor conflicts, such as the border war between Ecuador and Peru in 1995.

Primary to the current U.S. strategic vision on the hemisphere is a concern with the prevalence of narcotrafficking, arms dealing, and other transnational criminal enterprise, as well as the larger socioeconomic problems that are the root causes of national instability. As the phrase implies, these grey area phenomena are not black or white, military versus civilian (read police) issues, but instead overlap not only in terms of national boundaries but also in terms of jurisdictional responsibility. The narco-mafia is not only international in scope but has the ability to deploy armed forces and intelligence networks that surpass those of the police (and sometimes even the militaries) of the countries in which they are located. More insidiously, from a long-term perspective, these organizations are increasingly capable of exercising a dominant voice in national and regional politics.

As a result, the scope of their activities exceeds the capacity of local police forces and requires both national and international security cooperation, which makes for a blurring of the line between internal and external threats, police versus military responsibilities, and national versus regional responses to the problem. Add to this the ready access to increasingly sophisticated weapons on the international arms market, to include the potential acquisition by these criminal groups of weapons of mass destruction, and the changing and increasingly overlapped nature of the strategic environment becomes apparent. Thus, while the United States discourages the involvement of military forces in police roles, it understands that specific national circumstances ultimately dictate the involvement of military forces in ostensibly police matters. In such cases, the United States encourages that said involvement be carried out within very strict parameters that will prevent the corruption or compromising of military institutions.

What is interesting is that all this occurs at a time when national militaries have shown, at least in the case of the region's two largest neighbors, a propensity to engage in self-limiting strategies in which national programs to develop sophisticated weapons are canceled and transparency and cooperation on defense issues are emphasized (witness the elimination of the Cóndor ballistic missile program by Argentina and the closure of the Brazilian nuclear weapons research facility in the Amazonian province of Ceará, and the November 1996 signing of a mutual defense agreement between the two countries). Both Argentina and Brazil have committed themselves to join the Missile Technology Control Regime (MTCR) and along with Chile have ratified the Treaty of Tlatelolco nuclear nonproliferation accords. Similarly, albeit more unsuccessfully, the Central American Security Commission (CASC) established in 1990 continues to attempt to serve as a forum for arms control and verification.

Cooperative Security, Disarmament, Peacemaking, and Peacekeeping

"Our national security strategy is based on enlarging the community of market democracies while deterring and containing a range of threats to our nation, our allies and our interests. The more that democracy and political and economic liberalization take hold in the world, particularly in countries of geostrategic importance to the United States, the safer our nation is likely to be and the more our people are likely to prosper."

To that broad end, the "three central components of our strategy of engagement and enlargement [are]: our efforts to enhance our security by maintaining a strong defense capability and promoting cooperative security measures; our work to open foreign markets and spur global economic growth; and our promotion of democracy abroad."[13]

The current U.S. military strategy for the Western Hemisphere is part of the larger foreign policy platform of flexible and selective engagement and enlargement championed by the Clinton administration, as filtered by the U.S. National Security Strategy and U.S. National Military Strategies of February 1995. It is philosophically founded on the "Wilsonian realism" espoused by the "new internationalists" who hold sway over the U.S. foreign policy establishment, and it emphasizes the preferred use of cooperative multilateral vehicles such as the North American Free Trade Agreement, the Summit of the Americas, the Organization of American States, the Inter-American Defense Board, the recently convened Defense Ministerial of the Americas (where defense ministers from all of the region's democratically elected governments met for the first time), and other regional conventions like Southern Cone Common Market (MERCOSUR).[14] The three components of the U.S. national military strategy are peacetime engagement, deterrence and conflict prevention, and fighting and winning the nation's wars. In the Western Hemisphere, the main objective is to utilize peacetime engagement to deter aggression and obviate the need for U.S. involvement in the (more costly) options of conflict prevention or war.

The thrust of U.S. regional military policy is to promote the institutionalization of democratic civil-military relations, to reorient the strategic gaze of Latin American and Caribbean militaries toward external, multinational cooperative security and peacekeeping efforts, and to contain the spread of conventional arms and weapons of mass destruction in the region, be they employed by states or subnational and transnational actors formally unaffiliated with governmental bodies. This would be done via the promotion of a web of arms control and disarmament agreements under multilateral supervision that would encourage restraint in arms transfers, seek to remove incentives to engage in arms races, increase predictability regarding force size and structure, downplay national defense industries in favor of vital civilian industries, and increase confidence in compliance levels on the part of all parties. It is believed that a stable, calculable balance of power made possible through greater transparency, national responsibility, and institutional restraint contributes substantially to regional tranquility.[15] This allows for a reasoned and balanced approach toward military modernization that diminishes the offensive capabilities of each nation's armed forces while at the same time enabling them to acquire increasingly sophisticated defensive weapons as both a deterrent and response to potential aggression.

The United States actively supports a review of the role of the Inter-American Defense Board (IADB), the preeminent regional military forum and longest-standing multilateral military organization in the world, having been created in 1942 to plan for the collective defense of the hemisphere. Under consideration is either the adaptation of the IADB to carry out effective multilateral security-related operations in support of cooperative civilian policies, or its elimination as an anachronism in the post–cold war era. The IADB de-mining project in Central America is an example of the type of technomilitary assistance program that the board can offer in response to the needs and under the guidance of the OAS. In terms of regional military education, the United States also supports a curriculum review of the Inter-American Defense College in order to emphasize multilateral operations, confidence and security–building measures (CSBMs), and cooperative security. In parallel, the United States has moved to revamp U.S. Army School of the Americas and Inter-American Air Force Academy courses so that more emphasis be placed on human rights, support for democracy, cooperative security, and peacekeeping and peacemaking missions. The idea is to mesh professional development programs and established policy instruments into retooled vehicles for the achievement of the new strategic vision.

Central to the current foreign policy vision is the promotion of democracy and human rights. Promotion of democracy is to the Clinton administration what defense of human rights was to the Carter administration; in fact, one cannot exist without the other. In the field of civil-military relations, this has meant, among other things, U.S. support for the institutionalization of civilian control of military policy (such as through the establishment of civilian-run ministries of defense as opposed to military-run war ministries or service ministries, and through the promotion of strategic studies training for civilians that parallels or is a part of military strategic study programs). It has also meant U.S. support for the incorporation of human rights training into national and regional military training programs, and the establishment of more effective parliamentary and executive oversight mechanisms on military budgets and manpower issues. The United States strongly supports 1991 OAS Resolution 1080, which decrees that the interruption of a legitimate elected government is grounds for collective action. Resolution 1080 was invoked in Haiti in 1991, Peru in 1992, and Guatemala in 1993, in each case because of violations of electoral mandates. In order to continue to institutionalize regional military support for democracy, the U.S. Department of Defense hosted the first conference of hemispheric ministers of defense, representing the democratic regimes of the region, in July 1995, as a follow-up to the 1994 Summit of the Americas involving all of the freely elected presidents of the region (Cuban president Fidel Castro being the notable exclusion). The themes of the conference demonstrated the shift in strategic priority on the part of the United States: transparency and confidence building, defense cooperation, and the role of the military in the twenty-first century.

In parallel with the concern with supporting regional democratization is the approach toward multilateralism when settling disputes, be they economic, political, or military. The U.S. quest for OAS support and other military involvement in the occupation of Haiti is one such example, as is the involvement of the United States, Brazil, Argentina, and Chile in the negotiations to end the border conflict between Ecuador and Peru in 1995. Continued efforts to assert the security role of the OAS, the discussions about the future of the IADB, and the promotion of the Defense Ministerial serve to reaffirm the U.S. shift in strategic emphasis. The point to be underscored is that the United States is attempting to gradually relinquish some of its unilateral prerogatives in the region so that they can be gradually replaced by multilateral instruments that are conducive to the promotion of regional stability.

The second cornerstone of the new strategic policy is support for a reorientation of national military strategic perspectives toward external, multilateral peacekeeping and peacemaking missions. The idea is that professionalism could be fostered simultaneously with a change in perspective from internal security to external defense roles. This would in turn ease the incorporation into national military doctrines of notions of cooperative as opposed to collective security arrangements, in which mutual deterrence is achieved via the use of CSBMs that promote transparency in military-to-military relations. Cooperative security is believed to be to defense what preventive medicine is to health care: it seeks to prevent the international conflict by focusing on its causes, rather than by responding to the consequences of militarism. The goal of cooperative security is to facilitate peaceful conflict resolution in order to avoid serious crises.

In this light, traditional notions of collective security are akin to acute

278 Paul G. Buchanan

care: they respond to problems after the fact, deterring through superior force any would-be aggression, but not concentrating on the roots of aggression. The United States believes that the promotion of CSBMs throughout the region will diminish the prospect of military conflict between neighbors and ideological adversaries while at the same time laying the foundation for more durable and peaceful military alliances in the future.[16]

Likewise, the United States strongly believes that Latin American and Caribbean military involvement in both regional and extraregional peacekeeping missions will serve the purposes of military professionalization, civil-military democratization, and regional peace. The United States has taken its lead from Canada, which has a long history of professional international peacekeeping practice that could serve as a model for other military institutions in the hemisphere.[17] The exposure to other military establishments, the integration into multinational units, and the benefits of witnessing the international response to conflicts and crises are all believed to help encourage a reformulation of military strategic perspectives. Argentine, Brazilian, Chilean, Colombian, Uruguayan, and Venezuelan involvement in multinational operations as disparate as Nicaragua, the Persian Gulf, Bosnia, Cambodia, and Haiti during the last decade are believed to be major stepping-stones toward a gradual reorientation of national military strategies around the notion of external cooperative security.

In effect, although maintaining its self-appointed tutelar role in regional military affairs, the United States has attempted to shift its strategic orientation from that of regional policeman overseeing a network of counterinsurgency-minded allied militaries to that of a facilitator and advocate of multilateral military cooperation on both external and internal security issues. Forced by the changing world strategic context and domestic budgetary considerations to downsize the overall U.S. military presence, the United States has reformulated its regional military strategy and role in Latin America to conform with the new realities of the moment. That, plus the Clinton administration's belief in multilateralism, free trade, democracy, and the benefits of transparency, have all made for a recasting of the U.S. military presence in Latin America and the Caribbean. What remains to be seen is if this changed mission will be reproduced among the other military institutions in the hemisphere.

Instruments

The manner in which the U.S. security role is exercised is through a number of long-established instruments. But, whereas the instruments may not have changed, the content of the message they transmit is gradually being altered. Among the primary vehicles used are senior official counterpart visits, bi- and multilateral training exercises, and assistance at a variety of levels, from noncommissioned officer and enlisted specialist technical training to search and rescue exercises. Most recently, the move to convene Defense Ministerials of the Americas on a biannual basis adds another institutionalized forum for high-level strategic discussions, with the notable aspect being that all of the ministers involved are by fiat representatives of democratically elected regimes. At the level of commanders in chief, the Conferences of American Armies and Air Forces respectively bring together the service chiefs of each country around a common theme (not all of which agree with the stated U.S. foreign policy agenda: witness the theme of the 1990–91 Conference of American Armies: "Internal Subversion," which was defined to include left-leaning political parties as "Marxist Leninist fronts" in spite of their legal status and the absence of viable leftist insurgencies in a majority of countries. This points to the fact that in many cases the traditional tenets of the national security doctrine [NSD] have yet to be replaced with a viable strategic alternative, no matter what the United States proposes).

There are numerous Inter-American Service forums, including the above-mentioned Conference of American Armies (CAA), the System of Cooperation of American Air Forces (SICOFAA), the Inter-American Naval Conference, International Seapower Symposium, the Inter-American Defense Board and its Inter-American Defense College, and the Joint Mexican-U.S. Defense Commission.

Then there are the fore-mentioned military exchange and education programs, which run the gamut from enlisted personnel joint training programs to attendance at the Inter-American Defense College in Washington, D.C., the U.S. Army School of the Americas, the Inter-American Air Force Academy, a variety of M.A.-level U.S. Naval Postgraduate School professional development curricula, and placement of U.S. and Latin American officers in their respective war colleges and other institutions of military higher education. These include functional interaction programs such as the United States' international military education and training (IMET) program, and also U.S. military training opportunities of incidental benefit to other nations, including Deployments for Training (DFT), Humanitarian and Civic Action deployments (HCA), military Judge Advocate General (JAG) programs, and technical training at U.S. schools or the Panama-based Jungle Operations Training Center and Naval Small Craft Instruction and Technical Training School. In addition, the U.S. Drug Enforcement Agency, FBI, and other security agencies all conduct ongoing joint operations and training exercises with their Latin American and Caribbean counterparts, adding to the web of security cooperation vehicles currently in use. Finally, large-scale exercises such as the UNITAS naval training program and regular U.S. involvement with yearly Caribbean Regional Security System (RSS) training exercises round out the means by which the U.S. strategic perspective and doctrinal guidelines are shared with regional allies.

More broadly and, as mentioned above, as part of its strategic reorientation, the United States has sought to redefine the role of the IADB. Specifically, the United States has been willing to entertain the idea that the IADB should adopt a more formal security role on behalf of the Organization of American States, particularly with regard to multinational training exercises and regional security projects (such as the Central American de-mining efforts). This is complemented and reinforced by the U.S. withdrawal of the U.S. Southern Command (USSOUTHCOM) from Panama to the U.S. mainland, and its integration with the ongoing activities of the U.S. Atlantic Command (USACOM) based in Norfolk, Virginia. Likewise, the Inter-American Defense College would revise its course offerings to reflect this new posture, which would include offerings in peacekeeping, peacemaking, and cooperative security as part of its new curriculum.

Notwithstanding these changes, the United States recognizes the need to have U.S. forces prepared for regional contingencies, and to that end reserves the right to maintain a forward presence in the region. The United States currently has contingency mission plans for counterterrorism, noncombatant evacuation operations, foreign internal defense, peace enforcement and peacekeeping, and disaster relief. It prepares for these contingencies through training, joint and combined exercises, deployments, and a variety of military contacts. U.S. military forces assigned on a permanent basis to the region include the U.S. Army South at Fort Clayton, Panama, the U.S. Atlantic Fleet at Norfolk, Virginia, the U.S. 12th Air Force at Tucson, Arizona, and Marine Forces South, recently moved from Camp Lejeune, North Carolina, to Panama. The U.S. Southern Command also includes the Special Operations Command South, located at Ft. Albrook, Panama, and Joint Task Force Bravo at Soto Cano, Honduras. The U.S. Atlantic Command maintains a permanent presence at Roosevelt Roads, Puerto Rico, and at Guantanamo, Cuba, and serves as the joint force trainer and integrator for the Atlantic and Caribbean regions (or areas of responsibility, AOR). The departure of the U.S. Southern Command from Panama (scheduled to be completed by December 31, 1999) has resulted in a gradual withdrawal of the U.S. military presence in that country and will result in its integration with other U.S.-based commands (currently under discussion among the National Command Authorities and Joint Chiefs of Staff under the Unified Command Plan Process).

Even so, continued troop deployments under the training and assistance programs mentioned earlier, as well as the presence of defense attachés and their respective service counterparts, ensures that the United States will maintain a military presence in the region long after its forward-deployed elements are withdrawn. The continued strategic importance of the Panama Canal also ensures that, even with USSOUTHCOM's withdrawal, the United States will retain a forward military presence in close proximity to the region.

What should be apparent is that, in a continuation of long-standing practice, the United States has an abiding faith in institutionalized channels for the maintenance of military-to-military relations in the region. Overlapping in terms of scope, content, and practice, these institutional mechanisms are considered to be the primary means through which the new U.S. military role will be advertised throughout the hemisphere.

Rhetoric and Reality

However noble and altruistic the U.S.-stated strategic objectives in the Western Hemisphere, the translation of strategic theory into practice has been fraught with problems. First among these is the absence of a practicable praxis, that is, a strategy of action that melds theory and organizational practice into a coherent vehicle for addressing the strategic problems as defined. Thus, whatever its rhetorical championing of certain doctrinal shifts, the United States as of yet has not offered its neighbors a viable alternative to the NSD. Peacekeeping, cooperative security, and support for democracy have only been haphazardly and in piecemeal fashion incorporated into existing U.S. military curricula, and in those institutions where the changes have been most significant (such as at the School of the Americas), the changes have been instituted by mixed teams of outside civilian consultants and DOD officials (both civilian and military) rather than soldiers themselves.

Likewise, U.S. support for continued modernization of regional military forces has failed to account for or allay the traditional territorial disputes that, however dormant for the most part, continue to rend the region. As a result, military technologies may well be applied to other than the purported defensive purposes that the U.S. maintains as a guideline for such upgrading and may result in the increased destructiveness of relatively small armed conflicts.

For its part, U.S. support for a reorientation toward external roles flies in the face of its emphasis on "grey area" threats to national security. Particularly evident in the U.S. counterdrug program, which now stresses source country eradication over transit route interdiction, the concern with nontraditional threats to security reinforces the regional emphasis on internal military roles. This has been furthered by the emergence of a new transnational threat in the form of fundamentalist Islamic terrorism, which although different in its specific origins was behind the attempted coup in Trinidad and Tobago in 1990 and the bombings of the Israeli Embassy and Jewish Community Center in Buenos Aires, Argentina, in 1991 and 1993, all with considerable property damage and loss of life. Given the limitations of national police forces and the resources available to transnational narco-trafficking and terrorist groups, the emphasis on "grey area" phenomena serves to justify established strategic perspectives with a strong internal emphasis (such as the NSD) while simultaneously contradicting the U.S. interest in a switch to external military missions. The fact that the United States maintains contingency plans for "foreign internal defense" along with counterterrorism underscores the generalized ambivalence about external versus internal military professional roles.

Then there are the problems of definition; for example, the problem of trying to include the definition of *democracy* and *legitimate government* in a region that has very little historical experience with the concepts. The U.S. government has yet to distinguish between the procedural and substantive dimensions of democracy and has little conceptual basis for assessing the legitimacy of specific regimes. Nor does it have a focused approach toward democracy promotion at any level.[18] Moreover, the assumption that democracies are inherently peaceful is more an article of faith than an empirically corroborated fact. This is especially the case in the Western Hemisphere, where the United States—ostensibly the most mature democracy in the region—has repeatedly intervened in other democratic states—Guatemala, Chile, and the Dominican Republic being three of them—that held conflicting ideological or economic views. Moreover, there is evidence to suggest that elected politicians, particularly in newly democratic, unconsolidated, or immature democracies, are especially susceptible to nationalist pressures on territorial issues, which makes them prone to conflict with their neighbors.[19] The democratic peace thesis is thus a particularly difficult concept for Latin Americans and Caribbean islanders to accept, for both historical and conceptual reasons. The recent conflict between Ecuador and Peru can only reaffirm their skepticism.

There is also the problem of transplanting notions derived in one context, Europe and NATO, which evolved within the framework of a long-established collective security system, when applying them to another region where no such long-standing integrated frameworks exist, as in the case of promoting cooperative security and CSBMs in the Western Hemisphere. Moreover, the concepts of cooperative security and CSBMs have traditionally been applied to states, but in Latin America and the Caribbean many nontraditional sub- and transnational actors increasingly compete with duly constituted governmental actors for resources and influence (on this, see Ivelaw Griffith's chapter in this volume).

The unit of analysis problem is further complicated, as Caesar Sereseres points out elsewhere in this collection of essays, by the withdrawal of the formal state presence in many facets of civilian and military life. The ensuing vacuum has opened the door for the emergence of a host of new actors, many if not most of them criminal organizations, throughout the region, particularly in Central America and the Caribbean. This further complicates the facile transposing of security concepts derived from the European context. Finally, as if all of these problems of conceptualization and transfer were not enough, CSBMs have most often been used to establish a basis for trust with military adversaries, such as in the case of NATO and the former Warsaw Pact. Yet no movement has been made, for domestic political reasons, to incorporate Cuba into regional cooperative security schemes.

There are also serious questions about the feasibility of using the traditional vehicles for implementing U.S. regional military policy for the dissemination of the new strategic vision. High-level military-to-military contacts have been very useful at times in promoting the U.S. support for democracy and the new strategic vision. This was particularly evident in the prodemocratic intercession of high-ranking U.S. commanders with the coup plotters in Venezuela in 1992–93 and with the Guatemalan military hierarchy the latter year during President Serrano's abortive *auto-golpe*. On the other hand, the knowledge and complicity of U.S. military personnel in the coverup of military human rights violations in El Salvador and Guatemala in the 1980s and early 1990s points to the fact that their tacit agreement often serves to confirm in the minds of allied militaries that any behavior will be condoned if traditional U.S. interests are served.

The reason for this state of affairs lies in the nature of institutional contacts between the U.S. military and its regional partners. Most of these instruments are purely technical in nature. That is, they are strictly oriented toward the reproduction of technical expertise in various aspects of warfare. They are not oriented or conformed to reproduce a specific ideology or strategic mindset that involves notions such as those that underpin U.S. foreign and military policy. Only a full-scale reconversion of these instruments, so that they address the political-military context in which the technical expertise and military technologies are applied, can begin to seriously address the practical aspects of strategic change at the regional level. In other words, there needs to be an infusion of normative concerns to accompany the positive empirical aspects of U.S. military training in the arts of war.

Fundamental alterations in U.S. institutional morphology and good intentions may not be enough. Having a civilian Defense Ministry when de facto military authority rests within the officer corps, such as in the case of Chile, or having the armed forces refuse to relinquish control over service-led ministries or subordinate them to an overarching civilian-led Defense Ministry, such as in Brazil, only mystifies the obvious in the eyes of the U.S. foreign policy elite (but not the citizens of the countries in question). Fundamental change of the sort being championed by the United States requires internal acceptance on the part of the officer corps of allied militaries that such change is in their national interest. To this point, the extent to which this has occurred has been partial at best, with Argentina being the most "cooperative" (no pun intended) in reconciling its views with those of the United States. Even the Argentine strategic change of perspective may be due as much if not more to the defeat in the Falkland/Malvinas War and an attempt to curry favor with the United States than it is to sincere appreciation for the utility of the concepts being promoted. For militaries such as those of Peru, Venezuela, and Mexico, beset by political crises, internal unrest within the armed forces, and active insurgencies in two of the cases, the U.S. doctrinal reorientation is at odds with the realities of the national situation and thus takes a secondary place in the strategic perspective of these militaries.

Finally, there are the problems internal to the U.S. foreign policy and military establishments. Various agencies in the U.S. foreign policy apparatus, primarily but not exclusively the State and Defense Departments, often have different when not conflicting views on the best approach to regional military issues.[20] Moreover, different branches of the Defense Department, such as the Office of the Secretary of Defense (OSD) and Joint Chiefs of Staff (JCS), often differ on policy approach as well, as do many of their respective agencies (such as the deputy assistant secretary of defense for policy and plans and the deputy assistant secretary of defense for the inter-American region). Worse yet, in all cases the foreign policy apparatus of which the Defense Department is part is driven by reactive, reflexive, and crisis-driven logics of bureaucratic survival that is prone to ignore entire regions in the absence of pressing strategic concerns.

This has relegated Latin America and the Caribbean to a secondary position in the U.S. foreign policy landscape, which has further prevented the U.S. government from developing a responsive and proactive approach to the region, including its military affairs. Add to this the fact that many in the foreign policy bureaucracies, to include career civil servants engaged in the defense and international security fields, have a vested interest in seeing that crises remain unresolved (since placement on crisis task forces ensures higher visibility of individual civil servants by the political appointees who staff the uppermost positions in the foreign policy apparatus), and what emerges is a foreign policy that is determined as much by personalist and bureaucratic rationales as it is by the practicalities of the situation at hand. Such has been the case in the practice of U.S. Latin American policy over the years, and it has been echoed in the current approach toward redefining the U.S. role in regional security affairs.

To which can be added the shifting perspectives of the regional military commands with responsibilities in the hemisphere: the U.S. Atlantic Command (USACOM), which has authority over the Atlantic and Caribbean area and is nominally a Navy Command at the admiral (four star) level, the U.S. Southern Command (USSOUTHCOM), which is responsible for everything from Guatemala to Tierra del Fuego and is ostensibly an Army Command under the leadership of a general (four star), the U.S. Central Command (USCENCOM), another four-star billet, which includes Mexico within its jurisdictional purview, and the U.S. Special Operations Command (USSO-COM), which conducts ongoing operations throughout the hemisphere. Relocation of USSOUTHCOM to the continental United States in 1997 will directly overlap these commands' areas of responsibility (AOR), and it is possible, given the equal rank of the officers involved, that serious conflicts over jurisdiction and authority will emerge between the respective commanders in chief (CINCs) of the different commands. The absorption or integration of USACOM's naval responsibilities in the Caribbean and South America into the U.S. SOUTHCOM AOR might also generate serious interservice disputes, to which can be added the political implications such a move would have at the state and federal levels.

Domestic budgetary politics also have had an adverse impact on the U.S. military role in Latin America and the Caribbean. The pressures to reduce military expenditures, coupled with the fact that Latin America and the Caribbean are not considered to be regions in which high-priority threats exist, has led to a severe curtailment of virtually all U.S. military assistance and education programs in the region. As a result, the United States has attempted to consolidate many of these programs and integrate them into ongoing multilateral projects in which resource sharing serves as a force multiplier. The discussions with Great Britain about the future of the Regional Security System (RSS) is an example of one such program currently under review, and the full range of U.S. military projects in the region are the subject of both administration and congressional scrutiny. Thus, whatever the changed orientation of the U.S. military approach toward the Western Hemisphere, all of it remains contingent upon the budgetary constraints imposed by domestic political considerations rather than regional security requirements per se.

Then there is the lingering presence of traditional military perspectives in the U.S. command structure. When Mexico asked for military assistance in order to combat the Zapatista insurgency in Chiapas (specifically requesting helicopter gunships, armored personnel carriers, and counterinsurgency training), the U.S. Army, National Security Council, and State Department all agreed with the request over the objections of the Office of the Secretary of Defense, which held the view that military solutions do not address the fundamental socioeconomic and political issues that underpin the peasant revolt. Thus, the Mexican Army, long aloof from the United States, renowned for its uncooperative stance in the so-called war on drugs, and notoriously brutal in its approach to domestic unrest, was rewarded according to traditional foreign policy dictates rather than the new strategy of engagement and enlargement.[21]

The point of this digression into bureaucratic politics is to highlight the fact that U.S. military policy—and its attendant role—in the region is by no means uniform within the U.S. foreign policy apparatus. Instead, it is more akin to a patchwork of different perspectives variously informed by the exigencies of the field and the vicissitudes of the domestic political process, all of which often makes for rather disjointed when not contradictory policy implementation.

But the problems do not end there. In the current U.S. political context, symbolism often matters more than substance, and hypocrisy has become a common element in all foreign policy decisions. For example, while the United States denounced the attempted auto-coup by President Serrano in Guatemala in 1993 and condemned President Fujimori's assumption of dictatorial powers in Peru the year before, it said nothing negative about President Yeltsin's decision to bombard the Russian Parliament in 1993. The reason? Russia has nuclear weapons and is too strategically important a country to alienate at such a critical juncture in its history.

Reasonable enough logic, but it contradicts the ostensible championing of democracy as a foreign policy objective, and it makes clear to Latin Americans that the United States considers them, be it rightfully or wrongfully so, an area of secondary importance. Add to this the U.S. refusal to allow U.S. troops to serve under foreign commanders in the wake of the Somalia debacle of 1993–94, and the maintenance of its right to unilaterally intervene when and where it feels its national interests are at stake (even if purely domestic in nature, such as in Haiti in 1994–95), and the push for transparency and other indexes of a cooperative approach to regional security are given their lie.

There is a larger conceptual problem at stake in the promotion of cooperative security, as well. Cooperative security entails a loss of national autonomy over military decision making, or in other words, a loss of a basic measure of national sovereignty. Fine enough for large nations that are resource-endowed, self-sufficient, or militarily powerful, who can afford to give up some marginal measure of sovereignty in exchange for increased regional or international stability. But for smaller states, giving away any measure of military decision-making autonomy to foreign actors is tantamount to a surrender of sovereignty at its most basic level.

If we accept that the ultimate mission of the military is national defense, and national defense is construed as the sovereign right of nations, then the problems for small states when confronting efforts to have them accept the notion of cooperative security become apparent. For if the United States and other large states will not accept foreign oversight of their most important military assets (nuclear, chemical, and biological weapons), what is there to compel smaller states to do otherwise in the interest of some ill-defined regional peace and stability that appears to further subordinate them to the dictates of the regional military power? Chile and Brazil, most notably, have made these arguments against the rote acceptance of U.S.-promoted redefinitions of national military strategy in accord with the notions of cooperative security.[22]

But perhaps there is a method to the self-proclaimed U.S. role as champion of cooperative security and the new strategic vision. Although the United States holds as a threat in reserve its traditional prerogative to unilaterally intervene in the region and elsewhere, it may well be attempting to exercise symbolic leadership in order to set an example and the tone for future hemispheric military cooperation. Symbolic politics may well be as important as a starting block as substantive politics are to actual policy implementation. Moreover, on the latter score, the United States has absorbed most of the operational costs associated with Latin American involvement in OAS and UN peacekeeping operations and continues to actively promote the instruments and protocols required for the effective implementation of a cooperative security system in the hemisphere. So perhaps there is a strategy of action behind the rhetorical championing of the new strategic role of the United States.

There may be an understanding on the part of the United States that CS-BMs and other mechanisms that have worked well in other regions cannot readily be transposed onto the Latin American context but that the mere broaching of the subject may prompt a realistic adaptation of these models to the realities of the region. The United States has pointedly refrained from openly defining its posture as a leadership role, but instead it has repeatedly stressed the need for a regional approach to the problems of a new strategic environment. In this regard, more than a promotor, it has been a facilitator and supporter of initiatives such as that championed by OAS Special Committee on Hemispheric Security Chairman Ambassador Hernan Patiño Meyer, who has led the push to reaffirm that body's leadership role in regional security affairs under the umbrella of cooperative security.[23]

This issue for the United States ultimately revolves around the problem of simultaneously pursuing a proactive and self-limiting regional security policy in accord with the realities of the changing strategic context. Neither concept is part of the traditional U.S. approach to regional security issues, and it is an open question as to whether they are in fact the conceptual foundations of the purportedly new U.S. approach toward its security role in the hemisphere.

Conclusion

Although it appears that the United States has substantially reoriented its strategic posture in the Western Hemisphere in response to the changed global strategic environment and the ideological perspective of the Clinton administration, it is by no means clear that it has entirely given up some of its more traditional prerogatives, particularly in times of crisis. Nor is it apparent that Latin American militaries uniformly believe or share the ostensibly changed U.S. strategic perspective. But what is clear is that, for practical as well as ideological reasons, there is an ongoing reappraisal of the U.S. security role in Latin America and the Caribbean. The causes being championed, if not the instruments, have changed significantly over the last ten years, and this process of change appears to be increasingly solidified and ongoing. The question remains, however, if these changes are truly substantive, merely cosmetic, or somewhere in between, and whether they are in fact irreversible or just temporary alterations of a long established theme. For the time being, the taxonomical placement of the evolving U.S. strategy remains in limbo, pending further, if not definitive classification.

❀ Notes

Chapter 1. Security, Peace, and Democracy in Latin America and the Caribbean by Jorge I. Domínguez

1. This is not a freestanding chapter. Instead, it calls attention to and, to some degree, summarizes themes that emerge from the chapters in this book and in other work that has been part of the Inter-American Dialogue Project, "Securing Inter-American Peace and Security." This chapter relies occasionally on textual references to other chapters but my debt to the authors of this book is much greater than these citations suggest. I am also grateful to my coauthors and to Peter Hakim, Michael Shifter, and Viron P. Vaky for comments on various drafts of this chapter. The views expressed here are mine alone, however. The Inter-American Dialogue and the authors are at liberty to claim that all the errors in this chapter are mine and all the insights are theirs. All mistakes are certainly mine alone.

2. For a historical study, Jack Child, *Geopolitics and Conflict in South America: Quarrels Among Neighbors* (New York: Praeger Publishers, 1985).

3. The cold war has not ended in the Caribbean, of course. The hostility between the governments of the United States and Cuba remains severe; force might be used in the context of their relations. In this chapter, and in this book, for the most part we do not focus much attention on Cuba or on U.S.-Cuban relations, although several of my colleagues and I have done so in some of our other work. The purpose of this book is to analyze security issues that have received less international attention than those pertaining directly to Cuba and its relations with the United States.

4. For a discussion of international regimes more generally, Stephen D. Krasner, ed., *International Regimes* (Ithaca: Cornell University Press, 1983).

5. For the modern statement of these views, Kenneth Waltz, *Theory of International Politics* (New York: McGraw-Hill, 1979).

6. For studies of arms races in Latin America in the late 1960s and 1970s, see, among others, Luigi Einaudi, Hans Heymann Jr., David Ronfeldt, and Caesar Sereseres, *Arms Transfers to Latin America: Toward a Policy of Mutual Respect*, R-1173-DOS (Santa Monica: Rand Corporation, June 1973); and Michael A. Morris and Victor Millán, *Controlling Latin American Conflicts: Ten Approaches* (Boulder: Westview Press, 1983). For data, U.S. Arms Control and Disarmament Agency, *World Military Expenditures and Arms Transfers, 1967–1976* (Washington: U.S. Government Printing Office, 1978).

7. Much of this burgeoning scholarship responds to Michael Doyle, "Liberalism and World Politics," *American Political Science Review* 80, no. 4 (December 1986): 1151–69. See also Bruce Russett, *Grasping the Democratic Peace: Principles for a Post–Cold War World* (Princeton: Princeton University Press, 1993). For a statistical and analytical critique, David E. Spiro, "The Insignificance of the Liberal Peace," *International Security* 19 (fall 1994): 50–86. Joanne Gowa has indicated, moreover, that "the rates of war and other serious disputes are significantly lower between members of democratic pairs of states than between members of other country pairs only during the cold war." See her "Democratic States and International Disputes," *International Organization* 49, no. 3 (summer 1995): 512.

8. "Democratic states are less inclined to wage war against one another." *United States Security Strategy for the Americas* (Washington, D.C.: Office of International Security Affairs, U.S. Department of Defense, September 1995), 10.

9. For analysis and comparisons, Alfred Stepan, *The State and Society: Peru in Comparative Perspective* (Princeton: Princeton University Press, 1978), chapter 4.

10. For analysis and comparisons, Alfred Stepan, *Rethinking Military Politics: Brazil and the Southern Cone* (Princeton: Princeton University Press, 1988).

11. For evidence of this process under way, see Gabriel Marcella, "Up in Arms," *Hemisfile* 8, no. 1 (January–February 1997): 6–7.

12. Arms Control and Disarmament Agency, *World Military Expenditures and Arms Transfers, 1991–92* (Washington: U.S. Government Printing Office, 1994), 47–88; Francisco Rojas Aravena, "El proceso de asignación del gasto militar en América Latina," in *Gasto Militar en América Latina*, ed. Francisco Rojas Aravena (Santiago: CINDE-FLACSO, 1994); and Daniel P. Hewitt, "Military Expenditures 1972–1990: The Reasons Behind the Post-1985 Fall in World Military Spending," *IMF Working Paper* no. WP/93/18 (Washington, D.C.: International Monetary Fund, March 1993).

13. The first systematic study of the creation of this balance of power was Robert N. Burr's "The Balance of Power in Nineteenth Century South America: An Exploratory Essay," *Hispanic American Historical Review* 35 (1955): 37–60.

14. The word was first used by Bayless Manning, "The Congress, the Executive and Intermestic Affairs," *Foreign Affairs* 55, no. 2 (January 1977): 306–24. It has been applied to Latin America by Abraham F. Lowenthal; see his "Changing U.S. Interests and Policies in a New World," in *The United States and Latin America in the 1990s: Beyond the Cold War*, ed. Jonathan Hartlyn, Lars Schoultz, and Augusto Varas (Chapel Hill: University of North Carolina Press, 1992), 73–75.

15. In his chapter, David Mares finds that the end of the cold war had no impact on the likelihood of militarized interstate disputes in Latin America as a whole.

16. Anthony Maingot, "The Structure of Modern-Conservative Societies," in *Latin America, Its Problems and Its Promise: A Multidisciplinary Introduction*, ed. Jan Knippers Black (Boulder: Westview Press, 1984).

17. U.S. Assistant Secretary of State Bernard Aronson played a key role in both of these settlements.

18. As Zeledón shows, there are also various unresolved territorial disputes between Central American countries. The oldest kinds of security issues coexist with the new.

19. In part because one of its authors, William Perry, subsequently became U.S. secretary of defense, the most important work on cooperative security is by Ashton B. Carter, William J. Perry, and John D. Steinbruner, *A New Concept of Cooperative Security* (Washington, D.C.: Brookings Institution, 1992). In Latin America, discussions of cooperative security owe much to Hernán Patiño Meyer, who served in the early 1990s as Argentina's ambassador to the OAS and, from 1992 to 1995, as president of the OAS Special Committee on Hemisphere Security. His speeches and papers focused attention on these matters. Among others, see Permanent Council of the Organization of American States, Special Committee on Hemisphere Security, "Support for a New Concept of Hemisphere Security: Cooperative Security," OEA/Ser.G, CE/SH-12/93 rev. 1 (17 May 1993).

20. Karl W. Deutsch, Sidney A. Burrell, Robert A. Kann, Maurice Lee Jr., Martin Lichterman, Raymond E. Lindgren, Francis L. Loewenheim, and Richard W. Van Wagenen, *Political Community in the North Atlantic Area: International Organization in the Light of Historical Experience* (Princeton: Princeton University Press, 1957), 5–7.

21. For background, see Foreign Broadcast Information Service, FBIS-LAT-93-140 (23 July 1993), 22; FBIS-LAT-93-141 (26 July 1993), 33.

22. See Richard J. Bloomfield, "Making the Western Hemisphere Safe for Democracy," *Washington Quarterly* 17, no. 2 (spring 1994): 157–70.

23. See also Héctor Alejandro Gramajo Morales, "Political Transition in Guatemala, 1980–1990: A Perspective from Inside Guatemala's Army," in *Democratic Transitions in Central America,* ed. Jorge I. Domínguez and Marc Lindenberg (Gainesville: University Press of Florida, 1997).

24. Informal discussions have occurred between the United States and Cuba on these matters, and some confidence-building measures were implemented between the two countries in the 1990s around the U.S. naval base at Guantanamo and in the Straits of Florida.

25. For a comparative discussion, Fen Osler Hampson, "Building a Stable Peace: Opportunities and Limits to Security Co-Operation in Third World Regional Conflicts," *International Journal* 45 (spring 1990): 454–89.

26. See also his "The Increased Role of Latin American Armed Forces in UN Peacekeeping: Opportunities and Challenges," *Airpower Journal* 9 (Special Edition 1995): 17–28.

27. Nonetheless, even in 1996, after Argentina cut back and Brazil increased their respective deployments of forces in UN missions, Argentina's effort relative to the size of its military establishment was twice greater than Brazil's. In 1996, per one thousand troops in their respective armed forces, Argentina deployed eight peacekeepers, whereas Brazil deployed just four.

28. For background, see John Martz, "National Security and Politics: The Colombian-Venezuelan Border," *Journal of Interamerican Studies and World Affairs* 30, no. 4 (winter 1988–89): 117–35; Larry George, "Realism and Internationalism in the Gulf of Venezuela," *Journal of Interamerican Studies and World Affairs* 30, no. 4 (winter 1988–89): 139–63.

29. The existence of constitutional government is threatened by the persistence of this dispute. In 1992, Venezuela's military coup plotters claimed that unwarranted territorial concessions to Colombia were among the motivations for their efforts.

30. For historical discussion, see Alma H. Young and Dennis H. Young, "The Impact of the Anglo-Guatemalan Dispute on the Internal Politics of Belize," *Latin American Perspectives* 15, no. 2 (spring 1988): 6–30.

31. Foreign Broadcast Information Service, FBIS-LAT, as follows: 93-122 (28 June 1993): 13, 16–17; 93-123 (29 June 1993): 11–14; 93-124 (30 June 1993): 5; 93-126 (2 July 1993): 14; 93-127 (6 July 1993): 18; 93-127 (7 July 1993): 20–21; 93-237 (13 December 1993): 27–28. See also *Caribbean and Central America Report,* RC-93-06 (22 July 1993): 2–3; *Los Angeles Times,* 12 December 1993; *Financial Times,* 2 July 1993, 4; 20 July 1993; and 14 October 1993. I am also relying on confidential interviews.

32. For a history, Jack Child, *Unequal Alliance: The Inter-American Military System, 1938–1978* (Boulder: Westview Press, 1980).

33. For a historical discussion, J. Lloyd Mecham, *Inter-American Security Relations* (Austin: University of Texas Press, 1962).

34. In addition, the United States runs the U.S. Army School of the Americas, the Inter-American Air Forces Academy, and the Naval Small Craft and Technical Training School.

35. For discussion, see Ambassador Hernán Patiño Meyer (President of the OAS Special Committee on Hemisphere Security), "El futuro de la Junta Interamericana de Defensa," *Ser en el 2000* 5 (March 1994): 59–61.

36. Secretary of Defense William J. Perry, Defense Ministerial of the Americas, "Closing Remarks" (Williamsburg, Virginia, 26 July 1995).

37. "Declaración de San Carlos de Bariloche," *Fuerzas Armadas y sociedad* 11, no. 3 (July–September 1996): 33–37.

38. Confidential interviews. See also Pala's chapter for evidence of military collaboration with the Foreign Ministry with regard to United Nations peacekeeping missions.

39. The U.S. Southern Command completed its withdrawal from Panama in 1998, consistent with the U.S.-Panama treaty concerning the Panama canal.

40. For U.S. policy, *United States Security Strategy for the Americas,* 17–18, 24.

41. National Intelligence Estimate, "Conditions and Trends in Latin America," in *Foreign Relations of the United States, 1955–1957,* vol. 6, ed. Office of the Historian, U.S. Department of State (Washington: U.S. Government Printing Office, 1987), 24.

Chapter 2. The Use of Force in Latin American Interstate Relations by David R. Mares and Steven A. Bernstein

This essay was prepared for the Inter-American Dialogue Project on Inter-American Peace and Security. We would like to thank Randolf M. Siverson for providing the MID data base and project participants for helpful comments. The Institute on Global Conflict and Cooperation of the University of California provided partial funding for this study. Naturally, all responsibility for views expressed herein is ours alone.

1. Michael A. Morris and Victor Millán, eds., *Controlling Latin American Conflicts: Ten Approaches* (Boulder: Westview, 1983), 2–5; see also Jorge I. Domínguez, "Ghosts from the Past: War, Territorial and Boundary Disputes in Mainland Central and South America Since 1960," ms., Harvard University, Department of Government, 1977.

2. Charles S. Gochman and Zeev Maoz, "Militarized Interstate Disputes, 1816–1976," *Journal of Conflict Resolution* 28, no. 4 (December 1984): 605–12, combine figures for the United States and Latin America in an "Americas region." But their own study demonstrates that major powers are more likely to become involved in MIDs and thus the combined figure overstates Latin America's MID behavior. The MID data set examines disputes around the world between 1816 and 1993 in which force has been threatened, displayed, or used. A revised and extended version of the data base is discussed in Zeev Maoz and Bruce Russett, "Normative and Structural Causes of Democratic Peace, 1946–1986," *American Political Science Review* 87, no. 3 (1993): 624–38.

3. There are eight as defined by the standard one thousand battlefield deaths cutoff: the Second and Third Central American Wars of 1906 and 1907; Dominican Republic–Haiti 1937; Bolivia-Paraguay 1931–35; Ecuador-Peru 1939–41; El Salvador–Honduras, 1969; Argentina–Great Britain, 1982; and Ecuador-Peru 1995. Figures from the MID data set except for 1995, which are based on my confidential interviews with Ecuadorian, Peruvian, and U.S. military analysts, and on J. Lloyd Mecham, *The United States and Inter-American Security, 1889–1960* (Austin: University of Texas Press, 1962), 175–76, for Dominican Republic–Haiti. The Peru-Colombia clash in 1932 produced 868 deaths.

4. On Peru and Chile, CHIP News, Santiago: Chile Information Project, March 3, 1995. On the 1978 war between Chile and Argentina, see Thomas Princen, *Beagle Channel Negotiations* (Washington: Pew Case Study Center, 1988), no. 401, 14.

5. Jefferson's principle of "no-transfer" was a precursor to the Monroe Doctrine in 1823. Ernest R. May, *The Making of the Monroe Doctrine* (Cambridge: Harvard University Press, 1975).

6. For purposes of tractability, the relatively few MIDs with non–Western Hemisphere states (mainly Great Britain, France, Germany, and Japan) are omitted from the analysis, except for the Falklands War between Argentina and Great Britain.

7. Bryce Wood, *The United States and Latin American Wars, 1932–1942* (New York: Columbia University Press, 1966); Jorge I. Domínguez, "Los conflictos internacionales en America Latina y la amenaza de guerra," *Foro Internacional* 97, 25:1 (July–September 1984): 1–13.

8. David Spiro, "How Liberalism Produces Democratic Peace," *International Security* 19, no. 2 (fall 1994): 50–86.

9. Inter-American institutions could disagree with U.S. definitions and proposals, but they were incapable of stopping U.S. actions once the latter decided that U.S. security interests could not be protected in a multilateral context. For example, in the Panamanian case the United States preferred that the OAS remove General Noriega from power, but

Latin American members rejected the argument that his dictatorship in Panama threatened hemispheric security. Rather than altering its view about the threat, the United States undertook a unilateral invasion to remove what it defined as the "threat."

10. That analyst is Robert Rothstein, *Alliances and Small Powers* (New York: Columbia University Press, 1968), 5. The list of scholars who casually assert that the United States has been able to control interstate conflicts in Latin America is long; cf. Phillipe C. Schmitter, "Introduction," in Schmitter, ed., *Military Rule in Latin America* (Beverly Hills, Calif.: Sage, 1973), xi; Carlos Portales, "Seguridad regional en Sudamerica," in *Paz, desarme y desarrollo en América Latina*, ed. Augusto Varas (Buenos Aires: Grupo Editorial Latinoamericana, 1987), 333–82; Heraldo Muñoz, "Beyond the Malvinas Crisis," *Latin American Research Review* 19, no. 1 (1984): 158–72; Richard Millett, "The Limits of Influence: The United States and the Military in Central America and the Caribbean," in Louis W. Goodman, Johanna S. R. Mendelson, and Juan Rial, *The Military and Democracy* (Lexington: Lexington Books, 1990), 123–40. More developed discussions of the positive impact of the United States for Latin American security are found in Wood, *The United States and Latin American Wars, 1932–1942*; Domínguez, "Los conflictos internacionales en America Latina y la amenaza de guerra"; and Clifford E. Griffin, "Power Relations and Conflict Neutralization in Latin America," International Studies Working Paper, Hoover Institution, March 1992. Griffin attempts to test the hypothesis that power preponderance leads to peace by examining geographically contiguous dyads in Latin America from 1900 to 1980. His statistical analysis provides no support for the hypothesis, although he mysteriously concludes that "conflict prevention and conflict neutralization in Latin America may be due in large measure, although not exclusively, to the preponderance of US power in the region" (25). Because the same MID data he used demonstrate that conflict is not simply between contiguous nations, nor simply between Latin American countries, and he provides no justification for choosing the year 1900 as a starting point, we believe that our analysis is better suited to testing the preponderance proposition.

11. The Platt Agreement of 1901 established U.S. hegemony over the newly independent Cuba, but it took the Roosevelt Corollary to the Monroe Doctrine (1904) to eliminate European rivals in the Caribbean. For Central America, U.S. preponderance dates from the end of joint mediation with Mexico around 1907. Robert John Deger Jr., "Porfirian Foreign Policy and Mexican Nationalism: A Study of Cooperation and Conflict in Mexican-American Relations, 1884–1904," Ph.D. dissertation, Indiana University, 1979; David R. Mares, "Mexico's Policy as a Middle Power: The Nicaragua Connection, 1884–1986," *Latin American Research Review* 23, no. 3 (1988): 81–107; two books by Dana G. Munro, *The United States and the Caribbean Area* (Boston: World Peace Foundation, 1934), and *Intervention and Dollar Diplomacy in the Caribbean 1900–1921* (Princeton: Princeton University Press, 1964).

12. Wood, *The United States and Latin American Wars*.

13. Brian Loveman, "'Protected Democracies' and Military Guardianship: Political Transitions in Latin America, 1978–1993," *Journal of InterAmerican and World Affairs* 36, no. 2 (summer 1994): 105–89; on the general point, David Beetham, *Defining and Measuring Democracy* (Thousand Oaks: Sage, 1994).

14. Michael Doyle, "Liberalism and World Politics," *American Political Science Review* 80, no. 4 (1986): 1151–61.

15. Calculation of the dyads excludes Latin American dyads with European states. Six democratic-democratic MIDs were excluded by this decision. But to calculate total dyads with European states included would require either coming up with a set of politically relevant dyads for the states outside of the Western Hemisphere or developing an exhaustive set of international dyads with Latin American states. The former would produce biased results and the latter would produce statistically uninteresting results (i.e., we would have

an extremely large denominator, which would make the MID dyad/all dyad ratios insignificant.

16. Stanislav Andreski, "On the Peaceful Disposition of Military Dictatorships," *Journal of Strategic Studies* 3, no. 3 (December 3, 1980): 3–10. The logic of the argument applies to democratic polities in which the military retains sufficient autonomy to be a determinate influence on foreign policy.

17. Richard K. Betts, *Soldiers, Statesmen and Cold War Crises* (Cambridge: Harvard University Press, 1977).

18. Alfred Stepan, *The Military in Politics* (Princeton: Princeton University Press, 1971).

19. Discussion with Peruvian journalist Gustavo Gorritti, San Diego, Calif., June 5, 1995, and with Peruvian analyst Enrique Obando, Washington, D.C., September 30, 1995.

20. For the importance of the unexpected in strategy, see Edward N. Luttwak, *Strategy* (Cambridge: Belknap Press for Harvard University Press, 1987).

21. CLADDE-RIAL, *Estudio Estrategico de America Latina* (Santiago, Chile: FLACSO, 1988), section IV.

22. Centro de Estudios para la Nueva Mayoría, 1987, cited in Andrés Fontana, "Percepcion de amenazas y adquisición de armamentos: Argentina 1960–1989," in VA Rigoberto Cruz Johnson and Augusto Varas Fernández, eds., *Percepciones de Amenaza y Politicas de Defensa en América Latina* (Santiago: FLACSO, 1993), 112–13; Roy Braybrook, *Battle for the Falklands (3) Air Force* (London: Osprey, 1982), 8–9.

23. John Keegan and Andrew Wheatcroft, *Zones of Conflict* (New York: Simon and Schuster, 1986), 135.

24. Keegan and Wheatcroft, *Zones of Conflict*, 134.

25. Interview with Emilio Meneses, Director of National Security Studies at the Catholic University in Chile and a reserve officer in the Chilean Navy; see also note 5, above.

26. Virginia Gamba, *The Falklands/Malvinas War* (Boston: Allyn & Unwin, 1987), passim.

27. J. David Singer, National Capabilities Database, University of Michigan 1993.

28. For example, the Organization of American States created a committee to examine the relationship between the social-political-economic components of the organization and their military counterparts. Academic institutions in the United States, Canada, and Latin America (e.g., The North-South Center at the University of Miami; the Latin American Program of the Woodrow Wilson Center of the Smithsonian Institution; The Queens University, University of Montreal; and FLACSO-Chile) have organized conferences and research on this topic.

29. Mecham, *The United States and Inter-American Security, 1889–1960*, 48–111.

30. Even before Ronald Reagan took office, the Carter administration increased military aid to Honduras while economic aid to Nicaragua was retargeted to the private sector. Karl Bermann, *Under the Big Stick: Nicaragua and the United States since 1848* (Boston: South End Press, 1986), 261–74.

31. *Hoy* (Quito), March 14, 1995.

32. Jean-Philippe Therien, Michel Fortmann, and Guy Gosselin, "The Organization of American States: Restructuring Inter-American Multilateralism," University of Montreal, March 1995; see also committee reports for the Organization of American States: Working Group on Hemispheric Security; the Working Group on Cooperation for Hemispheric Security; and the Special Committee on Hemispheric Security.

33. *New York Times*, May 19, 1994, A1, 10.

34. Argentina has become very willing to utilize military force in the management of conflict. This new stance in Argentine foreign policy is the result of both its new foreign policy (which seeks to align itself closely with the United States, a country quite willing to

utilize military force as a tool of foreign policy) and the new civil-military relationship (in which a subordinate military and civilian politicians search for a nondomestic mission for the armed forces).

35. Hector Gros Espiell, *Conflictos Territoriales en Iberoamérica y Solución Pacífica de Controversias* (Madrid: Ediciones Cultura Hispana, 1986); and Wood, *The United States and Latin American Wars,* 6–8.

36. See Gros Espiell, *Conflictos Territoriales;* Mecham, *United States and Inter-American Security.*

37. The Pope's mediation, begun in 1979, was not successful until after Argentina was defeated by the British in 1982. Although the defeat in the Atlantic was probably necessary for the success of the mediation in the Beagle Channel, the Pope's willingness to mediate prevented an Argentine-Chilean war in December 1978.

38. Alicia Frohmann, "De Contadora al Grupo de los Ocho: El reaprendizaje de la concertación política regional," *Estudios Internacionales* 23, no. 87 (July–September 1989): 365–427.

39. Cf. Latin America Data Base, Latin American Institute, University of New Mexico, June 9, 1995.

40. Robert N. Burr, *By Reason or Force* (Berkeley: University of California Press, 1965).

41. John R. Redick, "The Tlatelolco Regime and Nonproliferation in Latin America," *International Organization* 35, no. 1 (winter 1981): 103–34.

42. Since 1987 the Latin American Center for Defense and Disarmament (CLADDE) and the Joint Study Program of Latin American International Relations (RIAL) have edited an annual study of progress in this area, *Estudio Estrategico de America Latina* (Santiago, Chile).

43. Ronald Bruce St. John, *The Foreign Policy of Peru* (Boulder: Lynne Reinner, 1992), 204, 210.

44. Israel's strategy that the "best defense is a strong offense" is a prime example. Many Chilean military analysts find important parallels between Israel's and Chile's strategic predicament. On the general subject of the relationship between capability and doctrine, see John Mearsheimer, *Conventional Deterrence* (Ithaca: Cornell University Press, 1982).

45. St. John, *Foreign Policy of Peru,* 203–05; Daniel M. Masterson, *Militarism and Politics in Latin America* (New York: Greenwood Press, 1991), 265; military expenditures can be found in Arms Control and Disarmament Agency, *World Military Expenditures and Arms Transfers,* various issues.

46. Venezuela had already been reinforcing border defenses after Colombian guerrillas crossed, but the appearance of a Colombian navy vessel in Venezuelan-claimed waters provoked a major interstate dispute. Leandro Area and Elke Nieschulz de Stockhausen, *El Golfo de Venezuela: Documentación y Cronología,* vol. 2 (1981–89) (Caracas: Universidad Central de Venezuela, 1991), 64–87.

47. E.g., Argentine Defense Minister Oscar Camilión (a civilian) argued at the Argentine-American Forum that the local balance of power must be maintained, that the United States should help keep the balance stable, and that Argentina would purchase what it needed wherever the market made it available. October 31–November 2, 1993.

48. See the discussions concerning the recent purchases of Skyhawk A4's with top-down radar from the United States. Although old, the Skyhawks had been responsible for destroying some of the British ships during the Malvinas War. Adrian J. English, *Battle for the Falklands (2) Naval Forces* (London: Osprey, 1982), 27–29.

49. CHIP News, March 20, 1995; *America Vuela* 25 (1995): 22–27.

50. "Encuesta," *Fuerzas Armadas y Sociedad* 7, no. 2: 26–35.

51. Cf., *New York Times,* January 31, 1995, A5.

Chapter 3. Argentina's Security Policies by Carlos Escudé and Andrés Fontana

1. In November 1979, during the military regime, a tripartite treaty was signed between Argentina, Brazil, and Paraguay that set the ground for future cooperative relations. An intense exchange of agreements between Argentina and Brazil followed immediately, which included the sensitive field of nuclear technology and which long preceded the integration project initiated by the civilian governments of both countries, starting in 1985. See M. Segré, "La Cuestión Itaipú-Corpus: El Punto de Inflexión en las Relaciones Argentino-Brasileñas," FLACSO Working Paper, Buenos Aires, September 1990.

2. See J. S. Tulchin, *Argentina-United States: A Conflicted Relationship* (Boston: Twayne Publishers, 1990). A word should be said here about the relation between democracy and the perspectives for peace and security. While it is true that the turning point in the bilateral relations between Argentina and Brazil took place at a time in which military regimes ruled over both countries, and while it is likewise true that the Peace and Friendship Treaty of 1985 between Argentina and Chile was signed between a democratic government (Argentina) and a military one (Chile), it is also true that the Falkland/Malvinas War was started by a military government, and that it would have been nearly impossible for an Argentine civilian government to sell such a war to the military. On the other hand, it also seems fair to say that, at least in the Argentine case, although military governments were able to sign honest peace treaties, and relations with other states did at times improve under them just as they did under democratic governments, they would seldom if ever carry the improvement of relations with other states to the point of actually spending less in defense or disarming, simply because such measures are contrary to their corporate interests.

3. See C. Díaz-Alejandro, *Essays on the Economic History of the Argentine Republic* (New Haven: Yale University Press, 1966).

4. See C. Escudé, "Education, Political Culture and Foreign Policy: The Case of Argentina," Duke-UNC Working Paper Series of Latin America, Durham, November 1992; *La "Riconquista" Argentina: Scuola e Nazionalismo* (Fiesole, Italy: Edizioni Cultura della Pace, 1992), *El Fracaso del Proyecto Argentino: Educación e Ideología* (Buenos Aires: Ed. Tesis/Instituto Torcuato Di Tella, 1990), and *Realismo Periférico: Fundamentos para la Nueva Política Exterior Argentina* (Buenos Aires: Planeta, 1992), chapter 4.

5. See C. Escudé, "The Argentine Eclipse: The International Factor in Argentina's Post-World War II Decline," Ph.D. diss., Yale University, 1981; "Argentina: The Costs of Contradiction," in *Exporting Democracy: The United States and Latin America,* ed. Abraham F. Lowenthal (Baltimore: Johns Hopkins University Press, 1991); "US Political Destabilisation and Economic Boycott of Argentina During the 1940s," in *Argentina Between the Great Powers 1939–46,* ed. G. Di Tella and D. Cameron Watt (London: Macmillan, 1989); and *Gran Bretaña, Estados Unidos y la Declinación Argentina, 1942–49* (Buenos Aires: Ed. de Belgrano, 1983). See also the chapter on "The United States' Persecution of Argentina," in J. S. Tulchin, op. cit.

6. For a full treatment of the citizen-centric approach versus its alternatives, see C. Escudé, *Foreign Policy Theory in Menem's Argentina* (Gainesville: University Press of Florida, 1997).

7. See, for example, R. Bouzas and R. Russell, eds., *Estados Unidos y la Transición Argentina* (Buenos Aires: Ed. Legasa, 1989). See also C. Escudé, "Política Exterior Argentina: Una Sobredosis Crónica de Confrontaciones," in *La Nueva Democracia Argentina,* ed. E. Garzón Valdés, M. Mols, and A. Spita (Buenos Aires: Sudamericana, 1988); *La Argentina vs. las Grandes Potencias: el Precio del Desafío* (Buenos Aires: Ed. de Belgrano, 1986); and *La Argentina, ¿Paria Internacional?* (Buenos Aires: Ed. de Belgrano, 1984). See also successive issues of the newsletter *América Latina/Internacional* published by FLACSO, Buenos Aires.

8. Curiously, in the pre-Menem era there did not exist a significant cleavage between democratic and militaristic forces with respect to some of the most relevant axes of foreign and security policy. True, the conservative and militaristic segments of the political spectrum bought the cold war logic, while the left and left-of-center segments did not and were more prone to sympathize with the socialist block. However, with respect to Falkland/Malvinas, the territorial disputes with Chile, and the issues of nuclear safeguards and nonproliferation, both the Left and the Right were united in a nationalist stance perhaps largely attributable to decades of classroom indoctrination. The Cóndor II missile project was initiated under Alfonsín and with his direct approval, and when the Menem administration scrapped the project, Alfonsín and his party protested loudly. They also protested what they considered was "caving in" to the British regarding Falkland/Malvinas, having implemented a far more hawkish policy themselves while in office. They were proud of Argentina's achievements in the field of nuclear technology, and they disapproved of accepting any formal international constraints to future developments and exports. Before Menem, both the militaristic and democratic sectors of society (including Menem's Justicialist party) were overwhelmingly enthusiastic about CONEA, the Argentine agency of atomic energy. From this point of view, what the post–Falkland/Malvinas intellectual debate achieved was not so much help consolidate the point of view of the democratic segments of society but challenge a previous consensus that included the majority of both the democratic and the militaristic forces. This consensus still prevails in Brazil and is one of the causes of the divergent strategic perspectives that presently divide the Argentine and Brazilian states, and which are dealt with below.

9. Probably the most important reason why the Alfonsín administration was not disposed to depart radically from Argentine diplomatic traditions lies in the belief systems of the major decision makers of that government, linked to the rhetoric of *dependencia* (and to some extent, of interdependence). The idea that the Alfonsín administration did not want to challenge the military on yet another issue, given the high contentiousness of human rights issues and the repeated military mutinies, does not satisfy us inasmuch as some facets of Alfonsín's confrontationist policies in Falkland/Malvinas were very displeasing to the military, and not precisely due to a government inclination toward appeasement. This is most noticeable in the case of the fishing agreements of October 1986 with the Soviet Union and Bulgaria, which included Falkland/Malvinas waters and which aimed at getting the Russians to fish in disputed waters under British control, with Argentine permission. When the agreements were defended in the Chamber of Deputies, the government acknowledged that its prime objective was not commercial but aimed at applying pressure to the British. This very dangerous move (which if successful would have brought the East-West conflict right into the South Atlantic) was very much opposed by the Argentine military, due basically to their rejection of everything associated with Communism and the Soviets. Yet Alfonsín and his foreign minister Caputo thought it worthwhile to thus escalate the conflict both with the British and with their own military. Fortunately for everyone concerned, the Russians used this agreement to fish only in undisputed Argentine waters. When they moved into Falkland/Malvinas it was with a joint Spanish-Soviet firm that purchased fishing licenses in London.

10. Foreign Minister Guido Di Tella has published a series of press articles in which he explains the rationale of Argentina's new foreign policies in the same terms as those presented in this chapter (albeit with the simplifications necessary when addressing a mass audience). See, for example, "Una política exterior al servicio del pueblo," *La Nación* (November 4, 1991): 7; "El 'realismo moral' de nuestra política exterior," *Clarín* (November 12, 1991): 13; "La ilusión 'Argentina potencia' resultó fatal," *El Cronista* (December 8, 1991): 6–7; "Moral y pragmatismo," *Somos* magazine (December 16, 1991): 24; and "Hay que atraer al capital extranjero," *Ambito Financiero* (December 19, 1991): 20.

11. This coincides with the perceptions of young military officers interviewed by

298 Notes to Pages 55–56

Fontana who expressed their satisfaction with their own belief that their participation in peacekeeping operations was their "first ever contribution to the welfare of society." See A. Fontana, "Percepciones Militares del Rol de las Fuerzas Armadas en Argentina," Serie Cuadernos no. 27 (Buenos Aires: Fundación Simón Rodríguez, August 1993).

12. Some local military sources claim that one of the reasons for the intense U.S. pressures to dismantle the Cóndor II was that the solid fuel technology used in the missile, of European origin, competed with U.S. liquid fuel technology. Although the present authors are not convinced by attempts to relativize the role of an authentic nonproliferation concern in these U.S. pressures (at least in the Argentine case), the perception is worth reporting.

13. As of mid-1996, the situation of the Argentine military industry was as follows: a) the *Tanque Argentino Mediano S.E.* (TAMSE) factory of Boulogne, Buenos Aires, dedicated to the production of the TAM family of armored vehicles (TAM, VCTP, VCTM, VCA, VCPC) has been liquidated (it will be totally closed down once the production of the last one hundred vehicles for the Argentine Army is finished); b) the *Area Material Córdoba* complex, dedicated to the maintenance of aircraft and to the production of aeronautical material (electronic systems, parachute breaks, etc.) is to be privatized; c) the *Fábrica Militar de Aviones* of Córdoba, dedicated to the production of the IA-63 Pampa training aircraft, has been sold to Lockheed, which will convert it into an aircraft maintenance center after finishing the production of a few more IA-63s for the Argentine Air Force; d) the *Astilleros Río Santiago* shipyards, of Río Santiago, Buenos Aires, dedicated to the production of destroyers and missile frigates of the MEKO family under license from the German firm Blhom & Voss, plus various other vessels, has been turned over to the government of the Province of Buenos Aires, which will reconvert them for the production of cargo vessels (the three MEKO-140 frigates under construction will be finished, after which an attempt will be made to export them); e) the *Astilleros Domeq García* shipyards of the city of Buenos Aires, dedicated to the production of class 1700 submarines under license from Thyssen Nordseewrke GmbH of Germany, will be closed down and all of its facilities will be liquidated (it will become a fancy harborside shopping mall); f) the *Altos Hornos Zapla* (of Palpala, Jujuy), *ACINDAR,* and *SOMISA* steel mills, formerly a part of the *Fabricaciones Militares* empire, have all been privatized; g) the *Fábrica Militar de Acido Sulfúrico* and the *Fábrica Militar de Tolueno Sintético,* respectively located in Berisso and Campana, Buenos Aires, dedicated to the manufacture of chemical inputs for the production of explosives, have both been privatized; h) the *Fábrica Militar Domingo Matheu* of Rosario, Santa Fe (dedicated to the manufacture of pistols and automatic rifles), the *Fábrica Militar Río Tercero* of Río Tercero, Córdoba (dedicated to the production of cannons, mortars, and their ammunition), and the *Fábrica Militar Fray Luis Beltrán* of Rosario (dedicated to the production of artillery ammunition and rockets) are all undergoing processes of reconversion; i) the *Fábrica Militar San Francisco* of San Francisco, Córdoba, dedicated to the production of ammunition for personal guns, electronic material, and parts for the TAM family of armored vehicles, is being privatized; j) the *Fábrica Militar de Materiales Pirotécnicos* of Pilar, Buenos Aires, dedicated to the production of light-generating projectiles, was liquidated, with part of its equipment reinstalled in some of the few surviving military factories; k) the *Fábrica Militar General San Martín* of San Martín, Buenos Aires, dedicated to the production of military communications equipment, was privatized and is actually used for the production of railway equipment, while part of its original facilities were relocated in the now privatized San Francisco factory; l) the *Fábrica Militar E.C.A.* of Avellaneda, Buenos Aires, dedicated to the production of tin, bronzes, and electric conductors, was privatized; m) the *Fábrica Militar Villa María* of Villa María, Córdoba, dedicated to the production of gunpowder, propulsion fuels, and explosives, was privatized, while part of its original equipment was relocated in the few remaining military factories; n) the *Tandanor* factory of the city of Buenos Aires, dedicated

to the maintenance of warships and civilian vessels, was privatized; and o) the *FANAZUL* factory of Azul, Buenos Aires, dedicated to the production of explosives, ammunition for cannons and light guns, and the Martín Pescador missile, is undergoing reconversion. (Sources: *Tecnología Militar,* December 1986 and August–September 1994, plus authors' personal sources. Grateful acknowledgement is due to Ignacio Montes de Oca and to IDECSI-CESPAL.)

14. R. Rosecrance, *The Rise of the Trading State: Commerce and Conquest in the Modern World* (New York: Basic Books, 1986).

15. In September 1994, Argentina had 1,765 participants in multilateral peace operations (without counting 107 gendarmes in Haiti), while Brazil had 138, Chile 34, Colombia 62, Ecuador 5, Honduras 16, Mexico 50, Uruguay 927, and Venezuela 32. The Latin American total, then, was 3,062. At the time, Argentina's contribution accounted for considerably more than half of that total and set off a sort of revolution in Southern Cone participation in this type of mission (see Antonio L. Pala and Frank O. Mora, "Unknown Peacekeepers: The Increased Role of Latin American Armed Forces with the UN," ms.). However, due to cost considerations, Argentina's participation in UN peacekeeping missions has hence decreased. As of September 30, 1996, it had 622 troops committed to the United Nations. Fortunately, Brazil has followed the good example, increasing its participation to 1,115, while Uruguay maintained its level of participation with 915. Contrariwise, Chile remains recalcitrant, with only six men committed to UN peacekeeping missions.

16. See A. Fontana, ed., *Argentina-NATO: Perspectives on Global Security* (Buenos Aires: GEL, 1994).

17. Among other measures, the declaration recommends: 1) the gradual adoption of a mechanism for a previous notification of all military maneuvers; 2) the participation of all the member states in the UN's register of conventional weapons and in the standardized international report on military expenditures; 3) the establishment of a system of consultations for the limitation and control of conventional weapons; and 4) the exchange of information on defense policies and doctrines.

18. The main objective is to reduce the probability of military incidents in the South Atlantic through a system of direct communication, information exchange, and reciprocal consultations with respect to naval and air traffic near the disputed area; common rules for naval and air traffic in the region; and common procedures for the case of emergencies. There is an accord to inform the other party about military maneuvers fourteen days in advance, whenever four or more ships or aircraft, or more than one thousand troops, are involved, if these maneuvers are to take place within fifty-five nautical miles of the disputed area. There is also an air traffic control agreement that links the Mount Pleasant base in Falkland/Malvinas with bases in southeastern Argentina. These arrangements have been evolving continuously, and favorably, from 1990 to the present.

19. F. Rojas Aravena, "Procesos de decisiones en el gasto militar latinoamericano," *Fuerzas Armadas y Sociedad* (July–September 1994): 27–33.

20. The International Institute for Strategic Studies (IISS), *The Military Balance, 1994–1995* (London: Brassey's, 1996), 205–11.

21. Notwithstanding, the degree of liberalization of the doctrine of top-level Argentine military officers is such that senior navy officers acknowledge that the Argentine aircraft carrier (whose return to operating conditions would cost some US$70 million) is not necessary for Argentina's defense, although (true to their corporate interests) they argue that it would be of immense symbolic value in the event of its participation in an international coalition.

22. L. S. Spector, *Nuclear Ambitions* (Cambridge, Mass.: Ballinger/Carnegie Endowment, 1990).

23. For a survey of the recent history of Argentine threat perceptions, see A. Fontana, *Percepción de Amenazas y Adquisición de Armamentos: Argentina, 1960–1989* (Buenos

Aires: Documento CEDES/48, 1990). See also A. Fontana, *Percepciones Militares del Rol de las Fuerzas Armadas en Argentina,* already cited.

24. According to the International Institute for Strategic Studies (IISS), Argentina has 266 main battle tanks and 166 light tanks, compared to Chile's 136 and 81. Argentina's navy has 2 submarines, 6 destroyers, and 7 frigates, as compared to Chile's 4 submarines, 6 destroyers, and 4 frigates. Argentina's naval aviation reportedly has 42 combat aircraft and 13 armed helicopters, vis-à-vis Chile's 14 and 16, respectively. Finally, the Argentine Air Force supposedly has 219 combat aircraft and 11 armed helicopters, while Chile's has 98 combat aircraft and no armed helicopters. Op. cit., loc. cit. As stated in the text, these data are almost meaningless.

25. It is deceiving to use Argentina's total defense budget for this computation because together with the budgets of the individual armed services, it includes factories, the *gendarmerie,* the coast guard, the ministry staff, etc. On the other hand, it should be born in mind that large investments in hardware usually come from special accounts, which the individual budgets of each armed service do not reflect. In Argentina, important acquisitions such as the thirty-six A4M Skyhawks (which have not yet been received nor paid for) are paid through the use of the legal figure of a "public credit," which entails a budgetary authorization for the contraction of debt and which is included in the annual national budget but is not a part of the defense budget, much less of the individual services.

Similar problems emerge from the Brazilian and Chilean defense budgets. For example, to the Chilean budget one must add 10 percent of annual copper exports, which is appropriated to be used exclusively for the purchase of equipment for the three armed services. To the Brazilian budget one must add 8 percent of offshore oil royalties, which is appropriated for the equipment of the navy. Clearly, this represents a problem because not every addition to the resources of the armed forces through this sort of appropriation can be identified. There is a consensus among Argentine officers that the defense budget should be consolidated, and that there should be budget transparency among the ABC countries, but apparently there is little enthusiasm for such action in Brazil and Chile. It is interesting to note that this idea is the equivalent of NATO's proposal to the former member states of the Warsaw Pact, which has been accepted by most of them including, very recently, Russia; it is also similar to NATO's 1990 proposal for the standardization of all military budgets.

26. These data and those presented in the next two paragraphs come out of interviews conducted in 1995 by A. Fontana for this essay. The interviewees were senior naval officers who asked to remain anonymous.

27. On this subject, see A. Fontana, "Relaciones Cívico-Militares y Agenda de Seguridad en América Latina," in *La Argentina y la Situación Internacional* (Buenos Aires: Agora/GEL, 1993).

28. This came out clearly from a meeting between high-level officials of both countries, held in Santiago on November 23, 1994, under the auspices of FLACSO-Chile and Universidad Torcuato Di Tella.

29. It is interesting to observe the differences between Western and Third World evaluations of Argentina's participation in UN peacekeeping forces. For example, in a 1994 interview Sir Brian Urquhart, former undersecretary-general of the United Nations, stated that: "Argentina has provided hospitals, troops, engineers, police, and electoral observers. I wish that all countries would participate at this level and diversity." Contrariwise, Prof. Raúl Benítez of UNAM, Mexico, in the context of a seminar held at the American University in May 1995, called the Argentine peacekeeping forces "mercenaries."

30. Such was the case, for example, of Deputy Raúl Alconada Sempé, former vice foreign minister of the Radical administration, who made public his support of the agreement immediately after its announcement but later retreated to headstrong opposition.

31. See C. Escudé, *La Argentina, ¿Paria Internacional?* (Buenos Aires: Belgrano, 1984); *La Argentina vs. las Grandes Potencias: El Precio del Desafío* (Buenos Aires: Belgrano, 1986), essays 3 and 4; "Argentine Territorial Nationalism," *Journal of Latin American Studies* (May 1988); *Realismo Periférico,* chapter 4; and especially "Education, Political Culture and Foreign Policy: The Case of Argentina."

32. Dr. Ferreira was absent but a reading of his official presentation was made in the meeting.

33. See AFP cable of June 8, 1995 (*La Nación,* June 9, 3, column 1).

34. This information has been acquired through interviews with top-level army and navy officers.

35. Revealed to the authors by two high-ranking Argentine military officers in separate interviews. Both officers had been witnesses to this Brazilian argument and repeated it in very similar terms.

36. This view (with an explicit quotation) was heartily endorsed by one of the Argentine organizers of a seminar held in Brasilia on May 26 and 27, 1995, which was the follow-up of the September 1994 seminar mentioned above.

37. This was official policy, and it was the Argentine reply to a poll conducted by the United Nations on the issue of the expansion of the Security Council. The situation changed somewhat when it became known that the United States wanted Germany and Japan to be permanent members of the Council, and that in order to seduce the General Assembly (whose majority support it needs to change the charter), it was willing to support the inclusion of three additional permanent members from the developing world, one from Africa, one from Asia, and one from Latin America. When this issue became a matter of public debate in August 1997, President Menem himself stated that Argentina was in favor of a "permanent" position for Latin America in which the three largest Latin American states should take turns. The Brazilian government was outraged with this statement, which generated a mini-crisis in the political relations between the two major MERCOSUR states. Voices of dissent against what was perceived as Menem's obstructionism of Brazil's probable candidacy were also raised in Argentina, and the official position now seems to be that if the "permanent yet rotational" mechanism proposed by Menem is rejected by the General Assembly (a likely case), Argentina will in its final instance support Brazil. Domestic politics underly this convoluted approach to the issue, inasmuch as the government was afraid that an outright support of Brazil would be exploited by the opposition through the manipulation of nationalist emotions. Menem's declaration was made in the campaign climate previous to the October 1997 elections, and the authors of this chapter have had an explicit confirmation of the government's political fears from very senior political officials, *previous* to Menem's statement.

38. Although public opinion polls conducted by the most prestigious firms in the country (the most complete being by Mora y Araujo, Noguera y Asociados) show that the great majority of the population supports the country's present-day foreign and security policies, and furthermore show that the United States is widely viewed as *the* model to be followed (this certainly being a novelty in Argentine and Latin American politics), the majority that thus expresses itself is a silent one (which time and time again has voted for Carlos Menem despite the media's dislike of the president), while significative and influential minorities express themselves loudly against what has pejoratively been labeled a policy of "carnal relations" with the United States. It is interesting to note that this is a label that was actually coined jokingly by the foreign minister himself and that has boomeranged strongly. It is one of few identified cases in which an anthropomorphic metaphor coined by a politician serves to alienate instead of to rally public opinion. See C. Escudé, "The Anthropomorphic Metaphor in International Relations Discourse," Paper No. 94-6, Center for International Affairs, Harvard University, August 1994.

39. Date in which Argentina entered the Paraguayan war, in league with Brazil and an Uruguayan faction, with the dubious excuse that Paraguayan forces had crossed Argentine territory without permission in order to engage with Brazilian forces.

Chapter 4. Transition and Civil-Military Relations in Chile by Francisco Rojas Aravena

1. Naciones Unidas, Comisión Económica para América Latina (CEPAL), "Desenvolvimiento de los procesos de integración en América Latina y el Caribe," Santiago, May 1995.

2. Special importance should be assigned to the conflict and confrontations between Ecuador and Peru in the Condor Mountain Range at the beginning of 1995. See Francisco Rojas Aravena, "Un desafío a la seguridad hemisférica," La Epoca, Santiago, 6 February 1995. Also at the beginning of 1995, tense situations emerged along the Colombia-Venezuela border. Likewise, the press highlighted the resurgence of some difficulties in border areas of Central America. See Jaime Delgado, "Un conflicto en la zona fronteriza tico-nicaragüense," in Una Informa (Heredia, Costa Rica: Universidad Nacional, April 1995). Likewise the Agency EFE reported on these same dates some incidents in the Gulf of Fonseca, which El Salvador, Honduras, and Nicaragua share. The armed confrontation in the Andean area changed the climate of regional relationships on border topics. It generated a perception of uncertainty that affected the image of the region.

3. Augusto Varas, "La seguridad hemisférica," in Paz y Seguridad en América Latina y el Caribe en los años noventa (Lima: Centro Regional de Naciones Unidas para el Desarme y el Desarrollo en América Latina y el Caribe, 1991).

4. Francisco Rojas Aravena, "Security Regimes in the Western Hemisphere: A View from Latin America," in Security, Democracy and Development in U.S.-Latin American Relations, ed. Lars Schoultz, William C. Smith, and Augusto Varas (New Brunswick: Transaction Publishers, 1994).

5. In all cases, more than two presidential elections have already taken place. In the Southern Cone, the last elections ratified a second term for the presidents of Argentina and Peru (Carlos Menem and Alberto Fujimori). In both cases, the incumbents obtained a majority in Congress.

6. Daniel Wisecarver, ed., El modelo económico chileno (Santiago: Centro Internacional para el Desarrollo Económico y el Instituto de Economía de la Pontificia Universidad Católica de Chile, 1992).

7. Oscar Muñoz, ed., Transición a la democracia: marco político y económico (Santiago: CIEPLAN, 1990).

8. Augusto Varas, "Las relaciones civil-militares en la democracia," in América Latina: militares y sociedad II, ed. Dirk Krujit and Edelberto Torres-Rivas (San José, Costa Rica: FLACSO-Costa Rica, 1991); Wendy Hunter, "Contradictions of Civilian Control: Argentina, Brazil and Chile in the 1990s," Third World Quarterly 15, no. 4 (1994): 635–55.

9. Joaquín Fermandois and Michael A. Morris, "Democracy in Chile: Transition and Consolidation 1987–2000," Conflict Studies no. 279 (London: Research Institute for the Study of Conflict and Terrorism, 1995).

10. Luciano Tomassini, ed., ¿Qué espera la sociedad del gobierno? (Santiago: Centro de Análisis de Políticas Públicas, Universidad de Chile, 1994).

11. Augusto Varas and Claudio Fuentes, Defensa Nacional, Chile 1990–1994 (Santiago: FLACSO, 1994).

12. Genaro Arriagada, "Modernización: el desafío crucial del segundo gobierno de la Concertación," in ¿Qué espera la sociedad del gobierno?, ed. Luciano Tomassini; José Joaquín Brunner, "La modernización del Estado," La Epoca, 30 April 1995.

13. Mark Ensalaco, "Military Prerogatives and the Stalemate of Chilean Civil-Military Relation," *Armed Forces & Society* 21, no. 2 (winter 1995): 225–70.

14. Eduardo Frei, *Mensaje Presidencial 1995* (Santiago: Secretaría de Comunicación y Cultura, Ministerio Secretaría General de Gobierno, May 1995); Carlos Figueroa, *Intervención en el 62 aniversario del Partido Socialista* (Santiago: 19 April 1995). A summary was published in *La Epoca*, April 1995.

15. Oscar Godoy, "La política aguachenta," interview in the magazine *Hoy*, no. 937 (3–9 July 1995): 13–15.

16. José Zalaquett, "Derechos humanos y limitaciones políticas en las transiciones democráticas del Cono Sur," *Colección Estudios Cieplan* 33 (December 1991): 147–86. See also José Zalaquett, "Balancing Ethical Imperatives and Political Constraints: The Dilemma of New Democracies Confronting Past Human Rights Violations," *Hasting Law Journal* 43, no. 6 (August 1992): 1425–38.

17. When faced with the Report from the Commission on Truth and Reconciliation, "Informe Rettig," which established the truth of the state on the issue, the army indicated that "the report has no historical nor juridical validity." The navy indicated that many aspects of the document "tend not to promote the harmonious integration of all sectors of the nation and can seriously affect the security of the nation." See *El Mercurio*, 28 March 1991.

18. Crisóstomo Pizarro, Dagmar Raczynsk, and Joaquín Vial, *Políticas económicas y sociales en el Chile democrático* (Santiago: CIEPLAN/UNICEF, 1995).

19. Francisco Rojas Aravena, "La reinserción internacional de Chile," in *Anuario de política exterior chilena 1990* (Santiago: FLACSO-Chile, 1991).

20. Francisco Rojas Aravena, "De la reinserción a los acuerdos," in *Anuario de política exterior chilena 1991* (Santiago: FLACSO-Chile, 1992). Francisco Rojas Aravena, "Consolidando una inserción múltiple en el sistema internacional," in *Anuario de política exterior chilena 1993* (Santiago: FLACSO-Chile, 1993); Francisco Rojas Aravena, "Construyendo un nuevo perfil externo: democracia, modernización, pluralismo," in *Anuario de política exterior chilena 1994* (Santiago: FLACSO-Chile, 1994).

21. Ministerio de Relaciones Exteriores, *Política exterior vecinal del gobierno del presidente Aylwin, 1990–1994* (Santiago, January 1994).

22. Edgardo Riveros Marín, "Los medios de solución pacífica de controversias en el tratado de paz y amistad," in *El tratado de paz y amistad entre Chile y Argentina* (Santiago: Editorial Universitaria, 1988), 73–79.

23. Carlos Figueroa, "La política exterior y los desafíos de la seguridad internacional," *Política y estrategia*, Revista ANEPE, no. 63 (Santiago: May–August 1994): 15–21.

24. Augusto Varas and Isaac Caro, eds., *Medidas de confianza mutua en América Latina* (Santiago: FLACSO, Stimson Center, SER, 1994).

25. Augusto Varas, "Las relaciones civil-militares en la democracia," in *América Latina: militares y sociedad II*.

26. Brian Loveman, *The Constitution of Tyranny* (Pittsburgh: University of Pittsburgh Press, 1993).

27. Gonzalo García and Juan Esteban Montes, *Subordinación democrática de los militares, éxitos y fracasos en Chile* (Santiago: CED, 1994). See also Augusto Varas and Claudio Fuentes, *Defensa Nacional, Chile 1990–1994*.

28. The statement by General Martín Balza appeared throughout the Argentine press on April 26, 1995. See, for example, *Página/12*. The debate continued for subsequent days. For Admiral Enrique Molina Pico's statements, see *Clarín*, 4 May 1995.

29. The issue of human rights, especially of those who were detained-disappeared, is a topic of special importance in the region. In Brazil, legal ways to overcome this three-decades-old problem are being sought in 1995. In Peru, an amnesty law was decreed. In Chile, the debate about human rights became a central issue. In Argentina, after the con-

victions and the pardon, a self-critique by the armed forces has emerged. In Honduras and Guatemala, there is an important debate on the role played by foreign forces and advisors on techniques of disappearance, execution, and torture.

30. Charlie Rose, "Democratic Control of the Armed Forces," *NATO Review* 5 (October 1994). A Spanish-language version was distributed by USIS. Brian A. Davenport, "Civil-Military Relations in the Post Soviet State: 'Loose Coupling' Uncoupled," *Armed Forces & Society* 21, no. 2 (winter 1995): 175–94. Robert Arnett, "Can Civilians Control the Military?," *Orbis* 38, no. 1 (winter 1994): 41–58.

31. Augusto Varas, *Chile: política de defensa y gran estrategia* (Santiago: FLACSO-Chile, Area de Relaciones Internacionales y Militares, 1994). For the platforms of the presidential candidates E. Frei and A. Alessandri, as well as the view of the army as expressed at the conference by General A. Pinochet, "Ejército de Chile: posibles elementos a considerar en su proyección futura," see *Fuerzas Armadas y Sociedad* 8, no. 4 (Santiago: FLACSO-Chile, October–December).

32. Edmundo Pérez Yoma, "Planteamientos programáticos del gobierno en el área de la defensa nacional," *Política y estrategia,* Revista de la ANEPE, no. 63 (Santiago, May–August 1994).

33. Bases programáticas del segundo gobierno de la Concertación, *Un gobierno para los nuevos tiempos* (Santiago, 1993).

34. Adrian J. English and Scott D. Tollefson, "National Security," in *Chile: A Country Study,* ed. Rex A. Hudson (Washington, D.C.: U.S. Department of Defense, 1994).

35. José Miguel Insulza, *Discurso inaugural año académico del magister del Instituto de Estudios Internacionales* (Santiago: Universidad de Chile, May 1995).

36. Raúl Sohr, *La industria militar chilena* (Santiago: Comisión Sudamericana de Paz, 1990). Augusto Varas and Claudio Fuentes, "La industria de bienes de uso militar en Chile," *Documento de Trabajo FLACSO* (Santiago, Chile: FLACSO, 1991). Patrice M. Franko, "Small Scale Competitiveness in the New International Arms Market: The Case of Chile," unpublished, 1995.

37. Augusto Varas and Rigoberto Cruz Johnson, *Percepciones de amenaza y políticas de defensa en América Latina* (Santiago: FLACSO-Chile/CEEA, 1993).

38. Edmundo Pérez Yoma, *Fundamentos y características de la política de defensa* (speech at the Armed Forces Academy, March 1995), Colección Documentos, Departamento de Difusión, SECC, Ministerio Secretaría General de Gobierno (June 1995).

39. One approach to these issues can be found in Claudio Fuentes, "Relaciones Internacionales en el campo de la defensa," *Cono Sur* 12, no. 1 (January–February 1993): 26–31.

40. Francisco Rojas Aravena, ed., *Gasto Militar en América Latina: procesos de decisiones y actores claves* (Santiago: FLACSO-Chile/CINDE, 1994).

41. Augusto Varas, *La seguridad hemisférica cooperativa de post guerra fría* (Santiago: FLACSO-Chile, Area of International and Military Relations, 1994). See the different reports from the Peace Program: Paz y seguridad en las Américas, developed jointly by FLACSO-Chile and the Latin American Program of the Wilson Center in Washington, D.C. See especially, "Políticas de seguridad hemisférica cooperativa."

42. Programa Paz y Seguridad en las Américas, *Reunión de Ministros de Defensa de las Américas* 3 (Santiago, June 1995).

43. O'Seadet Deger and Somnath Sen, "Desarme, desarrollo y gastos militares," *Desarme* 13, no. 3: 48.

Chapter 5. Security Policies, Democratization, and Regional Integration in the Southern Cone by Mônica Hirst

I would like to thank Elsa Llenderrozas for her valuable assistance in preparing this essay.

1. See Philippe Schmitter, "Idealism, Regime Change, and Regional Cooperation: Lessons from the Southern Cone of Latin America," *The New Interdependence in the Americas: Challenges to Economic Restructuring, Political Redemocratization, and Foreign Policy* (Stanford: Stanford University Press, 1991). For general analysis of Kant's theory of liberal internationalism, see Michael Doyle, "Liberalism and World Politics," *American Political Science Review* 80 (1986): 1151–69.

2. See Carlos Acuña and William Smith, "The Politics of 'Military Economics' in the Southern Cone: Comparative Perspectives on Democracy, Arms Production and the Arms Race Among Argentina, Brazil and Chile," mimeo, CEDES, Buenos Aires, 1994.

3. Bruce Russett, *Grasping the Democratic Peace* (Princeton: Princeton University Press, 1993), 34.

4. In 1979, Argentina and Brazil signed the Itaipú-Corpus Treaty, which settled the dispute over the exploitation of the Paraná River's hydroelectric resources. In 1984, Argentina and Chile signed a Peace and Friendship Treaty, which sealed negotiations regarding the Beagle Channel.

5. According to the International Institute for Strategic Studies (IISS), defense spending average in nineteen Latin American countries dropped 35.2 percent between 1985 and 1990. South America spends less on the military than any other region in the world. Argentina's defense spending fell from nearly 7 percent of national GDP to roughly 3 percent over this decade. See Patrice Franko, "De Facto Militarization: Budget-Driven Downsizing in Latin America," *Journal of Inter-American Studies and World Affairs* 36, no. 1 (spring 1994): 37–74.

6. The concept "spill-around effect" has been used by Philippe Schmitter when he analyzed the myriad of cooperative initiatives in Central America in the fifties. This concept is applied to describe the process by which "there is a proliferation of independent efforts at regional coordination in distinct functional spheres—i.e. an expansion in the scope of regional tasks—without, however, a concomitant devolution of authority to a single body—i.e., without an increase in the level of regional decision making." See Philippe Schmitter, "Central American Integration: Spill-Over, Spill-Around or Encapsulation?" *Journal of Common Market Studies* 9, no. 1 (September 1970): 39.

7. The Argentina-Brazil Economic Cooperation and Integration Program (PICE) involved a set of agreements in the economic field (including capital goods, commerce, wheat, food supply, iron and steel industry, and automobile industry), and in the military-technological field (including nuclear energy and armaments industry). Negotiations also involved technological cooperation for computers and biotechnology.

8. The Asunción Treaty was signed by Argentina, Brazil, Paraguay, and Uruguay in 1991. This treaty determines the formation of a common market with phased elimination of barriers leading to free movement of goods, services, capital, and labor throughout the region and a common external tariff by 1995.

9. The only programs fully maintained were the development and prototype construction of the Cóndor II missile and the Pampa 2000 jet trainer. See Acuña & Smith, op. cit., 13.

10. See Brian Loveman, "¿Misión Cumplida? Civil-Military Relations and the Chilean Political Transition," in *Journal of Inter-American Studies and World Affairs* 33, no. 3 (fall 1991): 35–74; Arturo Valenzuela, "Chile: Origins, Consolidation, and Breakdown of a Democratic Regime," in Larry Diamond, Juan Linz, and Seymour Lipset, eds., *Democracy in Developing Countries* (Boulder: Lynne Rienner Publishers, 1989).

11. These negotiations included an amnesty for political crimes committed between 1973 and 1978, an autonomous defense policy, an independent Central Bank, no inquiry about the prior privatization process, and the automatic transference of 10 percent of copper exports to the armed forces. See Brian Loveman, op. cit.; Manuel Garretón, *Discu-*

tir la 'transición': Estrategias y escenarios de la democratización política chilena (Santiago: FLACSO, 1991).

12. See Geraldo Cavagnari Filho, "Autonomía Militar e Construção da Potencia," in *As Forças Armadas no Brasil* (Rio de Janeiro: Espaço e Tempo, 1987).

13. According to the 1988 Constitution, the military were conceded the authority to intervene in domestic matters. According to Article 142 the armed forces are responsible for national defense and the protection of constitutional powers. Law and order shall be defended in accordance with constitutional powers.

14. Two examples to be mentioned are the diplomatic recognition of Cuba in 1987 and the nuclear cooperation agreements negotiated with Argentina since 1986.

15. See, for instance, Emanuel Adler, *The Power of Ideology: The Quest for Technological Autonomy in Argentina and Brazil* (Berkeley: University of California Press, 1987).

16. See Mônica Hirst and Maria Regina Soares de Lima, "Crisis y toma de decisión en la política exterior brasileña: el programa de integración Argentina-Brasil y las negociaciones sobre la informática con Estados Unidos," in Roberto Russell, ed., *Política Exterior y Toma de Decisiones en América Latina* (Buenos Aires: GEL, 1990).

17. Charles Gillespie and L. González, "Uruguay: The Survival of Old and Autonomous Institutions," in L. Diamond, J. Linz, and S. Lipset, eds., op. cit.; Aldo Solari, "Proceso de democratización en Uruguay," *Síntesis* 13 (January–April 1991): 147–65; Juan Rial, "Los militares en tanto 'partido político sustituto' frente a la redemocratización en Uruguay," *Síntesis* 13 (January–April 1991): 229–57.

18. Domingo Rivarola, "Política y sociedad en Paraguay contemporáneo. El autoritarismo y la democracia," *Síntesis* 10 (January–April 1990): 195–214.

19. See, for instance, Guillermo O'Donnell, "Challenges to Democratization in Brazil," *World Policy Journal* 5, no. 2 (spring 1988): 281–300.

20. The military rebellions that took place in Argentina during the democratic transition were Campo de Mayo, headed by Col. Aldo Rico (April 1987); Monte Caseros (Corrientes) led by Aldo Rico and collaborators (January 1988); Villa Martelli (Buenos Aires), headed by Col. Seineldin (December 1988); Palermo (Buenos Aires) led by midrange officials (December 1990).

21. After the 1973 military coup, a Copper Law was amended by which an appropriation of 10 percent of total copper exports (instead of a percentage of taxes on copper exports) was to be equally divided between the three branches of the armed forces. In 1986, the Copper Law was replaced by a *ley reservada* that doubled the minimum contribution from $90 to $180 million. In the event that copper exports are insufficient to cover this minimum contribution, the 1986 amendment mandates that the state will make up the difference to the armed forces. See Carlos Acuña and William Smith, op. cit., 16.

22. This reform would involve changes in the membership of the Constitutional Court and of the National Security Council as well as the elimination of life-tenure senators previously appointed by Pinochet. President Frei's proposals were also aimed to increase the presidential prerogatives to ask for the retirement of military authorities.

23. For a general view of postauthoritarian thought on the Brazilian military, see Mario Cesar Flores, *Base para uma política militar* (Campinas: Editora da Unicamp, 1992).

24. Uruguay's navy and air force had major budgetary constraints that affected the capacity of the armed forces to accomplish their objectives and missions. The navy possesses equipment to support professional development for ten years but with a low performance in some of their essential tasks such as coastal control. In fact, Uruguay's navy and air force are at risk to disappear in the near future. See Juan Rial, "Renovación o Reforma Militar," *Seguridad estratégica regional* 4 (Septiembre 1993): 66.

25. Uruguay has participated in the UN Group of Military Observation in Iran-Iraq (UNIMOG) from 1988 to 1990; and in the UN Group of Military Observation in Iraq-

Kuwait (UNIKOM) since 1991. Also, it has participated in UNTAC (Cambodia) since 1992 and in the UN Observer Mission in Mozambique (ONUMOZ) since 1993. See Ejército Nacional de la República Oriental del Uruguay, "Relaciones de los ejércitos de la región con la Organización de las Naciones Unidas," *Seguridad estratégica regional* 5 (Marzo 1994): 96.

26. See Marcial A. Riquelme, "Bases para la discusión de las relaciones Fuerzas Armadas-Sociedad Civil en el Paraguay," in J. L. Simon, ed., *La democracia en Paraguay cinco años después* (Asunción: Fundación Hans Seidel—Universidad Nacional de Asunción, 1994).

27. Hans Henrik Holm and Georg Sorensen use this distinction when they refer to post–cold war global transformations. According to this distinction there are two competing interpretations regarding the end of the cold war. One states that there has been a qualitative change in international politics, while the other downgrades the scope and level of the transformation, sustaining that "the end of the Cold War merely meant changes in the distribution of power within an anarchic system of states." See Holm and Sorensen, eds., *Whose World Order?* (Boulder: Westview Press, 1995).

28. See Carlos Escudé and Andrés Fontana, chapter 3 in this book.

29. For the importance of ideas in governmental strategies and a more precise analysis of the influence of belief systems on foreign policy, see Judith Goldstein and Robert O. Keohane, eds., *Ideas and Foreign Policy* (Ithaca: Cornell University Press, 1993).

30. For a comprehensive assessment of Collor de Mello's foreign policy, see Ademar Seabra de Cruz Jr., Antonio Ricardo Cavalcante, and Luiz Pedone, "Brazil's Foreign Policy Under Collor," *Journal of Inter-American Studies and World Affairs* 35, no. 1 (1993): 119–44. See also Mônica Hirst and Leiticia Pinheiro, "A política externa do Brasil em dois tempos," *Revista Brasileira de Política Internacional* (Brasilia: Univ. de Brasilia, July 1995).

31. The main decisions in this case were negotiation of a full-scope nuclear safeguards agreement with Argentina, the revision for full enforcement of the Tlatelolco Treaty, and the preparation of a bill to control arms and sensitive technology exports.

32. See Maria Regina Soares de Lima, "Ejes analíticos y conficto de paradigmas en la política exterior brasíleña," *América Latina/Internacional* 1, no. 2 (FLACSO-Argentina, 1994): 27–46. See also Paulo Nogueira Batista, "A Política Externa de Collor: Modernização ou Retrocesso," *Política Externa* 1, no. 4 (Sao Paulo, 1993): 106–35.

33. See Carlos Augusto Santos Neves, "O Brasil e o futuro: linhas para uma presença do Brasil na vida internacional," *Política Externa* 1, no. 4 (March 1993).

34. James Hoge, "Cardoso's Brazilian Dreams," *Foreign Affairs* 74, no. 4 (July–August 1995): 68.

35. Gleuber Vieira, "La variable estratégica en el processo de constitución del Mercosur," *Seguridad estratégica regional* no. 5 (marzo 1994): 10. For a broad analysis of present world transformations from a military perspective, see Leonel Itaussu Almeida Mello, "A Geopolítica do Poder Terrestre Revistada," *Lua Nova* no. 34 (1994): 55–69. According to this author, the post–cold war world will "continue to be anarchical, hierarchical and oligopolistic," 69.

36. Ibid., 9.

37. Brazil participated in the UN Observer Mission in El Salvador (ONUSAL), the UN Observer Mission in Mozambique (ONUMOZ), and the UN Mission in Angola (UNAVEM). Until December 1994, only 150 Brazilian officials participated in international missions, an amount lower than Argentina (1,300) and Uruguay (930). See *Gazeta Mercantil*, December 1, 1995, 9.

38. The SIVAM is intertwined with a broader concern in Brazil shared by governmental and political segments about the need for a more effective integration between the Amazon territory and the rest of the country. For this reason SIVAM belongs to a comprehensive project called SIPAN (Amazon Protection System), which involves the armed

forces, the secretary for strategic affairs, the Federal Police, the Ministry for Environmental Resources, and the National Indigenous Foundation.

39. This concept was developed and applied by Karl Deutsch to characterize the security cooperation and integration among Western European countries. See Karl Deutsch et al., *Political Community and the North Atlantic Area* (Princeton: Princeton University Press, 1957).

40. See Gustavo Druetta and Luis Tibiletti, "La seguridad estratégica regional en el Cono Sur," in *Cambios Globales y América Latina. Algunos Temas de la Transición Estratégica* (Santiago: CLADDE-FLACSO, 1993).

41. Claudio Fuentes, "El Mundo desde Chile," *Seguridad estratégica regional* no. 7 (marzo 1995): 70.

42. Thomaz Guedes da Costa, "Bases de la postura estratégica de los países sudamericanos en la década del noventa," in *Cambios Globales y América Latina* (Santiago: CLADDE-FLACSO, 1993), 81.

43. See K. J. Holsti, "Analyzing an Anomaly: Conflict and Peace in South America," in *The State, War, and the State of War* (Cambridge: Cambridge University Press, 1996).

44. Shared worldviews have been linked to ideological preferences, to partisan politics, to international influences and interests, and to a permanent process of contamination of economic and political developments between Argentina and Brazil.

45. See Mônica Hirst, "A Reação do Empresariado Argentino diante da Formação do Mercosul," Brasilia: IPEA, 1994.

46. Following this same kind of logic, when Argentina's goverment initiated military action to recuperate the South Atlantic islands, certain segments in Brazil's government and society supported Argentina not only by reason of this country's legitimate rights but also because of the admiration for their neighbor's audacity. A similar feeling was observed at first when Brazil broke relations with the Axis powers in 1942 and Argentina maintained the decision to keep neutral. Regarding economic policies, when Cavallo's stabilization program began showing positive results, different sectors of Brazilian elites were frustrated that Brazil would not copy the same formula.

47. Gleuber, op. cit.

48. Hoge, op. cit., 66.

49. As Holsti has stated, "no-war" zones are those "In which the possibility of armed conflict has been reduced to almost zero." See Holsti, op. cit., 158.

50. Holsti analyzes South America's legalistic diplomatic culture, suggesting that it could represent a compensation for the lack of other commanding doctrines, such as "manifest destiny" and "a civilizing mission," "world revolution," or "anti-communism." See Holsti, op. cit., 170.

51. Chile has resisted entering MERCOSUR for three basic reasons: It does not want to tie its tariff structure to a subregional Common External Tarriff, it fears that a significant increase in the importance of trade with other Southern Cone countries could make the Chilean economy more vulnerable to instability, and the Chilean agricultural sector would inevitably be affected by competition with Argentina's primary products. See Andrea Butelmann and Patricio Meller, *Evaluation of a Chile-U.S. FTA Trade Liberalization in the Western Hemisphere* (Washington, D.C.: IDB/ECLAC, 1995).

Chapter 6. Institutionalization, Cooperative Security, and Peacekeeping Operations by Ricardo E. Lagorio

1. Francis Fukuyama, "The End of History," *National Interest* 16 (summer 1989): 3–18.

2. Boutros Boutros-Ghali, "Empowering the UN," *Foreign Affairs* 71, no. 5 (winter 1992–93): 89–103.

3. Thomas G. Weiss, "Intervention: Whither the United Nations," *Washington Quarterly* 17, no. 1 (winter 1994): 109–29.

4. Marisol Touraine, *Le Bouleversement du Monde: Geopolitique du XXI Siecle* (Paris: Seuil, 1995).

5. Weiss, "Intervention."

6. Adam Roberts, "The Crisis in U.N. Peacekeeping," *Survival* 36, no. 3 (autumn 1994): 93–121.

7. John Lukacs, "The Short Century Is Over," *New York Times,* Feb. 17, 1991, sec. 4, 13.

8. Alexis de Tocqueville, *Democracy in America* (New York: Phillips Bradley, 1955).

9. Samuel P. Huntington, "Political Modernization: America vs. Europe," *World Politics* 18, no. 3 (1966): 378–414.

10. Joseph S. Nye Jr., *Understanding International Conflicts* (New York: Harper Collins College Publishers, 1993).

11. On purpose I refer to "country" because the Congress adopted a law supporting the executive's decision to participate in the coalition under the terms of the Security Council Resolution.

12. Memoria del Ejército Argentino, *Un ejército hacia el siglo XXI* (Buenos Aires, 1995).

13. Idem.

14. Ashton B. Carter, William J. Perry, John D. Steinbruner, *A New Concept of Cooperative Security* (Washington: Brookings Institution, 1992).

15. Idem.

16. Documento A/50/60, S/1995/1, January 3, 1995. Suplemento de "Un programa de paz": Documento de posición del Secretario General presentado con ocasión del cincuentenario de las Naciones Unidas.

Chapter 7. Peacekeeping and its Effects on Civil-Military Relations
by Antonio Palá

1. Jose C. d'Odorico, "Argentina Waiting in the Wings for a Chance to Join NATO," *Armed Forces Journal International* 130, no. 7 (February 1993): 38.

2. Manuel Mora-Araujo, Graciela Di Rado, and Paula Montoya, "La Política Exterior y la Opinión Pública Argentina," in Roberto Russell, ed., *La Política Exterior Argentina en el Nuevo Orden Mundial* (Buenos Aires: FLACSO, 1992), 237–38.

3. Germán Sopeña, "Boutros Ghali: El Gran Problema es el Nacionalismo Extremo," *La Nación,* March 21, 1994, 3.

4. "ONUCA Mission Deemed a Success," *UN Chronicle,* September 1990, 42.

5. For a more detailed explanation of the increased role of the UN, see William J. Durch, ed., *The Evolution of UN Peacekeeping: Case Studies and Comparative Analysis* (New York: St. Martin's Press, 1993).

6. For a complete discussion of Latin American peacekeeping experiences, see Jack Child, "Peacekeeping and the Inter-American System," *Military Review* 60, no. 10 (October 1980): 40–51.

7. Carlos Eduardo Azcoitia, *La Guerra Olvidada: Argentina en la Guerra del Congo* (Buenos Aires: Marymar Ediciones, 1992).

8. For a complete discussion of Uruguayan multilateral participation, see: "Fuerzas de Paz: La Experiencia del Ejército de Uruguay," *Seguridad y Estrategia Regional 2000* 5 (Marzo 1994): 88–98.

9. Ovidio Bellando, "EE.UU. venderá los aviones con radares," *La Nación,* February 2, 1994, 5.

10. Comando de Aviación del Ejército, "La Aeromovilidad y su Nuevo Enfoque," *Revista del Suboficial* 617 (Abril–Junio 1995): 32–33.

11. These comments were made during a one-day seminar on peacekeeping prior to the commencement of a peacekeeping exercise at the Army War College in August 1994. The seminar included civilian as well as military speakers, and Ambassador Airaldi represented the Cancilleria.

12. Interview with the author in Buenos Aires, 1995.

13. For a comparative discussion of political participation and civilian control, see Wendy Hunter, "Contradictions of Civilian Control: Argentina, Brazil and Chile in the 1990s," *Third World Quarterly* 15, no. 4 (1994): 633–53.

14. Gonzalo Pérez Tellado, "Cascos Azules Argentinos en Chipre" (part 1), *Revista del Suboficial* 616 (Jan.–Mar. 1995): 21.

15. Author interview with an Argentine Army lieutenant from an elite unit based in Buenos Aires.

16. For a complete account, see Carlos Eduardo Azcoitia, *La Guerra Olvidada: Argentina en la Guerra del Congo* (Buenos Aires: Maymar Ediciones, 1992).

17. Deborah Norden, "Keeping the Peace, Outside and In: Argentina's United Nations Missions," *International Peacekeeping* 2, no. 3 (autumn 1995): 330–49.

18. United States Information Agency (USIA) Message from Argentina dated 21 March 1994.

19. General de División Carlos María Zabala, "Una Oportunidad Histórica," *Revista del Suboficial* 611 (March–April 1994): 24–25.

20. María Luisa Mac Kay, "Blue Helmets, an Argentine Industry," *Clarín*, 6 November 1993, 16.

21. "Argentine Participation in United Nations Peacekeeping and the Possible Use of Force," Argentine Military Joint Staff, Senior War College, 1993, 5, photocopied.

22. UNCRO and UNPREDEP (UN Preventive Deployment in Macedonia) are part of what used to be called UNPROFOR. The two new denominations have been created to facilitate the management of the mandates for the different regions. UNPROFOR remains in place in Bosnia, but all three missions share an overall commander.

23. Norden, "Keeping the Peace," 7.

24. Speech by Admiral José Ferrer, chief of staff of the Argentine Navy, at the Eleventh International Seapower Symposium, October 1991.

25. Julio Horacio Rube, Teodoro Blanco, Arístides Bonino, and Hugo Galelli, "El Ejército Argentino: Fuerza de la Paz en la UN," *Revista Militar* 725 (1992): 10.

26. Alejandro Di Tella, "La Infantería de Marina Operando por la Paz," *Desembarco* 154 (April 1995): 48.

27. Gonzalo Pérez Tellado, "Cascos Azules Argentinos en Chipre" (part 2), *Revista del Suboficial* 617 (April–June 1995): 40–41.

28. Fuerza Aérea Argentina, "La Fuerza Aérea Argentina en Mozambique," an unpublished report of the operation of the field hospital in ONUMOZ.

29. From a report and personal interview with the first Argentine commander of the field hospital in Mozambique.

30. For a detailed explanation of collective goods, see Bruce M. Russett and John D. Sullivan, "Collective Goods and International Organization," *International Organization* 25, no. 4 (autumn 1971): 845–65.

31. Ivelaw L. Griffith, "The OAS and Confidence Building in the Americas," *North-South Magazine* (September–October 1994): 36–39.

32. Research questionnaire by author querying 250 Argentine officers for a Ph.D. dissertation in progress.

33. "El Rol de las Fuerzas Armadas en el MERCOSUR," proceedings of a symposium by the Consejo Argentino para las Relaciones Internacionales, Buenos Aires, 25–26 November 1993.

34. Virgilio Beltrán, "Buscando Nuevos Roles para los Ejércitos de América Latina"

(International Congress of Military Sociology, Valparaiso, Chile, 29–31 August 1992), 37–38.

35. Jack Child, "The Military and the Americas: Peacekeeping, Confidence-Building" (paper prepared for the Seventeenth Latin American Studies Association Congress, Atlanta, 12 March 1994), 14.

36. Virginia Page Fortna, *Regional Organizations and Peacekeeping: Experiences in Latin America and Africa,* Occasional Paper No. 11 (Washington, D.C.: The Henry L. Stimson Center, 1993), 16.

37. Alfredo Vega, "Entrenará Argentina tropas para misiones de paz de la UN," *La Nación,* 13 March 1994, 1A.

38. The United States has not been a colonial power but it is considered imperialist by most of the Third World, particularly Latin America. U.S. intervention in Central America and the Caribbean has fostered a sense of mistrust on the part of many leaders in this hemisphere.

39. Based on interviews with Uruguayan peacekeepers that had participated in UNTAG.

40. Tad Szulc, "Don't Take Canada for Granted," *Parade Magazine,* 20 February 1994, 5.

Chapter 8. Exporting Peace by Other Means by Carlos A. Romero

1. Adam Roberts and Benedict Kinsbury, *United Nations, Divided World: The U.N.'s Roles in International Relations* (Oxford: Clarendon Press, 1993).

2. Elsa Cardozo Da Silva, "Militares y política: Propuestas para el estudio del caso venezolano," in *Civiles y militares, fuerzas armadas y transición democrática,* ed. Carlos J. Moneta (Caracas: Editorial Nueva Sociedad, 1990).

3. Alberto Müller Rojas, "Los problemas de seguridad en la región Caribe. Perspectiva venezolana," in *La Nueva Agenda de Seguridad en el Caribe,* ed. Andrés Serbin (Caracas: INVESP, 1993), 45–51.

4. Carlos A. Romero, *Las relaciones entre Venezuela y la Unión Soviética: Diplomacia o Revolución* (Caracas: CDCH, Universidad Central de Venezuela, 1992).

5. Eloy Lanza, *El sub-imperialismo venezolano* (Caracas: Fondo Editorial Carlos Aponte, 1980).

6. Carlos A. Romero, "Planos y etapas de la política exterior de Venezuela," *Revista de la Facultad de Ciencias Jurídicas y Políticas* (Universidad Central de Venezuela) 35, no. 74 (1990): 183–231.

7. Alberto Müller Rojas, "Los problemas de seguridad en la región del Caribe."

8. Eloy Lanza, *El sub-imperialismo venezolano.*

9. Aníbal Romero, "La situación estratégica de Venezuela," *Política Internacional* (Caracas) no. 1 (January–March 1986): 6–14.

10. Ministerio de Relaciones Exteriores de Venezuela, *Libro Amarillo,* 1983, 1984, 1985, and 1986 (Caracas); Jack Child, *The Central American Peace Process, 1983–1991: Sheathing Swords, Building Confidence* (Boulder: Lynne Rienner, 1992); Alberto Müller Rojas, "Los problemas de seguridad en la región Caribe."

11. Jack Child, *The Central American Peace Process,* chapter 1.

12. Alberto Müller Rojas, "Los problemas de seguridad en la región Caribe."

13. Jack Child, *The Central American Peace Process,* part 3, 45–80.

14. Ibid., 48.

15. As part of the peace process. Alberto Müller Rojas, "Los problemas de seguridad en la región Caribe."

16. In the end, Venezuela did not take part in the TAG due to objections by Colombia. See Ministry of Foreign Affairs of Venezuela, *Classified document* (1988).

17. "Letter from the Secretary-General of the United Nations, Javier Pérez de Cuéllar to

the Chairman of the Security Council" (August 28, 1989). United Nations, *Resolutions and Decisions of the Security Council, 1990* (New York: United Nations, 1990), 20.

18. Brian D. Smith and William J. Durch, "U.N. Observer Group in Central America," *The Evolution of U.N. Peacekeeping: Case Studies and Comparative Analysis*, ed. William J. Durch (London: Macmillan Press, 1993), 436–62; Sally Morthet, "U.N. Peacekeeping and Election-Monitoring," in *United Nations, Divided World: The UN's Roles in International Relations*, ed. Adam Roberts and Benedict Kingsburn (Oxford: Clarendon Press, 1990); Morthet, ibid. (2d ed., 1993), 183–239; Alan James, *Peacekeeping in International Politics* (London: Macmillan, 1990); United Nations Security Council, Resolution 644/89, in United Nations, *Resolutions and Decisions of the Security Council 1989* (New York: United Nations, 1990), 21; "Letter from Javier Pérez de Cuéllar to the Chairman of the United Nations," *Resolutions and Decisions of the Security Council 1989* (New York: United Nations, 1990), 20.

19. United Nations, *Resolutions and Decisions of the Security Council 1989*, 21. See also Brian D. Smith and William J. Durch, op. cit., 440; Paul F. Dreal, *International Peacekeeping* (Baltimore: Johns Hopkins University Press, 1993); United Nations, *The Blue Helmets: A Review of United Nations Peace Keeping* (New York: United Nations, 1990), 396–99.

20. United Nations, *Resolutions and Decisions of the Security Council 1989*, 21; United Nations, *Index to Proceedings of the Security Council. Forty-fourth year, 1989* (New York: United Nations, 1990), 48; United Nations, *The Blue Helmets*, chap. 18; Brian D. Smith and William J. Durch, op. cit., 389–410.

21. United Nations, *Resolutions and Decisions of the Security Council 1990. Security Council Official Records: Forty-fifth Year* (New York: United Nations, 1991), 14–15 (Resolutions 650/90 and 653/90).

22. United Nations, *The Blue Helmets*, 389.

23. Alan James, *Peacekeeping in International Politics*, 50, 149; Edgardo Paz Barnica, "Peacekeeping Within the Inter-American System," in *Peacekeeping Appraisals and Proposals*, ed. Henry Wiseman (London: Pergamon Press, 1985), 237–55; United Nations, *The Blue Helmets*, 164–65.

24. Edgardo Paz Barnica, "Peacekeeping Within the Inter-American System," 249.

25. Virginia Page Fortna, "United Nations Transition Assistance Group," in *The Evolution of U.N. Peacekeeping*, 353–75.

26. William J. Durch, "The Iraq-Kuwait Observation Mission (UNIKOM)," in *The Evolution of U.N. Peacekeeping*, 258–71; William J. Durch, "United Nations, Mission for the Referendum in Western Sahara," in *ibid.*, 406–34.

27. Alan James, *Peacekeeping in International Politics*, 66; United Nations, *The Blue Helmets*, 398; Jack Child, *The Central American Peace Process*, 95; Brian D. Smith and William J. Durch, "U.N. Observer Group in Central America," 450–51.

28. United Nations, *Resolutions and Decisions of the Security Council 1990*, 14.

29. United Nations, *The Blue Helmets*, 360; Jack Child, *The Central American Peace Process*, 91; *El Nacional* (Caracas), March 23, 1990, D-2.

30. Brian D. Smith and William J. Durch, "U.N. Observer Group in Central America," 452–53; Alan James, *Peacekeeping in International Politics*, 66; United Nations, *The Blue Helmets*, 398; Agustín Quesada Gómez, "Operaciones de mantenimiento de la paz en las Naciones Unidas: ONUCA y Nicaragua," *Estudios internacionales* (Madrid, 1993): 367–82.

31. Jack Child, *Peacekeeping in Central America*, 95; United Nations, *The Blue Helmets*, 398.

32. Brian D. Smith and William J. Durch, "U.N. Observer Group in Central America," 453; Jack Child, *The Central American Peace Process*, 153; *Latin American World Report*, WR 90-13 (London), 5 April 1990; Alan James, *Peacekeeping in International Politics*, 66; United Nations, *The Blue Helmets*, 937.

33. Ibid.

34. Brian D. Smith and William J. Durch, "U.N. Observer Group in Central America," 454; Jack Child, *The Central American Peace Process,* 106; William J. Durch, "Paying the Tab: Financial Crisis," in *The Evolution of U.N. Peacekeeping,* 40; United Nations, *Resolutions and Decisions 1990,* 14.

35. *Latin American World Report,* WR 92-06, 13 February 1992, 1; *Latin American World Report,* WR 92-07, 20 February 1992, 4; Interview with Congressman Pastor Heydra (eyewitness to events from the time President Pérez arrived in Maiquetía on February 3, 1992) in Caracas in June 1992.

36. Fernando Spirito, "Un nuevo proyecto político para Venezuela," *Politeia* 13 (Caracas: Instituto de Estudios Políticos, Universidad Central de Venezuela, 1989): 231–53; Luis Salamanca, "El 27 de febrero: la política por otros medios," *Politeia* 13 (Caracas: Instituto de Estudios Políticos, Universidad Central de Venezuela, 1989): 187–218.

37. Ministerio de la Defensa de Venezuela, "Relación de oficiales participando en ONUSAL" (Caracas: Ministerio de la Defensa, 1992).

38. On several occasions, personal diplomacy became "parallel" diplomacy, formulated and guided by President Pérez, Diego Arria (Venezuelan ambassador to the United Nations), and Beatrice Rangel (vice minister and, later, minister of the Secretariat of the Presidency). The work done by Ambassador Arria at the United Nations, above all when he was a temporary member of the Security Council (1992–93), was considered very controversial and overly active for a small country such as Venezuela.

39. See Antonio L. Palá's chapter in this book.

Chapter 9. Security Collaboration and Confidence Building in the Americas
by Ivelaw L. Griffith

1. For a recent discussion on this subject, see James N. Rosenau, *Multilateral Governance and the Nation-State System: A Post-Cold War Assessment* (Washington, D.C.: Interamerican Dialogue Occasional Papers in Western Hemisphere Governance, no. 1, September 1995), esp. 16–21.

2. See, for example, Barry Buzan, *People, States, and Fear,* 2d ed. (Boulder: Lynne Rienner, 1991); Charles W. Kegley Jr., "The Neoidealist Moment in International Studies? Realist Myths and the New International Realities," *International Studies Quarterly* 37 (June 1993): 131–46; and Peter Gleick, "Environment, Resources, and Security," in Patrick M. Cronin, ed, *From Globalism to Regionalism: New Perspectives on U.S. Foreign and Defense Policies* (Washington, D.C.: National Defense University Press, 1993).

3. This formulation is from Theodore Sorensen, "America's First Post-Cold War President," *Foreign Affairs* 71 (fall 1992): 29.

4. For example, Gen. James R. Harding, "Security Challenges and Opportunities in the Americas," *North-South* 3 (February–March 1994): 48–51; Vice Adm. Jorge Patricio Arancibia Reyes, "View from Chile," in L. Erik Kjonnerod, ed., *Hemispheric Security in Transition: Adjusting to the Post-1995 Environment* (Washington, D.C.: National University Press, 1995); Gen. John J. Sheehan "Lessons of 1994; Outlook for the Future," LANTCOM—NDU—North-South Center Caribbean Security Symposium, Miami, April 18, 1995; and Gen. Barry R. McCaffrey, "Lessons of 1994: Prognosis for 1995 and Beyond," SOUTHCOM-NDU Annual Strategy Symposium, Miami, April 25, 1995.

5. For the views of one skeptic, see David R. Mares, "Inter-American Security Communities: Concepts and Challenges," in Lars Schoultz et al., eds., *Security, Democracy, and Development in U.S.-Latin American Relations* (Miami: University of Miami, 1994). For outright hostility, see Daniel Deudney, "Environment and Security: Muddled Thinking," *Bulletin of the Atomic Scientists* 47 (April 1991): 22–28.

6. See his "Theory, Realism, and World Security," in Michael T. Klare and Daniel C. Thomas, eds., *World Security: Trends and Challenges at Century's End* (New York: St. Martin's Press, 1991), 10.

7. United Nations, General Assembly, *General and Complete Disarmament: Concepts and Policies*, A/47/394, September 22, 1992, 11.

8. Ibid., 29.

9. For a useful survey of the contemporary security scene, see Kjonnerod, ed., *Hemispheric Security in Transition*; Schoultz et al., eds., *Security, Democracy, and Development in US-Latin American Relations*; Harding, "Security Challenges and Opportunities"; Hal P. Klepak, ed., *Canada and Latin American Security* (Quebec: Méridien, 1993); William Perry and Max Primorac, "The Inter-American Security Agenda," *Journal of Interamerican Studies and World Affairs* 36 (fall 1994): 111–27; Ivelaw L. Griffith, "Caribbean Security: Retrospect and Prospect," *Latin American Research Review* 30 (summer 1995): 3–32; and Jorge Rodríguez Beruff and Humberto García Muñiz, eds., *Security Problems and Policies in the Post-Cold War Caribbean* (London: Macmillan, 1996).

10. See "Indecent Proposal" and "Venezuela's Ultimatum," *Guyana Review* 27 (April 1995): 2–6; and "[Foreign Minister Clement] Rohee Says No," *Guyana Review* 29 (June 1995): 7. The summit was never held. Jagan himself died in March 1997.

11. See Francisco Rojas Aravena, "Latin American Military Expenditures," *Hemisphere* 6, no. 3 (1995): 29, 31.

12. Carlos H. Acuña and William C. Smith, "The Politics of Arms Production and the Arms Race Among the New Democracies of Argentina, Brazil, and Chile," in Schoultz et al., eds., *Security, Democracy, and Development in U.S.-Latin American Relations*, 226.

13. See Jack Child, "Geopolitical Conflicts in South America," in Georges Fauriol, ed., *Security in the Americas* (Washington, D.C.: National Defense University Press, 1989), 311.

14. See his "Post-Cold War Security Interests and Perceptions of Threat in the Western Hemisphere," in Schoultz et al., eds., *Security, Democracy, and Development in U.S.-Latin American Relations*, 9.

15. For a discussion of Caribbean geopolitics, see Andrés Serbin, *Caribbean Geopolitics: Toward Security Through Peace?* (Boulder: Lynne Rienner, 1991); and Ivelaw L. Griffith, *The Quest for Security in the Caribbean* (Armonk, N.Y.: M. E. Sharpe, 1993), 175–216. On the Canada–Latin America connection, see Klepak, ed., *Canada and Latin American Security*.

16. Francisco Rojas Aravena, "Security Regimes in the Western Hemisphere: A View from Latin America," in Schoultz et al., eds., *Security, Democracy, and Development in U.S.-Latin American Relations*, 184–89.

17. U.S. Department of State, *International Narcotics Control Strategy Report*, March 1995, 197.

18. Gen. McCaffrey, "Lessons of 1994."

19. For a full discussion, see Ivelaw L. Griffith, "From Cold War Geopolitics to Post-Cold War Geonarcotics," *International Journal* 49 (winter 1993–94): 1–36.

20. Eric Schmitt, "Colorado Bunker Built for Cold War Shifts Focus to Drug Battle," *New York Times*, July 18, 1993, 18. See also *Computer Technology: Air Attack Warning Systems Cannot Process all Radar/Track Data*, GAO Report to the Chairman, House Subcommittee on Defense, Committee on Appropriations, GAO/MTEC-91-15, May 1991.

21. For more on drug-related corruption in Latin America and the Caribbean, see Andrés Benavente Urbina, "Drug Traffic and State Stability," *North-South* 2 (August–September 1992): 34–37; Ethan A. Nadelmann, *Cops Across Borders* (Philadelphia: Pennsylvania State University Press, 1993), 251–312; Peter Andreas, "Profits, Poverty, and Illegality: The Logic of Drug Corruption," *NACLA Report on the Americas* 27 (November/December 1993): 22ff; and Anthony P. Maingot, "Confronting Corruption in the Hemisphere: A Soci-

ological Perspective," *Journal of Interamerican Studies and World Affairs* 36 (fall 1994): 49–74.

22. "Crackdown on Vigilantes," *New York Carib News*, June 23, 1993, 8.

23. Government of Jamaica, National Task Force on Crime, *Report of the National Task Force on Crime* (Kingston, Jamaica, April 1993), 42.

24. For a full discussion of regional and international narcotics collaboration in relation to the Caribbean, see Ivelaw L. Griffith, "Drugs and World Politics: The Caribbean Dimension," *Round Table* 332 (October 1994): 419–31; and Ivelaw L. Griffith, *Drugs and Security in the Caribbean: Sovereignty Under Siege* (University Park, Pa.: The Pennsylvania State University Press, 1997), chap. 7.

25. This is clear from what is so far the best account of the affair, in terms of the domestic political and geopolitical circumstances that precipitated the intervention, the intervention as planned and executed, and its aftermath: Mark Adkin, *Urgent Fury: The Battle for Grenada* (Lexington, Mass.: Lexington Books, 1989), written by a British officer on attachment to the RSS who participated in the affairs.

26. These and other details of the 1995 exercises were provided in telephone conversations with Brig. Rudyard Lewis, RSS coordinator, and Lt. Col. Trevor Thomas of the Antigua-Barbuda Defense Force on June 24, 1995.

27. For more on the RSS, see RSS Staff, "The Roles of the Regional Security System in the East Caribbean," *Bulletin of Eastern Caribbean Affairs* 11 (January–February 1986): 5–7; and Griffith, *The Quest for Security in the Caribbean*, 155–74.

28. See Johan J. Holst, "Confidence-Building Measures: A Conceptual Framework," *Survival* 25 (January–February 1983): esp. 2–5; and United Nations, *General and Complete Disarmament*, 53–65.

29. Ashton B. Carter, William J. Perry, and John D. Steinbruner, *A New Concept of Cooperative Security* (Washington, D.C.: Brookings Institution, 1992), 7.

30. Jill Sinclair, "The OAS and Hemispheric Security: A Canadian Approach," in *Hemispheric Security in Transition*, 135.

31. For the results of this project, see Michael A. Morris and Victor Millán, eds., *Controlling Latin American Conflicts: Ten Approaches* (Boulder: Westview, 1983).

32. Patiño Meyer left Washington in July 1995 to become Argentina's ambassador to Uruguay and was succeeded as chairman by Brazil's ambassador to the OAS, Luiz Augusto de Araújo Castro, who left Washington in March 1996. The chairmanship passed to El Salvador's ambassador, José Roberto Andino Salazar, and then, on an interim basis, to Minister Counselor Ricardo Mario Rodríguez of Venezuela. Ambassador Carmen Moreno of Mexico assumed leadership in late summer 1996 and then Ambassador Lionel Hurst of Antigua-Barbuda in summer 1997.

33. See *Address by the Secretary General of the OAS to the Opening Preparatory Session of the Meeting of Governmental Experts on Mutual Confidence Measures and Security Mechanisms in the Region, held on November 17, 1993*, OEA/Ser.K/XXIX, SEGRE/doc.3.93 February 28, 1994; and *The Role of the Organization of American States in Regard to the Hemispheric Security*, OEA/Ser.K/XXIX, SEGRE/doc.16/94 rev.1, March 8, 1994.

34. *New Concept of Security in the Hemisphere*, OEA/Ser.K/XXIX, SEGRE/doc.6/94, February 28, 1994, 5.

35. *Declaration of Santiago on Confidence- and Security-Building Measures*, OEA/Ser.K/XXXIX.2, COSEGRE/doc.18/95 rev. 1, November 9, 1995, 2–3. The first high-level meeting mentioned at item j of the Santiago Declaration was held in October 1996 in Washington. Canada presented to the meeting a special study on confidence building in the Caribbean that it had commissioned. The study, *Confidence Building: Managing Caribbean Security Concerns* (Ottawa: Ministry of Foreign Affairs and International Trade, 1996), was undertaken by James Macintosh of Canadian Security Research, a pri-

vate security consulting firm, and Ivelaw Griffith of Florida International University.

36. Some of the discussion that follows draws on *Statement by Professor Ivelaw L. Griffith to the Meeting of Experts on Confidence and Security Building in the Region,* OEA/Ser.K/XXIX, SEGRE/doc.16/91 add.1, March 18, 1994; and Ivelaw L. Griffith, "Challenges to Confidence-Building in the Americas," in J. Marshall Beier and Steven Mataija, eds., *Verification, Compliance, and Confidence-Building: The Global and Regional Interface* (Toronto: York University Center for International and Security Studies, 1996), 98–102.

37. *A New Concept of Cooperative Security,* 10.

38. See Edward N. Luttwak, "Toward Post-Heroic Warfare," *Foreign Affairs* 74 (May–June 1995): 112.

Chapter 10. The Illicit Drug Trade in the Caribbean by Anthony P. Maingot

1. *New York Times,* October 30, 1995, 1, 13.

2. Claire Sterling, *Thieves World* (New York: Simon and Schuster, 1994), 21.

3. For the background to the Cuntrera brothers' operations in Caracas, see Claire Sterling, *Octopus* (New York: W. W. Norton, 1990), 130–42. For their extradition to Italy see *Miami Herald,* September 24, 1992, 16.

4. A notable exception is the work of Ivelaw L. Griffith of Florida International University. Significant to this study is his "Drugs and Security in the Commonwealth Caribbean," *Journal of Commonwealth and Comparative Politics* 31 (July 1993): 70–102.

5. Anthony Lake, "The Reach of Diplomacy," *New York Times,* September 23, 1994, 15.

6. See Jonathan Beaty and S. C. Gwynne, *The Outlaw Bank* (New York: Random House, 1993); Rachel Ehrenfeld, *Evil Money* (New York: Harper Collins, 1992); Alberto Donadio, *Banqueros en el banquillo* (Bogotá: El Ancora Editores, 1983).

7. On the case of guns from Antigua, see Robert Coran, *Caribbean Timebomb* (New York: William Morrow, 1993); on the case of the arms discovered in Jamaica, see Ignacio Gómez G., *El complot del Copacabana* (Bogotá: Plus, 1989); on how all these plots and schemes are combatted by U.S. law enforcement agencies, see David McClintock, *Swordfish: A True Story of Ambition, Savagery, and Betrayal* (New York: Pantheon Books, 1993).

8. For a well-informed economist's view see the various works of Peter Reuter of the Rand Corporation, especially Peter Reuter and John Haaga, *The Organization of High-Level Drug Markets: An Exploratory Study,* N-2830-NIJ (Santa Monica: Rand Corporation, 1989).

9. "Mitchell Blasts Narcotics Report," *Barbados Advocate,* March 9, 1995.

10. U.S. Department of State, Bureau for International Narcotics and Law Enforcement Affairs, *International Narcotics Control Strategy Report* (Washington, D.C., March 1995), 39 (hereinafter cited as *The 1995 Report*).

11. *Ultima Hora,* September 14, 1995, 1.

12. The literature on corruption in the Dominican Republic is growing fast. The following works by M. A. Velázquez Mainardi are important: *El narcotráfico y el lavado de dólares en República Dominicana* (Santo Domingo: Editora Corripio, 1992); *Corrupción e impunidad* (Santo Domingo: Editora Tele-3, 1993).

13. *Miami Herald,* Oct. 12, 1995, 18.

14. I have demonstrated the success of the cartels in my book, *The United States and the Caribbean: Challenges of an Asymmetrical Relationship* (London: Macmillan, and Boulder: Westview, 1994), 163–82.

15. *El Nuevo Día,* May 18, 1995, 26.

16. Commissioner of Police, Col. Trevor MacMillan, at a private meeting of the Jamaica Think Tank, Montego Bay, Jamaica, October 29, 1994. The author was present.

17. *The 1995 Report,* 180.

18. See by Michael Manley, *The Politics of Change* (London: André Deutsch, 1973); *A Voice in the Workplace* (London: André Deutsch, 1975); *Jamaica: Struggle in the Periphery* (London: Writers and Readers Publishing Cooperative Society, Ltd., 1982); *Up and Down the Escalator* (London: André Deutsch, 1987).

19. *Jamaican Weekly Gleaner*, April 18, 1988.

20. *Jamaican Weekly Gleaner*, July 18, 1989.

21. This section draws heavily from A. P. Maingot, *The United States and the Caribbean* (London: Macmillan, 1994), 142–62.

22. See Carl Stone, *National Survey on the Use of Drugs in Jamaica* (Kingston, 1990), 35–40.

23. See the film, "The Harder They Fall," based on the novel by E. M. Thelwell by the same name. The study by Laurie Gunst, *Born Fi' Dead* (New York: Henry Holt, 1995), is more interested in condemning U.S. policy in the Caribbean than in explaining the consequences to Jamaica of this deadly trend toward gangsterism.

24. *Jamaican Weekly Gleaner*, November 18–24, 1994, 4.

25. Ibid., June 16–22, 1995, 1.

26. Ibid., June 23–29, 1995, 6.

27. Ibid., June 23–29, 1995, 2.

28. See Editorial, in ibid., September 17, 1993, 19.

29. *Financial Gleaner*, June 24, 1994, 1.

30. *Jamaican Weekly Gleaner*, June 23–29, 1995, 3.

31. Ibid., December 3, 1993, 9.

32. *Jamaican Weekly Gleaner*, June 16–22, 1995, 21.

33. See "In the Grip of the Cali Cartel: A Special Project," separata to the *Sunday Express*, November 6, 1994.

34. *The 1995 Report*, 189.

35. For Venezuelan confirmation of this, and the numerous murders occurring among the area's fishermen who are presumably involved, see "Mafia marina transporta drogas a las Antillas," *El Universal* (Caracas), March 22, 1995, 2–18.

36. *Trinidad Guardian*, May 26, 1995, 3.

37. G. Seaby, *Final Report for the Government of Trinidad and Tobago on Investigations Carried Out by Officers from New Scotland Yard* (London: July 20, 1993), paragraph 8.4.1.

38. *Sunday Guardian* (Trinidad), June 25, 1994, 141.

39. George Padmore in the *Sunday Guardian*, June 26, 1994, 6.

40. *Miami Herald*, July 29, 1995, 23.

41. *The 1995 Report*, 192.

42. Government of the Bahamas, *Report of the Commission of Inquiry into the Illegal Use of the Bahamas for the Transshipment of Dangerous Drugs Destined for the United States* (Nassau, 1984), 41.

43. Robert Coram's *Caribbean Time Bomb* (New York: Morrow, 1993), approximates such a compendium.

44. See Louis Blom-Cooper, "Guns for Antigua: Report of the Commission of Inquiry into the Circumstances Surrounding the Shipment of Arms from Israel to Antigua and Transshipment on 24 April, 1989 en route to Colombia" (November 2, 1990). References are to pages in the report.

45. Research by author in files of Antigua newspapers, *Outlet* and *Observer*, June 20–25, 1995.

46. *Daily Nation* (Barbados), January 9, 1989, 1.

47. See Alma H. Young, "The Territorial Dimensions of Caribbean Security: The Case of Belize," in Ivelaw L. Griffith, ed., *Strategy and Security in the Caribbean* (New York: Praeger, 1991), 143.

48. Cited in *Drug Policy Report* 1, no. 4 (May 1994): 7.

49. For further elaboration on this point, see A. P. Maingot, "Confronting Corruption in the Hemisphere: A Sociological Perspective," *Journal of Inter-American Studies and World Affairs* 36, no. 3 (fall 1994): 49–74.

50. *Weekend Nation* (Barbados), June 2, 1995, 1.

51. Police statistics reported in *Sunday Sun* (Barbados), May 28, 1995, 5.

52. Owen Arthur, "The Performance and Prospects of the Service Sector of Barbados," speech, Montego Bay, May 14, 1995.

53. *Barbados Saturday Advocate*, May 20, 1995, 3.

54. *Law Enforcement Sensitive Newsletter*, January 1995.

Chapter 11. Central American Regional Security by Caesar D. Sereseres

1. The nearly two-hundred-page document can be found in *Los Acuerdos de Paz* (Guatemala: Office of the Presidency, March 1997).

2. The reality is that the socioeconomic conditions of Central American societies have changed little since the late 1970s when the latest "round" of Central American wars began. For an overview of the socioeconomic context of the region's conflicts see John A. Booth, "Socioeconomic and Political Roots of National Revolts in Central America," *Latin American Research Review* 26, no. 1 (1991): 33–73.

3. For a discussion of U.S. policy in Central America and focused treatment of the U.S.-Sandinista conflict, see Robert Kagan, *A Twilight Struggle: American Power and Nicaragua, 1977–1990* (New York: The Free Press, 1996).

4. In an ironic twist of fate, the Central American democracies now face the long aftereffects of the region's war. As anti–illegal immigrant attitudes and legislation grow in the United States, thousands of Central Americans face deportation to their homelands. The consequences are serious for the families facing deportation and also for the economies and societies of the region. Currently, Central American immigrants (documented and undocumented) send over $1.5 billion annually to their families in the region. See Juanita Darling, "U.S. Immigration Law Dims Hopes in Central America," *Los Angeles Times*, May 25, 1997, A3; and Rodolfo de la Garza, Manuel Orozco, and Miguel Baraona, "Binational Impact of Latino Remittances," *Policy Brief* (Claremont, Calif.: The Tomas Rivera Policy Institute, March 1997).

5. For a review of the changing security environment in the region, see Gabriel Aguilera, "The Armed Forces, Democracy, and Transition in Central America," in *The Military and Democracy: The Future of Civil-Military Relations in Latin America*, ed. Louis W. Goodman, Johanna Mendelson, and Juan Rial (Lexington, Mass.: Lexington Books, 1990), 23–38; J. Samuel Fitch, "Democracy, Human Rights, and the Armed Forces in Latin America," in *The United States and Latin America in the 1990s: Beyond the Cold War*, ed. Jonathan Hartlyn, Lars Schoultz, and Augusto Varas (Chapel Hill: University of North Carolina Press, 1992), 181–213; and David Pion-Berlin, "Latin American National Security Doctrine: Hard and Softline Themes," *Armed Forces and Society* 15, no. 3 (1989): 41–49.

6. For a general assessment of the complexities of the transition from "war to peace," see Luis Guillermo Solís Rivera and Francisco Rojas Aravena, eds., *De La Guerra a La Integración: La Transición y La Seguridad en Centroamérica* (San Jose, Costa Rica: FLACSO–Fundación Arias, Costa Rica, 1994).

7. See the various articles in the February 1997 issue of *Current History*. The specific postwar environments of most of the Central American countries are described; the political and socioeconomic issues confronting the democracies are discussed in some detail.

8. For a discussion of these issues, see "Reshaping Cooperative Security Among Central American States," *Strategic Forum* (Washington, D.C.: Institute for National Strategic Studies, National Defense University, 1995).

9. Richard L. Millett and Michael Gold-Biss provide an insight into the civil-military discussions and the debates internal to the armed forces concerning postwar and post–cold war missions. See their *Beyond Praetorianism: The Latin American Military in Transition* (Miami: North-South Center Press, University of Miami, 1996).

10. See draft legislation *Iniciativa de Ley del Consejo Nacional de Seguridad y de la Secretaría de Inteligencia del Estado* (Guatemala: Office of the President, October 1994).

11. The region between the Mexico-Guatemala and the Panama-Colombian borders remains highly conflictive as international crime organizations and drug families and networks fight for control of borders. The same can be said for the U.S.-Mexico border! For an intriguing story of the battle for control of the Panama-Colombian border and thus drug routes into Central America and the Caribbean, see Juanita Darling, "A Casualty Decries Colombia's War on Guerrillas," *Los Angeles Times*, March 2, 1997, A6. For a similar description of the battle for controlling the U.S.-Mexico border, see Mark Fineman and Craig Pyes, "Border Ranchers Losing Drug War," *Los Angeles Times*, July 7, 1996, A1, A11.

12. For a brief history of the dispute from Belize's point of view, see *The Guatemalan Claim* (Belmopan, Belize: National Advisory Commission on Relations with Guatemala, Ministry of Foreign Affairs, 1993).

13. For an excellent chronology of the peace process, see Jack Child, *The Central American Peace Process, 1983–1991* (Boulder: Lynne Rienner, 1992).

14. See *Framework Treaty on Democratic Security in Central America* (Tegucigalpa: Central American Security Commission, December 15, 1995).

15. For a description of the command and its future, see General Barry R. McCaffrey, commander in chief, United States Southern Command, *End of Tour Summary* (Quarry Heights, Panama: February 29, 1996); ibid., "Remarks to the Ministers of Defense of the Hemisphere," *Defense Ministerial of the Americas* (Williamsburg, Va.: U.S. Department of Defense, July 24, 1995); and the briefing paper "US SouthCom: An Operational Concept" (Quarry Heights, Panama, U.S. Southern Command Headquarters, September 1995).

16. For the political dynamics of the negotiations and U.S.-Panama relations, see "Panama's Historic Transition Brings High Hopes, Uncertainties," *North-South Focus* 6, no. 1 (1997).

17. A draft report prepared in February 1997 by staff members of the Senate Foreign Relations Committee concluded that "Unless there is a change in current policy, all US military forces will withdraw from Panama on December 31, 1999. If US forces depart, the United States will remain without a significant military presence in Latin America."

18. An account of the U.S. security agenda and policies can be found in *United States Security Strategy for the Americas* (Washington, D.C.: Office of International Security Affairs, U.S. Department of Defense, September 1995).

19. See "Statement of General Barry R. McCaffrey, Commander in Chief, United States Southern Command," U.S. Senate, Committee on Armed Services, February 16, 1995.

20. For an articulate and insightful discussion of the dilemmas facing civilians and military alike, see Luigi R. Einaudi, "The Politics of Security in the Western Hemisphere," *Parameters* 26, no. 4 (winter 1996–97): 13–25. One of Ambassador Einaudi's core premises is that "the end of the Cold War has not meant the end of security problems."

Chapter 12. Security, Agenda, and Military Balance in Central America
by Fernando Zeledón Torres

1. The route dictated by the presidential accords of 1987–88 recognized the connections in the transition from the political (democracy) to the economic (common good); i.e., the idea that to achieve economic development it was necessary to agree to a cease-fire and to establish a minimum of political guarantees in divided societies. Except for Costa Rica, the Central American countries have moved from war and an economy of

320 Notes to Pages 223–26

war to an economy of structural adjustment following the cease-fire, along with the management of conflictive situations characteristic of structural adjustment. Guatemala is at an early stage in this transition. Long at peace, Costa Rica had to move from the phase of a populist, welfare, reformist, and stable state to the adjustment phase by applying the "neoliberal" recipe, which proposes the transformation of the state as an overall measure to address the economic crisis of the 1980s.

2. Oscar Arias S., Closing Address, Conference on Security and Militarism in Central America (Tegucigalpa, Honduras, February 1995).

3. Thus, it is important to highlight the recent creative effort of the Central American Dialogue for Peace and Disarmament, sponsored by the Center for Peace and National Reconciliation of the Arias Foundation and the Center for International Policy, with its respective national chapters involving politicians, academics, public officials, and military officials of the region.

4. On the topic of a new security agenda in the region, see also Abelardo Morales, *Oficios de paz y de posguerra en Centroamérica* (San José: FLACSO, 1995).

5. Panama and Belize are peripheral cases, separate from historic Central America. These countries have more ties to Afro-Caribbean traditions although in a remote way. Panama, because of the geostrategic importance of the canal, and Belize, because of its strong colonialist legacy that delayed its entry into the history of the region, continue to be unique case studies for analyzing the security of the region.

6. See Marta Cordero and Fernando Zeledón, "Gasto militar en Centroamérica: Apuntes para entender su discusión nacional en los recientes procesos políticos, 1990–93," in *Gasto militar en América Latina: Procesos de decisiones y actores claves* (Santiago: CINDE-FLACSO, 1994).

7. Gabriel Aguilera Peralta, *Seguridad, función militar y democracia* (Guatemala: FLACSO-Ebert, 1994), 27.

8. In the case of Costa Rica, we can mention the pressures of Senator Jesse Helms regarding the problems of expropriations of U.S. citizens' land and the defense of their interests before the state; and the pressures and threats of the AFL-CIO, in alliance with national unions, to change the country's labor legislation. These pressures included the threat of advocating the adoption of trade sanctions. Finally, we can mention the pressures of banana-exporting corporations such as United Brands or Dole in the negotiations over the banana quotas between Costa Rica and the European Union.

9. In this sense, it is initially desirable to distance oneself from the theory of systematic threats that refer to situations of conflict that small countries face as a result of their insertion into the international environment. In the case of the Central American region, most threats have less and less to do with the particular situation of coexistence in the zone of influence of the United States. For a discussion on the redefinition of the notion of national security, see Bengt Sundelius, "Coping with Structural Security Threats," in *Small States in Europe and Dependence,* ed. Otmar Höll (Boulder, Colo.: Westview Press, 1983).

10. Consider also the classic territorial problems between Guatemala and Belize and between Nicaragua and Colombia.

11. The "Soccer War" or the "100-hour War" began on 8 June 1969 with a soccer match between the national teams from both countries. Hostile confrontations began on July 14. It concluded on July 29 with the withdrawal of the Salvadoran troops from the territories they temporarily occupied. The civilian and military death toll reached a total of five thousand.

12. These 419.6 km² do not constitute a single territorial strip of land in and of itself, but rather, they are divided into 6 pockets and several islands. The territorial division is fashioned as follows: Goascoran (57 km²); Dolores (54.8 km²); Naguaterique (148.4 km²); Salazapa (51 km²); Cayaguanca (38.1 km²); Tepamgüisir (70.3 km²); Meanguera Island; Meanguerita Island; and El Tigre Island. An important part of the dispute involves the

very delimitation of the Fonseca Gulf. See "Honduras—El Salvador: Una frontera conflictiva," *Revista Aportes,* no. 58 (San José: August 1989): 41–42.

13. For the official text of this ruling, see International Court of Justice, Case Concerning the Land, Island and Maritime Frontier Dispute (El Salvador, Honduras: Nicaragua intervening), Report of Judgments, Advisory Opinions and Orders, Judgment of 11 September 1992. An important summary appears in Centro de Documentación Honduras (CEDOH), *Boletín Informativo,* no. 7, September 1992.

14. Following the ruling by the International Court of Justice of The Hague, more than four thousand Salvadorans who make up the "social base" of the FMLN in the zone of Nahuaterique, which belongs to Honduras, refused to leave their land and adopt Honduran citizenship. A communique from the FMLN maintains that "one of the concerns of the peasants is the change of nationality, hence they are requesting documents that confer on them dual citizenship and thereby resolve the problem of ownership of their land and their work activities. The rebels have asked the Government of Honduras not to establish military positions in the zones that were assigned to that country and that these be declared 'peace zones.'" *La República* (Costa Rica), September 18, 1992, 8A.

15. See *La República,* March 5, 1995, 4A. This means that approximately 300,000 undocumented people of Nicaraguan nationality live in Costa Rica.

16. Since 1992 the government of Costa Rica had discovered that part of the area where these peasants had settled was in Nicaraguan territory. However, it was not until 1995, because of diplomatic pressures, that the decision was made in favor of a group of approximately thirty-five families. See *La Nación,* June 29, 1995, 6A.

17. Abelardo Morales, *Oficios de paz y de posguerra en Centroamérica,* 39.

18. See "Atrapados por la in-seguridad ciudadana," *Revista centroamericana hombres de maíz,* no. 25 (San José, August 1994): 37.

19. Joel Burgos, "El Salvador: La metamórfosis de los escuadrones de la muerte" in *Revista centroamericana hombres de maíz,* no. 26 (San José, 1994): 18.

20. Ejército Popular Sandinista, "El ejército en Nicaragua hoy" (Managua: April 1993).

21. United Nations, *Nuevo informe del Secretario General sobre la misión de observadores de las Naciones Unidas en El Salvador (ONUSAL)* (New York: UN Security Council, August 30, 1993), 3–4. This report registers the destruction of the entire arsenal of the FMLN as follows: 10,230 weapons (9,851 individual and 379 supporting), 4,032,606 bullets, 140 rockets, 9,229 grenades, 5,107 kilograms of explosives, and 63 units of communications equipment, as well as 74 land-to-air missiles. All of this identified arsenal was found in 129 hiding places, spread throughout El Salvador (109), Nicaragua (14), and Honduras (5).

22. Marco Enríquez, "Visión del ejército de Guatemala respecto a las amenazas en Centroamérica," *Desmovilización, desmilitarización y democratización en Centroamérica* (San José: Centro para la Paz y Reconciliación and Centro Internacional para los Derechos Humanos y el Desarollo Democrático, 1995), 135.

23. The case of Panama is different not only in terms of the origin and evolution of the defense forces, but also because of their almost total disappearance following the 1989 U.S. invasion. The debate that occurred in the years prior to this action taken by the National Assembly focused on the type and requirements of security forces that would be needed in the new phase of democratic transition and not so much with the resurrection of an army.

24. In a timely fashion, Cristina Eguizábal has pointed out this paradox in several articles that discuss the topic of civil-military relations, and especially, in one article entitled "Paradojas Centroamericanas" (in press).

25. U.S. Arms Control and Disarmament Agency, *World Military Expenditures and Arms Transfers, 1993–1994* (Washington, D.C.: U.S. Government Printing Office).

26. In August 1995, UNDP made the Human Development Index results for recent years available.

27. For a better understanding of the role of the CIVS, see H. P. Klepack, "Peacekeeping in Central America," in *Peacekeeping and the Challenge of Civil Conflict Resolution,* ed. David A. Charters (Fredericton: University of New Brunswick, 1992).

28. The general headquarters of ONUCA was established in Tegucigalpa, Honduras, in 1989. The peace mission was under the command of Major General Agustín Quesada Gómez, a Spaniard who had substantial experience in UN peace missions in Angola. The first contingent was formed by military personnel from Canada, Colombia, Ireland, Spain, and Venezuela, and civilian pilots and medical corps from Germany. Klepack, "Peacekeeping in Central America," 86.

29. Abelardo Morales, *Oficios de paz y de posguerra en Centroamérica,* 184.

Chapter 13. Why Latin America May Miss the Cold War by Michael C. Desch

An early draft of this chapter was presented at the Inter-American Dialogue's Workshop on "Inter-American Peace and Security," 23–24 April 1995, Washington, D.C. For their very helpful comments, I would especially like to thank Mary Jo Desch, Jorge Domínguez, Carlos Escudé, and David Mares.

1. Abraham F. Lowenthal, "Latin America: Ready for Partnership?" *Foreign Affairs* 72, no. 1 (America and the World 1992–93): 74–92.

2. Suggesting this argument is Richard H. Ullman, "The United States, Latin America, and the World After the Cold War," and Haroldo Muñoz, "A New OAS for the New Times," in Abraham F. Lowenthal and Gregory F. Treverton, eds., *Latin America in a New World* (Boulder: Westview Press, 1994), 23–24 and 191–202.

3. Quoted in Howard LaFranchi, "A Little War Chills South America's Hopes," *Christian Science Monitor,* February 24, 1995, 1.

4. An example of such optimism is Abraham F. Lowenthal, *Partners in Conflict: The United States in Latin America* (Baltimore: Johns Hopkins University Press, 1987), 21–22.

The classic articulation of the argument that an increasing external threat worsens civil-military relations is Harold Lasswell, "The Garrison State," *The American Journal of Sociology* 46, no. 4 (January 1941): 544–68. Following this reasoning, the end of the cold war should improve civil-military relations.

5. The classic statements of this are Georg Simmel, *Conflict and the Web of Group Affiliation,* trans. Kurt H. Wolff and Rheinhard Bendix (New York: The Free Press, 1955), and Lewis Coser, *The Functions of Social Conflict* (Glencoe: The Free Press, 1956). I develop this argument at length in my "War and Strong States, Peace and Weak States?" *International Organization* 50, no. 2 (spring 1996): 237–68.

6. Obviously there remains the problem of "free riding" by individuals who realize that defense is a public good that will be provided whether they contribute their fair share or not. However, to avoid this problem, citizens allow the state to play a hegemonic role including sanctioning individuals who try to free ride. On the problem of free riding and the various means to ensure that it does not occur, see Mancur Olson, *The Logic of Collective Action: Public Goods and the Theory of Groups* (Cambridge: Harvard University Press, 1965).

7. The clearest articulation of this argument is Barry R. Posen, *The Sources of Military Doctrine: France, Britain, and Germany Between the World Wars* (Ithaca: Cornell University Press, 1984), 59. Also see Josef Joffe, "Bismarck or Britain? Toward an American Grand Strategy After Bipolarity," *Changing Security Environment and American National Interests Working Paper* (Cambridge: John M. Olin Institute, Harvard University, forthcoming), 10–12. In general, the Realist approach to the study of international relations assumes that because states always face threats due to international anarchy, it makes sense to talk about them as rational and coherent actors. The well-spring of modern Realist thinking is Kenneth N. Waltz, *Theory of International Politics* (Reading: Addison-Wesley, 1979).

8. Jon Elster, *Solomonic Judgements: Studies in the Limitations of Rationality* (Cambridge: Cambridge University Press, 1989), 4.

9. Elster, *Solomonic Judgments,* 7–17.

10. See, for example, Raymond Seitz, "From the Jaws of Victory," *Economist* (May 27, 1995): 21–23.

11. See, for example, Lars Schoultz, *National Security and United States Policy Toward Latin American* (Princeton: Princeton University Press, 1987), 330; William Leogrande, "A Splendid Little War: Drawing the Line in El Salvador," *International Security* 6, no. 1 (summer 1981): 27–52; and Jerome Slater, "Dominos in Central America: Will They Fall? Does It Matter?" *International Security* 12, no. 2 (fall 1987): 105–34.

12. Compare public's and leaders' ratings of "Vital Interests" in various Latin American countries in 1986 and 1990 in John E. Reilly, ed., *American Public Opinion and U.S. Foreign Policy 1991* (Chicago: Chicago Council on Foreign Relations, 1991), figure III-2, 19. Also see Mark Uhlig, "Central America Faces New U.S. Policy: The Cold Shoulder," *New York Times,* February 3, 1991, "Week in Review," 4.

13. I examine these periods at greater length in my book *When the Third World Matters: Latin America and U.S. Grand Strategy* (Baltimore: Johns Hopkins University Press, 1993).

14. These issues are discussed in Friedrich Katz, *The Secret War in Mexico: Europe, the United States, and the Mexican Revolution* (Chicago: University of Chicago Press, 1983), 160–61, 529–30.

15. Quoted in Katz, 302.

16. For more detailed discussion see Desch, *When the Third World Matters,* 19–45.

17. See the discussion in Edwin Lieuwen, *U.S. Policy in Latin America: A Short History* (New York: Praeger, 1965), 29–60.

18. Desch, *When the Third World Matters,* 88.

19. Ibid., 81–88.

20. Ibid., 89–114.

21. It is likely that U.S. policy toward Latin America will be more discriminate. For example, national security concerns will still play a role in U.S. policy toward Mexico. On this see Pierre Thomas and Bradley Graham, "U.S. Drafts Plan for Influx of Illegal Immigrants," *Washington Post,* April 8, 1995, 6, and Lisa Burgess, "Bracing for an Exodus," *Journal of Commerce,* April 7, 1995, 1. In fact, Mexico does not fall under the rubric of the U.S. Southern Command in Panama but rather under the U.S. Forces Command, which is responsible for the defense of the continental United States.

22. "To the Rescue," and "Scenes From a Border," *Economist* (February 4, 1995): 13–14, 24–25.

23. Elaine Sciolino, "Top U.S. Officials Divided in Debate On Invading Haiti," *New York Times,* August 4, 1994, 1, 10.

24. See Steven Greenhouse, "Clinton Opposes Move to Toughen Embargo on Cuba," *New York Times,* May 5, 1995, 1, 8; Peter Kornbluh, "From Here to Cuba," *New York Times,* May 17, 1995, 19; and Steven Lee Meyers, "Clinton Troubleshooter Discovers Big Trouble From Allies on Cuba," *New York Times,* October 23, 1996, 1, 14.

25. For a similarly pessimistic argument, see Jorge Castañeda, "Latin America and the End of the Cold War: An Essay in Frustration," in Lowenthal and Treverton, eds., *Latin America in a New World,* 28–52. Castaneda foresees an increase in hemispheric conflict due to "new issues" such as drugs and migration.

26. See John J. Mearsheimer, "The False Promise of International Institutions," *International Security* 19, no. 3 (winter 1994–95): 8.

27. See John J. Mearsheimer, "Back to the Future: Instability in Europe After the Cold War," *International Security* 15, no. 1 (summer 1990): 5–56; Stanley Hoffmann, Robert O. Keohane, and John J. Mearsheimer, "Back to the Future, Part II: International Relations

Theory and Post-Cold War Europe," *International Security* 15, no. 2 (fall 1990): 191–99; and Bruce M. Russett, Thomas Risse-Kappen, and John J. Mearsheimer, "Back to the Future, Part III: Realism and the Realities of European Security," *International Security* 15, no. 3 (winter 1990–91): 216–22. Richard Ullman also published a book on this debate entitled *Securing Europe* (Princeton: Princeton University Press, 1991).

28. This argument is developed most fully in Joseph Grieco, *Cooperation Among Nations: Europe, America, and Non-Tariff Barriers to Trade* (Ithaca: Cornell University Press, 1990), 27–50 and passim.

29. Mearsheimer, "The False Promise," 24–26.

30. Lieuwen, *U.S. Policy in Latin America*, 87. For a comprehensive historical account see J. Lloyd Mecham, *The United States and Inter-American Security: 1889–1960* (Austin: University of Texas Press, 1967), 278–484.

31. The standard works on U.S. policy toward Guatemala are Richard Immerman, *The CIA in Guatemala: The Foreign Policy of Intervention* (Austin: University of Texas Press, 1982), and Stephen Schlesinger and Stephen Kinzer, *Bitter Fruit: The Untold Story of the American Coup in Guatemala* (Garden City: Anchor Books, 1983).

32. Hugh Thomas, *The Cuban Revolution* (New York: Harper Torchbooks, 1971), and Jorge I. Domínguez, *Cuba: Order and Revolution* (Cambridge: Belknap Press of Harvard University Press, 1978).

33. The standard works include Abraham Lowenthal, *The Dominican Intervention* (Cambridge: Harvard University Press, 1972), and Jerome Slater, *Intervention and Negotiation* (New York: Harper and Row, 1970).

34. Samuel P. Huntington, *The Third Wave: Democratization in the Late Twentieth Century* (Norman: University of Oklahoma Press, 1991), table 5.4, 275.

35. The literature on this is extensive, beginning of course with Immanuel Kant's *Perpetual Peace*. More recent examples include Melvin Small and J. David Singer, "The War-Proneness of Democratic Regimes, 1816–1965," *Jerusalem Journal of International Relations* 1, no. 4 (summer 1976): 50–69; Michael Doyle, "Kant, Liberal Legacies and Foreign Affairs," part 1, *Philosophy and Public Affairs* 12, no. 3 (summer 1983): 205–35; Doyle, "Liberalism and World Politics," *American Political Science Review* 80, no. 4 (December 1986): 1151–69; and Bruce Russett, *Grasping the Democratic Peace: Principles for a Post-Cold War World* (Princeton: Princeton University Press, 1993).

36. Abraham F. Lowenthal, "Latin America and the United States in a New World: Prospects for Partnership," in Lowenthal and Treverton, eds., *Latin America in a New World*, 242.

37. For further discussion of this see David Mares's chapter in this volume.

38. See the Doyle articles cited above in note 35.

39. Christopher Layne, "Kant or Cant: The Myth of the Democratic Peace," *International Security* 19, no. 2 (fall 1994): 6.

40. See his "Kant or Cant," 5–49.

41. See his "The Insignificance of the Liberal Peace," *International Security* 19, no. 2 (fall 1994): 50–86.

42. Snyder and Mansfield, "Democratization and the Danger of War," *International Security* 20, no. 1 (summer 1995): 5–38.

43. Patti Lane, "Peru-Ecuador Conflict Slows Andean Pact Trade Reforms," *Journal of Commerce*, April 12, 1995, 1 and 8.

44. See his "On the Peaceful Disposition of Military Dictatorships," *Journal of Strategic Studies* 3, no. 3 (December 1980): 3–10.

45. J. David Singer and Melvin Small, *The Wages of War: 1816–1965—A Statistical Handbook* (New York: John Wiley and Sons, Inc., 1972), 295, table 12.3.

46. These include disputes between Argentina-Uruguay (border), Argentina-Chile (border), Argentina–United Kingdom (Malvinas), Belize-Guatemala (territory), Bolivia-

Chile (Rio Lauca and access to Pacific), Brazil-Paraguay (border), Brazil-Uruguay (border), Colombia-Nicaragua (Archipelago de San Andres y Providencia and Quita Sueno Bank), Colombia-Venezuela (Gulf of Venezuela), El Salvador-Honduras-Nicaragua (Gulf of Fonseca), French Guiana–Suriname (border), Guyana-Venezuela (territory to Essequibo River), and Guyana-Suriname (headwaters of Courantyne River). U.S. Central Intelligence Agency, *The World Factbook 1993* (Washington, D.C.: CIA, 1993).

47. The two dominant theoretical perspectives on civil-military relations that epitomize these two domestic approaches are Morris Janowitz, *The Professional Soldier: A Social and Political Portrait* (New York: The Free Press, 1971), and Samuel P. Huntington, *The Soldier and the State: The Theory and Politics of Civil-Military Relations* (Cambridge: Belknap Press of Harvard University Press, 1957).

48. Eric Nordlinger, *Soldiers in Politics: Military Coups and Governments* (Englewood Cliffs: Prentice-Hall, Inc., 1977).

49. I develop this argument more fully in my new book manuscript, *Soldiers, States, and Structure: Civil-Military Relations in a Changing Security Environment* (forthcoming).

50. Samuel P. Huntington, *Political Order in Changing Societies* (New Haven: Yale University Press, 1968), 194. I discuss how this was true of the cold war Soviet Army in my "Why the Soviet Military Supported Gorbachev and Why the Russian Military Might Only Support Yeltsin for a Price," *Journal of Strategic Studies* 16, no. 4 (December 1993): 455–89.

51. On these historical incidents see Gordon A. Craig, *The Politics of the Prussian Army: 1640–1945* (New York: Oxford University Press, 1956), 254–381, and John Steward Ambler, *The French Army in Politics: 1945–1962* (Columbus: Ohio State University Press, 1966).

52. See, for example, Alain Rouquie, *The Military and the State in Latin America,* Paul Sigmund, trans. (Berkeley: University of California Press, 1987).

53. Allan Millett, *The American Political System and Civilian Control of the Military: A Historical Perspective* (Columbus: Mershon Center of Ohio State University, April 1979), 38.

54. Proponents of the "crisis" school include Richard H. Kohn, "Out of Control: The Crisis in Civil-Military Relations," *National Interest* 35 (spring 1994): 3–17; Edward N. Luttwak, "Washington's Biggest Scandal," *Commentary* 97, no. 5 (May 1994): 29–33; and Col. Charles Dunlap, "Welcome to the Junta: The Erosion of Civilian Control of the U.S. Military," *Wake Forest Law Review* 29, no. 2 (summer 1994): 231–92.

55. See, for example, Colin L. Powell, "Why Generals Get Nervous," *New York Times,* October 8, 1992, 21.

56. My thoughts on this are laid out in "U.S. Civil-Military Relations in a Changing International Order," in Don Snider and Miranda A. Carlton-Carew, eds., *U.S. Civil-Military Relations: In Crisis or Transition?* (Washington, D.C.: Center for Strategic and International Studies, 1995), 166–84.

57. But there is definitely pressure from some Clinton appointees to do so. See letter from Deborah R. Lee, assistant secretary of defense for reserve affairs, "Our Civil-Military Program is Small, But It's Paying Big Dividends," *Washington Times,* May 24, 1995, 22.

58. There is also some evidence that the Brazilian military became more concerned about external threats in the wake of the Falkland/Malvinas War. On this see Stanley E. Hilton, "The Brazilian Military: Changing Strategic Perception and the Question of Mission," *Armed Forces and Society* 13, no. 3 (spring 1987): 346.

59. "Brazil's Justice Minister Tells of '93 Coup Plot," *New York Times,* January 7, 1994, 8.

60. On the Falklands War see the *Sunday Times* Insight Team, *The Falklands War: The Full Story* (London: Sphere Books, Ltd., 1982).

61. On the institutional crisis of the PDC see Michael Fleet, *The Rise and Fall of Chilean Christian Democracy* (Princeton: Princeton University Press, 1985).

326 Notes to Pages 261–67

62. See Mark Ensalaco, "Military Prerogatives and the Stalemate of Chilean Civil-Military Relations," *Armed Forces and Society* 21, no. 2 (winter 1995): 255–70.

63. Obviously, there remain some potential external threats to states in the region both from one another (e.g., Chile and Argentina, Argentina and Brazil, Bolivia and Chile, etc.) as well as from the United States.

64. Martin Edwin Andersen, "The Military Obstacle to Latin American Democracy," *Foreign Policy* 72 (winter 1988–89): 94–113, and Richard L. Millett, "An End to Militarism? Democracy and the Armed Forces in Central America," *Current History* 94, no. 589 (February 1995): 71–75.

65. Joseph Stiglitz, "On the Economic Role of the State," in Arnold Heertje, ed., *The Economic Role of the State* (New York: Oxford University Press, 1989), 14.

66. "Eat Your NAFTA," and "The Showdown," *Economist* (November 13, 1993): 15–16, 23–26.

67. The classic argument about how the "low politics" of complex interdependence leads to a less rational and coherent state is Robert O. Keohane and Joseph S. Nye, *Power and Interdependence: World Politics in Transition* (Boston: Little, Brown, and Co., 1977).

68. Mearsheimer, "Back to the Future," 11.

69. Samuel P. Huntington, "Why International Primacy Matters," *International Security* 17, no. 4 (spring 1993): 68–83.

70. Ironically, there is also pressure from the dovish side to broaden the definition of security. On this see Richard Ullman, "Redefining Security," *International Security* 8, no. 1 (summer 1983): 129–53, and Jessica Tuchman Matthews, "Redefining Security," *Foreign Affairs* 68, no. 2 (winter 1988): 162–77.

71. I discuss this throughout Desch, *When the Third World Matters*. Also see Ted Hopf, *Peripheral Visions: Deterrence Theory and American Foreign Policy in the Third World, 1965–1990* (Ann Arbor: University of Michigan Press, 1994).

72. "Nicaragua: Whose Trump?" *Economist* (March 26, 1988): 34–35, and "El Salvador: Another War Falls Out of Fashion," *Economist* (January 11, 1992): 40–41.

73. I have a somewhat unique insight into how the U.S. Department of State viewed Contadora during the early 1980s as I spent a summer as an intelligence analyst with the Office for Inter-American Affairs of the Bureau of Intelligence and Research where I had responsibility for this issue. My sense, reinforced by the fact that a temporary employee was assigned to cover it, was that the U.S. government did not consider the Contadora group to be a major player in the Central American crisis.

74. For a similar argument see Kenechi Ohmae, "The Rise of the Regional State," *Foreign Affairs* 72, no. 2 (spring 1993): 78–86, and Ohmae, "Beyond Friction to Fact: The Borderless Economy," *New Perspectives Quarterly* 7, no. 2 (spring 1990): 20–21.

75. Deborah Norden, "Keeping the Peace, Outside and In: Argentina's United Nations Missions," *International Peacekeeping* 2, no. 3 (autumn 1995): 330–49.

Chapter 14. Chameleon, Tortoise, or Toad by Paul G. Buchanan

Michael Kelly and Brian Sutliff helped in the research of this project, which was made possible by an International Affairs Fellowship administered by the Council on Foreign Relations. I am indebted to RADM (Ret.) Luther Schriefer, LTC Gerrold Gendron, LTC (Ret.) Patrick St. Clair, William Mock, Theodore Piccone, Raymond Ruga and Jorge Domínguez for their advice and assistance. None of the above is responsible for any errors of omission and commission. The views expressed herein are solely those of the author.

1. Jack Child, *Geopolitics and Conflict in South America: Quarrels Among Neighbors* (New York: Praeger Publishers, 1985).

2. S. Huntington, *The Third Wave: Democratization in the Late Twentieth Century* (Norman: University of Oklahoma Press, 1991).

3. On the history of U.S. intervention in the region, see C. Brown, ed., *With Friends Like These* (New York: Pantheon Books, 1985); R. Newfarmer, ed., *From Gunboats to Diplomacy* (Baltimore: Johns Hopkins University Press, 1984); and C. Blasier, *The Hovering Giant* (Pittsburgh: University of Pittsburgh Press, 1985).

4. On U.S. training of police and other counterinsurgency programs of the time, see NACLA, *Argentina: In the Hour of the Furnaces* (New York and Berkeley: NACLA, 1975), and C. Brown, ed., *With Friends Like These.*

5. It is worth noting that Argentine and Chilean military personnel were the original advisors of the Nicaraguan contras, serving as a cover for the U.S. government, which continued to supply financial and material assistance under the rationale of "plausible deniability" (a bureaucratic practice that involves purposely operating in a legal grey area in which reading and writing between the lines served as the authorization for covert action). The Argentines thought that their regional anticommunist service would curry them favor with the Reagan administration during the Falkland/Malvinas War, an assumption that proved to be mistaken.

6. Theoretical justification for this view was offered by Jeanne Kirkpatrick, "Dictatorships and Double Standards," *Commentary* 68, no. 5 (November 1979): 34–45.

7. The various strains of the NSD are examined in D. Pion-Berlin, "Latin American National Security Doctrines: Hard and Soft Themes," *Armed Forces and Society* 15, no. 1 (spring 1989): 411–30.

8. For a thorough review of geopolitical thought in Latin America, see J. Child, *Quarrels Among Neighbors,* and the works cited therein.

9. Concern with the changing strategic landscape preceded the Clinton administration. Beyond President Bush's allusions to a "New World Order," specific attention to the changing strategic environment in the Western Hemisphere has been offered in L. Erik Kjonnerod, ed., *Evolving U.S. Strategy for Latin America and the Caribbean* (Washington, D.C.: National Defense University Press, 1992); D. E. Schulz and G. Marcella, *Latin America: The Unfinished Business of Security* (Carlisle Barracks, Penn.: Strategic Studies Institute, U.S. Army War College, 1992); G. Marcella, "Forging New Strategic Relationships," *Military Review* 74, no. 10 (October 1994): 31–42; and LTC D. G. Bradford, "The Southern Theater: U.S. Interests Still Matter Here," *Strategic Review* 23, no. 1 (winter 1994): 43–50.

10. "Regional Security Strategy for Latin America" (Washington, D.C.: Assistant Secretary of Defense for International Security Affairs [Inter-American Affairs], draft version, April 1995), 5. The final version of the new regional strategy, with increased emphasis on the July 1995 Defense Ministerial Meetings in Williamsburg, Va., was published under the signature of Secretary of Defense William Perry with the title *United States Security Strategy for the Americas* (Washington, D.C.: Department of Defense, Office of International Security Affairs, September 1995). The thrust of the two documents is the same.

11. On the travails of the Latin American Left, see J. Castañeda, *Utopia Unarmed* (New York: Basic Books, 1994). Also see R. Barros, "The Left and Democracy: Recent Debates in Latin America," *TELOS* 68 (summer 1986): 49–70.

12. "Regional Security Strategy for Latin America," 6.

13. "A National Security Strategy of Engagement and Enlargement," draft presidential directive, National Security Council, July 1994, 2. The foundations of the Clinton foreign policy are further elaborated in the speech given by National Security Advisor Anthony Lake, "From Containment to Enlargement," at the Johns Hopkins School of Advanced International Studies, September 21, 1993.

14. On the notion that the Clinton administration practices Wilsonian realism (or pragmatic idealism, if you prefer), and how this has been translated into U.S. defense policy in the Western Hemisphere, see P. G. Buchanan and M. L. Jaramillo, "U.S. Defense Policy for the Western Hemisphere," *North-South* 4, no. 1 (July–August 1994): 5–9.

15. "Regional Security Strategy for Latin America," 19.

16. The notion of cooperative security offered here, including medical analogies, para-phrases the more complete discussion found in A. S. Carter, W. J. Perry, and J. D. Stein-brunner, *A New Concept of Cooperative Security* (Washington, D.C.: Brookings Occasional Papers, The Brookings Institution, 1992). An excellent overview of CSBMs in the South-ern Cone and elsewhere is provided by M. Krepon et al., *A Handbook of Confidence-Build-ing Measures for Regional Security* (Washington, D.C.: Henry L. Stimson Center, hand-book no. 1, September 1993).

17. Not that Canadian peacekeeping missions have been without problems. The con-viction of two Canadian soldiers on murder charges stemming from their activities in So-malia in 1993–94 points to the fact that not all those involved in such missions adhere to the standards upon which they are ostensibly based.

18. On the various dimensions of democracy and the problems of democratizing on all dimensions, see P. G. Buchanan, *State, Labor, Capital: Democratizing Class Relations in the Southern Cone* (Pittsburgh: University of Pittsburgh Press, 1995), chap. 1.

19. On the debate over the "democratic peace thesis," see, e.g., Christopher Layne, "Kant or Cant: The Myth of the Democratic Peace," *International Security* 19, no. 2 (fall 1994): 5–49; D. E. Spiro, "The Insignificance of the Liberal Peace," *International Security* 19, no. 2 (fall 1994): 50–86; J. Snyder and E. Mansfield, "Democratization and the Danger of War," *International Security* 20, no. 1 (summer 1995): 5–38.

20. In 1994, the Defense and State Departments took opposing stands on the subject of friendly nation shoot-downs of suspected drug-smuggling civilian aircraft. The specific issue revolved around the use of such a policy by the Colombian and Peruvian air forces when U.S.-supplied and -operated radar were used to track the suspect aircraft. State was in favor of the shoot-down policy, while Defense opposed it on legal grounds. As a result, U.S. radar coverage of drug-trafficking routes was suspended during the time it took these agencies and the governments in question to negotiate mutually acceptable terms of en-gagement, all in the midst of a very public diplomatic row.

21. The author was involved in preparing the initial Office of the U.S. Secretary of De-fense (OSD) position on the Mexican request and is familiar with the debate of the time. The materials in question remain classified.

22. On Brazilian concerns with U.S. promotion of cooperative security as being against its own national security interests, see J. Smith, "The Brazilian Military Ideology: Implica-tions for Institutionalized Democracy" (master's thesis, Latin American Studies, Universi-ty of Arizona, 1994).

23. For Patiño Meyer's proposals, see his "Support for a New Concept of Hemisphere Security: Cooperative Security" (Washington, D.C.: OEA/Ser.g.CE/SH-12/93, rev. 1, May 17, 1993).

❀ Contributors

Steven A. Bernstein is a doctoral candidate in the political science department at the University of California, San Diego. In addition to security studies, he has done extensive work in the field of international finance. Mr. Bernstein is coauthor of the *International Sourcebook of Housing Finance* and articles on financial systems in developing countries.

Paul G. Buchanan is senior lecturer in politics and Latin American Studies at the University of Auckland. Previously he taught at the Naval Postgraduate School, University of Arizona, and the New College of the University of South Florida. From 1993–94 he served as international affairs fellow of the Council on Foreign Relations, holding the position of regional policy analyst in the Office of the Secretary of Defense. He is the author of *State, Labor, Capital: Democratizing Class Relations in the Southern Cone.*

Michael C. Desch is assistant director and senior research associate at the John M. Olin Institute for Strategic Studies at Harvard University. He is the author of *When the Third World Matters: Latin America and U.S. Grand Strategy* and *Soldiers, States, and Structures: Civilian Control of the Military in a Changing Security Environment.*

Jorge I. Domínguez is Clarence Dillon Professor of International Affairs and director of the Weatherhead Center for International Affairs at Harvard University. With Abraham Lowenthal, he is coeditor and coauthor of *Constructing Democratic Governance: Latin America and the Caribbean in the 1990s;* he is also editor and coauthor of *Technopols: Freeing Politics and Markets in Latin America in the 1990s.* All of these books were published under the auspices of the Inter-American Dialogue.

Carlos Escudé is professor of international relations at Torcuato Di Tella University in Buenos Aires where he also is a researcher at its Argentine National Research Council. He has been Visiting Professor of Government at Harvard University. He has served as advisor to the foreign minister of Argentina on foreign policy strategy. He is the author of *Realismo Periférico: Fundamentos para una Nueva Política Exterior Argentina.*

Andrés Fontana has been the director of international security and military affairs research at the Fundación Simón Rodríguez in Buenos Aires since 1987. He has been a professor at the University of Buenos Aires and is the author of *Seguridad Cooperativa: Tendencias Globales y el Continente Americano* (1996).

Ivelaw L. Griffith is associate professor of political science at Florida International University. His publications include *Strategy and Security in the Caribbean* (Praeger 1991), *The Quest for Security in the Caribbean* (M.E. Sharpe 1993, 1994), *Caribbean Security in the Eve of the 21st Century* (National Defense University Press 1996), *Drugs and Security in the Caribbean: Sovereignty Under Siege* (Pennsylvania State University Press 1997), and *Democracy and Human Rights in the Caribbean* (Westview Press 1997).

Mônica Hirst is executive director of the Center of Brazilian Studies in Argentina and senior researcher at the Facultad Latinoamericana de Ciencias Sociales (FLACSO-Sede Buenos Aires). She was a history professor at Catholic University in Rio de Janeiro and has been a visiting professor at the Center for Latin American Studies of Stanford University. She is the author of *Argentina-Brasil: perspectivas, comparativas y ejes de integración* and of *Democracia, seguridad, e integración. América Latina en un mundo en transición.*

Ricardo Ernesto Lagorio is a career diplomat in Argentina. He was a professor of international relations theory at the Institute of Foreign Service and Universidad Católica Argentina. From 1982 to 1989, Lagorio was posted to the Argentine Mission to the United Nations. He has served as president of the Information Committee and vice president of the Committee on Peacekeeping Operations of the United Nations. In 1993, he served as chief of cabinet of the Ministry of Defense in Argentina. From January 1994 to August 1996, Lagorio served as undersecretary of defense. Currently, he is serving at the Argentine Ministry of Foreign Affairs.

Anthony P. Maingot is professor of sociology at the Florida International University. He has held positions at Yale University and the University of the West Indies, as well as a visiting appointment at the Rand Corporation in Santa Monica. He is the author of *The United States and the Caribbean: Chal-*

lenges of an Asymmetrical Relationship. Maingot is also the founding editor of the magazine *Hemisphere.*

David R. Mares is professor of political science and adjunct professor of international affairs at the University of California, San Diego. He has held positions at El Colegio de México, Universidad de Chile, and FLACSO-Ecuador. The author of numerous articles and chapters on Latin American international and comparative politics, he is also editor of *Civil-Military Relations: Building Peace and Democracy in Latin America, Southern Asia, and Central Europe,* and author of *Violent Peace: Managing Interstate Conflict in Latin America.*

Antonio L. Palá is a lieutenant colonel in the United States Air Force. He has served as the officer in charge of courses offered to Latin American military officers and has traveled throughout the hemisphere to evaluate training programs for the Latin American armed forces. Lt. Col. Palá is a doctoral candidate in international relations and is currently writing his dissertation on the Argentine military participation in United Nations peacekeeping. Lt. Col. Palá is presently an associate professor at the United States Air Force Academy.

Francisco Rojas Aravena is director of FLACSO-Chile and co-director of the Program Peace and Security in the Americas. He is a professor at the Instituto de Estudios Internacionales of the Universidad de Chile and at the University of Stanford in Santiago. He is author and editor of several books, and his most recent publications are *Balance Estratégico y Medidas de Confianza Mutua; Medidas de Confianza Mutua: Verificación; Gasto Militar en América Latina: Procesos de Decisiones y Actores Claves;* and *El Cono Sur y las Transformaciones Globales* (with William C. Smith).

Carlos A. Romero is professor of law and political studies and head of the Department of International Relations at the Central University of Venezuela (UCV). He has served as political advisor to the Venezuelan Ministry of Foreign Affairs and is a regular columnist in *El Diario de Caracas* and *Excelencia.* He is the author of *Las relaciones entre Venezuela y la Unión Soviética: diplomacia o revolución.*

Caesar D. Sereseres is associate dean for undergraduate studies at the School of Social Sciences, University of California, Irvine, and an adjunct professor of political science at the U.S. Air Force Special Operations School,

Hurlburt Field, Florida. He is the author of "The Guatemalan Counterinsurgency Campaign of 1982–1985: A Strategy of Going it Alone," in *Low Intensity Conflict*, ed. Edwin G. Corr and Stephen Sloan.

Fernando Zeledón Torres is instructor for the International Indigenous Program of the Peace University and consultant to the Center for Peace and National Reconciliation of the Oscar Arias Foundation in Costa Rica. Previously he was research director at the Political Science School of the University of Costa Rica. He is the author of several publications, including "Security and Militarism in Central America."

⚘ Index

ABACC, 57
Acción Democrática (Social Democratic Party) (Venezuela), 153
Ad Hoc Commission for the Purging of the Armed Forces (El Salvador), 240
AFL-CIO, 225
Africa, 148, 210, 241
Agreement on Economic Complementation, 89–90
Aguilera, Gabriel, 225
Airaldi, Eduardo, 136
Airrecú, 228
Alberdi, Juan Bautista, 121, 129
Alemán, Arnoldo, 213
Alfonsín, Raúl, 51, 53, 63, 104, 149, 172: and Argentine military policies, 63, 65–66; and Chile, 23, 54, 68; and Egypt, 63; and Iraq, 63
Allende, Salvador, 260, 262
Alliance for Progress, 269
Amaral de Oliveira, José do, 70–71
Amazonian Watch System (SIVAM), 112
Amazon River region, 17, 75, 105, 112, 114
Andreski, Stanislaw, 255
Angola, 112, 145, 164
Anguilla, 203
Antigua-Barbuda, 14, 177–78, 200, 203–06, 210
Antigua Defence Force, 204
Antonio Nicolás Briceño Battalion, 158–61, 164
APEC (Asia-Pacific Economic Council), 13, 90, 98
Arbenz, Jacobo, 253, 262
Argentina: armed forces and military policies of, 6–7, 13–14, 17–19, 23–24, 27, 37, 45–46, 49, 51, 53–58, 60–61, 63–70, 72–77, 103–07, 112–15, 117, 119–20, 123–50, 157, 166, 172, 260, 264–65, 269, 271, 274, 278, 284; and Bolivia, 58, 128; and Brazil, 7–9, 13, 24, 49–51, 53–54, 57–61, 69–70, 73–78, 102–03, 106, 112, 114–17, 124, 128, 145, 147, 155, 274; and Canada, 61–62; and CBMs, 56, 59, 62, 73–74, 77, 116–17, 184; and Chile, 7, 9, 13–14, 16, 22–24, 30, 38, 43–44, 46, 49–51, 53–54, 57–61, 63–69, 73–75, 77, 88–90, 99–100, 103, 114–15, 124, 128, 172, 184, 267, 274; and conflict management, 43; Constitution of (1984), 79; and the Contadora Support Group, 155; and co-

operative security, 13–17, 53, 56, 59, 77, 102–03, 114–17, 121–29, 278; coup attempt in (1987), 148–49; and the Cuba blockade (1962), 145; democracy and civilian government in, 21, 23–24, 46, 53, 56–57, 65–67, 71, 74–76, 83, 103, 105–07, 117, 119–20, 123–24, 127–50, 260, 264–65; and drugs, 75; economy of, 52–55, 74, 89, 103–06, 115, 148; and Ecuador, 58, 134, 277; educational system of, 52; and Egypt, 51, 63; foreign policies of, 49–63, 70–72, 76–77, 104–06, 109–10, 114–17, 119, 123–26, 132, 135–36, 172; geography of, 37, 52; guerrillas in, 260; and the Gulf War, 19, 54–56, 124, 132, 140–41, 145; human rights in, 106; and the IADB, 59–60; impact of end of cold war on, 109–10; intelligence services of, 6; international relations ideology of, 52–53; and Iraq, 51, 63; and Libya, 51; and NATO, 57, 77; and the OAS, 59–60; and Paraguay, 8–9, 13, 58, 60, 78, 113, 124, 128, 145 (see also Itaipú-Corpus Treaty; Treaty of Asunción); and peace-keeping, 18–21, 54–57, 61–62, 67, 73, 119–50, 157, 166, 264–65, 278; and Peru, 134, 155, 277; and Spain, 145; and the United Kingdom, 15, 19, 42–43, 46, 49, 53–56, 62–63, 65, 78–79, 135, 172, 270 (see also Falkland/Malvinas War); and the United States, 16, 19, 46, 49, 51–52, 54–58, 61–63, 70–72, 75–77, 106–07, 109–10, 115–16, 132, 135, 145, 250, 271, 284; and the UN Security Council, 56, 75, 77, 132, 135, 140; and Uruguay, 8–9, 13, 58, 60, 124, 128, 145, 155 (see also Treaty of Asunción); terrorism in, 15, 78, 282 (see also under non-state and substate forces)
Argentine Army War College, 135–36
Argentine Council on Foreign Relations (CARI), 125
Arias, Oscar, 155, 222–23. See also Arias Plan
Arias Plan, 44, 155–56
Arica, 88, 90
Aristide, Jean Bertrand, 144, 164, 166
Armed Forces Academy (Chile), 96
Arthur, Owen, 207–08
Arzú, Alvaro, 213
Asia-Pacific Economic Council. See APEC

333